Hadoop Application Architectures

Mark Grover, Ted Malaska,
Jonathan Seidman & Gwen Shapira

Beijing · Boston · Farnham · Sebastopol · Tokyo

Hadoop Application Architectures

by Mark Grover, Ted Malaska, Jonathan Seidman, and Gwen Shapira

Printed in the United States of America.

Published by O'Reilly Media, Inc., 1005 Gravenstein Highway North, Sebastopol, CA 95472.

O'Reilly books may be purchased for educational, business, or sales promotional use. Online editions are also available for most titles (*http://safaribooksonline.com*). For more information, contact our corporate/institutional sales department: 800-998-9938 or *corporate@oreilly.com*.

Editors: Ann Spencer and Brian Anderson	**Indexer:** Ellen Troutman
Production Editor: Nicole Shelby	**Interior Designer:** David Futato
Copyeditor: Rachel Monaghan	**Cover Designer:** Ellie Volckhausen
Proofreader: Elise Morrison	**Illustrator:** Rebecca Demarest

July 2015:   First Edition

Revision History for the First Edition
2015-06-26:   First Release

See *http://oreilly.com/catalog/errata.csp?isbn=9781491900086* for release details.

The O'Reilly logo is a registered trademark of O'Reilly Media, Inc. *Hadoop Application Architectures*, the cover image, and related trade dress are trademarks of O'Reilly Media, Inc.

978-1-491-90008-6

[LSI]

Table of Contents

Part I. Architectural Considerations for Hadoop Applications

Part II.   Case Studies

Foreword

Apache Hadoop has blossomed over the past decade.

It started in Nutch as a promising capability—the ability to scalably process petabytes. In 2005 it hadn't been run on more than a few dozen machines, and had many rough edges. It was only used by a few folks for experiments. Yet a few saw promise there, that an affordable, scalable, general-purpose data storage and processing framework might have broad utility.

By 2007 scalability had been proven at Yahoo!. Hadoop now ran reliably on thousands of machines. It began to be used in production applications, first at Yahoo! and then at other Internet companies, like Facebook, LinkedIn, and Twitter. But while it enabled scalable processing of petabytes, the price of adoption was high, with no security and only a Java batch API.

Since then Hadoop's become the kernel of a complex ecosystem. Its gained fine-grained security controls, high availability (HA), and a general-purpose scheduler (YARN).

A wide variety of tools have now been built around this kernel. Some, like HBase and Accumulo, provide online keystores that can back interactive applications. Others, like Flume, Sqoop, and Apache Kafka, help route data in and out of Hadoop's storage. Improved processing APIs are available through Pig, Crunch, and Cascading. SQL queries can be processed with Apache Hive and Cloudera Impala. Apache Spark is a superstar, providing an improved and optimized batch API while also incorporating real-time stream processing, graph processing, and machine learning. Apache Oozie and Azkaban orchestrate and schedule many of the above.

Confused yet? This menagerie of tools can be overwhelming. Yet, to make effective use of this new platform, you need to understand how these tools all fit together and which can help you. The authors of this book have years of experience building Hadoop-based systems and can now share with you the wisdom they've gained.

In theory there are billions of ways to connect and configure these tools for your use. But in practice, successful patterns emerge. This book describes best practices, where each tool shines, and how best to use it for a particular task. It also presents common-use cases. At first users improvised, trying many combinations of tools, but this book describes the patterns that have proven successful again and again, sparing you much of the exploration.

These authors give you the fundamental knowledge you need to begin using this powerful new platform. Enjoy the book, and use it to help you build great Hadoop applications.

—Doug Cutting
Shed in the Yard, California

Preface

It's probably not an exaggeration to say that Apache Hadoop has revolutionized data management and processing. Hadoop's technical capabilities have made it possible for organizations across a range of industries to solve problems that were previously impractical with existing technologies. These capabilities include:

- Scalable processing of massive amounts of data
- Flexibility for data processing, regardless of the format and structure (or lack of structure) in the data

Another notable feature of Hadoop is that it's an open source project designed to run on relatively inexpensive commodity hardware. Hadoop provides these capabilities at considerable cost savings over traditional data management solutions.

This combination of technical capabilities and economics has led to rapid growth in Hadoop and tools in the surrounding ecosystem. The vibrancy of the Hadoop community has led to the introduction of a broad range of tools to support management and processing of data with Hadoop.

Despite this rapid growth, Hadoop is still a relatively young technology. Many organizations are still trying to understand how Hadoop can be leveraged to solve problems, and how to apply Hadoop and associated tools to implement solutions to these problems. A rich ecosystem of tools, application programming interfaces (APIs), and development options provide choice and flexibility, but can make it challenging to determine the best choices to implement a data processing application.

The inspiration for this book comes from our experience working with numerous customers and conversations with Hadoop users who are trying to understand how to build reliable and scalable applications with Hadoop. Our goal is not to provide detailed documentation on using available tools, but rather to provide guidance on how to combine these tools to architect scalable and maintainable applications on Hadoop.

We assume readers of this book have some experience with Hadoop and related tools. You should have a familiarity with the core components of Hadoop, such as the Hadoop Distributed File System (HDFS) and MapReduce. If you need to come up to speed on Hadoop, or need refreshers on core Hadoop concepts, *Hadoop: The Definitive Guide* by Tom White remains, well, the definitive guide.

The following is a list of other tools and technologies that are important to understand in using this book, including references for further reading:

YARN

Up until recently, the core of Hadoop was commonly considered as being HDFS and MapReduce. This has been changing rapidly with the introduction of additional processing frameworks for Hadoop, and the introduction of YARN accelarates the move toward Hadoop as a big-data platform supporting multiple parallel processing models. YARN provides a general-purpose resource manager and scheduler for Hadoop processing, which includes MapReduce, but also extends these services to other processing models. This facilitates the support of multiple processing frameworks and diverse workloads on a single Hadoop cluster, and allows these different models and workloads to effectively share resources. For more on YARN, see *Hadoop: The Definitive Guide*, or the Apache YARN documentation (*http://bit.ly/oozie-yarn*).

Java

Hadoop and many of its associated tools are built with Java, and much application development with Hadoop is done with Java. Although the introduction of new tools and abstractions increasingly opens up Hadoop development to non-Java developers, having an understanding of Java is still important when you are working with Hadoop.

SQL

Although Hadoop opens up data to a number of processing frameworks, SQL remains very much alive and well as an interface to query data in Hadoop. This is understandable since a number of developers and analysts understand SQL, so knowing how to write SQL queries remains relevant when you're working with Hadoop. A good introduction to SQL is *Head First SQL* by Lynn Beighley (O'Reilly).

Scala

Scala is a programming language that runs on the Java virtual machine (JVM) and supports a mixed object-oriented and functional programming model. Although designed for general-purpose programming, Scala is becoming increasingly prevalent in the big-data world, both for implementing projects that interact with Hadoop and for implementing applications to process data. Examples of projects that use Scala as the basis for their implementation are Apache Spark and Apache Kafka. Scala, not surprisingly, is also one of the languages supported for implementing applications with Spark. Scala is used for many of the examples in this book, so if you need an introduction to Scala, see *Scala for the Impatient* by Cay S. Horstmann (Addison-Wesley Professional) or for a more in-depth overview see *Programming Scala*, 2nd Edition, by Dean Wampler and Alex Payne (O'Reilly).

Apache Hive

Speaking of SQL, Hive, a popular abstraction for modeling and processing data on Hadoop, provides a way to define structure on data stored in HDFS, as well as write SQL-like queries against this data. The Hive project also provides a metadata store, which in addition to storing metadata (i.e., data about data) on Hive structures is also accessible to other interfaces such as Apache Pig (a high-level parallel programming abstraction) and MapReduce via the HCatalog component. Further, other open source projects—such as Cloudera Impala, a low-latency query engine for Hadoop—also leverage the Hive metastore, which provides access to objects defined through Hive. To learn more about Hive, see the Hive website (*https://hive.apache.org/*), *Hadoop: The Definitive Guide*, or *Programming Hive* by Edward Capriolo, et al. (O'Reilly).

Apache HBase

HBase is another frequently used component in the Hadoop ecosystem. HBase is a distributed NoSQL data store that provides random access to extremely large volumes of data stored in HDFS. Although referred to as the *Hadoop database*, HBase is very different from a relational database, and requires those familiar with traditional database systems to embrace new concepts. HBase is a core component in many Hadoop architectures, and is referred to throughout this book. To learn more about HBase, see the HBase website (*http://hbase.apache.org/*), *HBase: The Definitive Guide* by Lars George (O'Reilly), or *HBase in Action* by Nick Dimiduk and Amandeep Khurana (Manning).

Apache Flume

Flume is an often used component to ingest event-based data, such as logs, into Hadoop. We provide an overview and details on best practices and architectures for leveraging Flume with Hadoop, but for more details on Flume refer to the Flume documentation (*http://bit.ly/flume-docs*) or *Using Flume* (O'Reilly).

Apache Sqoop

Sqoop is another popular tool in the Hadoop ecosystem that facilitates moving data between external data stores such as a relational database and Hadoop. We discuss best practices for Sqoop and where it fits in a Hadoop architecture, but for more details on Sqoop see the Sqoop documentation (*http://bit.ly/sqoop-docs*) or the *Apache Sqoop Cookbook* (O'Reilly).

Apache ZooKeeper

> The aptly named ZooKeeper project is designed to provide a centralized service to facilitate coordination for the zoo of projects in the Hadoop ecosystem. A number of the components that we discuss in this book, such as HBase, rely on the services provided by ZooKeeper, so it's good to have a basic understanding of it. Refer to the ZooKeeper site (*http://zookeeper.apache.org/*) or *ZooKeeper* by Flavio Junqueira and Benjamin Reed (O'Reilly).

As you may have noticed, the emphasis in this book is on tools in the open source Hadoop ecosystem. It's important to note, though, that many of the traditional enterprise software vendors have added support for Hadoop, or are in the process of adding this support. If your organization is already using one or more of these enterprise tools, it makes a great deal of sense to investigate integrating these tools as part of your application development efforts on Hadoop. The best tool for a task is often the tool you already know. Although it's valuable to understand the tools we discuss in this book and how they're integrated to implement applications on Hadoop, choosing to leverage third-party tools in your environment is a completely valid choice.

Again, our aim for this book is not to go into details on how to use these tools, but rather, to explain when and why to use them, and to balance known best practices with recommendations on when these practices apply and how to adapt in cases when they don't. We hope you'll find this book useful in implementing successful big data solutions with Hadoop.

A Note About the Code Examples

Before we move on, a brief note about the code examples in this book. Every effort has been made to ensure the examples in the book are up-to-date and correct. For the most current versions of the code examples, please refer to the book's GitHub repository at *https://github.com/hadooparchitecturebook/hadoop-arch-book*.

Who Should Read This Book

Hadoop Application Architectures was written for software developers, architects, and project leads who need to understand how to use Apache Hadoop and tools in the Hadoop ecosystem to build end-to-end data management solutions or integrate Hadoop into existing data management architectures. Our intent is not to provide deep dives into specific technologies—for example, MapReduce—as other references do. Instead, our intent is to provide you with an understanding of how components in the Hadoop ecosystem are effectively integrated to implement a complete data pipeline, starting from source data all the way to data consumption, as well as how Hadoop can be integrated into existing data management systems.

We assume you have some knowledge of Hadoop and related tools such as Flume, Sqoop, HBase, Pig, and Hive, but we'll refer to appropriate references for those who need a refresher. We also assume you have experience programming with Java, as well as experience with SQL and traditional data-management systems, such as relational database-management systems.

So if you're a technologist who's spent some time with Hadoop, and are now looking for best practices and examples for architecting and implementing complete solutions with it, then this book is meant for you. Even if you're a Hadoop expert, we think the guidance and best practices in this book, based on our years of experience working with Hadoop, will provide value.

This book can also be used by managers who want to understand which technologies will be relevant to their organization based on their goals and projects, in order to help select appropriate training for developers.

Why We Wrote This Book

We have all spent years implementing solutions with Hadoop, both as users and supporting customers. In that time, the Hadoop market has matured rapidly, along with the number of resources available for understanding Hadoop. There are now a large number of useful books, websites, classes, and more on Hadoop and tools in the Hadoop ecosystem available. However, despite all of the available materials, there's still a shortage of resources available for understanding how to effectively integrate these tools into complete solutions.

When we talk with users, whether they're customers, partners, or conference attendees, we've found a common theme: there's still a gap between understanding Hadoop and being able to actually leverage it to solve problems. For example, there are a number of good references that will help you understand Apache Flume, but how do you actually determine if it's a good fit for your use case? And once you've selected Flume as a solution, how do you effectively integrate it into your architecture? What best practices and considerations should you be aware of to optimally use Flume?

This book is intended to bridge this gap between understanding Hadoop and being able to actually use it to build solutions. We'll cover core considerations for implementing solutions with Hadoop, and then provide complete, end-to-end examples of implementing some common use cases with Hadoop.

Navigating This Book

The organization of chapters in this book is intended to follow the same flow that you would follow when architecting a solution on Hadoop, starting with modeling data on Hadoop, moving data into and out of Hadoop, processing the data once it's in

Hadoop, and so on. Of course, you can always skip around as needed. Part I covers the considerations around architecting applications with Hadoop, and includes the following chapters:

- Chapter 1 covers considerations around storing and modeling data in Hadoop—for example, file formats, data organization, and metadata management.

- Chapter 2 covers moving data into and out of Hadoop. We'll discuss considerations and patterns for data ingest and extraction, including using common tools such as Flume, Sqoop, and file transfers.

- Chapter 3 covers tools and patterns for accessing and processing data in Hadoop. We'll talk about available processing frameworks such as MapReduce, Spark, Hive, and Impala, and considerations for determining which to use for particular use cases.

- Chapter 4 will expand on the discussion of processing frameworks by describing the implementation of some common use cases on Hadoop. We'll use examples in Spark and SQL to illustrate how to solve common problems such as de-duplication and working with time series data.

- Chapter 5 discusses tools to do large graph processing on Hadoop, such as Giraph and GraphX.

- Chapter 6 discusses tying everything together with application orchestration and scheduling tools such as Apache Oozie.

- Chapter 7 discusses near-real-time processing on Hadoop. We discuss the relatively new class of tools that are intended to process streams of data such as Apache Storm and Apache Spark Streaming.

In Part II, we cover the end-to-end implementations of some common applications with Hadoop. The purpose of these chapters is to provide concrete examples of how to use the components discussed in Part I to implement complete solutions with Hadoop:

- Chapter 8 provides an example of clickstream analysis with Hadoop. Storage and processing of clickstream data is a very common use case for companies running large websites, but also is applicable to applications processing any type of machine data. We'll discuss ingesting data through tools like Flume and Kafka, cover storing and organizing the data efficiently, and show examples of processing the data.

- Chapter 9 will provide a case study of a fraud detection application on Hadoop, an increasingly common use of Hadoop. This example will cover how HBase can be leveraged in a fraud detection solution, as well as the use of near-real-time processing.

- Chapter 10 provides a case study exploring another very common use case: using Hadoop to extend an existing enterprise data warehouse (EDW) environment. This includes using Hadoop as a complement to the EDW, as well as providing functionality traditionally performed by data warehouses.

Conventions Used in This Book

The following typographical conventions are used in this book:

Italic
: Indicates new terms, URLs, email addresses, filenames, and file extensions.

`Constant width`
: Used for program listings, as well as within paragraphs to refer to program elements such as variable or function names, databases, data types, environment variables, statements, and keywords.

`Constant width bold`
: Shows commands or other text that should be typed literally by the user.

`Constant width italic`
: Shows text that should be replaced with user-supplied values or by values determined by context.

 This icon signifies a tip, suggestion, or general note.

 This icon indicates a warning or caution.

Using Code Examples

Supplemental material (code examples, exercises, etc.) is available for download at *https://github.com/hadooparchitecturebook/hadoop-arch-book*.

This book is here to help you get your job done. In general, if example code is offered with this book, you may use it in your programs and documentation. You do not need to contact us for permission unless you're reproducing a significant portion of the code. For example, writing a program that uses several chunks of code from this book does not require permission. Selling or distributing a CD-ROM of examples from O'Reilly books does require permission. Answering a question by citing this book and quoting example code does not require permission. Incorporating a significant amount of example code from this book into your product's documentation does require permission.

We appreciate, but do not require, attribution. An attribution usually includes the title, author, publisher, and ISBN. For example: "*Hadoop Application Architectures* by Mark Grover, Ted Malaska, Jonathan Seidman, and Gwen Shapira (O'Reilly). Copyright 2015 Jonathan Seidman, Gwen Shapira, Ted Malaska, and Mark Grover, 978-1-491-90008-6."

If you feel your use of code examples falls outside fair use or the permission given above, feel free to contact us at *permissions@oreilly.com*.

Safari® Books Online

Safari Books Online is an on-demand digital library that delivers expert content in both book and video form from the world's leading authors in technology and business.

Technology professionals, software developers, web designers, and business and creative professionals use Safari Books Online as their primary resource for research, problem solving, learning, and certification training.

Safari Books Online offers a range of plans and pricing for enterprise, government, education, and individuals.

Members have access to thousands of books, training videos, and prepublication manuscripts in one fully searchable database from publishers like O'Reilly Media, Prentice Hall Professional, Addison-Wesley Professional, Microsoft Press, Sams, Que, Peachpit Press, Focal Press, Cisco Press, John Wiley & Sons, Syngress, Morgan Kaufmann, IBM Redbooks, Packt, Adobe Press, FT Press, Apress, Manning, New Riders, McGraw-Hill, Jones & Bartlett, Course Technology, and hundreds more. For more information about Safari Books Online, please visit us online.

How to Contact Us

Please address comments and questions concerning this book to the publisher:

O'Reilly Media, Inc.
1005 Gravenstein Highway North
Sebastopol, CA 95472
800-998-9938 (in the United States or Canada)
707-829-0515 (international or local)
707-829-0104 (fax)

We have a web page for this book, where we list errata, examples, and any additional information. You can access this page at *http://bit.ly/hadoop_app_arch_1E*.

To comment or ask technical questions about this book, send email to *bookquestions@oreilly.com*.

For more information about our books, courses, conferences, and news, see our website at *http://www.oreilly.com*.

Find us on Facebook: *http://facebook.com/oreilly*

Follow us on Twitter: *http://twitter.com/oreillymedia*

Watch us on YouTube: *http://www.youtube.com/oreillymedia*

Acknowledgments

We would like to thank the larger Apache community for its work on Hadoop and the surrounding ecosystem, without which this book wouldn't exist. We would also like to thank Doug Cutting for providing this book's forward, and not to mention for co-creating Hadoop.

There are a large number of folks whose support and hard work made this book possible, starting with Eric Sammer. Eric's early support and encouragement was invaluable in making this book a reality. Amandeep Khurana, Kathleen Ting, Patrick Angeles, and Joey Echeverria also provided valuable proposal feedback early on in the project.

Many people provided invaluable feedback and support while writing this book, especially the following who provided their time and expertise to review content: Azhar Abubacker, Sean Allen, Ryan Blue, Ed Capriolo, Eric Driscoll, Lars George, Jeff Holoman, Robert Kanter, James Kinley, Alex Moundalexis, Mac Noland, Sean Owen, Mike Percy, Joe Prosser, Jairam Ranganathan, Jun Rao, Hari Shreedharan, Jeff Shmain, Ronan Stokes, Daniel Templeton, Tom Wheeler.

Andre Araujo, Alex Ding, and Michael Ernest generously gave their time to test the code examples. Akshat Das provided help with diagrams and our website.

Many reviewers helped us out and greatly improved the quality of this book, so any mistakes left are our own.

We would also like to thank Cloudera management for enabling us to write this book. In particular, we'd like to thank Mike Olson for his constant encouragement and support from day one.

We'd like to thank our O'Reilly editor Brian Anderson and our production editor Nicole Shelby for their help and contributions throughout the project. In addition, we really appreciate the help from many other folks at O'Reilly and beyond—Ann Spencer, Courtney Nash, Rebecca Demarest, Rachel Monaghan, and Ben Lorica—at various times in the development of this book.

Our apologies to those who we may have mistakenly omitted from this list.

Mark Grover's Acknowledgements

First and foremost, I would like to thank my parents, Neelam and Parnesh Grover. I dedicate it all to the love and support they continue to shower in my life every single day. I'd also like to thank my sister, Tracy Grover, who I continue to tease, love, and admire for always being there for me. Also, I am very thankful to my past and current managers at Cloudera, Arun Singla and Ashok Seetharaman for their continued support of this project. Special thanks to Paco Nathan and Ed Capriolo for encouraging me to write a book.

Ted Malaska's Acknowledgements

I would like to thank my wife, Karen, and TJ and Andrew—my favorite two boogers.

Jonathan Seidman's Acknowledgements

I'd like to thank the three most important people in my life, Tanya, Ariel, and Madeleine, for their patience, love, and support during the (very) long process of writing this book. I'd also like to thank Mark, Gwen, and Ted for being great partners on this journey. Finally, I'd like to dedicate this book to the memory of my parents, Aaron and Frances Seidman.

Gwen Shapira's Acknowledgements

I would like to thank my husband, Omer Shapira, for his emotional support and patience during the many months I spent writing this book, and my dad, Lior Shapira, for being my best marketing person and telling all his friends about the "big data book." Special thanks to my manager Jarek Jarcec Cecho for his support for the project, and thanks to my team over the last year for handling what was perhaps more than their fair share of the work.

## PART I

Architectural Considerations for Hadoop Applications

## CHAPTER 1

Data Modeling in Hadoop

At its core, Hadoop is a distributed data store that provides a platform for implementing powerful parallel processing frameworks. The reliability of this data store when it comes to storing massive volumes of data, coupled with its flexibility in running multiple processing frameworks makes it an ideal choice for your data hub. This characteristic of Hadoop means that you can store any type of data as is, without placing any constraints on how that data is processed.

A common term one hears in the context of Hadoop is *Schema-on-Read*. This simply refers to the fact that raw, unprocessed data can be loaded into Hadoop, with the structure imposed at processing time based on the requirements of the processing application.

This is different from *Schema-on-Write*, which is generally used with traditional data management systems. Such systems require the schema of the data store to be defined before the data can be loaded. This leads to lengthy cycles of analysis, data modeling, data transformation, loading, testing, and so on before data can be accessed. Furthermore, if a wrong decision is made or requirements change, this cycle must start again. When the application or structure of data is not as well understood, the agility provided by the Schema-on-Read pattern can provide invaluable insights on data not previously accessible.

Relational databases and data warehouses are often a good fit for well-understood and frequently accessed queries and reports on high-value data. Increasingly, though, Hadoop is taking on many of these workloads, particularly for queries that need to operate on volumes of data that are not economically or technically practical to process with traditional systems.

Although being able to store all of your raw data is a powerful feature, there are still many factors that you should take into consideration before dumping your data into Hadoop. These considerations include:

Data storage formats
> There are a number of file formats and compression formats supported on Hadoop. Each has particular strengths that make it better suited to specific applications. Additionally, although Hadoop provides the Hadoop Distributed File System (HDFS) for storing data, there are several commonly used systems implemented on top of HDFS, such as HBase for additional data access functionality and Hive for additional data management functionality. Such systems need to be taken into consideration as well.

Multitenancy
> It's common for clusters to host multiple users, groups, and application types. Supporting multitenant clusters involves a number of important considerations when you are planning how data will be stored and managed.

Schema design
> Despite the schema-less nature of Hadoop, there are still important considerations to take into account around the structure of data stored in Hadoop. This includes directory structures for data loaded into HDFS as well as the output of data processing and analysis. This also includes the schemas of objects stored in systems such as HBase and Hive.

Metadata management
> As with any data management system, metadata related to the stored data is often as important as the data itself. Understanding and making decisions related to metadata management are critical.

We'll discuss these items in this chapter. Note that these considerations are fundamental to architecting applications on Hadoop, which is why we're covering them early in the book.

Another important factor when you're making storage decisions with Hadoop, but one that's beyond the scope of this book, is security and its associated considerations. This includes decisions around authentication, fine-grained access control, and encryption—both for data on the wire and data at rest. For a comprehensive discussion of security with Hadoop, see *Hadoop Security* (*http://bit.ly/hadoop-security*) by Ben Spivey and Joey Echeverria (O'Reilly).

Data Storage Options

One of the most fundamental decisions to make when you are architecting a solution on Hadoop is determining how data will be stored in Hadoop. There is no such thing as a standard data storage format in Hadoop. Just as with a standard filesystem, Hadoop allows for storage of data in any format, whether it's text, binary, images, or something else. Hadoop also provides built-in support for a number of formats optimized for Hadoop storage and processing. This means users have complete control and a number of options for how data is stored in Hadoop. This applies to not just the raw data being ingested, but also intermediate data generated during data processing and derived data that's the result of data processing. This, of course, also means that there are a number of decisions involved in determining how to optimally store your data. Major considerations for Hadoop data storage include:

File format

There are multiple formats that are suitable for data stored in Hadoop. These include plain text or Hadoop-specific formats such as SequenceFile. There are also more complex but more functionally rich options, such as Avro and Parquet. These different formats have different strengths that make them more or less suitable depending on the application and source-data types. It's possible to create your own custom file format in Hadoop, as well.

Compression

This will usually be a more straightforward task than selecting file formats, but it's still an important factor to consider. Compression codecs commonly used with Hadoop have different characteristics; for example, some codecs compress and uncompress faster but don't compress as aggressively, while other codecs create smaller files but take longer to compress and uncompress, and not surprisingly require more CPU. The ability to split compressed files is also a very important consideration when you're working with data stored in Hadoop—we'll discuss splittability considerations further later in the chapter.

Data storage system

While all data in Hadoop rests in HDFS, there are decisions around what the underlying storage manager should be—for example, whether you should use HBase or HDFS directly to store the data. Additionally, tools such as Hive and Impala allow you to define additional structure around your data in Hadoop.

Before beginning a discussion on data storage options for Hadoop, we should note a couple of things:

- We'll cover different storage options in this chapter, but more in-depth discussions on best practices for data storage are deferred to later chapters. For example, when we talk about ingesting data into Hadoop we'll talk more about considerations for storing that data.

- Although we focus on HDFS as the Hadoop filesystem in this chapter and throughout the book, we'd be remiss in not mentioning work to enable alternate filesystems with Hadoop. This includes open source filesystems such as GlusterFS and the Quantcast File System, and commercial alternatives such as Isilon OneFS and NetApp. Cloud-based storage systems such as Amazon's Simple Storage System (S3) are also becoming common. The filesystem might become yet another architectural consideration in a Hadoop deployment. This should not, however, have a large impact on the underlying considerations that we're discussing here.

Standard File Formats

We'll start with a discussion on storing standard file formats in Hadoop—for example, text files (such as comma-separated value [CSV] or XML) or binary file types (such as images). In general, it's preferable to use one of the Hadoop-specific container formats discussed next for storing data in Hadoop, but in many cases you'll want to store source data in its raw form. As noted before, one of the most powerful features of Hadoop is the ability to store all of your data regardless of format. Having online access to data in its raw, source form—"full fidelity" data—means it will always be possible to perform new processing and analytics with the data as requirements change. The following discussion provides some considerations for storing standard file formats in Hadoop.

Text data

A very common use of Hadoop is the storage and analysis of logs such as web logs and server logs. Such text data, of course, also comes in many other forms: CSV files, or unstructured data such as emails. A primary consideration when you are storing text data in Hadoop is the organization of the files in the filesystem, which we'll discuss more in the section "HDFS Schema Design" on page 14. Additionally, you'll want to select a compression format for the files, since text files can very quickly consume considerable space on your Hadoop cluster. Also, keep in mind that there is an overhead of type conversion associated with storing data in text format. For example, storing 1234 in a text file and using it as an integer requires a string-to-integer conversion during reading, and vice versa during writing. It also takes up more space to store *1234* as text than as an integer. This overhead adds up when you do many such conversions and store large amounts of data.

Selection of compression format will be influenced by how the data will be used. For archival purposes you may choose the most compact compression available, but if the data will be used in processing jobs such as MapReduce, you'll likely want to select a splittable format. Splittable formats enable Hadoop to split files into chunks for processing, which is critical to efficient parallel processing. We'll discuss compression types and considerations, including the concept of splittability, later in this chapter.

Note also that in many, if not most cases, the use of a container format such as SequenceFiles or Avro will provide advantages that make it a preferred format for most file types, including text; among other things, these container formats provide functionality to support splittable compression. We'll also be covering these container formats later in this chapter.

Structured text data

A more specialized form of text files is structured formats such as XML and JSON. These types of formats can present special challenges with Hadoop since splitting XML and JSON files for processing is tricky, and Hadoop does not provide a built-in InputFormat for either. JSON presents even greater challenges than XML, since there are no tokens to mark the beginning or end of a record. In the case of these formats, you have a couple of options:

- Use a container format such as Avro. Transforming the data into Avro can provide a compact and efficient way to store and process the data.

- Use a library designed for processing XML or JSON files. Examples of this for XML include XMLLoader in the PiggyBank library (*http://bit.ly/piggybank-lib*) for Pig. For JSON, the Elephant Bird project (*http://bit.ly/elephant-bird*) provides the LzoJsonInputFormat. For more details on processing these formats, see the book *Hadoop in Practice* by Alex Holmes (Manning), which provides several examples for processing XML and JSON files with MapReduce.

Binary data

Although text is typically the most common source data format stored in Hadoop, you can also use Hadoop to process binary files such as images. For most cases of storing and processing binary files in Hadoop, using a container format such as SequenceFile is preferred. If the splittable unit of binary data is larger than 64 MB, you may consider putting the data in its own file, without using a container format.

Hadoop File Types

There are several Hadoop-specific file formats that were specifically created to work well with MapReduce. These Hadoop-specific file formats include file-based data structures such as sequence files, serialization formats like Avro, and columnar formats such as RCFile and Parquet. These file formats have differing strengths and weaknesses, but all share the following characteristics that are important for Hadoop applications:

Splittable compression

These formats support common compression formats and are also splittable. We'll discuss splittability more in the section "Compression" on page 12, but note that the ability to split files can be a key consideration for storing data in Hadoop because it allows large files to be split for input to MapReduce and other types of jobs. The ability to split a file for processing by multiple tasks is of course a fundamental part of parallel processing, and is also key to leveraging Hadoop's data locality feature.

Agnostic compression
The file can be compressed with any compression codec, without readers having to know the codec. This is possible because the codec is stored in the header metadata of the file format.

We'll discuss the file-based data structures in this section, and subsequent sections will cover serialization formats and columnar formats.

File-based data structures

The *SequenceFile* format is one of the most commonly used file-based formats in Hadoop, but other file-based formats are available, such as MapFiles, SetFiles, Array-Files, and BloomMapFiles. Because these formats were specifically designed to work with MapReduce, they offer a high level of integration for all forms of MapReduce jobs, including those run via Pig and Hive. We'll cover the SequenceFile format here, because that's the format most commonly employed in implementing Hadoop jobs. For a more complete discussion of the other formats, refer to *Hadoop: The Definitive Guide*.

SequenceFiles store data as binary key-value pairs. There are three formats available for records stored within SequenceFiles:

Uncompressed
For the most part, uncompressed SequenceFiles don't provide any advantages over their compressed alternatives, since they're less efficient for input/output (I/O) and take up more space on disk than the same data in compressed form.

Record-compressed
This format compresses each record as it's added to the file.

Block-compressed
This format waits until data reaches block size to compress, rather than as each record is added. Block compression provides better compression ratios compared to record-compressed SequenceFiles, and is generally the preferred compression option for SequenceFiles. Also, the reference to *block* here is unrelated to the HDFS or filesystem block. A *block* in block compression refers to a group of records that are compressed together within a single HDFS block.

Regardless of format, every SequenceFile uses a common header format containing basic metadata about the file, such as the compression codec used, key and value class names, user-defined metadata, and a randomly generated sync marker. This sync marker is also written into the body of the file to allow for seeking to random points in the file, and is key to facilitating splittability. For example, in the case of block compression, this sync marker will be written before every block in the file.

SequenceFiles are well supported within the Hadoop ecosystem, however their support outside of the ecosystem is limited. They are also only supported in Java. A common use case for SequenceFiles is as a container for smaller files. Storing a large number of small files in Hadoop can cause a couple of issues. One is excessive memory use for the NameNode, because metadata for each file stored in HDFS is held in memory. Another potential issue is in processing data in these files—many small files can lead to many processing tasks, causing excessive overhead in processing. Because Hadoop is optimized for large files, packing smaller files into a SequenceFile makes the storage and processing of these files much more efficient. For a more complete discussion of the small files problem with Hadoop and how SequenceFiles provide a solution, refer to *Hadoop: The Definitive Guide*.

Figure 1-1 shows an example of the file layout for a SequenceFile using block compression. An important thing to note in this diagram is the inclusion of the sync marker before each block of data, which allows readers of the file to seek to block boundaries.

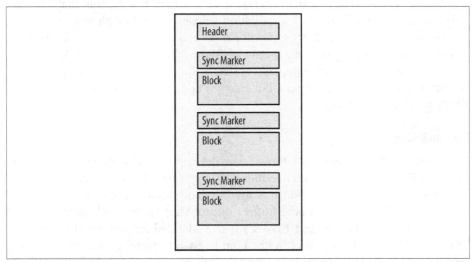

Figure 1-1. An example of a SequenceFile using block compression

Serialization Formats

Serialization refers to the process of turning data structures into byte streams either for storage or transmission over a network. Conversely, *deserialization* is the process of converting a byte stream back into data structures. Serialization is core to a distributed processing system such as Hadoop, since it allows data to be converted into a format that can be efficiently stored as well as transferred across a network connection. Serialization is commonly associated with two aspects of data processing in distributed systems: interprocess communication (remote procedure calls, or RPC) and data storage. For purposes of this discussion we're not concerned with RPC, so we'll focus on the data storage aspect in this section.

The main serialization format utilized by Hadoop is Writables. Writables are compact and fast, but not easy to extend or use from languages other than Java. There are, however, other serialization frameworks seeing increased use within the Hadoop ecosystem, including Thrift, Protocol Buffers, and Avro. Of these, Avro is the best suited, because it was specifically created to address limitations of Hadoop Writables. We'll examine Avro in more detail, but let's first briefly cover Thrift and Protocol Buffers.

Thrift

Thrift was developed at Facebook as a framework for implementing cross-language interfaces to services. Thrift uses an Interface Definition Language (IDL) to define interfaces, and uses an IDL file to generate stub code to be used in implementing RPC clients and servers that can be used across languages. Using Thrift allows us to implement a single interface that can be used with different languages to access different underlying systems. The Thrift RPC layer is very robust, but for this chapter, we're only concerned with Thrift as a serialization framework. Although sometimes used for data serialization with Hadoop, Thrift has several drawbacks: it does not support internal compression of records, it's not splittable, and it lacks native MapReduce support. Note that there are externally available libraries such as the Elephant Bird project to address these drawbacks, but Hadoop does not provide native support for Thrift as a data storage format.

Protocol Buffers

The Protocol Buffer (protobuf) format was developed at Google to facilitate data exchange between services written in different languages. Like Thrift, protobuf structures are defined via an IDL, which is used to generate stub code for multiple languages. Also like Thrift, Protocol Buffers do not support internal compression of records, are not splittable, and have no native MapReduce support. But also like Thrift, the Elephant Bird project can be used to encode protobuf records, providing support for MapReduce, compression, and splittability.

Avro

Avro is a language-neutral data serialization system designed to address the major downside of Hadoop Writables: lack of language portability. Like Thrift and Protocol Buffers, Avro data is described through a language-independent schema. Unlike Thrift and Protocol Buffers, code generation is optional with Avro. Since Avro stores the schema in the header of each file, it's self-describing and Avro files can easily be read later, even from a different language than the one used to write the file. Avro also provides better native support for MapReduce since Avro data files are compressible and splittable. Another important feature of Avro that makes it superior to Sequence-Files for Hadoop applications is support for *schema evolution*; that is, the schema used to read a file does not need to match the schema used to write the file. This makes it possible to add new fields to a schema as requirements change.

Avro schemas are usually written in JSON, but may also be written in Avro IDL, which is a C-like language. As just noted, the schema is stored as part of the file meta-data in the file header. In addition to metadata, the file header contains a unique sync marker. Just as with SequenceFiles, this sync marker is used to separate blocks in the file, allowing Avro files to be splittable. Following the header, an Avro file contains a series of blocks containing serialized Avro objects. These blocks can optionally be compressed, and within those blocks, types are stored in their native format, providing an additional boost to compression. At the time of writing, Avro supports Snappy and Deflate compression.

While Avro defines a small number of primitive types such as Boolean, int, float, and string, it also supports complex types such as array, map, and enum.

Columnar Formats

Until relatively recently, most database systems stored records in a row-oriented fashion. This is efficient for cases where many columns of the record need to be fetched. For example, if your analysis heavily relied on fetching all fields for records that belonged to a particular time range, row-oriented storage would make sense. This option can also be more efficient when you're writing data, particularly if all columns of the record are available at write time because the record can be written with a single disk seek. More recently, a number of databases have introduced columnar storage, which provides several benefits over earlier row-oriented systems:

- Skips I/O and decompression (if applicable) on columns that are not a part of the query.
- Works well for queries that only access a small subset of columns. If many columns are being accessed, then row-oriented is generally preferable.
- Is generally very efficient in terms of compression on columns because entropy within a column is lower than entropy within a block of rows. In other words, data is more similar within the same column, than it is in a block of rows. This can make a huge difference especially when the column has few distinct values.
- Is often well suited for data-warehousing-type applications where users want to aggregate certain columns over a large collection of records.

Not surprisingly, columnar file formats are also being utilized for Hadoop applications. Columnar file formats supported on Hadoop include the RCFile format, which has been popular for some time as a Hive format, as well as newer formats such as the Optimized Row Columnar (ORC) and Parquet, which are described next.

RCFile

The RCFile format was developed specifically to provide efficient processing for MapReduce applications, although in practice it's only seen use as a Hive storage format. The RCFile format was developed to provide fast data loading, fast query processing, and highly efficient storage space utilization. The RCFile format breaks files into row splits, then within each split uses column-oriented storage.

Although the RCFile format provides advantages in terms of query and compression performance compared to SequenceFiles, it also has some deficiencies that prevent optimal performance for query times and compression. Newer columnar formats such as ORC and Parquet address many of these deficiencies, and for most newer applications, they will likely replace the use of RCFile. RCFile is still a fairly common format used with Hive storage.

ORC

The ORC format was created to address some of the shortcomings with the RCFile format, specifically around query performance and storage efficiency. The ORC format provides the following features and benefits, many of which are distinct improvements over RCFile:

- Provides lightweight, always-on compression provided by type-specific readers and writers. ORC also supports the use of zlib, LZO, or Snappy to provide further compression.
- Allows predicates to be pushed down to the storage layer so that only required data is brought back in queries.
- Supports the Hive type model, including new primitives such as decimal and complex types.
- Is a splittable storage format.

A drawback of ORC as of this writing is that it was designed specifically for Hive, and so is not a general-purpose storage format that can be used with non-Hive MapReduce interfaces such as Pig or Java, or other query engines such as Impala. Work is under way to address these shortcomings, though.

Parquet

Parquet shares many of the same design goals as ORC, but is intended to be a general-purpose storage format for Hadoop. In fact, ORC came after Parquet, so some could say that ORC is a Parquet wannabe. As such, the goal is to create a format that's suitable for different MapReduce interfaces such as Java, Hive, and Pig, and also suitable for other processing engines such as Impala and Spark. Parquet provides the following benefits, many of which it shares with ORC:

- Similar to ORC files, Parquet allows for returning only required data fields, thereby reducing I/O and increasing performance.
- Provides efficient compression; compression can be specified on a per-column level.
- Is designed to support complex nested data structures.
- Stores full metadata at the end of files, so Parquet files are self-documenting.
- Fully supports being able to read and write to with Avro and Thrift APIs.
- Uses efficient and extensible encoding schemas—for example, bit-packaging/run length encoding (RLE).

Avro and Parquet. Over time, we have learned that there is great value in having a single interface to all the files in your Hadoop cluster. And if you are going to pick one file format, you will want to pick one with a schema because, in the end, most data in Hadoop will be structured or semistructured data.

So if you need a schema, Avro and Parquet are great options. However, we don't want to have to worry about making an Avro version of the schema and a Parquet version. Thankfully, this isn't an issue because Parquet can be read and written to with Avro APIs and Avro schemas.

This means we can have our cake and eat it too. We can meet our goal of having one interface to interact with our Avro and Parquet files, and we can have a block and columnar options for storing our data.

Comparing Failure Behavior for Different File Formats

An important aspect of the various file formats is failure handling; some formats handle corruption better than others:

- Columnar formats, while often efficient, do not work well in the event of failure, since this can lead to incomplete rows.
- Sequence files will be readable to the first failed row, but will not be recoverable after that row.

- Avro provides the best failure handling; in the event of a bad record, the read will continue at the next sync point, so failures only affect a portion of a file.

Compression

Compression is another important consideration for storing data in Hadoop, not just in terms of reducing storage requirements, but also to improve data processing performance. Because a major overhead in processing large amounts of data is disk and network I/O, reducing the amount of data that needs to be read and written to disk can significantly decrease overall processing time. This includes compression of source data, but also the intermediate data generated as part of data processing (e.g., MapReduce jobs). Although compression adds CPU load, for most cases this is more than offset by the savings in I/O.

Although compression can greatly optimize processing performance, not all compression formats supported on Hadoop are splittable. Because the MapReduce framework splits data for input to multiple tasks, having a nonsplittable compression format is an impediment to efficient processing. If files cannot be split, that means the entire file needs to be passed to a single MapReduce task, eliminating the advantages of parallelism and data locality that Hadoop provides. For this reason, splittability is a major consideration in choosing a compression format as well as file format. We'll discuss the various compression formats available for Hadoop, and some considerations in choosing between them.

Snappy

Snappy is a compression codec developed at Google for high compression speeds with reasonable compression. Although Snappy doesn't offer the best compression sizes, it does provide a good trade-off between speed and size. Processing performance with Snappy can be significantly better than other compression formats. It's important to note that Snappy is intended to be used with a container format like SequenceFiles or Avro, since it's not inherently splittable.

LZO

LZO is similar to Snappy in that it's optimized for speed as opposed to size. Unlike Snappy, LZO compressed files are splittable, but this requires an additional indexing step. This makes LZO a good choice for things like plain-text files that are not being stored as part of a container format. It should also be noted that LZO's license prevents it from being distributed with Hadoop and requires a separate install, unlike Snappy, which can be distributed with Hadoop.

Gzip

Gzip provides very good compression performance (on average, about 2.5 times the compression that'd be offered by Snappy), but its write speed performance is not as good as Snappy's (on average, it's about half of Snappy's). Gzip usually performs almost as well as Snappy in terms of read performance. Gzip is also not splittable, so it should be used with a container format. Note that one reason Gzip is sometimes slower than Snappy for processing is that Gzip compressed files take up fewer blocks, so fewer tasks are required for processing the same data. For this reason, using smaller blocks with Gzip can lead to better performance.

bzip2

bzip2 provides excellent compression performance, but can be significantly slower than other compression codecs such as Snappy in terms of processing performance. Unlike Snappy and Gzip, bzip2 is inherently splittable. In the examples we have seen, bzip2 will normally compress around 9% better than GZip, in terms of storage space. However, this extra compression comes with a significant read/write performance cost. This performance difference will vary with different machines, but in general bzip2 is about 10 times slower than GZip. For this reason, it's not an ideal codec for Hadoop storage, unless your primary need is reducing the storage footprint. One example of such a use case would be using Hadoop mainly for active archival purposes.

Compression recommendations

In general, any compression format can be made splittable when used with container file formats (Avro, SequenceFiles, etc.) that compress blocks of records or each record individually. If you are doing compression on the entire file without using a container file format, then you have to use a compression format that inherently supports splitting (e.g., bzip2, which inserts synchronization markers between blocks).

Here are some recommendations on compression in Hadoop:

- Enable compression of MapReduce intermediate output. This will improve performance by decreasing the amount of intermediate data that needs to be read and written to and from disk.
- Pay attention to how data is ordered. Often, ordering data so that like data is close together will provide better compression levels. Remember, data in Hadoop file formats is compressed in chunks, and it is the entropy of those chunks that will determine the final compression. For example, if you have stock ticks with the columns timestamp, stock ticker, and stock price, then ordering the data by a repeated field, such as stock ticker, will provide better compression than ordering by a unique field, such as time or stock price.

- Consider using a compact file format with support for splittable compression, such as Avro. Figure 1-2 illustrates how Avro or SequenceFiles support splittability with otherwise nonsplittable compression formats. A single HDFS block can contain multiple Avro or SequenceFile blocks. Each of the Avro or SequenceFile blocks can be compressed and decompressed individually and independently of any other Avro/SequenceFile blocks. This, in turn, means that each of the HDFS blocks can be compressed and decompressed individually, thereby making the data splittable.

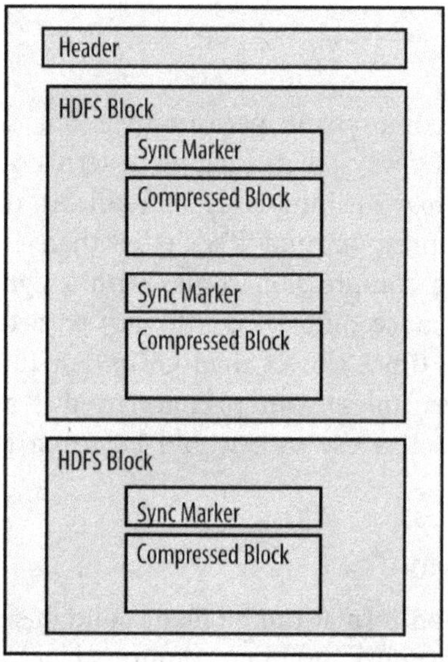

Figure 1-2. An example of compression with Avro

HDFS Schema Design

As pointed out in the previous section, HDFS and HBase are two very commonly used storage managers. Depending on your use case, you can store your data in HDFS or HBase (which internally stores it on HDFS).

In this section, we will describe the considerations for good schema design for data that you decide to store in HDFS directly. As mentioned earlier, Hadoop's Schema-on-Read model does not impose any requirements when loading data into Hadoop. Data can be simply ingested into HDFS by one of many methods (which we will discuss further in Chapter 2) without our having to associate a schema or preprocess the data.

While many people use Hadoop for storing and processing unstructured data (such as images, videos, emails, or blog posts) or semistructured data (such as XML documents and logfiles), some order is still desirable. This is especially true since Hadoop often serves as a data hub for the entire organization, and the data stored in HDFS is intended to be shared among many departments and teams. Creating a carefully structured and organized repository of your data will provide many benefits. To list a few:

- A standard directory structure makes it easier to share data between teams working with the same data sets.

- It also allows for enforcing access and quota controls to prevent accidental deletion or corruption.

- Oftentimes, you'd "stage" data in a separate location before all of it was ready to be processed. Conventions regarding staging data will help ensure that partially loaded data will not get accidentally processed as if it were complete.

- Standardized organization of data allows for reuse of some code that may process the data.

- Some tools in the Hadoop ecosystem sometimes make assumptions regarding the placement of data. It is often simpler to match those assumptions when you are initially loading data into Hadoop.

The details of the data model will be highly dependent on the specific use case. For example, data warehouse implementations and other event stores are likely to use a schema similar to the traditional star schema, including structured fact and dimension tables. Unstructured and semistructured data, on the other hand, are likely to focus more on directory placement and metadata management.

The important points to keep in mind when designing the schema, regardless of the project specifics, are:

- Develop standard practices and enforce them, especially when multiple teams are sharing the data.

- Make sure your design will work well with the tools you are planning to use. For example, the version of Hive you are planning to use may only support table partitions on directories that are named a certain way. This will impact the schema design in general and how you name your table subdirectories, in particular.

- Keep usage patterns in mind when designing a schema. Different data processing and querying patterns work better with different schema designs. Understanding the main use cases and data retrieval requirements will result in a schema that will be easier to maintain and support in the long term as well as improve data processing performance.

Location of HDFS Files

To talk in more concrete terms, the first decisions to make when you're designing an HDFS schema is the location of the files. Standard locations make it easier to find and share data between teams. The following is an example HDFS directory structure that we recommend. This directory structure simplifies the assignment of permissions to various groups and users:

/user/<username>

> Data, JARs, and configuration files that belong only to a specific user. This is usually scratch type data that the user is currently experimenting with but is not part of a business process. The directories under */user* will typically only be readable and writable by the users who own them.

/etl

> Data in various stages of being processed by an ETL (extract, transform, and load) workflow. The */etl* directory will be readable and writable by ETL processes (they typically run under their own user) and members of the ETL team. The */etl* directory tree will have subdirectories for the various groups that own the ETL processes, such as business analytics, fraud detection, and marketing. The ETL workflows are typically part of a larger application, such as clickstream analysis or recommendation engines, and each application should have its own subdirectory under the */etl* directory. Within each application-specific directory, you would have a directory for each ETL process or workflow for that application. Within the workflow directory, there are subdirectories for each of the data sets. For example, if your Business Intelligence (BI) team has a clickstream analysis application and one of its processes is to aggregate user preferences, the recommended name for the directory that contains the data would be */etl/BI/clickstream/aggregate_preferences*. In some cases, you may want to go one level further and have directories for each stage of the process: *input* for the landing zone where the data arrives, *processing* for the intermediate stages (there may be more than one *processing* directory), *output* for the final result, and *bad* where records or files that are rejected by the ETL process land for manual troubleshooting. In such cases, the final structure will look similar to */etl/<group>/<application>/<process>/{input,processing,output,bad}*

/tmp

> Temporary data generated by tools or shared between users. This directory is typically cleaned by an automated process and does not store long-term data. This directory is typically readable and writable by everyone.

/data

> Data sets that have been processed and are shared across the organization. Because these are often critical data sources for analysis that drive business deci-

sions, there are often controls around who can read and write this data. Very often user access is read-only, and data is written by automated (and audited) ETL processes. Since data in /data is typically business-critical, only automated ETL processes are typically allowed to write them—so changes are controlled and audited. Different business groups will have read access to different directories under /data, depending on their reporting and processing needs. Since /data serves as the location for shared processed data sets, it will contain subdirectories for each data set. For example, if you were storing all orders of a pharmacy in a table called *medication_orders*, we recommend that you store this data set in a directory named /data/medication_orders.

/app

Includes everything required for Hadoop applications to run, except data. This includes JAR files, Oozie workflow definitions, Hive HQL files, and more. The application code directory /app is used for application artifacts such as JARs for Oozie actions or Hive user-defined functions (UDFs). It is not always necessary to store such application artifacts in HDFS, but some Hadoop applications such as Oozie and Hive require storing shared code and configuration on HDFS so it can be used by code executing on any node of the cluster. This directory should have a subdirectory for each group and application, similar to the structure used in /etl. For a given application (say, Oozie), you would need a directory for each version of the artifacts you decide to store in HDFS, possibly tagging, via a symlink in HDFS, the latest artifact as *latest* and the currently used one as *current*. The directories containing the binary artifacts would be present under these versioned directories. This will look similar to: /app/<group>/<application>/<version>/<artifact directory>/<artifact>. To continue our previous example, the JAR for the latest build of our aggregate preferences process would be in a directory structure like /app/BI/clickstream/latest/aggregate_preferences/uber-aggregate-preferences.jar.

/metadata

Stores metadata. While most table metadata is stored in the Hive metastore, as described later in the "Managing Metadata" on page 31, some extra metadata (for example, Avro schema files) may need to be stored in HDFS. This directory would be the best location for storing such metadata. This directory is typically readable by ETL jobs but writable by the user used for ingesting data into Hadoop (e.g., Sqoop user). For example, the Avro schema file for a data set called movie may exist at a location like this: /metadata/movielens/movie/movie.avsc. We will discuss this particular example in more detail in Chapter 10.

Advanced HDFS Schema Design

Once the broad directory structure has been decided, the next important decision is how data will be organized into files. While we have already talked about how the for-

mat of the ingested data may not be the most optimal format for storing it, it's important to note that the default organization of ingested data may not be optimal either.
There are a few strategies to best organize your data. We will talk about partitioning,
bucketing, and denormalizing here.

Partitioning

Partitioning a data set is a very common technique used to reduce the amount of I/O
required to process the data set. When you're dealing with large amounts of data, the
savings brought by reducing I/O can be quite significant. Unlike traditional data
warehouses, however, HDFS doesn't store indexes on the data. This lack of indexes
plays a large role in speeding up data ingest, but it also means that every query will
have to read the entire data set even when you're processing only a small subset of the
data (a pattern called *full table scan*). When the data sets grow very big, and queries
only require access to subsets of data, a very good solution is to break up the data set
into smaller subsets, or partitions. Each of these partitions would be present in a subdirectory of the directory containing the entire data set. This will allow queries to
read only the specific partitions (i.e., subdirectories) they require, reducing the
amount of I/O and improving query times significantly.

For example, say you have a data set that stores all the orders for various pharmacies
in a data set called *medication_orders*, and you'd like to check order history for just
one physician over the past three months. Without partitioning, you'd need to read
the entire data set and filter out all the records that don't pertain to the query.

However, if we were to partition the entire orders data set so each partition included
only a single day's worth of data, a query looking for information from the past three
months will only need to read 90 or so partitions and not the entire data set.

When placing the data in the filesystem, you should use the following directory format for partitions: *<data set name>/<partition_column_name=partition_col-
umn_value>/{files}*. In our example, this translates to: *medication_orders/
date=20131101/{order1.csv, order2.csv}*

This directory structure is understood by various tools, like HCatalog, Hive, Impala,
and Pig, which can leverage partitioning to reduce the amount of I/O required during
processing.

Bucketing

Bucketing is another technique for decomposing large data sets into more managea-
ble subsets. It is similar to the hash partitions used in many relational databases. In
the preceding example, we could partition the orders data set by date because there
are a large number of orders done daily and the partitions will contain large enough
files, which is what HDFS is optimized for. However, if we tried to partition the data
by physician to optimize for queries looking for specific physicians, the resulting

number of partitions may be too large and resulting files may be too small in size. This leads to what's called the *small files problem*. As detailed in "File-based data structures" on page 6, storing a large number of small files in Hadoop can lead to excessive memory use for the NameNode, since metadata for each file stored in HDFS is held in memory. Also, many small files can lead to many processing tasks, causing excessive overhead in processing.

The solution is to *bucket* by *physician*, which will use a hashing function to map physicians into a specified number of buckets. This way, you can control the size of the data subsets (i.e., buckets) and optimize for query speed. Files should not be so small that you'll need to read and manage a huge number of them, but also not so large that each query will be slowed down by having to scan through huge amounts of data. A good average bucket size is a few multiples of the HDFS block size. Having an even distribution of data when hashed on the bucketing column is important because it leads to consistent bucketing. Also, having the number of buckets as a power of two is quite common.

An additional benefit of bucketing becomes apparent when you're joining two data sets. The word *join* here is used to represent the general idea of combining two data sets to retrieve a result. Joins can be done via SQL-on-Hadoop systems but also in MapReduce, or Spark, or other programming interfaces to Hadoop.

When both the data sets being joined are bucketed on the join key and the number of buckets of one data set is a multiple of the other, it is enough to join corresponding buckets individually without having to join the entire data sets. This significantly reduces the time complexity of doing a reduce-side join of the two data sets. This is because doing a reduce-side join is computationally expensive. However, when two bucketed data sets are joined, instead of joining the entire data sets together, you can join just the corresponding buckets with each other, thereby reducing the cost of doing a join. Of course, the buckets from both the tables can be joined in parallel. Moreover, because the buckets are typically small enough to easily fit into memory, you can do the entire join in the map stage of a Map-Reduce job by loading the smaller of the buckets in memory. This is called a *map-side join*, and it improves the join performance as compared to a reduce-side join even further. If you are using Hive for data analysis, it should automatically recognize that tables are bucketed and apply this optimization.

If the data in the buckets is *sorted*, it is also possible to use a merge join and not store the entire bucket in memory when joining. This is somewhat faster than a simple bucket join and requires much less memory. Hive supports this optimization as well. Note that it is possible to bucket any table, even when there are no logical partition keys. It is recommended to use both sorting and bucketing on all large tables that are frequently joined together, using the join key for bucketing.

As you can tell from the preceding discussion, the schema design is highly dependent on the way the data will be queried. You will need to know which columns will be used for joining and filtering before deciding on partitioning and bucketing of the data. In cases when there are multiple common query patterns and it is challenging to decide on one partitioning key, you have the option of storing the same data set multiple times, each with different physical organization. This is considered an anti-pattern in relational databases, but with Hadoop, this solution can make sense. For one thing, in Hadoop data is typically write-once, and few updates are expected. Therefore, the usual overhead of keeping duplicated data sets in sync is greatly reduced. In addition, the cost of storage in Hadoop clusters is significantly lower, so there is less concern about wasted disk space. These attributes allow us to trade space for greater query speed, which is often desirable.

Denormalizing

Although we talked about joins in the previous subsections, another method of trading disk space for query performance is denormalizing data sets so there is less of a need to join data sets. In relational databases, data is often stored in *third normal form*. Such a schema is designed to minimize redundancy and provide data integrity by splitting data into smaller tables, each holding a very specific entity. This means that most queries will require joining a large number of tables together to produce final result sets.

In Hadoop, however, joins are often the slowest operations and consume the most resources from the cluster. Reduce-side joins, in particular, require sending entire tables over the network. As we've already seen, it is important to optimize the schema to avoid these expensive operations as much as possible. While bucketing and sorting do help there, another solution is to create data sets that are prejoined—in other words, preaggregated. The idea is to minimize the amount of work queries have to do by doing as much as possible in advance, especially for queries or subqueries that are expected to execute frequently. Instead of running the join operations every time a user tries to look at the data, we can join the data once and store it in this form.

Looking at the difference between a typical Online Transaction Processing (OLTP) schema and an HDFS schema of a particular use case, you will see that the Hadoop schema consolidates many of the small dimension tables into a few larger dimensions by joining them during the ETL process. In the case of our pharmacy example, we consolidate frequency, class, admin route, and units into the medications data set, to avoid repeated joining.

Other types of data preprocessing, like aggregation or data type conversion, can be done to speed up processes as well. Since data duplication is a lesser concern, almost any type of processing that occurs frequently in a large number of queries is worth doing once and reusing. In relational databases, this pattern is often known as *Materi-*

alized Views. In Hadoop, you instead have to create a new data set that contains the same data in its aggregated form.

HDFS Schema Design Summary

To recap, in this section we saw how we can use partitioning to reduce the I/O overhead of processing by selectively reading and writing data in particular partitions. We also saw how we can use bucketing to speed up queries that involve joins or sampling, again by reducing I/O. And, finally, we saw how denormalization plays an important role in speeding up Hadoop jobs. Now that we have gone through HDFS schema design, we will go through the schema design concepts for HBase.

HBase Schema Design

In this section, we will describe the considerations for good schema design for data stored in HBase. While HBase is a complex topic with multiple books written about its usage and optimization, this chapter takes a higher-level approach and focuses on leveraging successful design patterns for solving common problems with HBase. For an introduction to HBase, see *HBase: The Definitive Guide*, or *HBase in Action*.

The first thing to understand here is that HBase is not a relational database management system (RDBMS). In fact, in order to gain a better appreciation of how HBase works, it's best to think of it as a huge hash table. Just like a hash table, HBase allows you to associate values with keys and perform fast lookup of the values based on a given key.

There are many details related to how regions and compactions work in HBase, various strategies for ingesting data into HBase, using and understanding block cache, and more that we are glossing over when using the hash table analogy. However, it's still a very apt comparison, primarily because it makes you think of HBase as more of a distributed key-value store instead of an RDBMS. It makes you think in terms of get, put, scan, increment, and delete requests instead of SQL queries.

Before we focus on the operations that can be done in HBase, let's recap the operations supported by hash tables. We can:

1. Put things in a hash table
2. Get things from a hash table
3. Iterate through a hash table (note that HBase gives us even more power here with *range scans*, which allow specifying a start and end row when scanning)
4. Increment the value of a hash table entry
5. Delete values from a hash table

It also makes sense to answer the question of why you would want to give up SQL for HBase. The value proposition of HBase lies in its scalability and flexibility. HBase is useful in many applications, a popular one being fraud detection, which we will be discussing in more detail in Chapter 9. In general, HBase works for problems that can be solved in a few get and put requests.

Now that we have a good analogy and background of HBase, let's talk about various architectural considerations that go into designing a good HBase schema.

Row Key

To continue our hash table analogy, a row key in HBase is like the key in a hash table. One of the most important factors in having a well-architected HBase schema is good selection of a row key. Following are some of the ways row keys are used in HBase and how they drive the choice of a row key.

Record retrieval

The row key is the key used when you're retrieving records from HBase. HBase records can have an unlimited number of columns, but only a single row key. This is different from relational databases, where the primary key can be a composite of multiple columns. This means that in order to create a unique row key for records, you may need to combine multiple pieces of information in a single key. An example would be a key of the type customer_id,order_id,timestamp as the row key for a row describing an order. In a relational database customer_id, order_id, and time stamp would be three separate columns, but in HBase they need to be combined into a single unique identifier.

Another thing to keep in mind when choosing a row key is that a get operation of a single record is the fastest operation in HBase. Therefore, designing the HBase schema in such a way that most common uses of the data will result in a single get operation will improve performance. This may mean putting a lot of information into a single record—more than you would do in a relational database. This type of design is called *denormalized*, as distinct from the *normalized* design common in relational databases. For example, in a relational database you will probably store customers in one table, their contact details in another, their orders in a third table, and the order details in yet another table. In HBase you may choose a very wide design where each order record contains all the order details, the customer, and his contact details. All of this data will be retrieved with a single get.

Distribution

The row key determines how records for a given table are scattered throughout various regions of the HBase cluster. In HBase, all the row keys are sorted, and each region stores a range of these sorted row keys. Each region is pinned to a region server (i.e., a node in the cluster).

A well-known anti-pattern is to use a timestamp for row keys because it would make most of the put and get requests focused on a single region and hence a single region server, which somewhat defeats the purpose of having a distributed system. It's usually best to choose row keys so the load on the cluster is fairly distributed. As we will see later in this chapter, one of the ways to resolve this problem is to *salt* the keys. In particular, the combination of device ID and timestamp or reverse timestamp is commonly used to salt the key in machine data.

Block cache

The block cache is a least recently used (LRU) cache that caches data blocks in memory. By default, HBase reads records in chunks of 64 KB from the disk. Each of these chunks is called an *HBase block*. When an HBase block is read from the disk, it will be put into the block cache. However, this insertion into the block cache can be bypassed if you desire. The idea behind the caching is that recently fetched records (and those in the same HBase block as them) have a high likelihood of being requested again in the near future. However, the size of block cache is limited, so it's important to use it wisely.

A poor choice of row key can lead to suboptimal population of the block cache. For example, if you choose your row key to be a hash of some attribute, the HBase block would have records that aren't necessarily *close* to each other in terms of relevance. Consequently, the block cache will be populated with these unrelated records, which will have a very low likelihood of resulting in a cache hit. In such a case, an alternative design would be to salt the first part of the row key with something meaningful that allows records fetched together in the same HBase block to be *close* to each other in the row key sort order. A salt is normally a hash mod on the original key or a part thereof, so it can be generated solely from the original key. We show you an example of salting keys in Chapter 9.

Ability to scan

A wise selection of row key can be used to co-locate related records in the same region. This is very beneficial in range scans since HBase will have to scan only a limited number of regions to obtain the results. On the other hand, if the row key is chosen poorly, range scans may need to scan multiple region servers for the data and subsequently filter the unnecessary records, thereby increasing the I/O requirements for the same request. Also, keep in mind that HBase scan rates are about eight times slower than HDFS scan rates. Therefore, reducing I/O requirements has a significant performance advantage, even more so compared to data stored in HDFS.

Size

The size of your row key will determine the performance of your workload. In general, a shorter row key is better than a longer row key due to lower storage overhead and faster read/write performance. However, longer row keys often lead to better get/scan properties. Therefore, there is always a trade-off involved in choosing the right row key length.

Let's take a look at an example. Table 1-1 shows a table with three records in HBase.

Table 1-1. Example HBase table

Row key	Timestamp	Column	Value
RowKeyA	Timestamp	ColumnA	ValueA
RowKeyB	Timestamp	ColumnB	ValueB
RowKeyC	Timestamp	ColumnC	ValueC

The longer the row key, the more I/O the compression codec has to do in order to store it. The same logic also applies to column names, so in general it's a good practice to keep the column names short.

 HBase can be configured to compress the row keys with Snappy. Since row keys are stored in a sorted order, having row keys that are close to each other when sorted will compress well. This is yet another reason why using a hash of some attribute as a row key is usually not a good idea since the sort order of row keys would be completely arbitrary.

Readability

While this is a very subjective point, given that the row key is so commonly used, its readability is important. It is usually recommended to start with something human-readable for your row keys, even more so if you are new to HBase. It makes it easier to identify and debug issues, and makes it much easier to use the HBase console as well.

Uniqueness

Ensuring that row keys are unique is important, since a row key is equivalent to a key in our hash table analogy. If your selection of row keys is based on a non-unique attribute, your application should handle such cases, and only put your data in HBase with a unique row key.

Timestamp

The second most important consideration for good HBase schema design is understanding and using the timestamp correctly. In HBase, timestamps serve a few important purposes:

- Timestamps determine which records are newer in case of a put request to modify the record.
- Timestamps determine the order in which records are returned when multiple versions of a single record are requested.
- Timestamps are also used to decide if a major compaction is going to remove the out-of-date record in question because the time-to-live (TTL) when compared to the timestamp has elapsed. "Out-of-date" means that the record value has either been overwritten by another put or deleted.

By default, when you are writing or updating a record, the timestamp on the cluster node at that time of write/update is used. In most cases, this is also the right choice. However, in some cases it's not. For example, there may be a delay of hours or days between when a transaction actually happens in the physical world and when it gets recorded in HBase. In such cases, it is common to set the timestamp to when the transaction actually took place.

Hops

The term *hops* refers to the number of synchronized get requests required to retrieve the requested information from HBase.

Let's take an example of a graph of relationships between people, represented in an HBase table. Table 1-2 shows a persons table that contains name, list of friends, and address for each person.

Table 1-2. Persons table

Name	Friends	Address
David	Barack, Stephen	10 Downing Street
Barack	Michelle	The White House
Stephen	Barack	24 Sussex Drive

Now, thinking again of our hash table analogy, if you were to find out the address of all of David's friends, you'd have to do a two-hop request. In the first hop, you'd retrieve a list of all of David's friends, and in the second hop you'd retrieve the addresses of David's friends.

Let's take another example. Table 1-3 shows a students table with an ID and student name. Table 1-4 shows a courses table with a student ID and list of courses that the student is taking.

Table 1-3. Students table

Student ID	Student name
11001	Bob
11002	David
11003	Charles

Table 1-4. Courses table

Student ID	Courses
11001	Chemistry, Physics
11002	Math
11003	History

Now, if you were to find out the list of courses that Charles was taking, you'd have to do a two-hop request. The first hop will retrieve Charles's student ID from the students table and the second hop will retrieve the list of Charles' courses using the student ID.

As we alluded to in "Advanced HDFS Schema Design" on page 17, examples like the preceding would be a good contender for denormalization because they would reduce the number of hops required to complete the request.

In general, although it's possible to have multihop requests with HBase, it's best to avoid them through better schema design (for example, by leveraging denormalization). This is because every hop is a round-trip to HBase that incurs a significant performance overhead.

Tables and Regions

Another factor that can impact performance and distribution of data is the number of tables and number of regions per table in HBase. If not done right, this factor can lead to a significant imbalance in the distribution of load on one or more nodes of the cluster.

Figure 1-3 shows a topology of region servers, regions, and tables in an example three-node HBase cluster.

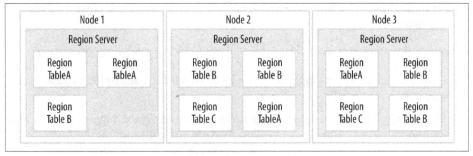

Figure 1-3. Topology of region servers, regions, and tables

The important things to note here are:

- There is one region server per node.
- There are many regions in a region server.
- At any time, a given region is pinned to a particular region server.
- Tables are split into regions and are scattered across region servers. A table must have at least one region.

There are two basic rules of thumb that you can use to select the right number of regions for a given table. These rules demonstrate a trade-off between performance of the put requests versus the time it takes to run a compaction on the region.

Put performance

All regions in a region server receiving put requests will have to share the region server's memstore. A *memstore* is a cache structure present on every HBase region server. It caches the writes being sent to that region server and sorts them in before it flushes them when certain memory thresholds are reached. Therefore, the more regions that exist in a region server, the less memstore space is available per region. This may result in smaller flushes, which in turn may lead to smaller and more HFiles and more minor compactions, which is less performant. The default configuration will set the ideal flush size to 100 MB; if you take the size of your memstore and divide that by 100 MB, the result should be the maximum number of regions you can reasonably put on that region server.

Compaction time

A larger region takes longer to compact. The empirical upper limit on the size of a region is around 20 GB, but there are very successful HBase clusters with upward of 120 GB regions.

You can assign regions to an HBase table in one of the two following ways:

- Create the table with a single default region, which then autosplits as data increases.
- Create the table with a given number of regions and set the region size to a high enough value (e.g., 100 GB per region) to avoid autosplitting.

For preselecting, you should make sure that you have the correct split policy selected. You will most likely want ConstantSizeRegionSplitPolicy or DisabledRegionSplitPolicy.

For most cases, we recommend preselecting the region count (the second option) of the table to avoid the performance impact of seeing random region splitting and suboptimal region split ranges.

However, in some cases, automatic splitting (the first option) may make more sense. One such use case is a forever-growing data set where only the most recent data is updated. If the row key for this table is composed of {Salt}{SeqID}, it is possible to control the distribution of the writes to a fixed set of regions. As the regions split, older regions will no longer need to be compacted (barring the periodic TTL-based compaction).

Using Columns

The concept of columns in an HBase table is very different than those in a traditional RDBMS. In HBase, unlike in an RDBMS, a record can have a million columns and the next record can have a million completely different columns. This isn't recommended, but it's definitely possible and it's important to understand the difference.

To illustrate, let's look into how HBase stores a record. HBase stores data in a format called HFile. Each column value gets its own row in HFile. This row has fields like row key, timestamp, column names, and values. The HFile format also provides a lot of other functionality, like versioning and sparse column storage, but we are eliminating that from the next example for increased clarity.

For example, if you have a table with two logical columns, foo and bar, your first logical choice is to create an HBase table with two columns named foo and bar. The benefits of doing so are:

- We can get one column at a time independently of the other column.

- We can modify each column independently of the other.

- Each column will age out with a TTL independently.

However, these benefits come with a cost. Each logical record in the HBase table will have two rows in the HBase HFile format. Here is the structure of such an HFile on disk:

```
|RowKey |TimeStamp  |Column  |Value
|101    |1395531114 |F       |A1
|101    |1395531114 |B       |B1
```

The alternative choice is to have both the values from foo and bar in the same HBase column. This would apply to all records of the table and bears the following characteristics:

- Both the columns would be retrieved at the same time. You may choose to disregard the value of the other column if you don't need it.

- Both the column values would need to be updated together since they are stored as a single entity (column).

- Both the columns would age out together based on the last update.

Here is the structure of the HFile in such a case:

```
|RowKey |TimeStamp  |Column  |Value
|101    |1395531114 |X       |A1|B1
```

The amount of space consumed on disk plays a nontrivial role in your decision on how to structure your HBase schema, in particular the number of columns. It determines:

- How many records can fit in the block cache

- How much data can fit through the Write-Ahead-Log maintained by HBase

- How many records can fit into the memstore flush

- How long a compaction would take

 Notice the one-character column names in the previous examples. In HBase, the column and row key names, as you can see, take up space in the HFile. It is recommended to not waste that space as much as possible, so the use of single-character column names is fairly common.

Using Column Families

In addition to columns, HBase also includes the concept of *column families*. A column family is essentially a container for columns. A table can have one or more column families. The takeaway here is that each column family has its own set of HFiles and gets compacted independently of other column families in the same table.

For many use cases, there is no need for more than one column family per table. The main reason to use more than one is when the operations being done and/or the rate of change on a subset of the columns of a table is significantly different from the other columns.

For example, let's consider an HBase table with two columns: column1 contains about 400 bytes per row and column2 contains about 20 bytes. Now let's say that the value of column1 gets set once and never changes, but that of column2 changes very often. In addition, the access patterns call get requests on column2 a lot more than on column1.

In such a case, having two column families makes sense for the following reasons:

Lower compaction cost
> If we had two separate column families, the column family with column2 will have memstore flushes very frequently, which will produce minor compactions. Because column2 is in its own column family, HBase will only need to compact 5% of the total records' worth of data, thereby making the compactions less impactful on performance.

Better use of block cache
> As you saw earlier, when a record is retrieved from HBase, the records near the requested record (in the same HBase block) are pulled into the block cache. If both column1 and column2 are in the same column family, the data for both columns would be pulled into the block cache with each get request on column2. This results in suboptimal population of the block cache because the block cache would contain column1 data, which will be used very infrequently since column 1 receives very few get requests. Having column1 and column2 in separate column families would result in the block cache being populated with values only from column2, thereby increasing the number of cache hits on subsequent get requests on column 2.

Time-to-Live

TTL is a built-in feature of HBase that ages out data based on its timestamp. This idea comes in handy in use cases where data needs to be held only for a certain duration of time. So, if on a major compaction the timestamp is older than the specified TTL in the past, the record in question doesn't get put in the HFile being generated by the major compaction; that is, the older records are removed as a part of the normal upkeep of the table.

If TTL is not used and an aging requirement is still needed, then a much more I/O-intensive operation would need to be done. For example, if you needed to remove all data older than seven years without using TTL, you would have to scan all seven years of data every day and then insert a delete record for every record that is older than seven years. Not only do you have to scan all seven years, but you also have to create new delete records, which could be multiple terabytes in size themselves. Then, finally, you still have to run a major compaction to finally remove those records from disk.

One last thing to mention about TTL is that it's based on the timestamp of an HFile record. As mentioned earlier, this timestamp defaults to the time the record was added to HBase.

Managing Metadata

Up until now, we have talked about data and the best way to structure and store it in Hadoop. However, just as important as the data is metadata about it. In this section, we will talk about the various forms of metadata available in the Hadoop ecosystem and how you can make the most out of it.

What Is Metadata?

Metadata, in general, refers to data about the data. In the Hadoop ecosystem, this can mean one of many things. To list a few, metadata can refer to:

Metadata about logical data sets
> This includes information like the location of a data set (e.g., directory in HDFS or the HBase table name), the schema associated with the data set,[1] the partitioning and sorting properties of the data set, if any, and the format of the data set, if applicable (e.g., CSV, TSV, SequenceFile, etc.). Such metadata is usually stored in a separate metadata repository.

Metadata about files on HDFS
> This includes information like permissions and ownership of such files and the location of various blocks of that file on data nodes. Such information is usually stored and managed by Hadoop NameNode.

---

1 Note that Hadoop is Schema-on-Read. Associating a schema doesn't take that away, it just implies that it is one of the ways to interpret the data in the data set. You can associate more than one schema with the same data.

Metadata about tables in HBase

This includes information like table names, associated namespace, associated attributes (e.g., MAX_FILESIZE, READONLY, etc.), and the names of column families. Such information is stored and managed by HBase itself.

Metadata about data ingest and transformations

This includes information like which user generated a given data set, where the data set came from, how long it took to generate it, and how many records there are or the size of the data loaded.

Metadata about data set statistics

This includes information like the number of rows in a data set, the number of unique values in each column, a histogram of the distribution of data, and maximum and minimum values. Such metadata is useful for various tools that can leverage it for optimizing their execution plans but also for data analysts, who can do quick analysis based on it.

In this section, we will be talking about the first point in the preceding list: metadata about logical data sets. From here on in this section, the word *metadata* will refer to metadata in that context.

Why Care About Metadata?

There are three important reasons to care about metadata:

- It allows you to interact with your data through the higher-level logical abstraction of a table rather than as a mere collection of files on HDFS or a table in HBase. This means that the users don't need to be concerned about where or how the data is stored.

- It allows you to supply information about your data (e.g., partitioning or sorting properties) that can then be leveraged by various tools (written by you or someone else) while populating and querying data.

- It allows data management tools to "hook" into this metadata and allow you to perform data discovery (discover what data is available and how you can use it) and lineage (trace back where a given data set came from or originated) analysis.

Where to Store Metadata?

The first project in the Hadoop ecosystem that started storing, managing, and leveraging metadata was Apache Hive. Hive stores this metadata in a relational database called the *Hive metastore*. Note that Hive also includes a service called the *Hive metastore service* that interfaces with the Hive metastore database. In order to avoid confusion between the database and the Hive service that accesses this database, we will call the former *Hive metastore database* and the latter *Hive metastore service*. When we refer to something as *Hive metastore* in this book, we are referring to the collective logical system comprising both the service and the database.

Over time, more projects wanted to use the same metadata that was in the Hive metastore. To enable the usage of Hive metastore outside of Hive, a separate project called HCatalog was started. Today, HCatalog is a part of Hive and serves the very important purpose of allowing other tools (like Pig and MapReduce) to integrate with the Hive metastore. It also opens up access to the Hive metastore to a broader ecosystem by exposing a REST API to the Hive metastore via the WebHCat server.

You can think of HCatalog as an accessibility veneer around the Hive metastore. See Figure 1-4 for an illustration.

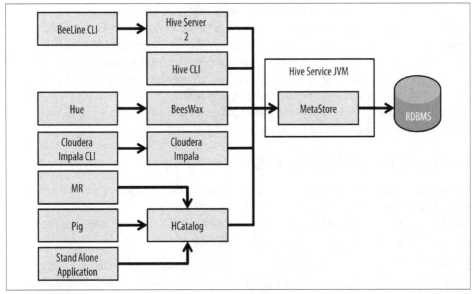

Figure 1-4. HCatalog acts as an accessibility veneer around the Hive metastore

Now MapReduce, Pig, and standalone applications could very well talk directly to the Hive metastore through its APIs, but HCatalog allows easy access through its WebHCat Rest APIs and it allows the cluster administrators to lock down access to the Hive metastore to address security concerns.

Note that you don't have to use Hive in order to use HCatalog and the Hive metastore. HCatalog just relies on some infrastructure pieces from Hive to store and access metadata about your data.

Hive metastore can be deployed in three modes: embedded metastore, local metastore, and remote metastore. Although we won't be able to do justice to the details of each of these modes here, we recommend that you use the Hive metastore in remote mode, which is a requirement for using HCatalog on top of the Hive metastore. A few of the popular databases that are supported as Hive metastore databases are MySQL, PostgreSQL, Derby, and Oracle. MySQL is by far the most commonly used in industry. You can, of course, run a new database instance, create a user for Hive and assign it the right permissions, and use this database as your metastore. If you already have a relational database instance in the organization that you can utilize, you have the option of using it as the Hive metastore database. You can simply create a new schema for Hive along with a new user and associated privileges on the existing instance.

Whether you should reuse the existing database instance instead of creating a new one depends on usage patterns of the database instance, existing load on the database instance, and other applications using the database instance. On one hand, it's good from an operational perspective to not have a new database instance for every new application (in this case the Hive metastore service, which handles metadata in the Hadoop ecosystem) but on the other hand, it makes sense to not have your Hadoop infrastructure cross-depend on a rather uncoupled database instance. Other considerations may matter as well. For example, if you already have an existing highly available database cluster in your organization, and want to use it to have high availability for your Hive metastore database, it may make sense to use the existing HA database cluster for the Hive metastore database.

Examples of Managing Metadata

If you are using Hive or Impala, you don't have to do anything special to create or retrieve metadata. These systems integrate directly with the Hive metastore, which means a simple CREATE TABLE command creates metadata, ALTER TABLE alters metadata, and your queries on the tables retrieve the stored metadata.

If you are using Pig, you can rely on HCatalog's integration with it to store and retrieve metadata. If you are using a programming interface to query data in Hadoop (e.g., MapReduce, Spark, or Cascading), you can use HCatalog's Java API to store and retrieve metadata. HCatalog also has a command-line interface (CLI) and a REST API that can be used to store, update, and retrieve metadata.

Limitations of the Hive Metastore and HCatalog

There are some downsides to using the Hive metastore and HCatalog, some of which are outlined here:

Problems with high availability
   To provide HA for the Hive metastore, you have to provide HA for the metastore database as well as the metastore service. The metastore database is a database at the end of the day and the HA story for databases is a solved problem. You can use one of many HA database cluster solutions to bring HA to the Hive meta-

store database. As far as the metastore services goes, there is support concurrently to run multiple metastores on more than one node in the cluster. However, at the time of this writing, that can lead to concurrency issues related to data definition language (DDL) statements and other queries being run at the same time.[2] The Hive community is working toward fixing these issues.

Fixed schema for metadata

While Hadoop provides a lot of flexibility on the type of data that can be stored, especially because of the Schema-on-Read concept, the Hive metastore, since it's backed by a relational backend, provides a fixed schema for the metadata itself. Now, this is not as bad as it sounds since the schema is fairly diverse, allowing you to store information all the way from columns and their types to the sorting properties of the data. If you have a rare use case where you want to store and retrieve metainformation about your data that currently can't be stored in the metastore schema, you may have to choose a different system for metadata. Moreover, the metastore is intended to provide a tabular abstraction for the data sets. If it doesn't make sense to represent your data set as a table, say if you have image or video data, you may still have a need for storing and retrieving metadata, but the Hive metastore may not be the right tool for it.

Another moving part

Although not necessarily a limitation, you should keep in mind that the Hive metastore service is yet one more moving part in your infrastructure. Consequently you have to worry about keeping the metastore service up and securing it like you secure the rest of your Hadoop infrastructure.

Other Ways of Storing Metadata

Using Hive metastore and HCatalog is the most common method of storing and managing table metadata in the Hadoop ecosystem. However, there are some cases (likely one of the limitations listed in the previous section) in which users prefer to store metadata outside of the Hive metastore and HCatalog. In this section, we describe a few of those methods.

Embedding metadata in file paths and names

As you may have already noticed in the section "HDFS Schema Design" on page 14, we recommend embedding some metadata in data set locations for organization and consistency. For example, in case of a partitioned data set, the directory structure would look like:

```
<data set name>/<partition_column_name=partition_column_value>/{files}
```

---

2 See HIVE-4759 (*http://bit.ly/hive-4759*), for example.

Such a structure already contains the name of the data set, the name of the partition column, and the various values of the partitioning column the data set is partitioned on. Tools and applications can then leverage this metadata in filenames and locations when processing. For example, listing all partitions for a data set named medication_orders would be a simple ls operation on the */data/medication_orders* directory of HDFS.

Storing the metadata in HDFS

You may decide to store the metadata on HDFS itself. One option to store such metadata is to create a hidden directory, say *.metadata*, inside the directory containing the data in HDFS. You may decide to store the schema of the data in an Avro schema file. This is especially useful if you feel constrained by what metadata you can store in the Hive metastore via HCatalog. The Hive metastore, and therefore HCatalog, has a fixed schema dictating what metadata you can store in it. If the metadata you'd like to store doesn't fit in that realm, managing your own metadata may be a reasonable option. For example, this is what your directory structure in HDFS would look like:

```
/data/event_log
/data/event_log/file1.avro
/data/event_log/.metadata
```

The important thing to note here is that if you plan to go this route, you will have to create, maintain, and manage your own metadata. You may, however, choose to use something like Kite SDK[3] to store metadata. Moreover, Kite supports multiple metadata providers, which means that although you can use it to store metadata in HDFS as just described, you can also use it to store data in HCatalog (and hence the Hive metastore) via its integration with HCatalog. You can also easily transform metadata from one source (say HCatalog) to another (say the *.metadata* directory in HDFS).

Conclusion

Although data modeling in any system is a challenging task, it's especially challenging in the Hadoop ecosystem due to the vast expanse of options available. The larger number of options exists partly due to Hadoop's increased flexibility. Even though Hadoop is still Schema-on-Read, choosing the right model for storing your data provides a lot of benefits like reducing storage footprint, improving processing times, making authorization and permission management easier, and allowing for easier metadata management.

---

3 Kite (*http://kitesdk.org/*) is a set of libraries, tools, examples, and documentation focused on making it easier to build systems on top of the Hadoop ecosystem. Kite allows users to create and manage metadata on HDFS as described in this section.

As we discussed in this chapter, you have a choice of storage managers, HDFS and HBase being the most common ones. If you're using HDFS, a number of file formats exist for storing data, with Avro being a very popular choice for row-oriented formats, and ORC and Parquet being a popular choice for column-oriented ones. A good choice of compression codecs to use for HDFS data exists as well, Snappy being one of the more popular ones. If you're storing data in HBase, the choice of row key is arguably the most important design decision from a modeling perspective.

The next important modeling choice relates to managing metadata. Although *metadata* can refer to many things, in this chapter we focused on schema-related metadata and types of fields associated with the data. The Hive metastore has become the de-facto standard for storing and managing metadata, but there are cases when users manage their own.

Choosing the right model for your data is one of the most important decisions you will make in your application, and we hope that you spend the appropriate amount of time and effort to get it right the first time.

## CHAPTER 2

Data Movement

Now that we've discussed considerations around storing and modeling data in Hadoop, we'll move to the equally important subject of moving data between external systems and Hadoop. This includes ingesting data into Hadoop from systems such as relational databases or logs, and extracting data from Hadoop for ingestion into external systems. We'll spend a good part of this chapter talking about considerations and best practices around data ingestion into Hadoop, and then dive more deeply into specific tools for data ingestion, such as Flume and Sqoop. We'll then discuss considerations and recommendations for extracting data from Hadoop.

Data Ingestion Considerations

Just as important as decisions around how to store data in Hadoop, which we discussed in Chapter 1, are the architectural decisions on getting that data into your Hadoop cluster. Although Hadoop provides a filesystem client that makes it easy to copy files in and out of Hadoop, most applications implemented on Hadoop involve ingestion of disparate data types from multiple sources and with differing requirements for frequency of ingestion. Common data sources for Hadoop include:

- Traditional data management systems such as relational databases and mainframes
- Logs, machine-generated data, and other forms of event data
- Files being imported from existing enterprise data storage systems

There are a number of factors to take into consideration when you're importing data into Hadoop from these different systems. As organizations move more and more data into Hadoop, these decisions will become even more critical. Here are the considerations we'll cover in this chapter:

Timeliness of data ingestion and accessibility
> What are the requirements around how often data needs to be ingested? How soon does data need to be available to downstream processing?

Incremental updates
> How will new data be added? Does it need to be appended to existing data? Or overwrite existing data?

Data access and processing
> Will the data be used in processing? If so, will it be used in batch processing jobs? Or is random access to the data required?

Source system and data structure
> Where is the data coming from? A relational database? Logs? Is it structured, semistructured, or unstructured data?

Partitioning and splitting of data
> How should data be partitioned after ingest? Does the data need to be ingested into multiple target systems (e.g., HDFS and HBase)?

Storage format
> What format will the data be stored in?

Data transformation
> Does the data need to be transformed in flight?

We'll start by talking about the first consideration: the timeliness requirements for the data being ingested.

Timeliness of Data Ingestion

When we talk about timeliness of data ingestion, we're referring to the time lag from when data is available for ingestion to when it's accessible to tools in the Hadoop ecosystem. The time classification of an ingestion architecture will have a large impact on the storage medium and on the method of ingestion. For purposes of this discussion we're not concerned with streaming processing or analytics, which we'll discuss separately in Chapter 7, but only with when the data is stored and available for processing in Hadoop.

In general, it's recommended to use one of the following classifications before designing the ingestion architecture for an application:

Macro batch
> This is normally anything over 15 minutes to hours, or even a daily job.

Microbatch

This is normally something that is fired off every 2 minutes or so, but no more than 15 minutes in total.

Near-Real-Time Decision Support

This is considered to be "immediately actionable" by the recipient of the information, with data delivered in less than 2 minutes but greater than 2 seconds.

Near-Real-Time Event Processing

This is considered under 2 seconds, and can be as fast as a 100-millisecond range.

Real Time

This term tends to be very overused, and has many definitions. For purposes of this discussion, it will be anything under 100 milliseconds.

It's important to note that as the implementation moves toward real time, the complexity and cost of the implementation increases substantially. Starting off at batch (e.g., using simple file transfers) is always a good idea; start simple before moving to more complex ingestion methods.

With more lenient timeliness requirements, HDFS will likely be the preferred source as the primary storage location, and a simple file transfer or Sqoop jobs will often be suitable tools to ingest data. We'll talk more about these options later, but these ingestion methods are well suited for batch ingestion because of their simple implementations and the validation checks that they provide out of the box. For example, the `hadoop fs -put` command will copy a file over and do a full checksum to confirm that the data is copied over correctly.

One consideration when using the `hdfs fs -put` command or Sqoop is that the data will land on HDFS in a format that might not be optimal for long-term storage and processing, so using these tools might require an additional batch process to get the data into the desired format. An example of where such an additional batch process would be required is loading Gzip files into HDFS. Although Gzip files can easily be stored in HDFS and processed with MapReduce or other processing frameworks on Hadoop, as we discussed in the previous chapter Gzip files are not splittable. This will greatly impact the efficiency of processing these files, particularly as the files get larger. In this case a good solution is to store the files in Hadoop using a container format that supports splittable compression, such as SequenceFiles or Avro.

As your requirements move from batch processing to more frequent updates, you should consider tools like Flume or Kafka. Sqoop and file transfers are not going to be a good selection, as the delivery requirements get shorter than two minutes. Further, as the requirements become shorter than two minutes, the storage layer may need to change to HBase or Solr for more granular insertions and read operations. As the requirements move toward the real-time category, we need to think about memory first and permanent storage second. All of the parallelism in the world isn't going to help for response requirements under 500 milliseconds as long as hard drives remain in the process. At this point, we start to enter the realm of stream processing, with tools like Storm or Spark Streaming. It should be emphasized that these tools are actually focused on data processing, as opposed to data ingest like Flume or Sqoop. Again, we'll talk more about near-real-time streaming with tools like Storm and Spark Streaming in Chapter 7. Flume and Kafka will be discussed further in this chapter.

Incremental Updates

This decision point focuses on whether the new data is data that will append an existing data set or modify it. If the requirements are for append only—for example, when you're logging user activity on a website—then HDFS will work well for the vast majority of implementations. HDFS has high read and write rates because of its ability to parallelize I/O to multiple drives. The downside to HDFS is the inability to do appends or random writes to files after they're created. Within the requirements of an "append only" use case, this is not an issue. In this case it's possible to "append" data by adding it as new files or partitions, which will enable MapReduce and other processing jobs to access the new data along with the old data.

> Note that Chapter 1 provides a full discussion of partitioning and organizing data stored in HDFS.

A very important thing to note when you're appending to directories with additional files is that HDFS is optimized for large files. If the requirements call for a two-minute append process that ends up producing lots of small files, then a periodic process to combine smaller files will be required to get the benefits from larger files. There are a number of reasons to prefer large files, one of the major reasons being how data is read from disk. Using a long consecutive scan to read a single file is faster than performing many seeks to read the same information from multiple files.

> We briefly discuss methods to manage small files later in this chapter, but a full discussion is beyond the scope of this book. See *Hadoop: The Definitive Guide* or *Hadoop in Practice* for detailed discussions on techniques to manage small files.

If the requirements also include modifying existing data, then additional work is required to land the data properly in HDFS. HDFS is read only—you can't update records in place as you would with a relational database. In this case we first write a "delta" file that includes the changes that need to be made to the existing file. A *com-*

paction job is required to handle the modifications. In a compaction job, the data is sorted by a primary key. If the row is found twice, then the data from the newer delta file is kept and the data from the older file is not. The results of the compaction process are written to disk, and when the process is complete the resulting compaction data will replace the older, uncompacted data. Note that this compaction job is a batch process—for example, a MapReduce job that's executed as part of a job flow. It may take several minutes depending on the data size, so it will only work for multi-minute timeliness intervals.

Table 2-1 is an example of how a compaction job works. Note in this example that the first column will be considered the primary key for the data.

Table 2-1. Compaction

Original data	New data	Resulting data
A,Blue,5	B,Yellow,3	A,Blue,5
B,Red,6	D,Gray,0	B,Yellow,3
C,Green,2		C,Green,2
		D,Gray,0

There are many ways to implement compaction with very different performance results. We'll provide some examples of implementing this in Chapter 4.

Another option to consider beyond HDFS and file compactions is to use HBase instead. HBase handles compactions in the background and has the architecture to support deltas that take effect upon the completion of an HBase put, which typically occurs in milliseconds.

Note that HBase requires additional administration and application development knowledge. Also, HBase has much different access patterns than HDFS that should be considered—for example, scan rates. HBase scan rates are about 8–10 times slower than HDFS. Another difference is random access; HBase can access a single record in milliseconds, whereas HDFS doesn't support random access other than file seeking, which is expensive and often complex.

Access Patterns

This decision point requires deep understanding of the underlying requirements for information delivery. How is the data going to be used once it is in Hadoop? For example: if the requirements call for random row access, HDFS may not be the best fit, and HBase might be a better choice. Conversely, if scans and data transformations are required, HBase may not be a good selection. Even though there can be many variables to consider, we suggest this basic guiding principle: for cases where simplicity, best compression, and highest scan rate are called for, HDFS is the default selection. In addition, in newer versions of HDFS (Hadoop 2.3.0 and later) caching data into memory is supported. This allows tools to read data directly from memory for files loaded into the cache. This moves Hadoop towards a massively parallel in-memory database accessible to tools in the Hadoop ecosystem. When random access is of primary importance, HBase should be the default, and for search processing you should consider Solr.

For a more detailed look, Table 2-2 includes common access patterns for these storage options.

Table 2-2. Access patterns for Hadoop storage options

Tool	Use cases	Storage device
MapReduce	Large batch processes	HDFS is preferred. HBase can be used but is less preferred.
Hive	Batch processing with SQL-like language	HDFS is preferred. HBase can be used but is less preferred.
Pig	Batch processing with a data flow language	HDFS is preferred. HBase can be used but is less preferred.
Spark	Fast interactive processing	HDFS is preferred. HBase can be used but is less preferred.
Giraph	Batch graph processing	HDFS is preferred. HBase can be used but is less preferred.
Impala	MPP style SQL	HDFS is preferred for most cases, but HBase will make sense for some use cases even through the scan rates are slower, namely near-real-time access of newly updated data and very fast access to records by primary key.
HBase API	Atomic puts, gets, and deletes on record-level data	HBase

Original Source System and Data Structure

When ingesting data from a filesystem, you should consider the following items:

Read speed of the devices on source systems

Disk I/O is often a major bottleneck in any processing pipeline. It may not be obvious, but optimizing an ingestion pipeline often requires looking at the system from which the data is being retrieved. Generally, with Hadoop we'll see read speeds of anywhere from 20 MBps to 100 MBps, and there are limitations on the motherboard or controller for reading from all the disks on the system. To maximize read speeds, make sure to take advantage of as many disks as possible on the source system. On some network attached storage (NAS) systems, additional mount points can increase throughput. Also note that a single reading thread may not be able to maximize the read speed of a drive or device. Based on our experience, on a typical drive three threads is normally required to maximize throughput, although this number will vary.

Original file type

Data can come in any format: delimited, XML, JSON, Avro, fixed length, variable length, copybooks, and many more. Hadoop can accept any file format, but not all formats are optimal for particular use cases. For example, consider a CSV file. CSV is a very common format, and a simple CSV file can generally be easily imported into a Hive table for immediate access and processing. However, many tasks converting the underlying storage of this CSV file may provide more optimal processing; for example, many analytical workloads using Parquet as a storage format may provide much more efficient processing while also reducing the storage size of the file.

Another consideration is that not all file formats can work with all tools in the Hadoop ecosystem. An example of this would be variable-length files. Variable-length files are similar to flat files in that columns are defined with a fixed length. The difference between a fixed-length file and a variable-length file is that in the variable-length file one of the leftmost columns can decide the rules to read the rest of the file. An example of this is if the first two columns are an 8-byte ID followed by a 3-byte type. The ID is just a global identifier and reads very much like a fixed-length file. The type column, however, will set the rules for the rest of the record. If the value of the type column is *car*, the record might contain columns like max speed, mileage, and color; however, if the value is *pet*, then there might be columns in the record such as size and breed. These different columns will have different lengths, hence the name "variable length." With this understanding we can see that a variable-length file may not be a good fit for Hive, but can still be effectively processed by one of the processing frameworks available for Hadoop, such as a Java MapReduce job, Crunch, Pig, or Spark.

Compression

There is a pro and a con to compressing data on the original filesystem. The pro is that transferring a compressed file over the network requires less I/O and network bandwidth. The con is that most compression codecs applied outside of Hadoop are not splittable (e.g., Gzip), although most of these compression codecs are splittable in Hadoop if you use them with a splittable container format like SequenceFiles, Parquet files, or Avro files as we discussed in Chapter 1. Normally the way to do this is to copy the compressed file to Hadoop and convert the files in a post-processing step. It's also possible to do the conversion as the data is streamed to Hadoop, but normally it makes more sense to use the distributed processing power of the Hadoop cluster to convert files, rather than just the edge nodes that are normally involved in moving data to the cluster.

 We discussed compression considerations with HDFS in Chapter 1, and we'll look at concrete examples of ingestion and post-processing in the case studies later in the book.

Relational database management systems

It is common for Hadoop applications to integrate data from RDBMS vendors like Oracle, Netezza, Greenplum, Vertica, Teradata, Microsoft, and others. The tool of choice here is almost always Apache Sqoop. Sqoop is a very rich tool with lots of options, but at the same time it is simple and easy to learn compared to many other Hadoop ecosystem projects. These options will control which data is retrieved from the RDBMS, how the data is retrieved, which connector to use, how many map tasks to use, split patterns, and final file formats.

Sqoop is a batch process, so if the timeliness of the data load into the cluster needs to be faster than batch, you'll likely have to find an alternate method. One alternative for certain use cases is to split data on ingestion, with one pipeline landing data in the RDBMS, and one landing data in HDFS. This can be enabled with tools like Flume or Kafka, but this is a complex implementation that requires code at the application layer.

Note that with the Sqoop architecture the DataNodes, not just the edge nodes, are connecting to the RDBMS. In some network configurations this is not possible, and Sqoop will not be an option. Examples of network issues are bottlenecks between devices and firewalls. In these cases, the best alternative to Sqoop is an RDBMS file dump and import into HDFS. Most relational databases support creating a delimited file dump, which can then be ingested into Hadoop via a simple file transfer. Figure 2-1 shows the difference between a file export with Sqoop versus RMDBS.

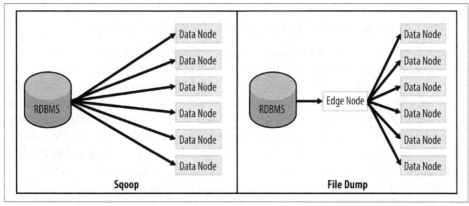

Figure 2-1. Sqoop versus RDBMS file export

We'll discuss more considerations and best practices for using Sqoop later in this chapter.

Streaming data

Examples of streaming input data include Twitter feeds, a Java Message Service (JMS) queue, or events firing from a web application server. In this situation a tool like Flume or Kafka is highly recommended. Both systems offer levels of guarantees and provide similar functionality, with some important differences. Later in this chapter we will drill down deeper into both Flume and Kafka.

Logfiles

Logfiles get their own section because they're a cross between filesystem and streaming input. An anti-pattern is to read the logfiles from disk as they are written because this is almost impossible to implement without losing data. The correct way of ingesting logfiles is to stream the logs directly to a tool like Flume or Kafka, which will write directly to Hadoop instead.

Transformations

In general, *transformation* refers to making modifications on incoming data, distributing the data into partitions or buckets, or sending the data to more than one store or location. Here are some simple examples of each option:

Transformation
    XML or JSON is converted to delimited data.

Partitioning
    Incoming data is stock trade data and partitioning by ticker is required.

Splitting
The data needs to land in HDFS and HBase for different access patterns.

Making a decision on how to transform data will depend on the timeliness of the requirements. If the timeliness of the data is batch, then the preferred solution will most likely be a file transfer followed by a batch transformation. Note that these transformations can be accomplished with tools like Hive, Pig, or Java MapReduce, or newer tools like Spark. The use of post-processing for this batch transformation step is preferred because of the checkpoints for failure provided by this processing, including the checksum on the file transfer and the all-or-nothing success/failure behavior of MapReduce. An important thing to note: MapReduce can be configured to transfer, partition, and split data beyond all-or-nothing processing. You would do so by configuring MapReduce with two output directories: one for records that were processed successfully and one for failures. In some cases, the timeliness of the data requirements will not allow for the simplicity of a file transfer followed by MapReduce processing. Sometimes the work has to be done as the data is in flight to the cluster with a stream ingestion tool like Flume. When using Flume, this can be done using interceptors and selectors. We'll cover Flume in more detail later in this chapter, but we'll briefly cover the roles of interceptors and selectors here.

Interceptors

A Flume interceptor is a Java class that allows for in-flight enrichment of event data. Since it's implemented in Java it provides great flexibility in the functionality that can be implemented. The interceptor has the capability to transform an event or a batch of events, including functionality to add or remove events from a batch. You must take special care when implementing it because it is part of a streaming framework, so the implementation should not cause the pipe to be slowed by things like calls to external services or garbage collection issues. Also remember that when transforming data with interceptors, you have a limit on processing power because normally Flume is only installed on a subset of nodes in a cluster.

Selectors

In Flume a selector object acts as a "fork in the road." It will decide which of the roads (if any) an event will go down. We'll provide an example of this in the following discussion of Flume patterns.

Network Bottlenecks

When you're ingesting into Hadoop the bottleneck is almost always the source system or the network between the source system and Hadoop. If the network is the bottleneck, it will be important to either add more network bandwidth or compress the data over the wire. You can do this by compressing the files before sending them over the wire or using Flume to compress the data between agents on different sides of the network bottleneck.

The easiest way to know if the network is the bottleneck is to look at your throughput numbers and at the network configuration: if you are using 1 Gb ethernet, the expected throughput is around 100 MBps. If this is the throughput you are seeing with Flume, than indeed you maximized the network capacity and need to consider compressing the data. For a more accurate diagnostic, you can use a network monitoring tool to determine your network utilization.

Network Security

Sometimes you need to ingest data from sources that you can access only by going outside the company's firewalls. Depending on the data, it may be important to encrypt the data while it goes over the wire. You can do so by simply encrypting the files before sending them, for example using OpenSSL. Alternatively, Flume includes support for encrypting data sent between Flume agents. Note that Kafka does not currently support encryption of data within a Kafka data flow, so you'll have to do additional work to encrypt and decrypt the data outside of Kafka.

Push or Pull

All the tools discussed in this chapter can be classified as either pushing or pulling tools. The important thing to note is the actor in the architecture because in the end that actor will have additional requirements to consider, such as:

- Keeping track of what has been sent
- Handling retries or failover options in case of failure
- Being respectful of the source system that data is being ingested from
- Access and security

We'll cover these requirements in more detail in this chapter, but first we'll discuss two common Hadoop tools—Sqoop and Flume—to help clarify the distinction between push and pull in the context of data ingestion and extraction with Hadoop.

Sqoop

Sqoop is a pull solution that is used to extract data from an external storage system such as a relational database and move that data into Hadoop, or extract data from Hadoop and move it into an external system. It must be provided various parameters about the source and target systems, such as connection information for the source database, one or more tables to extract, and so on. Given these parameters, Sqoop will run a set of jobs to move the requested data.

In the example where Sqoop is extracting (pulling) data from a relational database, we have considerations such as ensuring that we extract data from the source database at a defined rate, because Hadoop can easily consume too many resources on the source system. We also need to ensure that Sqoop jobs are scheduled to not interfere with the source system's peak load time. We'll provide further details and considerations for Sqoop later in this chapter and provide specific examples in the case studies later in the book.

Flume

Note that Flume can be bucketed in both descriptions depending on the source used. In the case of the commonly used Log4J appender, Flume is pushing events through a pipeline. There are also several Flume sources, such as the spooling directory source or the JMS source, where events are being pulled. Here again, we'll get into more detail on Flume in this section and in our case studies later in the book.

Failure Handling

Failure handling is a major consideration when you're designing an ingestion pipeline; how to recover in case of failure is a critical question. With large distributed systems, failure is not a question of *if*, but of *when*. We can put in many layers of protection when designing an ingestion flow (sometimes at great cost to performance), but there is no silver bullet that can prevent all possible failures. Failure scenarios need to be documented, including failure delay expectations and how data loss will be handled.

The simplest example of a failure scenario is with file transfers—for example, performing a `hadoop fs -put <filename>` command. When the `put` command has finished, the command will have validated that the file is in HDFS, replicated three times, and passed a checksum check. But what if the `put` command fails? The normal way of handling the file transfer failure is to have multiple local filesystem directories that represent different bucketing in the life cycle of the file transfer process. Let's look at an example using this approach.

In this example, there are four local filesystem directories: *ToLoad*, *InProgress*, *Failure*, and *Successful*. The workflow in this case is as simple as the following:

1. Move the file into *ToLoad*.

2. When the `put` command is ready to be called, move the file into *InProgress*.

3. Call the `put` command.

4. If the `put` command fails, move the file into the *Failures* directory.

5. If the `put` was successful, move the file into the *Successful* directory.

Note that a failure in the middle of a file put will require a complete resend. Consider this carefully when doing a `hadoop fs -put` with very large files. If a failure on the network happens five hours into a file transfer, the entire process has to start again.

File transfers are pretty simple, so let's take an example with streaming ingestion and Flume. In Flume, there are many areas for failure, so to keep things simple, let's just focus on the following three:

- A "pull" source such as the spooling directory source could fail to load events to the channel because the channel is full. In this case, the source must pause before retrying the channel, as well as retain the events.

- An event receiving source could fail to load the event to the channel because the channel is full. In this case, the source will tell the Flume client it was unsuccessful in accepting the last batch of events and then the Flume client is free to re-send to this source or another source.

- The sink could fail to load the event into the final destination. A sink will take a number of events from the channel and then try to commit them to the final destination, but if that commit fails then the batch of events needs to be returned to the channel.

The big difference between Flume and file transfers is that with Flume, in the case of a failure there is a chance of duplicate records getting created in Hadoop. This is because in the case of failure the event is always returned to the last step, so if the batch was half successful we will get duplicates. There are methods that try to address this issue with Flume and other streaming solutions like Kafka, but there is a heavy performance cost in trying to remove duplicates at the time of streaming. We'll see examples of processing to handle deduplication later in the book.

Level of Complexity

The last design factor that needs to be considered is complexity for the user. A simple example of this is if users need to move data into Hadoop manually. For this use case, using a simple `hadoop fs -put` or a mountable HDFS solution, like FUSE (Filesystem in Userspace) or the new NFS (Network File System) gateway, might provide a solution. We'll discuss these options next.

Data Ingestion Options

Now that we've discussed considerations around designing data ingestion pipelines, we'll dive more deeply into specific tools and methods for moving data into Hadoop. These range from simply loading files into HDFS to using more powerful tools such as Flume and Sqoop. As we've noted before, we're not attempting to provide in-depth introductions to these tools, but rather to provide specific information on effectively leveraging these tools as part of an application architecture. The suggested references will provide more comprehensive and in-depth overviews for these tools.

We'll start by discussing basic file transfers in the next section, and then move on to discussing Flume, Sqoop, and Kafka as components in your Hadoop architectures.

File Transfers

The simplest and sometimes fastest way to get data into (and out of) Hadoop is by doing file transfers—in other words, using the `hadoop fs -put` and `hadoop fs -get` commands. For this reason file transfers should be considered as the first option when you are designing a new data processing pipeline with Hadoop.

Before going into more detail, let's review the characteristics of file transfers with Hadoop:

- It's an all-or-nothing batch processing approach, so if an error occurs during file transfer no data will be written or read. This should be contrasted with ingestion methods such as Flume or Kafka, which provide some level of failure handling and guaranteed delivery.

- By default file transfers are single-threaded; it's not possible to parallize file transfers.

- File transfers are from a traditional filesystem to HDFS.

- Applying transformations to the data is not supported; data is ingested into HDFS as is. Any processing of the data needs to be done after it lands in HDFS, as opposed to in-flight transformations that are supported with a system like Flume.

- It is a byte-by-byte load, so any types of file can be transferred (text, binary, images, etc.).

HDFS client commands

As noted already, the `hadoop fs -put` command is a byte-by-byte copy of a file from a filesystem into HDFS. When the `put` job is completed, the file will be on HDFS as one or more blocks with each block replicated across different Hadoop DataNodes. The number of replicas is configurable, but the normal default is to replicate three times. To make sure that the blocks don't get corrupted, a checksum file accompanies each block.

When you use the `put` command there are normally two approaches: the *double-hop* and *single-hop*. The double-hop, shown in Figure 2-2, is the slower option because it involves an additional write and read to and from the disks on the Hadoop edge node. Sometimes, though, this is the only option because the external source filesystem isn't available to be mounted from the Hadoop cluster.

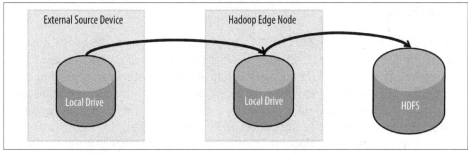

Figure 2-2. Double-hop file uploads

The alternative is the single-hop approach as shown in Figure 2-3, which requires that the source device is mountable—for example, a NAS or SAN. The external source can be mounted, and the put command can read directly from the device and write the file directly to HDFS. This approach has the benefits of improved performance. It also lessens the requirement to have edge nodes with large local drives.

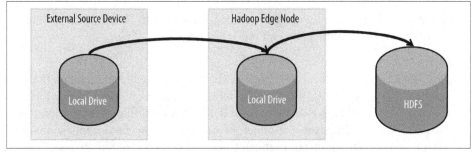

Figure 2-3. Single-hop file uploads

Mountable HDFS

In addition to using the commands available as part of the Hadoop client, there are several options available that allow HDFS to be mounted as a standard filesystem. These options allow users to interact with HDFS using standard filesystem commands such as ls, cp, mv, and so forth. Although these options can facilitate access to HDFS for users, they're of course still subject to the same limitations as HDFS:

- Just as with HDFS, none of these options offer full POSIX semantics.[1]
- Random writes are not supported; the underlying filesystem is still "write once, read many."

Another pitfall with mountable HDFS is the potential for misuse. Although it makes it easier for users to access HDFS and ingest files, this ease of access may encourage the ingestion of many small files. Since Hadoop is tuned for a relatively small number of large files, this scenario should be guarded against. Note that "many small files" could mean millions of files in a reasonably sized cluster. Still, for storage and processing efficiency it's better to store fewer large files in Hadoop. If there is a need to ingest many small files into Hadoop, there are several approaches that can be used to mitigate this:

- Use Solr for storing and indexing the small files. We'll discuss Solr in more detail in Chapter 7.
- Use HBase to store the small files, using the path and filename as the key. We'll also discuss HBase in more detail in Chapter 7.
- Use a container format such as SequenceFiles or Avro to consolidate small files.

There are several projects providing a mountable interface to Hadoop, but we'll focus on two of the more common choices, Fuse-DFS and NFS:

Fuse-DFS

Fuse-DFS is built on the FUSE project,which was designed to facilitate the creation of filesystems on UNIX/Linux systems without the need to modify the kernel. Fuse-DFS makes it easy to mount HDFS on a local filesystem, but as a user space module, it involves a number of hops between client applications and HDFS, which can significantly impact performance. Fuse-DFS also has a poor consistency model. For these reasons you should carefully consider it before deploying it as a production solution.

NFSv3

A more recent project adds support for the NFSv3 protocol to HDFS (see Figure 3-4). This provides a scalable solution with a minimal performance hit. The design involves an NFS gateway server that streams files to HDFS using the DFSClient. You can scale this solution by adding multiple NFS gateway nodes.

---

1 POSIX refers to a set of standards that operating systems should adhere to in order to support portability, including filesystem specifications. While HDFS is "POSIX-like," it does not fully support all the features expected of a POSIX-compliant filesystem.

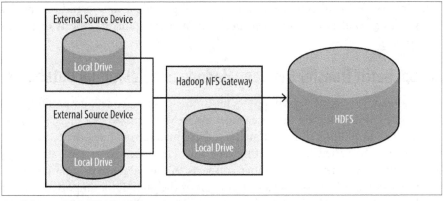

Figure 2-4. The HDFS NFSv3 gateway

Note that with the NFS gateway, writes are sent by the kernel out of order. This requires the NFS server to buffer and reorder the writes before sending them to HDFS, which can have an impact with high data volumes, both in performance and disk consumption. Before you deploy any mountable HDFS solution, it's highly recommended that you perform testing with sufficient data volumes to ensure that the solution will provide suitable performance. In general, these options are recommended for only small, manual data transfers, not for ongoing movement of data in and out of your Hadoop cluster.

Considerations for File Transfers versus Other Ingest Methods

Simple file transfers are suitable in some cases, particularly when you have an existing set of files that needs to be ingested into HDFS, and keeping the files in their source format is acceptable. Otherwise, the following are some considerations to take into account when you're trying to determine whether a file transfer is acceptable, or whether you should use a tool such as Flume:

- Do you need to ingest data into multiple locations? For example, do you need to ingest data into both HDFS and Solr, or into HDFS and HBase? In this case using a file transfer will require additional work after the files are ingested, and using Flume is likely more suitable.

- Is reliability important? If so, remember that an error mid-transfer will require a restart of the file transfer process. Here again, Flume is likely a more appropriate solution.

- Is transformation of the data required before ingestion? In that case, Flume is almost certainly the correct tool.

One option to consider if you have files to ingest is using the Flume spooling direc-tory source (*http://bit.ly/flume-spool*). This allows you to ingest files by simply placing them into a specific directory on disk. This will provide a simple and reliable way to ingest files as well as the option to perform in flight transformations of the data if required.

Sqoop: Batch Transfer Between Hadoop and Relational Databases

We've already discussed Sqoop quite a bit in this chapter, so let's get into more detail on considerations and best practices for it. As we've discussed, Sqoop is a tool used to import data in bulk from a relational database management system to Hadoop and vice versa. When used for importing data into Hadoop, Sqoop generates map-only MapReduce jobs where each mapper connects to the database using a Java database connectivity (JDBC) driver, selects a portion of the table to be imported, and writes the data to HDFS. Sqoop is quite flexible and allows not just importing full tables, but also adding where clauses to filter the data we import and even supply our own query.

For example, here is how you can import a single table:

```
sqoop import --connect jdbc:oracle:thin:@localhost:1521/oracle \
--username scott --password tiger \
--table  HR.employees --target-dir /etl/HR/landing/employee \
--input-fields-terminated-by "\t" \
--compression-codec org.apache.hadoop.io.compress.SnappyCodec --compress
```

And here is how to import the result of a join:

```
sqoop import \
  --connect jdbc:oracle:thin:@localhost:1521/oracle \
--username scott  --password tiger \
--query 'SELECT a.*, b.* FROM a JOIN b on (a.id == b.id) WHERE $CONDITIONS' \
--split-by a.id --target-dir /user/foo/joinresults
```

Note that in this example, $CONDITIONS is a literal value to type in as part of the command line. The $CONDITIONS placeholder is used by Sqoop to control the parallelism of the job, and will be replaced by Sqoop with generated conditions when the command is run.

In this section we'll outline some patterns of using Sqoop as a data ingestion method.

Choosing a split-by column

When importing data, Sqoop will use multiple mappers to parallelize the data ingest and increase throughput. By default, Sqoop will use four mappers and will split work between them by taking the minimum and maximum values of the primary key column and dividing the range equally among the mappers. The split-by parameter lets you specify a different column for splitting the table between mappers, and num-mappers lets you control the number of mappers. As we'll discuss shortly, one reason to specify a parameter for split-by is to avoid data skew. Note that each mapper will have its own connection to the database, and each will retrieve its portion of the table when we specify its portion limits in a `where` clause. It is important to choose a split column that has an index or is a partition key to avoid each mapper having to scan the entire table. If no such key exists, specifying only one mapper is the preferred solution.

Using database-specific connectors whenever available

Different RDBMSs support different dialects of SQL language. In addition they each have their own implementation and their own methods of optimizing data transfers. Sqoop ships with a generic JDBC connector that will work with any database that supports JDBC, but there are also vendor-specific connectors that translate across different dialects and optimize data transfer. For example, the Teradata connector will use Teradata's FastExport utility to optimally execute data import, while the Oracle connector will disable parallel queries to avoid bottlenecks on the query coordinator.

Using the Goldilocks method of Sqoop performance tuning

In most cases, Hadoop cluster capacity will vastly exceed that of the RDBMS. If Sqoop uses too many mappers, Hadoop will effectively run a denial-of-service attack against your database. If we use too few mappers, data ingest rates may be too slow to meet requirements. It is important to tune the Sqoop job to use a number of mappers that is "just right"—that is, one that adheres to the Goldilocks principle.[2]

Since the risk of overloading the database is much greater than the risk of a slower ingest, we typically start with a very low number of mappers and gradually increase it to achieve a balance between Sqoop ingest rates and keeping the database and network responsive to all users.

Loading many tables in parallel with fair scheduler throttling

There is a very common use case of having to ingest many tables from the same RDBMS. There are two different approaches to implementing fair scheduler throttling:[3]

Load the tables sequentially
   This solution is by far the simplest but has the drawback of not optimizing the bandwidth between the RDBMS and the Hadoop cluster. To illustrate this, imagine that we have five tables. Each table is ingested using a different number of

---

2 The Goldilocks principle states that something must fall within certain margins, as opposed to reaching extremes.

3 Fair schedulers are a method of sharing resources between jobs that allocate, on average, an equal share of the resources to each job. To read more on the Hadoop fair scheduler and how it can be used, see Chapter 7, "Resource Management" in Hadoop Operations (*http://bit.ly/hadoop-ops*) by Eric Sammer (O'Reilly).

mappers because not all table sizes require allocating the full number of allowed mappers. The result of this example will look like Figure 2-5.

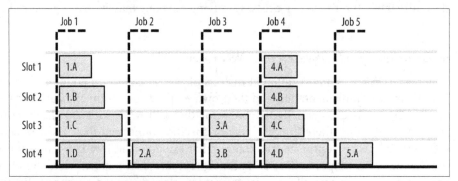

Figure 2-5. Sqoop tasks executing sequentially

As you can see from the figure, there are mappers left idle during certain jobs. This leads to the idea of running these jobs in parallel so we can optimally leverage the available mappers and decrease the processing and network time.

Load the tables in parallel

Running Sqoop jobs in parallel will allow you to use resources more effectively, but it adds the complexity of managing the total number of mappers being run against the RDBMS at the same time. You can solve the problem of managing the total number of mappers by using the fair scheduler to make a pool that has the maximum mappers set to the maximum number of mappers Sqoop should be allowed to use to interact with the RDBMS. If done correctly, the execution of the five jobs illustrated in the synchronized solution will look like Figure 2-6.

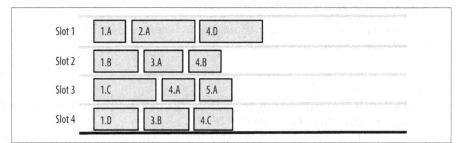

Figure 2-6. Sqoop tasks executing in parallel with number of tasks limited to four by the fair scheduler

Diagnosing bottlenecks

Sometimes we discover that as we increase the number of mappers, the ingest rate does not increase proportionally. Ideally, adding 50% more mappers will result in

50% more rows ingested per minute. While this is not always realistic, if adding more mappers has little impact on ingest rates, there is a bottleneck somewhere in the pipe.

Here are a few likely bottlenecks:

Network bandwidth

 The network between the Hadoop cluster and the RDBMS is likely to be either 1 GbE or 10 GbE. This means that your ingest rate will be limited to around 120 MBps or 1.2 GBps, respectively. If you are close to these rates, adding more mappers will increase load on the database, but will not improve ingest rates.

RDBMS

 Reading data from the database requires CPU and disk I/O resources on the database server. If either of these resources is not available, adding more mappers is likely to make matters worse. Check the query generated by the mappers. When using Sqoop in incremental mode, we expect it to use indexes. When Sqoop is used to ingest an entire table, full table scans are typically preferred. If multiple mappers are competing for access to the same data blocks, you will also see lower throughput. It is best to discuss Sqoop with your enterprise database administrators and have them monitor the database while importing data to Hadoop. Of course, it is also ideal to schedule Sqoop execution times when the database utilization is otherwise low.

Data skew

 When using multiple mappers to import an entire table, Sqoop will use the primary key to divide the table between the mappers. It will look for the highest and lowest values of the key and divide the range equally between the mappers. For example, if we are using two mappers, `customer_id` is the primary key of the table, and `select min(customer_id),max(customer_id) from customers` returns 1 and 500, then the first mapper will import customers 1—250 and the second will import customers 251—500. This means that if the data is skewed, and parts of the range actually have less data due to missing values, some mappers will have more work than others. You can use `--split-by` to choose a better split column, or `--boundary-query` to use your own query to determine the way rows will be split between mappers.

Connector

 Not using an RDBMS-specific connector, or using an old version of the connector, can lead to using slower import methods and therefore lower ingest rates.

Hadoop

 Because Sqoop will likely use very few mappers compared to the total capacity of the Hadoop cluster, this is an unlikely bottleneck. However, it is best to verify that Sqoop's mappers are not waiting for task slots to become available and to check disk I/O, CPU utilization, and swapping on the DataNodes where the mappers are running.

Inefficient access path

When a primary key does not exist, or when importing the result of a query, you will need to specify your own split column. It is incredibly important that this column is either the partition key or has an index. Having multiple mappers run full-table scans against the same table will result in significant resource contention on the RDBMS. If no such split column can be found, you will need to use only one mapper for the import. In this case, one mapper will actually run faster than multiple mappers with a bad split column.

Keeping Hadoop updated

Ingesting data from an RDBMS to Hadoop is rarely a single event. Over time the tables in the RDBMS will change and the data in Hadoop will require updating. In this context it is important to remember that HDFS is a read-only filesystem and the data files cannot be updated (with the exception of HBase tables, where appends are supported). If we wish to update data, we need to either replace the data set, add partitions, or create a new data set by merging changes.

In cases where the table is relatively small and ingesting the entire table takes very little time, there is no point in trying to keep track of modifications or additions to the table. When we need to refresh the data in Hadoop, we simply re-run the original Sqoop import command, ingest the entire table including all the modifications, and then replace the old version with a newer one.

When the table is larger and takes a long time to ingest, we prefer to ingest only the modifications made to the table since the last time we ingested it. This requires the ability to identify such modifications. Sqoop supports two methods for identifying new or updated rows:

Sequence ID

When each row has a unique ID, and newer rows have higher IDs than older ones, Sqoop can track the last ID it wrote to HDFS. Then the next time we run Sqoop it will only import rows with IDs higher than the last one. This method is useful for fact tables where new data is added, but there are no updates of existing rows.

For example, first create a job:

```
sqoop job --create movie_id --import  --connect \
jdbc:mysql://localhost/movielens  \
--username training --password training \
--table movie --check-column id --incremental append
```

Then, to get an incremental update of the RDBMS data, execute the job:

```
sqoop job --exec movie_id
```

Timestamp

When each row has a timestamp indicating when it was created or when it was last updated, Sqoop can store the last timestamp it wrote to HDFS. In the next execution of the job, it will only import rows with higher timestamps. This method is useful for slowly changing dimensions where rows are both added and updated.

When running Sqoop with the `--incremental` flag, you can reuse the same directory name, so the new data will be loaded as additional files in the same directory. This means that jobs running on the data directory will see all incoming new data without any extra effort. The downside of this design is that you lose data consistency —jobs that start while Sqoop is running may process partially loaded data. We recommend having Sqoop load the incremental update into a new directory. Once Sqoop finishes loading the data (as will be indicated by the existence of a _*SUCCESS* file), the data can be cleaned and preprocessed before it is copied into the data directory. The new directory can also be added as a new partition to an existing Hive table.

When the incremental ingest contains not only new rows but also updates to existing rows, we need to merge the new data set with the existing one. Sqoop supports this with the command `sqoop-merge`. It takes the merge key (typically the primary key of the table), the old and new directories, and a target location as parameters. Sqoop will read both data sets and when two rows exist for the same key, it will keep the latest version. `sqoop-merge` code is fairly generic and will work with any data set created by Sqoop. If the data sets are known to be sorted and partitioned, the merge process can be optimized to take advantage of these facts and work as a more efficient map-only job.

Flume: Event-Based Data Collection and Processing

Flume is a distributed, reliable, and available system for the efficient collection, aggregation, and movement of streaming data. Flume is commonly used for moving log data, but can be used whenever there's a need to move massive quantities of event data such as social media feeds, message queue events, or network traffic data. We'll provide a brief overview of Flume here and then cover considerations and recommendations for its use. For more details on Flume, refer to the Flume documentation (*http://bit.ly/flume-docs*) or *Using Flume* by Hari Shreedharan (O'Reilly).

Flume architecture

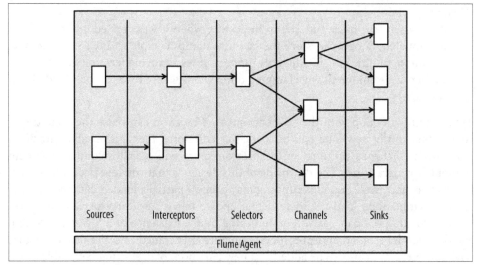

Figure 2-7. Flume components

Figure 2-7 shows the main components of Flume:

- Flume sources consume events from external sources and forward to channels. These external sources could be any system that generates events, such as a social media feed like Twitter, machine logs, or message queues. Flume sources are implemented to consume events from specific external sources, and many sources come bundled with Flume, including AvroSource, SpoolDirectorySource, HTTPSource, and JMSSource.

- Flume interceptors allow events to be intercepted and modified in flight. This can be transforming the event, enriching the event, or basically anything that can be implemented in a Java class. Some common uses of interceptors are formatting, partitioning, filtering, splitting, validating, or applying metadata to events.

- Selectors provide routing for events. Selectors can be used to send events down zero or more paths, so they are useful if you need to fork to multiple channels, or send to a specific channel based on the event.

- Flume channels store events until they're consumed by a sink. The most commonly used channels are the memory channel and the file channel. The memory channel stores events in memory, which provides the best performance among the channels, but also makes it the least reliable, because events will be lost if the process or host goes down. More commonly used is the disk channel, which provides more durable storage of events by persisting to disk. Choosing the right channel is an important architectural decision that requires balancing performance with durability.

- Sinks remove events from a channel and deliver to a destination. The destination could be the final target system for events, or it could feed into further Flume processing. An example of a common Flume sink is the HDFS sink, which, as its name implies, writes events into HDFS files.
- The Flume agent is a container for these components. This is a JVM process hosting a set of Flume sources, sinks, channels, and so on.

Flume provides the following features:

Reliability
Events are stored in the channel until delivered to the next stage.

Recoverable
Events can be persisted to disk and recovered in the event of failure.

Declarative
No coding is required. The configuration specifies how components are wired together.

Highly customizable
Although Flume includes a number of sources, sinks, and more out of the box, it provides a highly pluggable architecture that allows for the implementation of custom components based on requirements.

A Note About Guarantees

Although Flume provides "guaranteed" delivery, in the real world there's no way to provide a 100% guarantee. Failures can happen at many levels: memory can fail, disks can fail, even entire nodes can fail. Even though Flume can't provide 100% guarantees of event delivery, the level of guarantee can be tuned through configuration. Higher levels of guarantee of course come with a price in performance. It will be the responsibility of the architect to decide the level of guarantee required, keeping in mind the performance trade-offs. We'll discuss some of these considerations further in this section.

Flume patterns

The following patterns illustrate some common applications of Flume for data ingestion:

Fan-in
Figure 2-8 shows an example of a fan-in architecture, probably the most common Flume architecture. In this example, there's a Flume agent on each source system, say web servers, which send events to agents on Hadoop edge nodes.

These edge nodes should be on the same network as the Hadoop cluster. Using multiple edge nodes provides reliability: if one edge node goes down, you don't lose events. It's also recommended to compress events before you send them to reduce network traffic. SSL can also be used to encrypt data on the wire if security is a concern. We'll see a full example of a Flume fan-in configuration in the case study on clickstream processing.

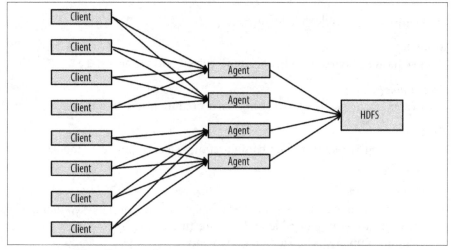

Figure 2-8. Flume fan-in architecture

Splitting data on ingest

Another very common pattern is to split events for ingestion into multiple targets. A common use of this is to send events to a primary cluster and a backup cluster intended for disaster recovery (DR). In Figure 2-9, we're using Flume to write the same events into our primary Hadoop cluster as well as a backup cluster. This DR cluster is intended to be a failover cluster in the event that the primary cluster is unavailable. This cluster also acts as a data backup, since effectively backing up Hadoop-sized data sets usually requires a second Hadoop cluster.

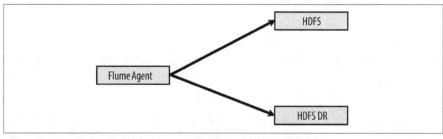

Figure 2-9. Flume event splitting architecture

Partitioning data on ingest

Flume can also be used to do partitioning of data as it's ingested, as shown in Figure 2-10. For example, the HDFS sink can partition events by timestamp.

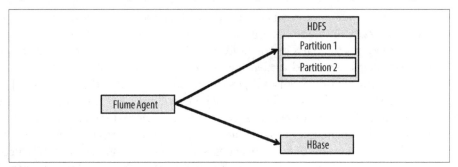

Figure 2-10. Flume partitioning architecture

Splitting events for streaming analytics

Up until now we have only talked about a persistent layer as final targets for Flume, but another common use case is sending to a streaming analytics engine such as Storm or Spark Streaming where real-time counts, windowing, and summaries can be made. In the case of Spark Streaming, the integration is simple since Spark Streaming implements the interface for the Flume Avro source, so all we have to do is point a Flume Avro sink to Spark Streaming's Flume Stream.

File formats

The following are some file format considerations when you're ingesting data into HDFS with Flume (we talked more about storage considerations in Chapter 1).

Text files

Text is a very common format for events processed through Flume, but is not an optimal format for HDFS files for the reasons discussed in Chapter 1. In general, when you're ingesting data through Flume it's recommended to either save to SequenceFiles, which is the default for the HDFS sink, or save as Avro. Note that saving files as Avro will likely require some extra work to convert the data, either on ingestion or as post-processing step. We'll provide an example of Avro conversion in the clickstream processing case study. Both SequenceFiles and Avro files provide efficient compression while also being splittable. Avro is preferred because it stores schema as part of the file, and also compresses more efficiently. Avro also checkpoints, providing better failure handling if there's an issue writing to a file.

Columnar formats

Columnar file formats such as RCFile, ORC, or Parquet are also not well suited for Flume. These formats compress more efficiently, but when you use them with

Flume, they require batching events, which means you can lose more data if there's a problem. Additionally, Parquet requires writing schema at the end of files, so if there's an error the entire file is lost.

Writing to these different formats is done through Flume *event serializers*, which convert a Flume event into another format for output. In the case of text or sequence files, writing events to HDFS is straightforward because they're well supported by the Flume HDFS sink. As noted earlier, ingesting data as Avro will likely require additional work, either on ingest or as a post-processing step. Note that there is an Avro event serializer available for the HDFS sink, but it will use the event schema for creating the Avro data, which will most likely not be the preferred schema for storing the data. It's possible, though, to override the EventSerializer interface to apply your own logic and create a custom output format. Creating custom event serializers is a common task, since it's often required to make the format of the persisted data look different from the Flume event that was sent over the wire. Note that interceptors can also be used for some of this formatting, but event serializers are closer to the final output to disk, while the interceptor's output still has to go through a channel and a sink before getting to the serialization stage.

Recommendations

The following are some recommendations and best practices for using Flume.

Flume sources. A Flume source is of course the origin for a Flume pipeline. This is where data is either pushed to Flume (say, in the case of the Avro source), or where Flume is pulling from another system for data (for example, in the case of the JMS source). There are two main considerations in configuring Flume sources that are critical to optimal Flume performance:

Batch size
> The number of events in a Flume batch can have dramatic effects on performance. Let's take the Avro source as an example. In this example, a client sends a batch of events to the Avro source, and then must wait until those events are in the channel and the Avro source has responded back to the client with an acknowledgment of success. This seems simple enough, but network latency can have a large impact here; as Figure 2-11 shows, even a couple of milliseconds of delay in a ping could add up to a significant delay in processing events. In this diagram there is a 12-millisecond delay to get a batch through. Now, if you are loading a million events with a batch size of 1 versus a batch size of 1,000, it would take 3.33 hours for the first batch, versus 12 seconds for the second batch. As you can see, setting an appropriate batch size when configuring Flume is important to optimal performance. Start with 1,000 events in a batch and adjust up or down from there based on performance.

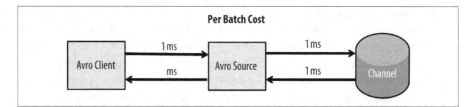

Figure 2-11. Effect of latency on flume performance

Threads

Understanding how Flume sources utilize threads will allow you to optimally take advantage of multithreading with those sources. In general, more threads are good up to the point at which your network or CPUs are maxed out. Threading is different for different sources in Flume. Let's take the Avro source as an example; the Avro source is a Netty server[4] and can have many connections to it at the same time, so to make the Avro source multithreaded you simply add more clients or client threads. A JMS source is very different; this source is a pull source, so to get more threads you need to configure more sources in your Flume agent.

Flume sinks.   Remember, sinks are what cause your data to land in its final destination. Here are some considerations for configuring Flume sinks in your Flume agents:

Number of sinks

A sink can only fetch data from a single channel, but many sinks can fetch data from that same channel. A sink runs in a single thread, which has huge limitations on a single sink—for example, throughput to disk. Assume with HDFS you get 30 MBps to a single disk; if you only have one sink writing to HDFS then all you're going to get is 30 MBps throughput with that sink. More sinks consuming from the same channel will resolve this bottleneck. The limitation with more sinks should be the network or the CPU. Unless you have a really small cluster, HDFS should never be your bottleneck.

Batch Sizes

Remember with all disk operations, buffering adds significant benefits in terms of throughput. Also remember for a Flume sink to guarantee to the channel that an event is committed, that event needs to be on disk. This means that the output stream to disk needs to be flushed, which requires the overhead of an fsync system call. If the sink is getting small batches, then a lot of time will be lost to executing these system calls. The only big downside to large batches with a sink is an

---

4 Netty is a Java-based software framework that's designed to support simplified development of client-server networking applications.

increased risk of duplicate events. For example, if a Flume process dies after some events have been written to HDFS but not acknowledged, those events might get rewritten when the process restarts. It's therefore important to carefully tune batch sizes to provide a balance between throughput and potential duplicates. However, as we noted earlier, it's relatively easy to add a post-processing step to remove duplicate records, and we'll show an example later in the book.

Flume interceptors. Interceptors can be a very useful component in Flume. The capability to take an event or group of events and modify them, filter them, or split them provides powerful functionality, but this comes with a warning. A custom interceptor is of course custom code, and custom code comes with risk of issues like memory leaks or consuming excessive CPU. Just remember with great power comes greater risk of introducing bugs in production, so it's very important to carefully review and test any custom interceptor code.

Flume memory channels. If performance is your primary consideration, and data loss is not an issue, then memory channel is the best option. Keep in mind that with the memory channel, if a node goes down or the Java process hosting the channel is killed, the events still in the memory channel are lost forever. Further, the number of events that can be stored is limited by available RAM, so the memory channel's ability to buffer events in the event of downstream failure is limited.

Flume file channels. As noted before, since the file channel persists events to disk, it's more durable than the memory channel. It's important to note, though, that it's possible to make trade-offs between durability and performance depending on how file channels are configured.

Before we proceed with recommendations for file channels, note that in addition to maintaining events on disk, the file channel also writes events to periodic checkpoints. These checkpoints facilitate restart and recovery of file channels, and should be taken into consideration when you're configuring file channels to ensure reliability.

Here are some considerations and recommendations for using file channels:

- Configuring a file channel to use multiple disks will help to improve performance because the file channel will round-robin writes between the different disks. Further, if you have multiple file channels on a single node, use distinct directories, and preferably separate disks, for each channel.

- In addition to the preceding point, using an enterprise storage system such as NAS can provide guarantees against data loss, although at the expense of performance and cost.

- Use dual checkpoint directories. A backup checkpoint directory should be used to provide higher guarantees against data loss. You can configure this by setting

`useDualCheckpoint` to `true`, and setting a directory value for `backupCheckpoint`
`Dir`.

We should also note the much less commonly used JDBC channel that persists events
to any JDBC-compliant data store, such as a relational database. This is the most
durable channel, but also the least performant due to the overhead of writing to a
database. The JDBC channel is generally not recommended because of performance,
and should only be used when an application requires maximum reliability.

A Note About Channels

Although we've been discussing the difference between the memory channel and file channel and why you might prefer one over
the other, there are times when you'll want to use both in the same
architecture. For example, a common pattern is to split events
between a persistent sink to HDFS, and a streaming sink, which
sends events to a system such as Storm or Spark Streaming for
streaming analytics. The persistent sink will likely use a file channel
for durability, but for the streaming sink the primary requirements
will likely be maximum throughput. Additionally, with the streaming data flow dropping events is likely acceptable, so the best-effort
and high-performance characteristics of the memory channel make
it the better choice.

Sizing Channels. When configuring a Flume agent, you'll often face questions around
whether to have more channels or fewer, or how to size the capacity of those channels. Here are some simple pointers:

Memory channels
> Consider limiting the number of memory channels on a single node. Needless to
> say, the more memory channels you configure on a single node, the less memory
> is available to each of those channels. Note that a memory channel can be fed by
> multiple sources and can be fetched from by multiple sinks. It's common for a
> sink to be slower than the corresponding source, or vice versa, making it neces-
> sary to have more of the slower component connected to a single channel. You
> would want to consider more memory channels on a node in the case where you
> have different pipelines, meaning the data flowing through the pipeline is either
> different or going to a different place.

File channels
> When the file channel only supported writing to one drive, it made sense to con-
> figure multiple file channels to take advantage of more disks. Now that the file
> channel can support writing to multiple drives or even to multiple files on the
> same drive, there's no longer as much of a performance benefit to using multiple

file channels. Here again, the main reason to configure multiple file channels on a node is the case where you have different pipelines. Also, whereas with the memory channel you need to consider the amount of memory available on a node when configuring your channels, with the file channel you of course need to consider the amount of disk space available.

Channel size

Remember the channel is a buffer, not a storage location. Its main goal is to store data until it can be consumed by sinks. Normally, the buffer should only get big enough so that its sinks can grab the configured batch sizes of data from the channel. If your channel is reaching max capacity, you most likely need more sinks or need to distribute the writing across more nodes. Larger channel capacities are not going to help you if your sinks are already maxed out. In fact, a larger channel may hurt you; for example, a very large memory channel could have garbage collection activity that could slow down the whole agent.

Finding Flume bottlenecks

There are many options to configure Flume, so many that it may be overwhelming at first. However, these options are there because Flume pipelines are meant to be built on top of a variety of networks and devices. Here is a list of areas to review when you're trying to identify performance issues with Flume:

Latency between nodes

Every client-to-source batch commit requires a full round-trip over the network. A high network latency will hurt performance if the batch size is low. Using many threads or larger batch sizes can help mitigate this issue.

Throughput between nodes

There are limits to how much data can be pushed through a network. Short of adding more network capacity, consider using compression with Flume to increase throughput.

Number of threads

Taking advantage of multiple threads can help improve performance in some cases with Flume. Some Flume sources support multiple threads, and in other cases an agent can be configured to have more than one source.

Number of sinks

HDFS is made up of many drives. A single HDFS sink will only be writing to one spindle at a time. As we just noted, consider writing with more than one sink to increase performance.

Channel

If you're using file channels, understand the performance limitations of writing to disk. As we previously noted, a file channel can write to many drives, which can help improve performance.

Garbage collection issues

When using the memory channel, you might experience full garbage collections; this can happen when event objects are stored in the channel for too long.

Kafka

Apache Kafka is a distributed publish-subscribe messaging system. It maintains a feed of messages categorized into topics. Applications can publish messages on Kafka, or they can subscribe to topics and receive messages that are published on those specific topics. Messages are published by *producers* and are pulled and processed by *consumers*. As a distributed system Kafka runs in a cluster, and each node is called a *broker*.

For each topic, Kafka maintains a *partitioned log*. Each partition is an ordered subset of the messages published to the topic. Partitions of the same topic can be spread across many brokers in the cluster, as a way to scale the capacity and throughput of a topic beyond what a single machine can provide. Messages are ordered within a partition and each message has a unique *offset*. A combination of topic, partition, and offset will uniquely identify a message in Kafka. Producers can choose which partition each message will be written to based on the message key, or they can simply distribute the messages between partitions in a round-robin fashion.

Consumers are registered in *consumer groups*; each group contains one or more consumers, and each consumer reads one or more partitions of a topic. Each message will be delivered to only one consumer within a group. However, if multiple groups are subscribed to the same topic, each group will get all messages. Having multiple consumers in a group is used for load balancing (supporting higher throughput than a single consumer can handle) and high availability (if one consumer fails, the partitions it was reading will be reassigned to other consumers in the group).

As you know from the preceding discussion, a topic is the main unit of application-level data separation. A consumer or consumer group will read all data in each topic it is subscribed to, so if only a subset of the data is of interest for each application, it should be placed in two different topics. If sets of messages are always read and processed together, they belong in the same topic.

A partition, on the other hand, is the main unit of parallelism. Each partition has to fit in a single server, but a topic can be as large as the sum of its partitions. In addition, each partition can be consumed by at most one consumer from the same group, so while you can add more consumers to increase read throughput, you are effectively limited by the number of partitions available in a topic. Therefore, we recommend at least as many partitions per node as there are servers in the cluster, possibly planning for a few years of growth. There are no real downsides to having a few hundred partitions per topic.

Kafka stores all messages for a preconfigured length of time (typically weeks or months) and only keeps track of the offset of the last message consumed by each consumer. This allows consumers to recover from crashes by rereading the topic partitions starting from the last good offset. Consumers can also rewind the state of the queue and reconsume messages. The rewind feature is especially useful for debugging and troubleshooting. By storing all messages for a period of time and not tracking acknowledgments for individual consumers and messages, Kafka can scale to more than 10,000 consumers, support consumers that read data in infrequent batches (MapReduce jobs, for example), and maintain low latency even with very high messaging throughput. Traditional message brokers that track individual acknowledgments typically need to store all unacknowledged messages in memory. With large number of consumers or consumers that read data in batches, this often causes swapping and severe degradation of performance as a result.

The following are some common use cases for Kafka:

- Kafka can be used in place of a traditional message broker or message queue in an application architecture in order to decouple services.
- Kafka's most common use case is probably high rate activity streams, such as website clickstream, metrics, and logging.
- Another common use case is stream data processing, where Kafka can be used as both the source of the information stream and the target where a streaming job records its results for consumption by other systems. We'll see examples of this in Chapter 7.

Kafka fault tolerance

Each topic partition can be replicated to multiple brokers, to allow continued service and no data loss in case of broker crash. For each partition, one replica is designated as a *leader* and the rest as followers. All reads and writes are done from the leader. The followers serve as insurance: if the leader crashes, a new leader will be elected from the list of synchronized replicas. A follower is considered synchronized if it did not fall too far behind the leader in replication.

When writing data, the producer can choose whether the write will be acknowledged by all synchronized replicas or just the leader, or to not wait for acknowledgments at all. The more acknowledgments the producer waits for, the more it can be sure the data written will not be lost in a crash. However, if reliability is not a concern, then waiting for fewer acknowledgements will allow for higher throughput. Administrators can also specify a minimum threshold for the number of synchronized replicas—if the number of synchronized replicas falls below this limit, writes that require acknowledgment from all synchronized replicas will be rejected. This provides extra assurance that messages will not be accidentally written to just a single broker, where they may be lost if this broker crashes.

Note that if a network failure occurs after a message was sent but before it was acknowledged, the producer has no way to check if it was written to a broker. It is up to the producer to decide whether to resend the message and risk duplicates or to skip it and risk missing data.

When reading data, the consumer will only read *committed* messages—that is, messages that were written to all synchronized replicas. This means that consumers don't need to worry about accidentally reading data that will later disappear when a broker crashes.

Kafka guarantees that all messages sent by a producer to a specific topic partition will be written to the partition in the order they were sent. The consumers will see those messages in the order they were sent. And if a partition was defined with replication factor of N, a failure of $N-1$ nodes will not cause any message loss.

Kafka can support *at least once*, *at most once*, and *exactly once* delivery semantics, depending on the configuration of the consumer:

- If the consumer advances the offset in Kafka after processing messages (default settings), it is possible that a consumer will crash after processing the data but before advancing the offset. This means that a new consumer will reread messages since the last offset; messages will be processed *at least once*, but there may be duplicates.

- If the consumer first advances the offset and then processes the messages, it may crash after the offset was advanced but before data was processed. In this case, the new consumer will read data from the new offset, skipping messages that were read but not processed by the crashed consumer. Messages will be processed *at most once*, but there may be data loss.

- If the consumer uses a two-phase commit to process data and advance the offset at the same time, messages will be processed *exactly once*. Since two-phase commits have high overhead, this is best done in batch consumers and not streaming processes. Camus, a Hadoop consumer that we'll discuss later, has *exactly once* semantics—both data and offset are getting written to HDFS by the mapper, and both will be removed if a mapper fails.

To complete the review of Kafka's high availability guarantees, we'll mention that Kafka can be deployed in multiple data centers. In this setup, one cluster serves as a consumer of another cluster, and as such replicates all messages with the same HA guarantees available to all consumers.

Kafka and Hadoop

Kafka is a generic message broker and was not written specifically for Hadoop. However, there are several use cases that combine both systems. One use case involves consuming messages from Kafka and storing them in HDFS for offline processing. For example, when tracking clickstream activity on a website, you can use Kafka to publish site activities such as page views and searches. These messages can then be consumed by real-time dashboards or real-time monitors, as well as stored in HDFS for offline analysis and reporting.

Another common use case is real-time stream processing. Kafka provides a reliable stream of messages as the data source for Spark Streaming or Storm. This use case will be covered in detail in Chapter 7.

A common question is whether to use Kafka or Flume for ingest of log data or other streaming data sources into Hadoop. As usual, this depends on requirements:

- Flume is a more complete Hadoop ingest solution; it has very good support for writing data to Hadoop, including HDFS, HBase, and Solr. It is configuration-based, so Hadoop administrators can deploy and use Flume without writing any code. Flume handles many common issues in writing data to HDFS, such as reliability, optimal file sizes, file formats, updating metadata, and partitioning.

- Kafka is a good fit as a reliable, highly available, high performance data source. If the requirements involve fault-tolerant message delivery, message replay, or a large number of potential consumers, Kafka is an excellent choice. However, this means you will have to develop your own producers and consumers rather than rely on existing sources and sinks.

Looking at how Flume and Kafka compare, it seems that they are complementary—Kafka provides a flexible, high-throughput, and reliable message bus, whereas Flume provides an easy-to-use collection of sources, interceptors, and Hadoop integration. It therefore can make a lot of sense to use both.

Flume includes a Kafka source, Kafka sink, and Kafka channel. These allow for sending events from Kafka to Flume sinks (such as HDFS, HBase, and Solr), or from Flume sources (such as Log4j and Netcat) to Kafka, and they even use Kafka to enhance Flume with a reliable channel.

Flume's Kafka source is a Kafka consumer, which reads data from Kafka and sends it to the Flume channel where it can continue flowing through the Flume topology. Configuring the source is as simple as setting a topic, the ZooKeeper server used by Kafka, and the channel. The source allows for tuning the batch sizes that will be sent from the source to the channel. Use smaller batches for low latency and larger batches for higher throughput and reduced CPU utilization.

By default, Flume uses the groupId `flume` when reading from Kafka. Adding multiple Flume sources with the same groupId will mean that each Flume agent will get a subset of the messages and can increase throughput. In addition, if one of the sources fails, the remaining sources will rebalance so that they can continue consuming all messages. Flume's Kafka source is reliable and will not lose messages if a source, channel, sink, or agent fails.

Flume's Kafka sink is a Kafka producer, which sends data from a Flume channel to Kafka. Configuring a Kafka sink requires setting a topic and a list of Kafka brokers. Similar to the Kafka source, it is also possible to tune the batch size on the Kafka sink for improved throughput or reduced latency.

Flume's Kafka channel combines a producer and a consumer. When a Flume source sends messages to the Kafka channel, these events will be sent to a Kafka topic. Each batch will be sent to a separate Kafka partition, so the writes will be load-balanced. When the Kafka sink reads from the channel, the events will be consumed from Kafka. The Kafka channel is highly reliable. When used with a properly configured Kafka server, it can guarantee that messages will not be lost, or even significantly delayed, in the event of server crashes.

Streaming data is not always appropriate. Batching typically supports better throughputs, and is a better fit for compressed columnar storage such as Parquet. For batch loads from Kafka, we recommend using Camus (*https://github.com/linkedin/camus*), a separate open source project that allows for ingesting data from Kafka to HDFS. Camus is flexible and relatively well maintained. It features automatic discovery of Kafka topics from ZooKeeper, conversion of messages to Avro and Avro schema management, and automatic partitioning. In the setup stage of the job, it fetches the list of topics and the ID of the first messages to consume from ZooKeeper, and then splits the topics among the map tasks. Each map task pulls messages from Kafka and writes them to HDFS directories based on timestamps. Camus map tasks will only move the messages to the final output location when the task finishes successfully. This allows the use of Hadoop's speculative execution without the risk of writing duplicate messages in HDFS.

Figure 2-12 is a high-level diagram to help give you an idea of how Camus works.

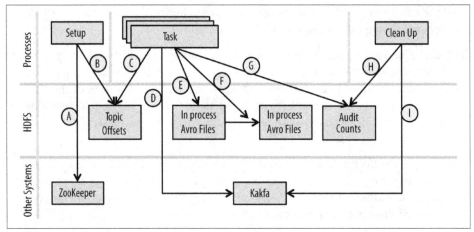

Figure 2-12. Camus execution flow

This diagram details the following series of steps:

- A: The setup stage fetches broker URLs and topic information from ZooKeeper.
- B: The setup stage persists information about topics and offsets in HDFS for the tasks to read.
- C: The tasks read the persisted information from the setup stage.
- D: The tasks get events from Kafka.
- E: The tasks write data to a temporary location in HDFS in the format defined by the user-defined decoder, in this case Avro-formatted files.
- F: The tasks move the data in the temporary location to a final location when the task is cleaning up.
- G: The task writes out audit counts on its activities.
- H: A clean-up stage reads all the audit counts from all the tasks.
- I: The clean-up stage reports back to Kafka what has been persisted.

To use Camus, you may need to write your own decoder to convert Kafka messages to Avro. This is similar to a serializer in Flume's HDFSEventSink.

Data Extraction

The bulk of this chapter has been concerned with getting data into Hadoop, which is where you generally spend more time when designing applications on Hadoop. Getting data out of Hadoop is, of course, also an important consideration though, and many of the considerations around getting data into Hadoop also apply to getting it out. The following are some common scenarios and considerations for extracting data from Hadoop:

Moving data from Hadoop to an RDBMS or data warehouse

A common pattern is to use Hadoop for transforming data for ingestion into a data warehouse—in other words, using Hadoop for ETL. In most cases, Sqoop will be the appropriate choice for ingesting the transformed data into the target database. However, if Sqoop is not an option, using a simple file extract from Hadoop and then using a vendor-specific ingest tool is an alternative. When you're using Sqoop it's important to use database-specific connectors when they're available. Regardless of the method used, avoid overloading the target database—data volumes that are easily managed in Hadoop may overwhelm a traditional database. Do yourself and your database administrator a favor and carefully consider load on the target system.

Another consideration is that as Hadoop matures and closes the gap in capabilities with traditional data management systems, we'll see more workloads being moved to Hadoop from these systems, reducing the need to move data out of Hadoop.

Exporting for analysis by external applications

Related to the previous item, Hadoop is a powerful tool for processing and summarizing data for input to external analytical systems and applications. For these cases a simple file transfer is probably suitable—for example, using the `Hadoop fs -get` command or one of the mountable HDFS options.

Moving data between Hadoop clusters

Transferring data between Hadoop clusters is also common—for example, for disaster recovery purposes or moving data between multiple clusters. In this case the solution is DistCp, which provides an easy and efficient way to transfer data between Hadoop clusters. DistCp uses MapReduce to perform parallel transfers of large volumes of data. DistCp is also suitable when either the source or target is a non-HDFS filesystem—for example, an increasingly common need is to move data into a cloud-based system, such as Amazon's Simple Storage System (S3).

Conclusion

There's a seemingly overwhelming array of tools and mechanisms to move data into and out of Hadoop, but as we discussed in this chapter, if you carefully consider your requirements it's not difficult to arrive at a correct solution. Some of these considerations are:

- The source systems for data ingestion into Hadoop, or the target systems in the case of data extraction from Hadoop

- How often data needs to be ingested or extracted

- The type of data being ingested or extracted

- How the data will be processed and accessed

Understanding the capabilities and limitations of available tools and the requirements for your particular solution will enable you to design a robust and scalable architecture.

## CHAPTER 3

Processing Data in Hadoop

In the previous chapters we've covered considerations around modeling data in Hadoop and how to move data in and out of Hadoop. Once we have data loaded and modeled in Hadoop, we'll of course want to access and work with that data. In this chapter we review the frameworks available for processing data in Hadoop.

With processing, just like everything else with Hadoop, we have to understand the available options before deciding on a specific framework. These options give us the knowledge to select the correct tool for the job, but they also add confusion for those new to the ecosystem. This chapter is written with the goal of giving you the knowledge to select the correct tool based on your specific use cases.

We will open the chapter by reviewing the main execution engines—the frameworks directly responsible for executing data processing tasks on Hadoop clusters. This includes the well-established MapReduce framework, as well as newer options such as data flow engines like Spark.

We'll then move to higher-level abstractions such as Hive, Pig, Crunch, and Cascading. These tools are designed to provide easier-to-use abstractions over lower-level frameworks such as MapReduce.

For each processing framework, we'll provide:

- An overview of the framework
- A simple example using the framework
- Rules for when to use the framework
- Recommended resources for further information on the framework

After reading this chapter, you will gain an understanding of the various data processing options, but not deep expertise in any of them. Our goal in this chapter is to give you confidence that you are selecting the correct tool for your use case. If you want more detail, we'll provide references for you to dig deeper into a particular tool.

Shared Nothing Architectures

Before we dive into a specifics of each framework, note one thing they all have in common: as much as possible, they attempt to implement a shared nothing architecture. In distributed systems, this is an architecture where each node is completely independent of other nodes in the system. There are no shared resources that can become bottlenecks. The lack of shared resources refers to physical resources such as memory, disks, and CPUs—instead of using centralized storage, Hadoop's processing framework uses the distributed HDFS storage. It also refers to lack of shared data—in those frameworks, each node is processing a distinct subset of the data and there's no need to manage access to shared data. Shared nothing architectures are very scalable: because there are no shared resources, addition of nodes adds resources to the system and does not introduce further contention. These architectures are also fault-tolerant: each node is independent, so there are no single points of failure, and the system can quickly recover from a failure of an individual node. As you read this chapter, notice how each framework preserves the principles of shared nothing architecture whereas its other details differ.

MapReduce

The MapReduce model was introduced in a white paper by Jeffrey Dean and Sanjay Ghemawat from Google called *MapReduce: Simplified Data Processing on Large Clusters* (*http://bit.ly/dean-ghemawat*). This paper described a programming model and an implementation for processing and generating large data sets. This programming model provided a way to develop applications to process large data sets in parallel, without many of the programming challenges usually associated with developing distributed, concurrent applications. The shared nothing architecture described by this model provided a way to implement a system that could be scaled through the addition of more nodes, while also providing fault tolerance when individual nodes or processes failed.

MapReduce Overview

The MapReduce programming paradigm breaks processing into two basic phases: a map phase and a reduce phase. The input and output of each phase are key-value pairs.

The processes executing the map phase are called *mappers*. Mappers are Java processes (JVMs) that normally start up on nodes that also contain the data they will process. Data locality is an important principle of MapReduce; with large data sets, moving the processing to the servers that contain the data is much more efficient than moving the data across the network. An example of the types of processing typically performed in mappers are parsing, transformation, and filtering. When the mapper has processed the input data it will output a key-value pair to the next phase, the sort and shuffle.

In the sort and shuffle phase, data is sorted and partitioned. We will discuss the details of how this works later in the chapter. This partitioned and sorted data is sent over the network to reducer JVMs that read the data ordered and partitioned by the keys. When a reducer process gets these records, the `reduce0` function can do any number of operations on the data, but most likely the reducer will write out some amount of the data or aggregate to a store like HDFS or HBase.

To summarize, there are two sets of JVMs. One gets data unsorted and the other gets data sorted and partitioned. There are many more parts to MapReduce that we will touch on in a minute, but Figure 3-1 shows what has been described so far.

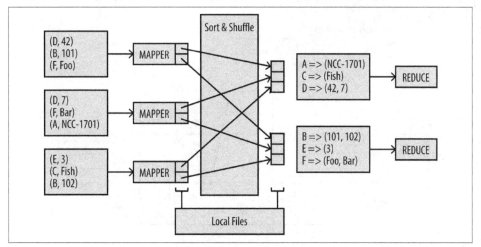

Figure 3-1. MapReduce sort and shuffle

The following are some typical characteristics of MapReduce processing:

- Mappers process input in key-value pairs and are only able to process a single pair at a time. The number of mappers is set by the framework, not the developer.
- Mappers pass key-value pairs as output to reducers, but can't pass information to other mappers. Reducers can't communicate with other reducers either.

- Mappers and reducers typically don't use much memory and the JVM heap size is set relatively low.

- Each reducer typically, although not always, has a single output stream—by default a set of files named *part-r-00000*, *part-r-00001*, and so on, in a single HDFS directory.

- The output of the mapper and the reducer is written to disk. If the output of the reducer requires additional processing, the entire data set will be written to disk and then read again. This pattern is called *synchronization barrier* and is one of the major reasons MapReduce is considered inefficient for iterative processing of data.

Before we go into the lower-level details of MapReduce, it is important to note that MapReduce has two major weaknesses that make it a poor option for iterative algorithms. The first is the startup time. Even if you are doing almost nothing in the MapReduce processing, there is a loss of 10—30 seconds just to startup cost. Second, MapReduce writes to disk frequently in order to facilitate fault tolerance. Later on in this chapter when we study Spark, we will learn that all this disk I/O isn't required. Figure 3-2 illustrates how many times MapReduce reads and writes to disk during typical processing.

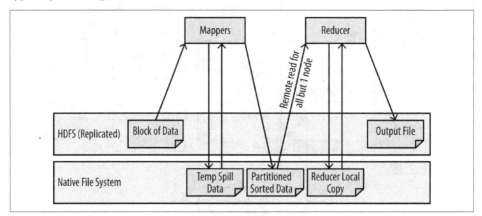

Figure 3-2. MapReduce I/O

One of the things that makes MapReduce so powerful is the fact that it is made not just of map and reduce tasks, but rather multiple components working together. Each one of these components can be extended by the developer. Therefore, in order to make the most out of MapReduce, it is important to understand its basic building blocks in detail. In the next section we'll start with a detailed look into the map phase in order to work toward this understanding.

There are a number of good references that provide more detail on MapReduce than we can go into here, including implementations of various algorithms. Some good resources are *Hadoop: The Definitive Guide* (*http://bit.ly/hadoop_tdg_4e*), *Hadoop in Practice*, and *MapReduce Design Patterns* (*http://bit.ly/mapreduce-patterns*) by Donald Miner and Adam Shook (O'Reilly).

Map phase

Next, we provide a detailed overview of the major components involved in the map phase of a MapReduce job.

InputFormat.   MapReduce jobs access their data through the `InputFormat` class. This class implements two important methods:

`getSplits()`
> This method implements the logic of how input will be distributed between the map processes. The most commonly used Input Format is the `TextInputFormat`, which will generate an input split per block and give the location of the block to the map task. The framework will then execute a mapper for each of the splits. This is why developers usually assume the number of mappers in a MapReduce job is equal to the number of blocks in the data set it will process.

> This method determines the number of map processes and the cluster nodes on which they will execute, but because it can be overridden by the developer of the MapReduce job, you have complete control over the way in which files are read. For example, the `NMapInputFormat` in the HBase code base allows you to directly set the number of mappers executing the job.

`getReader()`
> This method provides a reader to the map task that allows it to access the data it will process. Because the developer can override this method, MapReduce can support any data type. As long as you can provide a method that reads the data into a writable object, you can process it with the MapReduce framework.

RecordReader.   The `RecordReader` class reads the data blocks and returns key-value records to the map task. The implementation of most `RecordReader`s is surprisingly simple: a `RecordReader` instance is initialized with the start position in the file for the block it needs to read and the URI of the file in HDFS. After seeking to the start position, each call to `nextKeyValue()` will find the next row delimiter and read the next record. This pattern is illustrated in Figure 3-3.

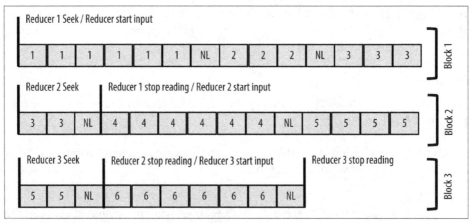

Figure 3-3. MapReduce RecordReader

The MapReduce framework and other ecosystem projects provide `RecordReader` implementations for many file formats: text delimited, SequenceFile, Avro, Parquet, and more. There are even `RecordReader`s that don't read any data—`NMapInputFormat` returns a `NullWritable` as the key and value to the mapper. This is to make sure the `map()` method gets called once.

Mapper.setup(). Before the map method of the map task gets called, the mapper's `setup()` method is called once. This method is used by developers to initialize variables and file handles that will later get used in the map process. Very frequently the `setup()` method is used to retrieve values from the configuration object.

Every component in Hadoop is configured via a `Configuration` object, which contains key-value pairs and is passed to the map and reduce JVMs when the job is executed. The contents of this object can be found in *job.xml*. By default the `Configuration` object contains information regarding the cluster that every JVM requires for successful execution, such as the URI of the NameNode and the process coordinating the job (e.g., the JobTracker when Hadoop is running within the Map-Reduce v1 framework or the Application Manager when it's running with YARN).

Values can be added to the `Configuration` object in the setup phase, before the map and reduce tasks are launched. After the job is executed, the mappers and reducers can access the `Configuration` object at any time to retrieve these values. Here is a simple example of a `setup()` method that gets a `Configuration` value to populate a member variable:

```
public String fooBar;
public final String FOO_BAR_CONF = "custom.foo.bar.conf";

@Override
```

```
public void setup(Context context) throws IOException {
    foobar = context.getConfiguration().get(FOO_BAR_CONF);
}
```

Note that anything you put in the Configuration object can be read through the Job-Tracker (in MapReduce v1) or Application Manager (in YARN). These processes have a web UI that is often left unsecured and readable to anyone with access to its URL, so we recommend against passing sensitive information such as passwords through the Configuration object. A better method is to pass the URI of a password file in HDFS, which can have proper access permissions. The map and reduce tasks can then read the content of the file and get the password if the user executing the Map-Reduce job has sufficient privileges.

Mapper.map. The map() method is the heart of the mapper. Even if you decide to use the defaults and not implement any other component of the map task, you will still need to implement a map() method. This method has three inputs: key, value, and a context. The key and value are provided by the RecordReader and contain the data that the map() method should process. The context is an object that provides common actions for a mapper: sending output to the reducer, reading values from the Configuration object, and incrementing counters to report on the progress of the map task.

When the map task writes to the reducer, the data it is writing is buffered and sorted. MapReduce will attempt to sort it in memory, with the available space defined by the io.sort.mb configuration parameter. If the memory buffer is too small, not all the output data can be sorted in memory. In this case the data is spilled to the local disk of the node where the map task is running and sorted on disk.

Partitioner. The partitioner implements the logic of how data is partitioned between the reducers. The default partitioner will simply take the key, hash it using a standard hash function, and divide by the number of reducers. The remainder will determine the target reducer for the record. This guarantees equal distribution of data between the reducers, which will help ensure that reducers can begin and end at the same time. But if there is any requirement for keeping certain values together for processing by the reducers, you will need to override the default and implement a custom partitioner.

One such example is a secondary sort. Suppose that you have a time series—for example, stock market pricing information. You may wish to have each reducer scan all the trades of a given stock ticker ordered by the time of the trade in order to look for correlations in pricing over time. In this case you will define the key as *ticker-time*. The default partitioner could send records belonging to the same stock ticker to different reducers, so you will also want to implement your own partitioner to make sure the ticker symbol is used for partitioning the records to reducers, but the time-stamp is not used.

Here is a simple code example of how this type of partitioner method would be implemented:

```
public static class CustomPartitioner extends Partitioner<Text, Text> {
    @Override
    public int getPartition(Text key, Text value, int numPartitions) {
      String ticker = key.toString().substring(5);
      return ticker.hashCode() % numPartitions;
    }
}
```

We simply extract the ticker symbol out of the key and use only the hash of this part for partitioning instead of the entire key.

Mapper.cleanup(). The `cleanup()` method is called after the `map()` method has exe-cuted for all records. This is a good place to close files and to do some last-minute reporting—for example, to write a message to the log with final status.

Combiner. Combiners in MapReduce can provide an easy method to reduce the amount of network traffic between the mappers and reducers. Let's look at the famous word count example. In word count, the mapper takes each input line, splits it into individual words and writes out each word with "1" after it, to indicate current count, like the following:

    the => 1
    cat => 1
    and => 1
    the => 1
    hat => 1

If a `combine()` method is defined it can aggregate the values produced by the mapper. It executes locally on the same node where the mapper executes, so this aggregation reduces the output that is later sent through the network to the reducer. The reducer will still have to aggregate the results from different mappers, but this will be over sig-nificantly smaller data sets. It is important to remember that you have no control on whether the combiner will execute. Therefore, the output of the combiner has to be identical in format to the output of the mapper, because the reducer will have to pro-cess either of them. Also note that the combiner executes after the output of the map-per is already sorted, so you can assume that the input of the combiner is sorted.

In our example, this would be the output of a combiner:

    and => 1
    cat => 1

hat => 1
the => 2

Reducer

The reduce task is not as complex as the map task, but there are a few components of which you should be aware.

Shuffle.   Before the reduce stage begins, the reduce tasks copy the output of the mappers from the map nodes to the reduce nodes. Since each reducer will need data to aggregate data from multiple mappers, we can have each reducer just read the data locally in the same way that map tasks do. Copying data over the network is mandatory, so a high-throughput network within the cluster will improve processing times significantly. This is the main reason why using a combiner can be very effective; aggregating the results of the mapper before sending them over the network will speed up this phase significantly.

Reducer.setup().   The reducer `setup()` step is very similar to the map `setup()`. The method executes before the reducer starts processing individual records and is typically used to initialize variables and file handles.

Reducer.reduce().   Similar to the `map()` method in the mapper, the `reduce()` method is where the reducer does most of the data processing. There are a few significant differences in the inputs, however:

- The keys are sorted.
- The `value` parameter has changed to `values`. So for one key the input will be all the values for that key, allowing you to then perform any type of aggregation and processing for all the values of the key. It is important to remember that a key and all its values will never be split across more than one reducer; this seems obvious, but often developers are surprised when one reducer takes significantly longer to finish than the rest. This is typically the result of this reducer processing a key that has significantly more values than the rest. This kind of skew in the way data is partitioned is a very common cause of performance concerns, and as a result a skilled MapReduce developer will invest significant effort in making sure data is partitioned between the reducers as evenly as possible while still aggregating the values correctly.
- In the `map()` method, calling `context.write(K,V)` stores the output in a buffer that is later sorted and read by the reducer. In the `reduce()` method, calling `context.write(Km,V)` sends the output to the `outputFileFormat`, which we will discuss shortly.

Reducer.cleanup().   Similar to the mapper `cleanup()` method, the reducer `cleanup()` method is called after all the records are processed. This is where you can close files and log overall status.

OutputFormat.   Just like the `InputFormat` class handled the access to input data, the `OutputFormat` class is responsible for formatting and writing the output data, typically to HDFS. Custom output formats are rare compared to input formats. The main reason is that developers rarely have control over the input data, which often arrives in legacy formats from legacy systems. On the other hand, the output data can be standardized and there are several suitable output formats already available for you to use. There is always a client with a new and unique input format, but generally one of the available output formats will be suitable. In the first chapter we discussed the most common data formats available and made recommendations regarding which ones to use in specific situations.

The `OutputFormat` class works a little bit differently than `InputFormat`. In the case of a large file, `InputFormat` would split the input to multiple map tasks, each handling a small subset of a single input file. With the `OutputFormat` class, a single reducer will always write a single file, so on HDFS you will get one file per reducer. The files will be named something like *part-r-00000* with the numbers ascending as the task numbers of the reducers ascend.

It is interesting to note that if there are no reducers, the output format is called by the mapper. In that case, the files will be named *part-m-0000N*, replacing the *r* with *m*. This is just the common format for naming, however, and different output formats can use different variations. For example, the Avro output format uses *part-m-00000.avro* as its naming convention.

Example for MapReduce

Of all the approaches to data processing in Hadoop that will be included in this chapter, MapReduce requires the most code by far. As verbose as this example will seem, if we included every part of MapReduce here, it would easily be another 20 pages. We will look at a very simple example: joining and filtering the two data sets shown in Figure 3-4.

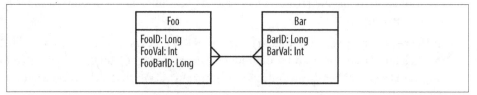

Figure 3-4. Data sets for joining and filtering example

The data processing requirements in this example include:

- Join Foo to Bar by FooBarId and BarId.

- Filter Foo and remove all records where FooVal is greater than a user-defined value, `fooValueMaxFilter`.

- Filter the joined table and remove all records where the sum of FooVal and BarVal is greater than another user parameter, `joinValueMaxFilter`.

- Use counters to track the number of rows we removed.

MapReduce jobs always start by creating a Job instance and executing it. Here is an example of how this is done:

```
public int run(String[] args) throws Exception {
    String inputFoo = args[0];
    String inputBar = args[1];
    String output = args[2];
    String fooValueMaxFilter = args[3];
    String joinValueMaxFilter = args[4];
    int numberOfReducers = Integer.parseInt(args[5]);

    Job job = Job.getInstance();                            ❶

    job.setJarByClass(JoinFilterExampleMRJob.class);
    job.setJobName("JoinFilterExampleMRJob");               ❷

    Configuration config = job.getConfiguration();
    config.set(FOO_TABLE_CONF, inputFoo);                   ❸
    config.set(BAR_TABLE_CONF, inputBar);
    config.set(FOO_VAL_MAX_CONF, fooValueMaxFilter);
    config.set(JOIN_VAL_MAX_CONF, joinValueMaxFilter);

    job.setInputFormatClass(TextInputFormat.class);
    TextInputFormat.addInputPath(job, new Path(inputFoo));  ❹
    TextInputFormat.addInputPath(job, new Path(inputBar));
    job.setOutputFormatClass(TextOutputFormat.class);
    TextOutputFormat.setOutputPath(job, new Path(output));

    job.setMapperClass(JoinFilterMapper.class);             ❺
    job.setReducerClass(JoinFilterReducer.class);
    job.setPartitionerClass(JoinFilterPartitioner.class);
    job.setOutputKeyClass(NullWritable.class);
    job.setOutputValueClass(Text.class);
    job.setMapOutputKeyClass(Text.class);
    job.setMapOutputValueClass(Text.class);

    job.setNumReduceTasks(numberOfReducers);                ❻

    job.waitForCompletion(true);                            ❼
    return 0;
}
```

Let's drill down into the job setup code:

❶ This is the constructor of the Job object that will hold all the information needed for the execution of our MapReduce job.

❷ While not mandatory, it is a good practice to name the job so it will be easy to find in various logs or web UIs.

❸ As we discussed, when setting up the job, you can create a Configuration object with values that will be available to all map and reduce tasks. Here we add the values that will be used for filtering the records, so they are defined by the user as arguments when the job is executed, not hardcoded into the map and reduce tasks.

❹ Here we are setting the input and output directories. There can be multiple input paths, and they can be either files or entire directories. But unless a special output format is used, there is only one output path and it must be a directory, so each reducer can create its own output file in that directory.

❺ This is where we configure the classes that will be used in this job: mapper, reducer, partitioner, and the input and output formats. In our example we only need a mapper, reducer, and partitioner. We will soon show the code used to implement each of those. Note that for the output format we use Text as the value output, but NullWritable as the key output. This is because we are only interested in the values for the final output. The keys will simply be ignored and not written to the reducer output files.

❻ While the number of mappers is controlled by the input format, we have to configure the number of reducers directly. If the number of reducers is set to 0, we would get a map-only job. The default number of reducers is defined at the cluster level, but is typically overridden by the developers of specific jobs because they are more familiar with the size of the data involved and how it is partitioned.

❼ Finally, we fire off the configured MapReduce job to the cluster and wait for its success or failure.

Now let's look at the mapper:

```
public class JoinFilterMapper extends
  Mapper<LongWritable, Text, Text, Text> {

  boolean isFooBlock = false;
  int fooValFilter;

  public static final int FOO_ID_INX = 0;
```

```
public static final int FOO_VALUE_INX = 1;
public static final int FOO_BAR_ID_INX = 2;
public static final int BAR_ID_INX = 0;
public static final int BAR_VALUE_INX = 1;

Text newKey = new Text();
Text newValue = new Text();

@Override
public void setup(Context context) {

  Configuration config = context.getConfiguration();   ❶
  fooValFilter = config.getInt(JoinFilterExampleMRJob.FOO_VAL_MAX_CONF, -1);


  String fooRootPath =
    config.get(JoinFilterExampleMRJob.FOO_TABLE_CONF);   ❷
  FileSplit split = (FileSplit) context.getInputSplit();
  if (split.getPath().toString().contains(fooRootPath)) {
    isFooBlock = true;
  }
}

@Override
public void map(LongWritable key, Text value, Context context)
    throws IOException, InterruptedException {

  String[] cells = StringUtils.split(value.toString(), "|");


  if (isFooBlock) {      ❸
    int fooValue = Integer.parseInt(cells[FOO_VALUE_INX]);

    if (fooValue <= fooValFilter) {    ❹
      newKey.set(cells[FOO_BAR_ID_INX] + "|"
          + JoinFilterExampleMRJob.FOO_SORT_FLAG);
      newValue.set(cells[FOO_ID_INX] + "|" + cells[FOO_VALUE_INX]);
      context.write(newKey, newValue);
    } else {
      context.getCounter("Custom", "FooValueFiltered").increment(1);  ❺
    }
  } else {
    newKey.set(cells[BAR_ID_INX] + "|" +
        JoinFilterExampleMRJob.BAR_SORT_FLAG);        ❻
    newValue.set(cells[BAR_VALUE_INX]);
    context.write(newKey, newValue);
  }
}
}
```

❶ As we discussed, the mapper's `setup()` method is used to read predefined values from the `Configuration` object. Here we are getting the `fooValMax` filter value that we will use later in the `map()` method for filtering.

❷ Each map task will read data from a file block that belongs either to the Foo or Bar data sets. We need to be able to tell which is which, so we can filter only the data from Foo tables and so we can add this information to the output key—it will be used by the reducer for joining the data sets. In this section of the code, the `setup()` method identifies which block we are processing in this task. Later, in the `map()` method, we will use this value to separate the logic for processing the Foo and Bar data sets.

❸ This is where we use the block identifier we defined earlier.

❹ And here we use the `fooValMax` value for filtering.

❺ The last thing to point out here is the method to increment a counter in MapReduce. A counter has a group and counter name, and both can be set and incremented by the map and reduce tasks. They are reported at the end of the job and are also tracked by the various UIs while the job is executing, so it is a good way to give users feedback on the job progress, as well as give the developers useful information for debugging and troubleshooting.

❻ Note how we set the output key: first there is the value used to join the data sets, followed by "|" and then a flag marking the record with *A* if it arrived from the Bar data set and *B* if it arrived from Foo. This means that when the reducer receives a key and an array of values to join, the values from the Bar data set will appear first (since keys are sorted). To perform the join we will only have to store the Bar data set in memory until the Foo values start arriving. Without the flag to assist in sorting the values, we will need to store the entire data set in memory when joining.

Now let's look into the partitioner. We need to implement a customer partitioner because we are using a multipart key that contains the join key plus the sort flag. We need to partition only by ID, so both records with the same join key will end up in the same reducer regardless of whether they originally arrived from the data set Foo or Bar. This is essential for joining them because a single reducer will need to join all values with the same key. To do this, we need only partition on the ID and entire composite key as shown:

```
public class JoinFilterPartitioner extends Partitioner<Text, Text>{

    @Override
    public int getPartition(Text key, Text value, int numberOfReducers) {
```

```
    String keyStr = key.toString();

    String pk = keyStr.substring(0, keyStr.length() - 2);

    return Math.abs(pk.hashCode() % numberOfReducers);
  }

}
```

In the partitioner we get the join key out of the key in the map output and apply the partitioning method using this part of the key only, as we discussed previously.

Next we'll look at the reducer and how it joins the two data sets:

```
public class JoinFilterReducer extends Reducer<Text, Text, NullWritable, Text> {

  int joinValFilter;
  String currentBarId = "";
  List<Integer> barBufferList = new ArrayList<Integer>();

  Text newValue = new Text();

  @Override
  public void setup(Context context) {
    Configuration config = context.getConfiguration();
    joinValFilter = config.getInt(JoinFilterExampleMRJob.JOIN_VAL_MAX_CONF, -1);
  }

  @Override
  public void reduce(Text key, Iterable<Text> values, Context context)
      throws IOException, InterruptedException {

    String keyString = key.toString();
    String barId = keyString.substring(0, keyString.length() - 2);
    String sortFlag = keyString.substring(keyString.length() - 1);

    if (!currentBarId.equals(barId)) {
      barBufferList.clear();
      currentBarId = barId;
    }

    if (sortFlag.equals(JoinFilterExampleMRJob.BAR_SORT_FLAG)) { ❶
      for (Text value : values) {
        barBufferList.add(Integer.parseInt(value.toString())); ❷
      }
    } else {
      if (barBufferList.size() > 0) {
        for (Text value : values) {
          for (Integer barValue : barBufferList) { ❸

            String[] fooCells = StringUtils.split(value.toString(), "|");

            int fooValue = Integer.parseInt(fooCells[1]);
```

```
        int sumValue = barValue + fooValue;

        if (sumValue < joinValFilter) {

            newValue.set(fooCells[0] + "|" + barId + "|" + sumValue);
            context.write(NullWritable.get(), newValue);
        } else {
            context.getCounter("custom", "joinValueFiltered").increment(1);
        }
      }
    }
  } else {
    System.out.println("Matching with nothing");
  }
      }
    }
  }
}
```

❶   Because we used a flag to assist in sorting, we are getting all the records from the
Bar data set for a given join key first.

❷   As we receive them, we store all the Bar records in a list in memory.

❸   As we process the Foo records, we'll loop through the cached Bar records to execute the join. This is a simple implementation of a *nested-loops join*.

When to Use MapReduce

As you can see from the example, MapReduce is a very low-level framework. The
developer is responsible for very minute details of operation, and there is a significant
amount of setup and boilerplate code. Because of this MapReduce code typically has
more bugs and higher costs of maintenance.

However, there is a subset of problems, such as file compaction,[1] distributed file-copy,
or row-level data validation, which translates to MapReduce quite naturally. At other
times, code written in MapReduce can take advantage of properties of the input data
to improve performance—for example, if we know the input files are sorted, we can
use MapReduce to optimize merging of data sets in ways that higher-level abstractions can't.

We recommend MapReduce for experienced Java developers who are comfortable
with the MapReduce programming paradigm, especially for problems that translate
to MapReduce naturally or where detailed control of the execution has significant
advantages.

---

1 We discuss compaction in more detail in Chapter 4.

Spark

In 2009 Matei Zaharia and his team at UC Berkeley's AMPLab researched possible improvements to the MapReduce framework. Their conclusion was that while the MapReduce model is useful for large-scale data processing, the MapReduce framework is limited to a very rigid data flow model that is unsuitable for many applications. For example, applications such as iterative machine learning or interactive data analysis can benefit from reusing a data set cached in memory for multiple processing tasks. MapReduce forces writing data to disk at the end of each job execution and reading it again from disk for the next. When you combine this with the fact that jobs are limited to a single map step and a single reduce step, you can see how the model can be significantly improved by a more flexible framework.

Out of this reseach came Spark, a new processing framework for big data that addresses many of the shortcomings in the MapReduce model. Since its introduction, Spark has grown to be the second largest Apache top-level project (after HDFS) with 150 contributors.

Spark Overview

Spark is different from MapReduce in several important ways.

DAG Model

Looking back at MapReduce you only had two processing phases: map and/or reduce. With the MapReduce framework, it is only possible to build complete applications by stringing together sets of map and reduce tasks. These complex chains of tasks are known as *directed acyclic graphs*, or *DAGs*, illustrated in Figure 3-5.

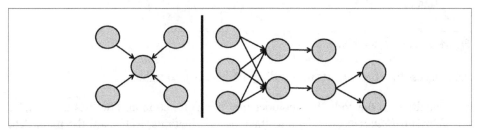

Figure 3-5. Directed acyclic graphs

DAGs contain series of actions connected to each other in a workflow. In the case of MapReduce, the DAG is a series of map and reduce tasks used to implement the application. The use of DAGs to define Hadoop applications is not new—MapReduce developers implemented these, and they are used within all high-level abstractions that use MapReduce. Oozie even allows users to define these workflows of MapReduce tasks in XML and use an orchestration framework to monitor their execution.

What Spark adds is the fact that the engine itself creates those complex chains of steps from the application's logic, rather than the DAG being an abstraction added externally to the model. This allows developers to express complex algorithms and data processing pipelines within the same job and allows the framework to optimize the job as a whole, leading to improved performance.

For more on Spark, see the Apache Spark site (*http://spark.apache.org/*). There are still relatively few texts available on Spark, but *Learning Spark* by Holden Karau, et al. (O'Reilly) will provide a comprehensive introduction to Spark. For more advanced Spark usage, see the *Advanced Analytics with Spark* by Sandy Ryza, et al. (O'Reilly).

Overview of Spark Components

Before we get to the example, it is important to go over the different parts of Spark at a high level. Figure 3-6 shows the major Spark components.

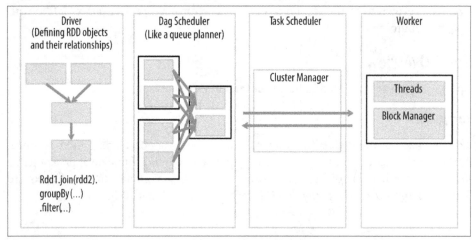

Figure 3-6. Spark components

Let's discuss the components in this diagram from left to right:

- The driver is the code that includes the "main" function and defines the *resilient distributed datasets* (RDDs) and their transformations. RDDs are the main data structures we will use in our Spark programs, and will be discussed in more detail in the next section.

- Parallel operations on the RDDs are sent to the DAG scheduler, which will optimize the code and arrive at an efficient DAG that represents the data processing steps in the application.

- The resulting DAG is sent to the *cluster manager*. The cluster manager has information about the workers, assigned threads, and location of data blocks and is responsible for assigning specific processing tasks to workers. The cluster manager is also the service that handles DAG play-back in the case of worker failure. As we explained earlier, the cluster manager can be YARN, Mesos, or Spark's cluster manager.

- The worker receives units of work and data to manage. The worker executes its specific task without knowledge of the entire DAG, and its results are sent back to the driver application.

Basic Spark Concepts

Before we go into the code for our filter-join-filter example, let's talk about the main components of writing applications in Spark.

Resilient Distributed Datasets

RDDs are *collections* of serializable elements, and such a collection may be *partitioned*, in which case it is stored on multiple nodes. An RDD may reside in memory or on disk. Spark uses RDDs to reduce I/O and maintain the processed data set in memory, while still tolerating node failures without having to restart the entire job.

RDDs are typically created from a Hadoop input format (a file on HDFS, for example), or from transformations applied on existing RDDs. When creating an RDD from an input format, Spark determines the number of partitions by the input format, very similar to the way splits are determined in MapReduce jobs. When RDDs are transformed, it is possible to shuffle the data and repartition it to any number of partitions.

RDDs store their *lineage*—the set of transformations that was used to create the current state, starting from the first input format that was used to create the RDD. If the data is lost, Spark will replay the lineage to rebuild the lost RDDs so the job can continue.

Figure 3-7 is a common image used to illustrate a DAG in spark. The inner boxes are RDD partitions; the next layer is an RDD and single chained operation.

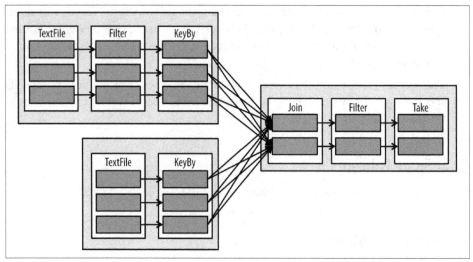

Figure 3-7. Spark DAG

Now let's say we lose the partition denoted by the black box in Figure 3-8. Spark would replay the "Good Replay" boxes and the "Lost Block" boxes to get the data needed to execute the final step.

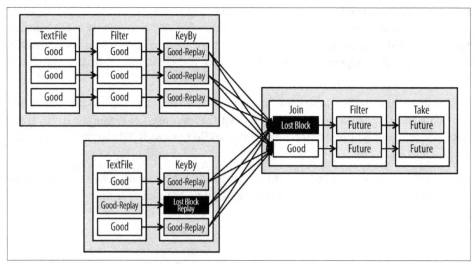

Figure 3-8. Spark DAG after a lost partition

Note that there are multiple types of RDDs, and not all transformations are possible on every RDD. For example, you can't join an RDD that doesn't contain a key-value pair.

Shared variables

Spark includes two types of variables that allow sharing information between the execution nodes: *broadcast* variables and *accumulator* variables. Broadcast variables are sent to all the remote execution nodes, where they can be used for data processing. This is similar to the role that Configuration objects play in MapReduce. Accumulators are also sent to the remote execution nodes, but unlike broadcast variables, they can be modified by the executors, with the limitation that you only add to the accumulator variables. Accumulators are somewhat similar to MapReduce counters.

SparkContext

SparkContext is an object that represents the connection to a Spark cluster. It is used to create RDDs, broadcast data, and initialize accumulators.

Transformations

Transformations are functions that take one RDD and return another. RDDs are *immutable*, so transformations will never modify their input, only return the modified RDD. Transformations in Spark are always *lazy*, so they don't compute their results. Instead, calling a transformation function only creates a new RDD with this specific transformation as part of its lineage. The complete set of transformations is only executed when an *action* is called. This improves Spark's efficiency and allows it to cleverly optimize the execution graph. The downside is that it can make debugging more challenging: exceptions are thrown when the action is called, far from the code that called the function that actually threw the exception. It's important to remember to place the exception handling code around the action, where the exception will be thrown, not around the transformation.

There are many transformations in Spark. This list will illustrate enough to give you an idea of what a transformation function looks like:

map()
> Applies a function on every element of an RDD to produce a new RDD. This is similar to the way the MapReduce map() method is applied to every element in the input data. For example: lines.map(s=>s.length) takes an RDD of Strings ("lines") and returns an RDD with the length of the strings.

filter()
> Takes a Boolean function as a parameter, executes this function on every element of the RDD, and returns a new RDD containing only the elements for which the function returned true. For example, lines.filter(s=>(s.length>50)) returns an RDD containing only the lines with more than 50 characters.

`keyBy()`
> Takes every element in an RDD and turns it into a key-value pair in a new RDD. For example, `lines.keyBy(s=>s.length)` return, an RDD of key-value pairs with the length of the line as the key, and the line as the value.

`join()`
> Joins two key-value RDDs by their keys. For example, let's assume we have two RDDs: lines and more_lines. Each entry in both RDDs contains the line length as the key and the line as the value. `lines.join(more_lines)` will return for each line length a pair of `Strings`, one from the `lines` RDD and one from the more_lines RDD. Each resulting element looks like `<length,<line,more_line>>`.

`groupByKey()`
> Performs a group-by operation on a RDD by the keys. For example: `lines.group ByKey()` will return an RDD where each element has a length as the key and a collection of lines with that length as the value. In Chapter 8 we use `groupBy Key()` to get a collection of all page views performed by a single user.

`sort()`
> Performs a sort on an RDD and returns a sorted RDD.

Note that transformations include functions that are similar to those that MapReduce would perform in the map phase, but also some functions, such as `groupByKey()`, that belong to the reduce phase.

Action

Actions are methods that take an RDD, perform a computation, and return the result to the driver application. Recall that transformations are lazy and are not executed when called. Actions trigger the computation of transformations. The result of the computation can be a collection, values printed to the screen, values saved to file, or similar. However, an action will never return an RDD.

Benefits of Using Spark

Next, we'll outline several of the advantages of using Spark.

Simplicity

Spark APIs are significantly cleaner and simpler than those of MapReduce. As a result, the examples in this section are significantly shorter than their MapReduce equivalents and are easy to read by someone not familiar with Spark. The APIs are so usable that there is no need for high-level abstractions on top of Spark, as opposed to the many that exist for MapReduce, such as Hive or Pig.

Versatility

Spark was built from the ground up to be an extensible, general-purpose parallel processing framework. It is generic enough to support a stream-processing framework called Spark Streaming and a graph processing engine called GraphX. With this flexibility, we expect to see many new special-purpose libraries for Spark in the future.

Reduced disk I/O

MapReduce writes to local disk at the end of the map phase, and to HDFS at the end of the reduce phase. This means that while processing 1 TB of data, you might write 4 TB of data to disk and send 2 TB of data over the network. When the application is stringing multiple MapReduce jobs together, the situation is even worse.

Spark's RDDs can be stored in memory and processed in multiple steps or iterations without additional I/O. Because there are no special map and reduce phases, data is typically read from disk when processing starts and written to disk when there's a need to persist results.

Storage

Spark gives developers a great deal of flexibility regarding how RDDs are stored. Options include: in memory on a single node, in memory but replicated to multiple nodes, or persisted to disk. It's important to remember that the developer controls the persistence. An RDD can go through multiple stages of transformation (equivalent to multiple map and reduce phases) without storing anything to disk.

Multilanguage

While Spark itself is developed in Scala, Spark APIs are implemented for Java, Scala, and Python. This allows developers to use Spark in the language in which they are most productive. Hadoop developers often use Java APIs, whereas data scientists often prefer the Python implementation so that they can use Spark with Python's powerful numeric processing libraries.

Resource manager independence

Spark supports both YARN and Mesos as resource managers, and there is also a standalone option. This allows Spark to be more receptive to future changes to the resource manager space. This also means that if the developers have a strong preference for a specific resource manager, Spark doesn't force them to use a different one. This is useful since each resource manager has its own strengths and limitations.

Interactive shell (REPL)

Spark jobs can be deployed as an application, similar to how MapReduce jobs are executed. In addition, Spark also includes a shell (also called a REPL, for *read-eval-print loop*). This allows for fast interactive experimentation with the data and easy validation of code. We use the Spark shell while working side by side with our customers, rapidly examining the data and interactively answering questions as we think of them. We also use the shell to validate parts of our programs and for troubleshooting.

Spark Example

With the introduction behind us, let's look at the first code example. It uses the same data sets as the example in the MapReduce section and processes the data in the same way:

```
var fooTable = sc.textFile("foo")                                    ❶

var barTable = sc.textFile("bar")

var fooSplit = fooTable.map(line => line.split("\\|"))                ❷

var fooFiltered = fooSplit.filter(cells => cells(1).toInt <= 500)     ❸

var fooKeyed = fooFiltered.keyBy(cells => cells(2))                   ❹

var barSplit = barTable.map(line => line.split("\\|"))               ❺

var barKeyed = barSplit.keyBy(cells => cells(0))

var joinedValues = fooKeyed.join(barKeyed)                           ❻

var joinedFiltered =                                                 ❼
joinedValues.filter(joinedVal =>
  joinedVal._2._1(1).toInt + joinedVal._2._2(1).toInt <= 1000)

joinedFiltered.take(100)                                            ❽
```

This code will do the following:

❶ Load Foo and Bar data sets into two RDDs.

❷ Split each row of Foo into a collection of separate cells.

❸ Filter the split Foo data set and keep only the elements where the second column is smaller than 500.

❹ Convert the results into key-value pairs using the ID column as the key.

❺ Split the columns in Bar in the same way we split Foo and again convert into key-value pairs with the ID as the key.

❻ Join Bar and Foo.

❼ Filter the joined results. The `filter()` function here takes the value of the join-edVal RDD, which contains a pair of a Foo and a Bar row. We take the first column from each row and check if their sum is lower than 1,000.

❽ Show the first 100 results. Note that this is the only action in the code, so the entire chain of transformations we defined here will only be triggered at this point.

This example is already pretty succinct, but it can be implemented in even fewer lines of code:

```
//short version
var fooTable = sc.textFile("foo")
  .map(line => line.split("\\|"))
  .filter(cells => cells(1).toInt <= 500)
  .keyBy(cells => cells(2))

var barTable = sc.textFile("bar")
  .map(line => line.split("\\|"))
  .keyBy(cells => cells(0))

var joinedFiltered = fooTable.join(barTable)
  .filter(joinedVal =>
    joinedVal._2._1(1).toInt + joinedVal._2._2(1).toInt <= 1000)

joinedFiltered.take(100)
```

The execution plan this will produce looks like Figure 3-9.

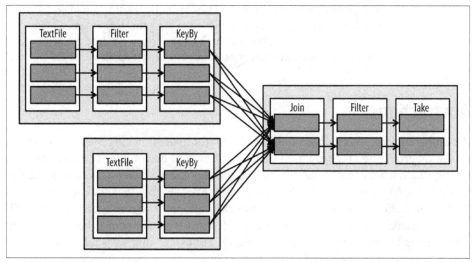

Figure 3-9. Spark execution

When to Use Spark

While Spark is a fairly new framework at the moment, it is easy to use, extendable, highly supported, well designed, and fast. We see it rapidly increasing in popularity, and with good reason. Spark still has many rough edges, but as the framework matures and more developers learn to use it, we expect Spark to eclipse MapReduce for most functionality. Spark is already the best choice for machine-learning applications because of its ability to perform iterative operations on data cached in memory.

In addition to replacing MapReduce, Spark offers SQL, graph processing, and streaming frameworks. These projects are even less mature than Spark, and it remains to be seen how much adoption they will have and whether they will become reliable parts of the Hadoop ecosystem.

Apache Tez: An Additional DAG-Based Processing Framework

Apache Tez (*http://tez.apache.org*) was introduced to the Hadoop ecosystem to address limitations in MapReduce. Like Spark, Tez is a framework that allows for expressing complex DAGs for processing data. The architecture of Tez is intended to provide performance improvements and better resource management than MapReduce. These enhancements make Tez suitable as a replacement for MapReduce as the engine for executing workloads such as Hive and Pig tasks.

While Tez shows great promise in optimizing processing on Hadoop, in its current state it's better suited as a lower-level tool for supporting execution engines on Hadoop, as opposed to a higher-level developer tool. Because of this we're not providing a detailed discussion in this chapter, but as Tez matures we might see it become a stronger contender as a tool to develop applications on Hadoop.

Abstractions

A number of projects have been developed with the goal of making MapReduce easier to use by providing an abstraction that hides much of its complexity as well as providing functionality that facilitates the processing of large data sets. Projects such as Apache Pig, Apache Crunch, Cascading, and Apache Hive fall into this category. These abstractions can be broken up into two different programming models: ETL (extract, transform, and load) and query. First we will talk about the ETL model, which includes Pig, Crunch, and Cascading. Following this we'll talk about Hive, which follows the query model.

So what makes the ETL model different from the query model? ETL is optimized to take a given data set and apply a series of operations on it to produce a set of outcomes, whereas query is used to ask a question of the data to get an answer. Note that these are not hard and fast categories: Hive is also a popular tool for performing ETL, as we'll see in our data warehousing case study in Chapter 10. However, there are cases where a tool like Pig can offer more flexibility in implementing an ETL work-flow than a query engine like Hive.

Although all of these tools were originally implemented as abstractions over MapReduce, for the most part these are general-purpose abstractions that can be layered on top of other execution engines; for example, Tez is supported as an engine for executing Hive queries, and at the time of this writing work was actively under way to provide Spark backends for Pig and Hive.

Before digging into these abstractions, let's talk about some aspects that differentiate them:

Apache Pig

- Pig provides a programming language known as *Pig Latin* that facilitates implementing complex transformations on large data sets.
- Pig facilitates interactive implementation of scripts by providing the *Grunt* shell, a console for rapid development.
- Pig provides functionality to implement UDFs to support custom functionality.
- Based on experience with customers and users, Pig is the most widely used tool for processing data on Hadoop.
- Pig is a top-level Apache project with over 200 contributors.
- As we noted before, although the main execution engine for Pig is currently MapReduce, Pig is code independent, meaning the Pig code doesn't need to change if the underlying execution engine changes.

Apache Crunch

- Crunch applications are written in Java, so for developers already familiar with Java there's no need to learn a new language.
- Crunch provides full access to all MapReduce functionality, which makes it easy to write low-level code when necessary.
- Crunch provides a separation of business logic from integration logic for better isolation and unit testing.
- Crunch is a top-level Apache project with about 13 contributors.
- Unlike Pig, Crunch is not 100% engine independent; because Crunch allows for low-level MapReduce functionality, those features will not be present when you switch engines.

Cascading
- Like Crunch, Cascading code is written in Java.
- Also like Crunch, full access is provided to all MapReduce functionality, which makes it easy to go low level.
- Once again like Crunch, Cascading provides separation of business logic from integration logic for better isolation and unit testing.
- Cascading has about seven total contributors.
- While not an Apache project, Cascading is Apache licensed.

Let's take a deeper dive into these abstractions, starting with Pig.

Pig

Pig is one of the oldest and most widely used abstractions over MapReduce in the Hadoop ecosystem. It was developed at Yahoo, and released to Apache in 2007.

Pig users write queries in a Pig-specific workflow language called Pig Latin, which gets compiled for execution by an underlying execution engine such as MapReduce. The Pig Latin scripts are first compiled into a logical plan and then into a physical plan. This physical plan is what gets executed by the underlying engine (e.g., MapReduce, Tez, or Spark). Due to Pig's distinction between the logical and physical plan for a given query, only the physical plan changes when you use a different execution engine.

For more details on Pig, see the Apache Pig site (*http://pig.apache.org/*) or *Programming Pig* by Alan Gates (O'Reilly).

Pig Example

As you can see in this example, Pig Latin is fairly simple and self-expressive. As you review the code, you might note that it's close to Spark in spirit:

```
fooOriginal = LOAD 'foo/foo.txt' USING PigStorage('|')
    AS (fooId:long, fooVal:int, barId:long);

fooFiltered = FILTER fooOriginal BY (fooVal <= 500);

barOriginal = LOAD 'bar/bar.txt' USING PigStorage('|')
    AS (barId:long, barVal:int);

joinedValues = JOIN fooFiltered by barId, barOriginal by barId;

joinedFiltered = FILTER joinedValues BY (fooVal + barVal <= 500);

STORE joinedFiltered INTO 'pig/out' USING PigStorage ('|');
```

Note the following in the preceding script:

Data container

This refers to identifiers like fooOriginal and fooFiltered that represent a data set. These are referred to as *relations* in Pig, and they are conceptually similar to the notion of RDDs in Spark (even though the actual persistence semantics of RDDs are very different). Speaking a little more about terminology, a relation is a *bag*, where a bag is a collection of *tuples*. A tuple is a collection of values/objects, which themselves could be bags, which could contain bags of more tuples, which could contain bags, and so on.

Transformation functions

This refers to operators like FILTER and JOIN that can transform relations. Again, logically just like Spark, these transformation functions do not force an action immediately. No execution is done until the STORE command is called, and nothing is done until the saveToTextFile is called.

Field definitions

Unlike in Spark, fields and their data types are called out (e.g., fooId:long). This makes dealing with field data easier and allows for other external tools to track lineage at a field level.

No Java

There are no commands for importing classes or objects in the preceding example. In some ways, you are limited by the dialect of Pig Latin, but in other ways, you get rid of the additional complexity of a programming language API to run your processing jobs. If you'd like a programming interface to your processing jobs, you will find later sections on Crunch and Cascading useful.

Pig also offers insight into its plan for running a job when issued a command like Explain JoinedFiltered from the previous example. Here is the output from our filter-join-filter job:

```
#------------------------------------------------
# MapReduce Plan
#------------------------------------------------
MapReduce node scope-43
Map Plan
Union[tuple] - scope-44
|
|---joinedValues: Local Rearrange[tuple]{long}(false) - scope-27
|   |   |
|   |   Project[long][2] - scope-28
|   |
|   |---fooFiltered: Filter[bag] - scope-11
|       |   |
|       |   Less Than or Equal[boolean] - scope-14
|       |   |
```

```
|       |   |---Project[int][1] - scope-12
|       |   |
|       |   |---Constant(500) - scope-13
|       |   |
|       |---fooOriginal: New For Each(false,false,false)[bag] - scope-10
|       |       |   |
|       |       |   Cast[long] - scope-2
|       |       |   |
|       |       |   |---Project[bytearray][0] - scope-1
|       |       |   |
|       |       |   Cast[int] - scope-5
|       |       |   |
|       |       |   |---Project[bytearray][1] - scope-4
|       |       |   |
|       |       |   Cast[long] - scope-8
|       |       |   |
|       |       |   |---Project[bytearray][2] - scope-7
|       |       |
|       |       |---fooOriginal: Load(hdfs://localhost:8020/foo/foo.txt:\
PigStorage('|')) - scope-0
|
|---joinedValues: Local Rearrange[tuple]{long}(false) - scope-29
    |   |
    |   Project[long][0] - scope-30
    |
    |---barOriginal: New For Each(false,false)[bag] - scope-22
        |   |
        |   Cast[long] - scope-17
        |   |
        |   |---Project[bytearray][0] - scope-16
        |   |
        |   Cast[int] - scope-20
        |   |
        |   |---Project[bytearray][1] - scope-19
        |
        |---barOriginal: Load(hdfs://localhost:8020/bar/bar.txt:\
PigStorage('|')) - scope-15--------
Reduce Plan
joinedFiltered: Store(fakefile:org.apache.pig.builtin.PigStorage) - scope-40
|
|---joinedFiltered: Filter[bag] - scope-34
    |   |
    |   Less Than or Equal[boolean] - scope-39
    |   |
    |   |---Add[int] - scope-37
    |   |   |
    |   |   |---Project[int][1] - scope-35
    |   |   |
    |   |   |---Project[int][4] - scope-36
    |   |
    |   |---Constant(500) - scope-38
    |
```

```
 |---POJoinPackage(true,true)[tuple] - scope-45--------
Global sort: false
```

From the explain plan, you can see that there is one MapReduce job just like in our MapReduce implementation, and we also see that Pig performs the filtering in the same places we did it in the MapReduce code. Consequently, at the core, the Pig code will be about the same speed as our MapReduce code. In fact, it may be faster because it stores the values in their native types, whereas in MapReduce we convert them back and forth to strings.

When to Use Pig

To wrap up our discussion of Pig, here is a list of reasons that make Pig a good choice for processing data on Hadoop:

- Pig Latin is very easy to read and understand.

- A lot of the complexity of MapReduce is removed.

- A Pig Latin script is very small compared to the size (in terms of number of lines and effort) of an equivalent MapReduce job. This makes the cost of maintaining Pig Latin scripts much lower than MapReduce jobs.

- No code compilation is needed. Pig Latin scripts can be run directly in the Pig console.

- Pig provides great tools to figure out what it is going on under the hood. You can use DESCRIBE joinedFiltered; to figure out what data types are in the collection and use Explain joinedFiltered; to figure out the MapReduce execution plan that Pig will use to get the results.

The biggest downside to Pig is the need to come up to speed on a new language—the concepts related to bags, tuples, and relations can present a learning curve for many developers.

Accessing HDFS from the Pig Command Line

Pig also offers a unique capability: a simple command-line interface to access HDFS. When using the Pig shell, you can browse the HDFS filesystem as if you were on a Linux box with HDFS mounted on it. This helps if you have really long folder hierarchies and you would like to stay in a given directory and execute filesystem commands like rm, cp, pwd, and so on. You can even access all the hdfs fs commands by preceding the command with fs in the prompt, and the commands will execute within the context of the given directory. So even if you don't use Pig for application development, you may still find the Pig shell and its access to HDFS helpful.

Crunch

Crunch is based on Google's *FlumeJava*,[2] a library that makes it easy for us to write data pipelines in Java without having to dig into the details of MapReduce or think about nodes and vertices of a DAG graph. The resulting code has similarities to Pig, but without field definitions since Crunch defaults to reading the raw data on disk.

Just like Spark centers on the `SparkContext`, Crunch centers on the `Pipeline` object (`MRPipeline` or `SparkPipeline`). The `Pipeline` object will allow you to create your first `PCollections`. `PCollections` and `PTables` in Crunch play a very similar role to RDDs in Spark and relations in Pig.

The actual execution of a Crunch pipeline occurs with a call to the `done()` method. Crunch differs here from Pig and Spark in that Pig and Spark start executing when they hit an action that demands for work to happen. Crunch instead defers execution until the `done()` method is called. The `Pipeline` object also holds the logic for compiling the Crunch code into the MapReduce or Spark workflow that is needed to get the requested results.

Earlier we noted that Crunch supports Spark and MapReduce with the caveat that Crunch is not 100% code transferable. This limitation centers on the `Pipeline` object. From the different `Pipeline` implementations you will get different core functionality, such as collection types and function types. Part of the reason for these differences is conflicting requirements on Crunch's side; Crunch wants to give you access to low-level MapReduce functionality, but some of that functionality just doesn't exist in Spark.

 For more on Crunch, see the Apache Crunch home page (*http://crunch.apache.org/*). Additionally, *Hadoop in Practice* includes some coverage of Crunch, and fourth edition of *Hadoop: The Definitive Guide* includes a chapter on Crunch.

Crunch Example

The next example is a Crunch program that will execute our filter-join-filter use case. You will notice the main body of logic is in the `run()` method. Outside the `run()` method are all the definitions of the business logic that will fire at different points in the pipeline. This is similar to the way this would be implemented with Java in Spark, and offers a nice separation of workflow and business logic:

---

2 Note that FlumeJava is used internally at Google, and is not a publicly available project.

```
public class JoinFilterExampleCrunch implements Tool {

  public static final int FOO_ID_INX = 0;
  public static final int FOO_VALUE_INX = 1;
  public static final int FOO_BAR_ID_INX = 2;

  public static final int BAR_ID_INX = 0;
  public static final int BAR_VALUE_INX = 1;

  public static void main(String[] args) throws Exception {
    ToolRunner.run(new Configuration(), new JoinFilterExampleCrunch(), args);
  }

  Configuration config;

  public Configuration getConf() {

    return config;
  }

  public void setConf(Configuration config) {
    this.config = config;

  }

  public int run(String[] args) throws Exception {

    String fooInputPath = args[0];
    String barInputPath = args[1];
    String outputPath = args[2];
    int fooValMax = Integer.parseInt(args[3]);
    int joinValMax = Integer.parseInt(args[4]);
    int numberOfReducers = Integer.parseInt(args[5]);

    Pipeline pipeline =
      new MRPipeline(JoinFilterExampleCrunch.class, getConf()); ❶

    PCollection<String> fooLines = pipeline.readTextFile(fooInputPath); ❷
    PCollection<String> barLines = pipeline.readTextFile(barInputPath);

    PTable<Long, Pair<Long, Integer>> fooTable = fooLines.parallelDo( ❸
        new FooIndicatorFn(),
        Avros.tableOf(Avros.longs(),
        Avros.pairs(Writables.longs(), Writables.ints())));

    fooTable = fooTable.filter(new FooFilter(fooValMax)); ❹

    PTable<Long, Integer> barTable = barLines.parallelDo(new BarIndicatorFn(),
        Avros.tableOf(Avros.longs(), Avros.ints()));

    DefaultJoinStrategy<Long, Pair<Long, Integer>, Integer> joinStrategy = ❺
        new DefaultJoinStrategy
```

```java
          <Long, Pair<Long, Integer>, Integer>
          (numberOfReducers);

  PTable<Long, Pair<Pair<Long, Integer>, Integer>> joinedTable =
    joinStrategy ❻
      .join(fooTable, barTable, JoinType.INNER_JOIN);

  PTable<Long, Pair<Pair<Long, Integer>, Integer>> filteredTable =
      joinedTable.filter(new JoinFilter(joinValMax));

  filteredTable.write(At.textFile(outputPath), WriteMode.OVERWRITE); ❼

  PipelineResult result = pipeline.done();

  return result.succeeded() ? 0 : 1;
}

public static class FooIndicatorFn extend
    MapFn<String, Pair<Long, Pair<Long, Integer>>> {

  private static final long serialVersionUID = 1L;

  @Override
  public Pair<Long, Pair<Long, Integer>> map(String input) {
    String[] cells = StringUtils.split(input.toString(), "|");

    Pair<Long, Integer> valuePair = new Pair<Long, Integer>(
        Long.parseLong(cells[FOO_ID_INX]),
        Integer.parseInt(cells[FOO_VALUE_INX]));

    return new Pair<Long, Pair<Long, Integer>>(
        Long.parseLong(cells[FOO_BAR_ID_INX]), valuePair);
  }
}

public static class FooIndicatorFn extends
    MapFn<String, Pair<Long, Pair<Long, Integer>>> {

  private static final long serialVersionUID = 1L;

  @Override
  public Pair<Long, Pair<Long, Integer>> map(String input) {
    String[] cells = StringUtils.split(input.toString(), "|");

    Pair<Long, Integer> valuePair = new Pair<Long, Integer>(
        Long.parseLong(cells[FOO_ID_INX]),
        Integer.parseInt(cells[FOO_VALUE_INX]));

    return new Pair<Long, Pair<Long, Integer>>(
        Long.parseLong(cells[FOO_BAR_ID_INX]), valuePair);
  }
}
```

```java
public static class FooFilter extends
    FilterFn<Pair<Long, Pair<Long, Integer>>> {

  private static final long serialVersionUID = 1L;

  int fooValMax;

  FooFilter(int fooValMax) {
    this.fooValMax = fooValMax;
  }

  @Override
  public boolean accept(Pair<Long, Pair<Long, Integer>> input) {
    return input.second().second() <= fooValMax;
  }
}

public static class FooFilter extends
    FilterFn<Pair<Long, Pair<Long, Integer>>> {

  private static final long serialVersionUID = 1L;

  int fooValMax;

  FooFilter(int fooValMax) {
    this.fooValMax = fooValMax;
  }

  @Override
  public boolean accept(Pair<Long, Pair<Long, Integer>> input) {
    return input.second().second() <= fooValMax;
  }
}

public static class BarIndicatorFn extends MapFn<String, Pair<Long, Integer>> {

  private static final long serialVersionUID = 1L;

  @Override
  public Pair<Long, Integer> map(String input) {
    String[] cells = StringUtils.split(input.toString(), "|");

    return new Pair<Long, Integer>(Long.parseLong(cells[BAR_ID_INX]),
        Integer.parseInt(cells[BAR_VALUE_INX]));
  }
}

public static class JoinFilter extends
    FilterFn<Pair<Long, Pair<Pair<Long, Integer>, Integer>>> {

  private static final long serialVersionUID = 1L;
```

```
        int joinValMax;

        JoinFilter(int joinValMax) {
          this.joinValMax = joinValMax;
        }

        @Override
        public boolean accept(Pair<Long,
                        Pair<Pair<Long, Integer>,
                        Integer>> input) {

          return input.second().first().second() +
              input.second().second() <= joinValMax;
        }

      }
    }
```

Let's walk through this code to see what's going on:

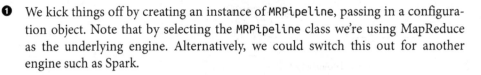

❶ We kick things off by creating an instance of MRPipeline, passing in a configuration object. Note that by selecting the MRPipeline class we're using MapReduce as the underlying engine. Alternatively, we could switch this out for another engine such as Spark.

❷ These two lines are where we add inputs to our newly created pipeline, sorting them in a PCollection. This idea is very in line with what we saw from Spark with RDDs. Think of this as an immutable distributed collection, and any operations on it will also most likely have to be distributed. Also like Spark, a PCollection may not always be physical; in other words, it might be stored in memory or on disk.

❸ Here we see our first parallelDo, which is like an RDD map() function in Spark. It will run over all the items in the PCollection in a distributed way and return either another PCollection, or in this case a PTable. Note this calls a method called FooIndicatorFn(). We will go into this method in a minute, but for now just know it gets called for each record in a distributed manner across the data set. The rest of the parameters tell Crunch what we intend to return in terms of a new PTable. The PTable is different from a PCollection in that we now need a key and value—this will help when we start joining.

❹ Generate a new PTable via a distributed filter.

❺ Define a join strategy for the join that will happen on the next line. We'll be using the DefaultJoinStrategy, but there are many other options, like BloomFilterJoin-

Strategy, MapsideJoinStrategy, and ShardedJoinStrategy. It's always important to understand your data set before selecting a join strategy.

 Here is our first example of a join operation. We're using our newly created join strategy, the input PTables, and an inner or outer definition.

 Finally, we write out our data to disk. Remember that this is still a distributed write, so it's highly likely that you will see many files in the output directory, one file per thread.

When to Use Crunch

Given its similarities to Spark, is it reasonable to assume that Crunch will eventually be replaced by Spark for most developers? This will likely vary based on several factors. If you're using Crunch over Spark, you get the benefits of an abstraction, while being shielded from the potential for something replacing Spark as the underlying engine.

However, these benefits of abstraction come at a cost. To truly be good at an abstraction you have to understand the underlying engine as well, so now you will have to learn Spark *and* Crunch. Also, there may be new functionality in Spark that hasn't reached Crunch and thus will be inaccessible to you until Crunch is updated.

Most likely, some developers who are currently using Crunch will continue to use it. But in addition to competition from the other abstractions—like Pig, and to a lesser extent Cascading—just like MapReduce Crunch also has competition from the underlying execution engine. Despite this, Crunch may be a good choice if you like Java, and you like the idea of an abstraction layer between you and the underlying execution engine.

Cascading

Of the three ETL abstractions Cascading is the least used in our experience, but those who do use it find it to be a valuable tool. When looking at the code you will find that Cascading presents somewhat of a middle ground between Crunch and Pig. It's similar to Crunch in that:

- Code is implemented in Java.
- Cascading supports a separation of business logic from workflow.
- Cascading provides the ability to go low level.

It's similar to Pig in that:

- Cascading includes the concept of strict fields, which allows for column-level lineage.

- You can separate business logic and implement custom functionality through UDFs.

 More information on Cascading is available at the Cascading home page (*http://www.cascading.org/*), or *Enterprise Data Workflows with Cascading* (*http://bit.ly/enterprise-data-workflows*) by Paco Nathan (O'Reilly).

Cascading Example

The following example is an implementation of the filter-join-filter code in Cascading. When you're first reading this code it may feel complex and different from Crunch and Spark, but on further examination you will see that they are very much alike:

```
public class JoinFilterExampleCascading {
  public static void main(String[] args) {
    String fooInputPath = args[0];
    String barInputPath = args[1];
    String outputPath = args[2];
    int fooValMax = Integer.parseInt(args[3]);
    int joinValMax = Integer.parseInt(args[4]);
    int numberOfReducers = Integer.parseInt(args[5]);

    Properties properties = new Properties();
    AppProps.setApplicationJarClass(properties,
        JoinFilterExampleCascading.class);
    properties.setProperty("mapred.reduce.tasks",
                      Integer.toString(numberOfReducers));
    properties.setProperty("mapreduce.job.reduces",
                      Integer.toString(numberOfReducers));

    SpillableProps props = SpillableProps.spillableProps()
        .setCompressSpill( true )
        .setMapSpillThreshold( 50 * 1000 );



    HadoopFlowConnector flowConnector = new HadoopFlowConnector(properties); ❶

    // create source and sink taps
    Fields fooFields = new Fields("fooId", "fooVal", "foobarId");
    Tap fooTap = new Hfs(new TextDelimited(fooFields, "|"), fooInputPath);
    Fields barFields = new Fields("barId", "barVal");
    Tap barTap = new Hfs(new TextDelimited(barFields, "|"), barInputPath); ❷
```

```
    Tap outputTap = new Hfs(new TextDelimited(false, "|"), outputPath); ❸

    Fields joinFooFields = new Fields("foobarId");
    Fields joinBarFields = new Fields("barId"); ❹

    Pipe fooPipe = new Pipe("fooPipe");
    Pipe barPipe = new Pipe("barPipe"); ❺

    Pipe fooFiltered = new Each(fooPipe, fooFields, new FooFilter(fooValMax)); ❻

    Pipe joinedPipe = new HashJoin(fooFiltered, joinFooFields, barPipe,
        joinBarFields); ❼
    props.setProperties( joinedPipe.getConfigDef(), Mode.REPLACE );


    Fields joinFields = new Fields("fooId", "fooVal", "foobarId", "barVal");
    Pipe joinedFilteredPipe = new Each(joinedPipe, joinFields,
        new JoinedFilter(joinValMax));

    FlowDef flowDef = FlowDef.flowDef().setName("wc") ❽
        .addSource(fooPipe, fooTap).addSource(barPipe, barTap)
        .addTailSink(joinedFilteredPipe, outputTap);

    Flow wcFlow = flowConnector.connect(flowDef); ❾
    wcFlow.complete();
}

public static class FooFilter extends BaseOperation implements Filter {

    int fooValMax;

    FooFilter(int fooValMax) {
        this.fooValMax = fooValMax;
    }

    @Override
    public boolean isRemove(FlowProcess flowProcess, FilterCall filterCall) {

        int fooValue = filterCall.getArguments().getTuple().getInteger(1);

        return fooValue <= fooValMax;
    }
}

public static class JoinedFilter extends BaseOperation implements Filter {

    int joinValMax;

    JoinedFilter(int joinValMax) {
        this.joinValMax = joinValMax;
    }
```

```
@Override
public boolean isRemove(FlowProcess flowProcess, FilterCall filterCall) {

    int fooValue = filterCall.getArguments().getTuple().getInteger(1);
    int barValue = filterCall.getArguments().getTuple().getInteger(3);

    return fooValue + barValue <= joinValMax;
  }
 }
}
```

Let's look at what's happening in our Cascading code:

❶ Cascading applications are normally broken up into four sections: first is the configuration stage, then integration, processing, and finally scheduling. At this point we are setting up the configuration and making a HadoopFlowConnector.

❷ Next we set up our Taps, which are the data inputs for our application.

❸ Before we leave the integration section of our Cascading code, note how we define our output, which is also a Tap object. Cascading includes the concept of source and sink taps; here we're creating a sink tap for the output.

❹ At this point we're entering the processing part of our Cascading program and defining the join keys before we do our join later on.

❺ This is where we define our Pipe objects. Unlike Crunch where we're basically working in Java but with distributed collections, with Cascading we are thinking about pipes and taps. These two pipes will take data from our two source taps and join them to flow out to our sink tap. You will find that these pipes feel and act pretty much like Crunch PCollections and Spark RDDs.

❻ Use an Each() call to apply a FooFilter() method to every tuple passing through fooPipe.

❼ Here is our first example of joining with Cascading. As with Crunch and SQL (discussed shortly), we will have many options for joins.

❽ Now we are leaving the processing stage for the scheduling stage. This is kind of the glue stage for Cascading. Here we put together our original source taps with our sink taps.

❾ Finally, this is where we select our flows and the output location, and start our execution.

When to Use Cascading

The recommendation in the Cascading case is the same as with Crunch. Much of it comes down to personal preferences, previous experience, and comfort with a particular programming model. Otherwise, for the most part the gaps between the various abstractions are small.

Note that we've discussed abstractions following the ETL model; in the next section we'll turn to the query model and discuss Hive and Impala.

Hive

Hive was one of the first abstraction engines to be built on top of MapReduce. It was started at Facebook to enable data analysts to analyze data in Hadoop by using familiar SQL syntax without having to learn how to write MapReduce.

Hive Overview

Like Pig, Hive has been around for some time in the Hadoop ecosystem. Unlike Pig, which requires you to learn a new language, Hive allows users to use a familiar abstraction: SQL. This SQL support made Hive a popular choice for data analysis on Hadoop from its inception, and even today it is the cornerstone of newer SQL implementations on Hadoop like Impala, Presto (*http://prestodb.io/*), and Spark SQL.

While Hive is a mature and widely used project, historically its biggest drawback has been performance. However, any comment about Hive and its performance must be followed by an explanation that Hive is going through some changes (for the better) that will help address some of these issues.

Much of the performance concerns can be attributed to the use of MapReduce as Hive's execution engine (up until Hive 0.12). MapReduce is great for a good number of things, but is not a good choice for running ad hoc, interactive queries. There are a number of reasons for this, but mainly it is because MapReduce reads and writes to disk extensively, and there is a high startup cost for MapReduce jobs. Therefore, a multijoin query could take minutes, not because of data size but just because of the number of read and writes to disk.

The Hive community is well aware of these performance issues and there are different approaches people are taking to resolve this. The approaches that involve changes to the Hive project are:

Hive-on-Tez
> This effort involves enabling Tez—a more performant batch engine than MapReduce—to be Hive's underlying execution engine. Running Hive on Tez is supported as of release 0.13.0 of Apache Hive.

Hive-on-Spark

This is similar to the preceding but instead involves allowing Spark to be Hive's underlying execution engine. This work is currently under development and is tracked by HIVE-7292 (*http://bit.ly/hive-7292*).

Vectorized query execution

This effort involves reducing the CPU overhead required by Hive queries by processing a batch of rows at a time and reducing the number of conditional branches when processing these batches. Apache Hive 0.13 is the first version of Hive to come with support for vectorized query execution, and you need to store your data in particular formats like ORC and Parquet to take advantage of this support.

Outside of the Hive project, there are new projects emerging like Impala, Spark SQL, Presto, and Apache Drill that provide faster SQL-on-Hadoop. We will talk about Impala in more detail later in this chapter.

All the aforementioned changes in the ecosystem, both within and outside the Hive project are making the SQL-on-Hadoop story better and faster every day. An important point to note is that all the redesign efforts to the Hive project and the new projects still rely on the Hive metastore for storing metadata. This allows various systems to share the metadata, which makes it easier to transition from one system to the other or interoperate between more than one system. Sharing metadata implies, for example, that when you create a table or add a partition to an existing table in Hive, the table or partition would also become available for use in Impala and other systems, and vice versa. This is very important and a great benefit for developers and users of Hadoop. The Hive metastore has emerged as the standard place for users to store and manage their metadata.

Figure 3-10 shows Hive's high-level architecture. Hive includes a server called Hive-Server2 to which Java database connectivity (JDBC), open database connectivity (ODBC), and Thrift clients connect. HiveServer2 supports multiple sessions, each of which comprises a Hive driver, compiler, and executor. HiveServer2 also communicates with a metastore server and uses a relational database to store metadata. As we covered in Chapter 1, the metastore service and the corresponding relational database are often collectively referred to as the Hive metastore.

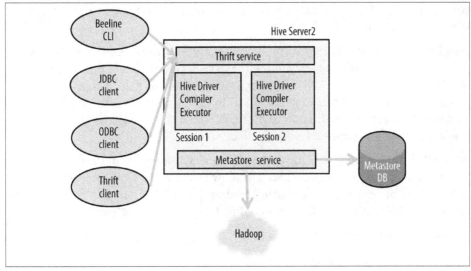

Figure 3-10. Hive architecture

For more on Hive, see the Apache Hive site (*https://hive.apache.org/*), or *Programming Hive* (*http://bit.ly/prog-hive*).

Example of Hive Code

Continuing the example of filter-join-filter, let's see an implementation in Hive.

First, we will need to make tables for our data sets, shown in the following code. We will use external tables because that way if we were to delete the table, only the metadata (information about the name of table, column names, types, etc. in the metastore) will get deleted. The underlying data in HDFS still remains intact:

```
CREATE EXTERNAL TABLE foo(fooId BIGINT, fooVal INT, fooBarId BIGINT)
  ROW FORMAT DELIMITED
    FIELDS TERMINATED BY '|'
STORED AS TEXTFILE
LOCATION 'foo';

CREATE EXTERNAL TABLE bar(barId BIGINT, barVal INT)
  ROW FORMAT DELIMITED
    FIELDS TERMINATED BY '|'
STORED AS TEXTFILE
LOCATION 'bar';
```

You'll notice this syntax is a little different from a typical RDBMS system, but any user familiar with SQL should be able to get the idea of what is going on. In short, we are making two tables named *foo* and *bar*. Their data is stored in text files with "|" as a column delimiter, and the files containing the data are located in the *foo* and *bar* directories, respectively, in HDFS.

Another thing to note is that we're also defining the storage format in these statements. In this case we're simply storing the data as delimited text files, but in a production application we'll likely use an optimized binary format, such as Parquet, for storage. We'll see a concrete example of this in Chapter 8. This is in contrast to most traditional data stores, such as an RDBMS, in which data is automatically converted into a proprietary, optimized format for that database.

Now, when that is done we can optionally (but it's always recommended) run the command to compute statistics. This will allow Hive to select join strategies and execution plans better suited to the data based on its distribution. The commands for computing statistics in Hive for the preceding tables would look like:

```
ANALYZE TABLE foo COMPUTE STATISTICS;

ANALYZE TABLE bar COMPUTE STATISTICS;
```

The automatic population of Hive statistics is controlled by a property named `hive.stats.autogather`, which is set to `true` by default. However, the stats are only automatically computed if you are inserting data via a Hive `insert` statement, like `INSERT OVERWRITE TABLE`. If you are moving data into HDFS outside of Hive or using something like Flume to stream data into your Hive table's HDFS location, you will have to run an `ANALYZE TABLE` *TABLE NAME* `COMPUTE STATISTICS` command explicitly to update the table statistics.

This will run map-only jobs that will read through the data and compute various statistics about it (min, max, etc.), which can then be used by the Hive query planner for queries on these tables later on.

When compute stats are done, we are ready to go. The following code shows how we would execute the filter-join-filter query in Hive:

```
SELECT
  *
FROM
  foo f JOIN bar b ON (f.fooBarId = b.barId)
WHERE
  f.fooVal < 500 AND
  f.fooVal + b.barVal < 1000;
```

As you'll notice this is quite simple, especially for someone who is already familiar with SQL. There is no need to learn MapReduce, Pig, Crunch, Cascading, and so on.

A word of caution here is that Hive is not the best at optimization and sometimes, even to optimize, you may have to set a few configuration properties. For example, Hive supports various kinds of distributed joins: map join (also known as hash join), bucketed join, sorted bucketed merge join, and regular join. If your data sets meet certain prerequisites, some joins may lead to much better performance than others. However, older versions of Hive didn't select the right join automatically, so the Hive compiler would rely on hints supplied by the query author to choose the right join for the query in question. Newer versions of Hive select the right join automatically, and as the project evolves more and more of these optimizations are being done automatically.

Also note that even though SQL is great for querying, it's not the best language for expressing all forms of processing. For every processing problem that you are expressing in SQL, you should ask whether SQL is a good fit, or if you're shoehorning the problem into it. Problems that use simple filtering and aggregation are a good fit for SQL. For example, if you need to find the user who was most active on Twitter in the past month, that is fairly easy to do in SQL (assuming you have access to the Twitter data set); you need to count Twitter activity for each user and then find the user with the highest count. On the other hand, machine learning, text processing, and graph algorithms are typically a poor fit for SQL. If you need to choose which advertisement to show to each Twitter user based on that user's interests and friends, it is unlikely that SQL is the right tool.

Similar to Pig, Hive is an abstraction over MapReduce, unless you're using one of the newer execution engines noted earlier. This means that Hive also hides all the MapReduce work behind the scenes. You should still make a habit of reviewing what Hive is doing under the hood to ensure it's doing what you intend. You can do this by simply adding the word EXPLAIN before the query command. The next example shows what the explain plan looks like for our filter-join-filter query.

As you'll see in the explain plan, the SQL query is mapped to three stages in Hive processing. Notice in the plan for stage 3 that in this example, Hive automatically figured out to do a map join (instead of the less performant regular join). Stage 3 populates a hash table equivalent to the query SELECT * FROM foo f WHERE f.fooVal < 500. This hash table is held in memory in all nodes of the cluster doing the join. Then, as shown in stage 4, the values from the bar table are simply read and joined against the in-memory hash table containing prefiltered values from the foo table:

```
EXPLAIN SELECT *
    > FROM foo f JOIN bar b ON (f.fooBarId = b.barId)
    > WHERE f.fooVal < 500 AND
    > f.fooVal + b.barVal < 1000
    > ;
OK
ABSTRACT SYNTAX TREE:

STAGE DEPENDENCIES:
  Stage-4 is a root stage
  Stage-3 depends on stages: Stage-4
  Stage-0 is a root stage
```

```
STAGE PLANS:
  Stage: Stage-4
    Map Reduce Local Work
      Alias -> Map Local Tables:
        f
          Fetch Operator
            limit: -1
      Alias -> Map Local Operator Tree:
        f
          TableScan
            alias: f
            Filter Operator
              predicate:
                  expr: (fooval < 500)
                  type: boolean
              HashTable Sink Operator
                condition expressions:
                  0 {fooid} {fooval} {foobarid}
                  1 {barid} {barval}
                handleSkewJoin: false
                keys:
                  0 [Column[foobarid]]
                  1 [Column[barid]]
                Position of Big Table: 1

  Stage: Stage-3
    Map Reduce
      Alias -> Map Operator Tree:
        b
          TableScan
            alias: b
            Map Join Operator
              condition map:
                  Inner Join 0 to 1
              condition expressions:
                0 {fooid} {fooval} {foobarid}
                1 {barid} {barval}
              handleSkewJoin: false
              keys:
                0 [Column[foobarid]]
                1 [Column[barid]]
              outputColumnNames: _col0, _col1, _col2, _col5, _col6
              Position of Big Table: 1
              Filter Operator
                predicate:
                    expr: ((_col1 < 500) and ((_col1 + _col6) < 1000))
                    type: boolean
                Select Operator
                  expressions:
                        expr: _col0
                        type: bigint
```

```
                    expr: _col1
                    type: int
                    expr: _col2
                    type: bigint
                    expr: _col5
                    type: bigint
                    expr: _col6
                    type: int
          outputColumnNames: _col0, _col1, _col2, _col3, _col4
          File Output Operator
            compressed: false
            GlobalTableId: 0
            table:
            input format: org.apache.hadoop.mapred.TextInputFormat
            output format:\
            org.apache.hadoop.hive.ql.io.HiveIgnoreKeyTextOutputFormat
            serde: org.apache.hadoop.hive.serde2.lazy.LazySimpleSerDe
    Local Work:
      Map Reduce Local Work

  Stage: Stage-0
    Fetch Operator
      limit: -1
```

When to Use Hive

While this section mainly answers the question of when to use Hive for processing
and querying data, it's important to point out that one part of Hive, the Hive metastore, has become the de facto standard for storing metadata (table names, column
names and types, etc.) in the Hadoop ecosystem, as explained in the section "Managing Metadata" on page 31. Therefore, regardless of what engine you use, you will most
likely always set up and use the Hive metastore to store metadata.

Hive of course is a good choice for queries that lend themselves to being expressed in
SQL, particularly long-running queries where fault tolerance is desirable. Aside from
queries, Hive can be a good choice if you'd like to write feature-rich, fault-tolerant,
batch (i.e., not near-real-time) transformation or ETL jobs in a pluggable SQL engine.
Let's talk about these features in more detail:

SQL

> Hive is a SQL engine for Hadoop. So is Impala and other engines not discussed
> here, like Apache Drill and Spark-SQL. So, if you care about writing your queries
> in SQL, you should probably only look at engines in this category.

Pluggable

> Hive is arguably the most pluggable SQL engine in the ecosystem. *Pluggability*
> here can refer to several things. Hive supports writing custom data formats and

writing code to serialize and deserialize (Hive `SerDes`) that data. Also, you can change the underlying execution engine in Hive from MapReduce to Tez to Spark (still pending at the time of writing). So, if switching between underlying general-purpose execution engines is important to you, Hive would be a good choice.

Batch

Hive is a batch engine. This means that you can't expect results in real time. Certain other engines, like Impala, are, in general, faster than Hive. So, if speed is your primary motive, Hive may not be the best fit.

Fault-tolerant

Hive is fault-tolerant, whereas other engines, like Impala at the time of this writing, are not. That means if a node processing a part of the query fails while running, the entire query will fail in Impala, but in Hive the underlying task would be retried. If your queries are hours long, this is very likely undesirable, but if your queries are shorter a simple retry from the client should suffice. Therefore, if fault tolerance is very important to you, Hive is usually a good choice.

Feature-rich

So, if Hive is slow, why use it at all? Hive is the oldest SQL engine on Hadoop; therefore, at the time of this writing, it has more features, in general, than newer engines. For example, at the time of this writing, Impala doesn't support nested data types (structs, arrays, maps, etc.). If representing data natively in those nested types is important to you, Hive is likely a very good choice.

Impala

By 2012 Hadoop had found a significant niche in many use cases, but it was still mainly used as a low-cost platform for storage and batch ETL. As it so happens, Google had published two white papers describing low-latency query engines: a fault-tolerant, distributed SQL database called F1 (*http://bit.ly/f1-data*) and a scalable, interactive ad-hoc query engine called Dremel (*http://bit.ly/dremel-engine*). In 2012, Impala—an open source, low-latency SQL engine on Hadoop—was released, inspired by Google's Dremel paper.

Impala differs from most of the Hadoop ecosystem projects that existed at the time in that it is not based on MapReduce. Designed to optimize latency, its architecture is similar to that of traditional massively parallel processing (MPP) data warehouses, such as Netezza, Greenplum, and Teradata. Impala delivers query latency and concurrency similar to traditional data warehouses, and significantly lower than that of Hive running on MapReduce.

To avoid creating silos of data within Hadoop, Impala uses the same SQL dialect as Hive and uses the Hive metastore. This allows users to define tables once and use them in Hive, Pig, and Impala. Similar to Hive, Impala supports both HDFS and HBase as data sources, and most of the popular data formats (delimited text, SequenceFiles, Avro, and Parquet). This allows Impala to query all data in Hadoop without requiring special transformations.

 More details on Impala are available at the Impala site (*http://impala.io/*) and in the book *Getting Started with Impala* by John Russell (O'Reilly).

Additionally, as we noted previously in this chapter there are other open source projects supporting low-latency query processing on Hadoop. These include the Presto project (*http://prestodb.io/*) and Apache Drill (*http://drill.apache.org/*).

Impala Overview

Impala has a shared nothing architecture, which allows for system-level fault tolerance and huge scalability that allows Impala to remain performant as the number of users and concurrent queries increases.

Impala's architecture includes the Impala daemons (*impalad*), the *catalog service*, and the *statestore*. Impala daemons run on every node in the cluster, and each daemon is capable of acting as the query planner, the query coordinator, and a query execution engine. To connect to Impala, the client uses JDBC, ODBC, impala-shell, or connects directly via Apache Thrift (*https://thrift.apache.org/*) to connect to one of the Impala daemons. All Impala daemons are identical and interchangeable, so the client will typically connect to a load balancer that will direct the connection to an active daemon. The daemon the client connects to will act as a query planner and coordinator for this query.

The query planner is responsible for parsing out the given SQL query and producing an execution plan. The query coordinator takes the plan and then assigns parts of it to the rest of the Impala daemons to execute. The Impala architecture is illustrated in Figure 3-11.

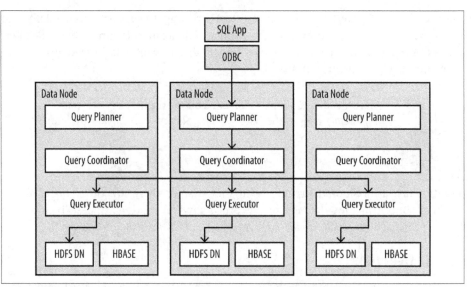

Figure 3-11. Impala architecture

Note that unlike other database management systems such as an RDBMS, Impala does not have to implement the underlying data store, because this is off-loaded to HDFS and HBase. Impala also doesn't have to implement the table and database management solution since this is implemented by the Hive metastore. This allows Impala to focus on its core functionality, which is executing queries as fast as possible.

Because Impala aims to be a distributed MPP database on top of Hadoop, the intent is to implement various distributed join strategies commonly found in such MPP databases. At the time of this writing, two such join strategies have been implemented: *broadcast hash joins* and *partitioned hash joins*. If you'd like to review the internals of such join strategies and how they are implemented in Impala, please see Appendix A.

Speed-Oriented Design

There are several design decisions that reduce Impala's query latency compared to other SQL-in-Hadoop solutions.

Efficient use of memory

As a completely rewritten query engine, Impala is not bound by the limitations of the MapReduce engine. Data is read from the disk when the tables are initially scanned, and then remains in memory as it goes through multiple phases of processing. Even when data is being shuffled between different nodes, it is sent through the network without being written to disk first. This means that as queries become more complex and require more stages of processing, Impala's performance benefits become more pronounced. Contrast this with Hive, which is forced to perform relatively slow disk reads and writes between each stage.

This does not mean that Impala can only process queries for which the results of intermediate computation can all fit in the aggregate memory. The initial versions of Impala had such a limitation for queries that relied heavily on memory. Examples of such queries are joins (where the smaller table, after filtering had to fit in the aggregate memory of the cluster), order by (where each individual node did some part of the ordering in memory), and group by and distinct (where each of the distinct keys were stored in memory for aggregation). However, with Impala 2.0 and later, Impala spills to disk when the intermediate data sets exceed the memory limits of any node. Consequently, with newer versions of Impala, queries are not simply limited to those whose intermediate data sets can fit within certain memory constraints. Impala will still favor fitting data in memory and running computations that way, but when necessary will spill data to disk and later reread the data, albeit at the expense of performance overhead due to higher I/O.

In general, for faster performance, Impala requires significantly more memory per node than MapReduce-based processing. A minimum of 128 GB to 256 GB of RAM is usually recommended. There is still one downside to using Impala due to its favoring memory over disk as much as possible: Impala queries can't recover from the loss of a node in the way that MapReduce and Hive can. If you lose a node while a query is running, your query will fail. Therefore, Impala is recommended for queries that run quickly enough that restarting the entire query in case of a failure is not a major event. Restarting a query that took a few seconds or even five minutes is usually OK. However, if a query takes over an hour to execute, then Hive might be a better tool.

Long running daemons

Unlike the MapReduce engine in Hive, Impala daemons are long-running processes. There is no startup cost incurred and no moving of JARs over the network or loading class files when a query is executed, because Impala is always running. The question comes up sometimes of whether to run the Impala daemons on the same nodes that run MapReduce tasks or on a separate set of nodes. We highly recommend running Impala on all the DataNodes in the cluster, side by side with MapReduce and other processing engines. This allows Impala to read data from the local node rather than over the network (aka *data locality*), which is essential for reducing latency. Much of the resource contention between Impala and other processing engines can be managed dynamically via YARN or statically by Linux CGroups.

Efficient execution engine

Impala is implemented in C++. This design decision makes Impala code highly efficient, and also allows a single Impala process to use large amounts of memory without the latency added by Java's garbage collection. Moreover, in general, it allows

Impala to take better advantage of vectorization and certain CPU instructions for text parsing, CRC32 computation, and more because it doesn't have to access these hardware features through the JVM.

Use of LLVM

One of the main performance improvement techniques used in Impala is the use of Low Level Virtual Machine (*http://llvm.org/*) (LLVM) to compile the query and all the functions used in this query into optimized machine code. This gives Impala query execution a performance boost in multiple ways. First, machine code improves the efficiency of the code execution in the CPU by getting rid of the polymorphism that you'd have to deal with when implementing something similar in, say, Java. Second, the machine code generated uses optimizations available in modern CPUs (such as Sandy Bridge) to improve its I/O efficiency. Third, because the entire query and its functions are compiled into a single context of execution, Impala doesn't have the same overhead of context switching because all function calls are inlined and there are no branches in the instruction pipeline, which makes execution even faster.

It is possible to turn off the LLVM code generation in Impala by setting the `disable_codegen` flag. This is used mostly for troubleshooting, but using it allows you to see exactly how much your query benefits from the code generation.

Impala Example

Although the inner workings of Impala can seem quite complex, using Impala is actually fairly easy. You can start *impala-shell*, the Impala command-line interface, and begin submitting queries like so:

```
CONNECT <impalaDaemon host name or loadbalancer>;

-- Make sure Impala has the latest metadata about which tables exist, etc.
-- from the Hive metastore
INVALIDATE METADATA;

SELECT
  *
FROM
  foo f JOIN bar b ON (f.fooBarId = b.barId)
WHERE
  f.fooVal < 500 AND
  f.fooVal + b.barVal < 1000;
```

This code connects to Impala, updates the metadata from Hive, and runs our query. You can immediately see why most developers prefer the SQL version of this code to the MapReduce version we saw earlier in the chapter.

To see the execution plan of a query in Impala, you simply add the word EXPLAIN before your query. The syntax is identical to that of Hive, but the resulting query plan is completely different. Because Impala is implemented as an MPP data warehouse, the execution plans use similar operators and look similar to those of Oracle and Netezza. These are very different from the MapReduce-based plans that are produced by Hive.

Here is the explain plan of the query just shown:

```
+----------------------------------------------------------------------+
| Explain String                                                       |
+----------------------------------------------------------------------+
| Estimated Per-Host Requirements: Memory=32.00MB VCores=2             |
| WARNING: The following tables are missing relevant table             |
|   and/or column statistics.                                          |
| default.bar, default.foo                                             |
|                                                                      |
| 04:EXCHANGE [PARTITION=UNPARTITIONED]                                |
| |                                                                    |
| 02:HASH JOIN [INNER JOIN, BROADCAST]                                 |
| |   hash predicates: f.fooBarId = b.barId                            |
| |   other predicates: f.fooVal + b.barVal < 1000                     |
| |                                                                    |
| |--03:EXCHANGE [BROADCAST]                                           |
| |  |                                                                 |
| |  01:SCAN HDFS [default.bar b]                                      |
| |      partitions=1/1 size=7.61KB                                    |
| |                                                                    |
| 00:SCAN HDFS [default.foo f]                                         |
|     partitions=1/1 size=1.04KB                                       |
|     predicates: f.fooVal < 500                                       |
+----------------------------------------------------------------------+
```

We can see that Impala first scans table foo and filters it with the predicate in the query. The plan shows the filtering predicate and the table size after the filtering as estimated by the Impala optimizer. The results of the filter operation are joined with table bar via a broadcast join, and the plan also shows the join columns and the additional filter.

Impala also has a web UI, by default on port 25000 on each Impala daemon. This web UI gives access to query profiles. Query profiles look similar to execution plans, but they are created after the query is executed—so in addition to the estimated size, a query profile also contains additional runtime information such as the rates at which tables were scanned, the actual data sizes, the amount of memory used, the execution times, and so on. This information is very useful for improving query performance.

When to Use Impala

As we've discussed, there are a few options for running SQL on data in Hadoop, Hive being the most popular of them. So when to use Hive versus Impala?

We think the answer to that question depends on your use case, but more interesting is that it will change with time as both Hive and Impala evolve. As of this writing, even though Impala is much faster than Hive on MapReduce and is highly concurrent, it is not fault-tolerant like Hive, nor does it have all the features that Hive has (like complex data types—maps, structs, arrays, etc.). Therefore, our recommendation is to use Impala where possible to make use of the higher speed. In particular, if your organization has hundreds of users who will need to run SQL queries on Hadoop concurrently, Impala is known to scale very well (*http://bit.ly/impala-scale*) to fit such a requirement. However, let's say your query needs to scan so much data (e.g., hundreds of terabytes) that even with Impala's performance the query will take hours due to the sheer amount of I/O needed. In that scenario, the ability to recover the query from a node failure without restarting is critical. Hive offers this functionality and would be our recommendation in such a case. Also worth pointing out is the fact that at the time of this writing, Impala lacks certain features that exist in Hive. The most important one is the ability to process nested data types (that's currently under development in Impala). Therefore, if using nested data types is critical to your application, we recommend you use Hive. As Hive and Impala evolve, this gap is expected to change.

Another important decision factor is the support for custom file formats. Hive supports all the popular file formats in the ecosystem (e.g., delimited text, Parquet, Avro, RCFile, SequenceFile) as well as custom file formats (e.g., JSON) by means of writing a pluggable SerDe (serializer/deserializer). However, Impala only supports the same popular Hadoop file formats; it doesn't provide support for writing custom file formats. In such cases, you can use Hive to read data directly in the format in question, or convert the data in Hive to a popular file format in the Hadoop ecosystem and then use Impala to query that data set.

Also note that while the choice between Impala and Hive may seem complicated now, it's relatively simple to switch between the two since they share the same metadata. For example, a table created and populated via Hive is readable via Impala and vice versa without any additional steps required to transfer between the two systems.

Conclusion

As we stated in the introduction to this chapter, our intention is not to give in-depth overviews of all of the processing engines available for Hadoop. Instead, our goal for this chapter was to give enough of an overview of the most-used processing options that you can confidently determine the correct tool for your particular applications as well as to provide you the appropriate resources to learn more about a selected tool.

In the next chapter we'll cover implementation of some common patterns using some of the tools we've covered here, and in Chapter 5 we'll discuss a specific set of libraries and APIs, such as GraphX and Giraph, to support graph processing on Hadoop, but there are a number of other libraries and APIs providing support for implementing applications on Hadoop. We don't have space to cover all these tools, but depending on your applications some of them may be worth exploring further. This includes projects such as:

RHadoop (http://bit.ly/RHadoop)
The R language has long been popular for data analysis, so not surprisingly there's a great deal of interest in being able to apply it to big data problems. The implementation of the R language presents some challenges to processing large volumes of data, but several open source projects have been developed to provide an R interface to process Hadoop data. The most prominent of these projects is probably RHadoop. RHadoop is actually a collection of projects, including *rmr*, which provides an interface to implement MapReduce applications in the R language.

Apache Mahout (http://mahout.apache.org/)
Mahout is a library providing implementations of common machine learning tasks such as recommendation systems, classification, and clustering. Although the goal of the project is to provide scalable implementations for scalable machine learning algorithms, note that not all of the algorithms implemented by Mahout lend themselves to parallelization and they are not designed to run on Hadoop. In addition to common machine learning algorithms, the Mahout project also includes libraries that can be applied to other processing tasks. See the Mahout website or *Mahout in Action* by Sean Owen, et al. (Manning).

Oryx (http://bit.ly/oryx-project)
The Oryx project is designed to facilitate building machine-learning applications that leverage the Lambda Architecture (*http://lambda-architecture.net/*). Although still in alpha, the project is intended to provide a platform for deploying analytical models at Hadoop scale.

Python
Python, of course, is a popular language, particularly with data science folks. If Python is your language of choice, you'll be happy to know that there are a number of frameworks intended to facilitate using Python with Hadoop. For a good overview of the available frameworks, see *A Guide to Python Frameworks for Hadoop* by Uri Laserson (O'Reilly).

## CHAPTER 4

Common Hadoop Processing Patterns

With an understanding of how to access and process data on Hadoop, we'd like to move on to discuss how to solve some fairly common problems in Hadoop using some of the tools we discussed in Chapter 3. We'll cover the following data processing tasks, which in addition to being common patterns in processing data on Hadoop, also have a fairly high degree of complexity in implementation:

- Removing duplicate records by primary key (compaction)
- Using windowing analytics
- Updating time series data

We'll go into more detail on these patterns next, and take a deep dive into how they're implemented. We'll present implementations of these patterns in both Spark and SQL (for Impala and Hive). You'll note that we're not including implementations in Map-Reduce; this is because of the size and complexity of the code in MapReduce, as well as the move toward newer processing frameworks such as Spark and abstractions such as SQL.

Pattern: Removing Duplicate Records by Primary Key

Duplicate records are a common occurrence when you are working with data in Hadoop for two primary reasons:

Resends during data ingest
  As we've discussed elsewhere in the book, it's difficult to ensure that records are sent exactly once, and it's not uncommon to have to deal with duplicate records during ingest processing.

Deltas (updated records)

HDFS is a "write once and read many" filesystem. Making modifications at a record level is not a simple thing to do. In the use case of deltas we would have an existing data set with a primary key (or composite key), and we will have updated records being added to that data set.

We cover methods for dealing with the first case, fully duplicate records, elsewhere in this book—for example, in the clickstream case study in Chapter 8—so we'll discuss the second case, record updates, in this example. This will require implementing processing to rewrite an existing data set so that it only shows the newest versions of each record.

If you're familiar with HBase, you might have noted that this is similar to the way HBase works; at a high level, a region in HBase has an HFile that has values linked to a key. When new data is added, a second HFile is added with keys and values. During cleanup activities called *compactions*, HBase does a merge join to execute this deduplication pattern, as shown in Figure 4-1.

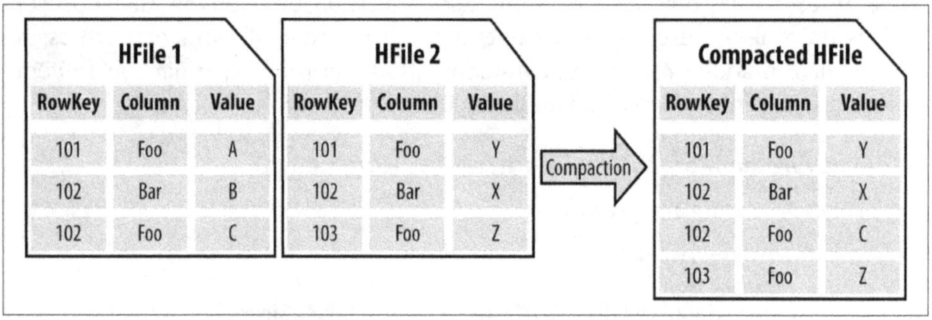

Figure 4-1. HBase compaction

Note that we're omitting some additional complexity, such as HBase's support for versioning, in the preceding example.

Data Generation for Deduplication Example

Before we get into examples of implementing this pattern, let's first look at some code to create test data. We are going to use the Scala object GenDedupInput, which uses the HDFS API to create a file on HDFS and write out records in the following format:

```
{PrimaryKey},{timeStamp},{value}
```

We'll write *x* records and *y* unique primary keys. This means if we set *x* to 100 and *y* to 10, we will get something close to 10 duplicate records for every primary key as seen in this example:

```
object GenDedupInput {
  def main(args:Array[String]): Unit = {
```

```
if (args.length < 3) {
  println("{outputPath} {numberOfRecords} {numberOfUniqueRecords}")
  return
}

// The output file that will hold the data
val outputPath = new Path(args(0))
// Number of records to be written to the file
val numberOfRecords = args(1).toLong
// Number of unique primary keys
val numberOfUniqueRecords = args(2).toInt

// Open fileSystem to HDFS
val fileSystem = FileSystem.get(new Configuration())

// Create buffered writer
val writer = new BufferedWriter(
  new OutputStreamWriter(fileSystem.create(outputPath)))

val r = new Random()

// This loop will write out all the records
// Every primary key will get about
// numberOfRecords/numberOfUniqueRecords records
for (i <- 0 until numberOfRecords) {
  val uniqueId = r.nextInt(numberOfUniqueRecords)
  // Format: {key}, {timeStamp}, {value}
  writer.write(uniqueId + "," + i + "," + r.nextInt(10000))
  writer.newLine()
}

writer.close()
  }
}
```

Code Example: Spark Deduplication in Scala

Now that we've created our test data in HDFS, let's look at the code to deduplicate
these records in the SparkDedupExecution object:

```
object SparkDedupExecution {
  def main(args:Array[String]): Unit = {
    if (args.length < 2) {
      println("{inputPath} {outputPath}")
      return
    }

    // set up given parameters
    val inputPath = args(0)
    val outputPath = args(1)

    // set up spark conf and connection
```

```
val sparkConf = new SparkConf().setAppName("SparkDedupExecution")
sparkConf.set("spark.cleaner.ttl", "120000");
val sc = new SparkContext(sparkConf)

// Read data in from HDFS
val dedupOriginalDataRDD = sc.hadoopFile(inputPath,
  classOf[TextInputFormat],
  classOf[LongWritable],
  classOf[Text],
  1)

// Get the data in a key-value format
val keyValueRDD = dedupOriginalDataRDD.map(t => {
  val splits = t._2.toString.split(",")
  (splits(0), (splits(1), splits(2)))})

// reduce by key so we will only get one record for every primary key
val reducedRDD =
    keyValueRDD.reduceByKey((a,b) => if (a._1.compareTo(b._1) > 0) a else b)

// Format the data to a human-readable format and write it back out to HDFS
reducedRDD
  .map(r => r._1 + "," + r._2._1 + "," + r._2._2)
  .saveAsTextFile(outputPath)
  }
}
```

Let's break this code down to discuss what's going on. We'll skip the setup code, which just gets the user arguments and sets up the SparkContext, and skip to the following code that will get our duplicate record data from HDFS:

```
val dedupOriginalDataRDD = sc.hadoopFile(inputPath,
  classOf[TextInputFormat],
  classOf[LongWritable],
  classOf[Text],
  1)
```

There are many ways to read data in Spark, but for this example we'll use the hadoop File() method so we can show how the existing input formats can be used. If you have done much MapReduce programing, you will be familiar with the TextInputFormat, which is one of the most basic input formats available. The TextInputFormat provides functionality that will allow Spark or MapReduce jobs to break up a directory into files, which are then broken up into blocks to be processed by different tasks.

The next item of code is the first map() function:

```
val keyValueRDD = dedupOriginalDataRDD.map(t => {
  val splits = t._2.toString.split(",")
  (splits(0), (splits(1), splits(2)))})
```

This code will run in parallel across different workers and parse the incoming records into a `Tuple` object that has two values representing a key and a value.

This key-value structure is required for the next piece of code, which will use the `reduceByKey()` method. As you might guess by the name, in order to use the `reduceByKey()` method we need a key.

Now let's look at the code that calls `reduceByKey()`:

```
val reducedRDD =
    keyValueRDD.reduceByKey((a,b) => if (a._1.compareTo(b._1) > 0) a else b)
```

The `reduceByKey()` method takes a function that takes a left and right value and returns a value of the same type. The goal of `reduceByKey()` is to combine all values of the same key. In the word count example, it is used to add all the counts of a single word to get the total count. In our example, the a and b are strings, and we will return a or b depending on which is greater. Since the key we're reducing by is the primary key, this function will make sure that we only have one record per primary key— hence, deduplicating the data based on the greatest primary key-value.

The last bit of code will just write the results back to HDFS:

```
reducedRDD
    .map(r => r._1 + "," + r._2._1 + "," + r._2._2)
    .saveAsTextFile(outputPath)
```

We will get a text output file for every partition in Spark, similar to the way MapReduce will output a file for each mapper or reducer at the end of a MapReduce job.

Code Example: Deduplication in SQL

Now we'll turn to the venerable SQL—well, more accurately, HiveQL, although the examples in this chapter will work with either Hive or Impala. First, we need to put our test data into a table using this data definition language (DDL) query:

```
CREATE EXTERNAL TABLE COMPACTION_TABLE (
   PRIMARY_KEY STRING,
   TIME_STAMP BIGINT,
   EVENT_VALUE STRING
   )
ROW FORMAT DELIMITED FIELDS TERMINATED BY ','
STORED AS TEXTFILE
LOCATION 'compaction_data';
```

Now that we have a table, let's look at the query to perform the deduplication:

```
SELECT
A.PRIMARY_KEY,
A.TIME_STAMP,
MAX(A.EVENT_VALUE)
FROM COMPACTION_TABLE A JOIN (
```

```
SELECT
 PRIMARY_KEY AS P_KEY,
 MAX(TIME_STAMP) as TIME_SP
 FROM COMPACTION_TABLE
 GROUP BY PRIMARY_KEY
) B
WHERE A.PRIMARY_KEY = B.P_KEY AND A.TIME_STAMP = B.TIME_SP
GROUP BY A.PRIMARY_KEY, A.TIME_STAMP
```

Here we have a two-level-deep SQL query. The deepest SELECT is getting the latest TIME_STAMP for all the PRIMARY_KEY records. The outer SELECT statement is taking the results from the inner SELECT statement to pull out the latest EVENT_VALUE. Also note that we apply a MAX() function to the EVENT_VALUE value; this is because we only want a single value, so if we have two EVENT_VALUEs with the same timestamp we'll select the one with the greatest value to keep for our new record.

Pattern: Windowing Analysis

Windowing functions provide the ability to scan over an ordered sequence of events over some window—for example, a specific slice of time. This pattern is very powerful and is useful in many industries:

- It can be used in finance to gain a better understanding of changing security prices.

- In sensor monitoring, it's useful in predicting failure from abnormalities in readings.

- It can be used in churn analysis for trying to predict if a customer will leave you based on behavior patterns.

- In gaming, it can help to identify trends as users progress from novice to expert.

To illustrate, we'll use an example that relates to the finance use case: finding peaks and valleys in equity prices in order to provide some insight into price changes. A *peak* is a record that has a lower price before it and a lower price after it, while a *valley* is just the opposite, with higher prices on both sides, as shown in Figure 4-2.

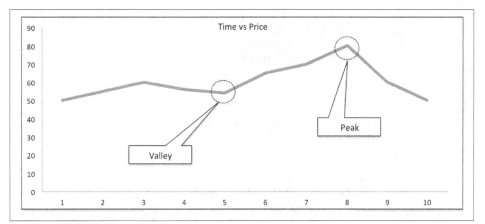

Figure 4-2. Peaks and valleys in stock prices over time

To implement this example we'll need to maintain a window of stock prices in order to determine where the peaks and valleys occur.

Note that a simple example like this makes it possible for us to show the solution in both SQL and Spark. As windowing analysis gets more complex, SQL becomes a less suitable solution.

Data Generation for Windowing Analysis Example

Let's create some test data containing records with a value that goes up and down, similar to stock prices. The following code example takes the same input parameters as our last data generation tool—numberOfRecords and numberOfUniqueIds— although the resulting records will be somewhat different:

Primary key
> An identifier for each sequence of events we are analyzing—for example, a stock ticker symbol. This will be based on the numberOfUniqueIds input parameter.

Incrementing counter
> This will be unique for every record in the generated data.

Event value
> This will have a value that increases and decreases for a random set of records for a given primary key.

Let's take a look at the code to generate this test data:

```
def main(args: Array[String]): Unit = {
  if (args.length == 0) {
    println("{outputPath} {numberOfRecords} {numberOfUniqueIds}")
    return
  }
```

```scala
val outputPath = new Path(args(0))
val numberOfRecords = args(1).toInt
val numberOfUniqueIds = args(2).toInt

val fileSystem = FileSystem.get(new Configuration())

val writer =
    new BufferedWriter( new OutputStreamWriter(fileSystem.create(outputPath)))

val r = new Random()

var direction = 1
var directionCounter = r.nextInt(numberOfUniqueIds * 10)
var currentPointer = 0

for (i <- 0 until numberOfRecords) {
  val uniqueId = r.nextInt(numberOfUniqueIds)

  currentPointer = currentPointer + direction
  directionCounter = directionCounter - 1
  if (directionCounter == 0) {
    var directionCounter = r.nextInt(numberOfUniqueIds * 10)
    direction = direction * -1
  }

  writer.write(uniqueId + "," + i + "," + currentPointer)
  writer.newLine()
}

writer.close()
}
```

Code Example: Peaks and Valleys in Spark

Now, let's look at the code to implement this pattern in Spark. There's quite a bit going on in the following code example, so after we present the code we'll drill down further to help you to understand what's going on.

You'll find this code in the *SparkPeaksAndValleysExecution.scala* file:

```scala
object SparkPeaksAndValleysExecution {
  def main(args: Array[String]): Unit = {
    if (args.length == 0) {
      println("{inputPath} {outputPath} {numberOfPartitions}")
      return
    }

    val inputPath = args(0)
    val outputPath = args(1)
    val numberOfPartitions = args(2).toInt
```

```
val sparkConf = new SparkConf().setAppName("SparkTimeSeriesExecution")
sparkConf.set("spark.cleaner.ttl", "120000");

val sc = new SparkContext(sparkConf)

// Read in the data
var originalDataRDD = sc.hadoopFile(inputPath,                    ❶
  classOf[TextInputFormat],
  classOf[LongWritable],
  classOf[Text],
  1).map(r => {
  val splits = r._2.toString.split(",")
  (new DataKey(splits(0), splits(1).toLong), splits(2).toInt)
})

// Partitioner to partition by primaryKey only
val partitioner = new Partitioner {                              ❷
  override def numPartitions: Int = numberOfPartitions

  override def getPartition(key: Any): Int = {
    Math.abs(key.asInstanceOf[DataKey].uniqueId.hashCode() % numPartitions)
  }
}

// Partition and sort
val partedSortedRDD =                                            ❸
  new ShuffledRDD[DataKey, Int, Int](
    originalDataRDD,
    partitioner).setKeyOrdering(implicitly[Ordering[DataKey]])

// MapPartition to do windowing
val pivotPointRDD = partedSortedRDD.mapPartitions(it => {        ❹

  val results = new mutable.MutableList[PivotPoint]

  // Keeping context
  var lastUniqueId = "foobar"                                    ❺
  var lastRecord: (DataKey, Int) = null
  var lastLastRecord: (DataKey, Int) = null

  var position = 0

  it.foreach( r => {
    position = position + 1

    if (!lastUniqueId.equals(r._1.uniqueId)) {

      lastRecord = null
      lastLastRecord = null
    }

    // Finding peaks and valleys
```

```scala
        if (lastRecord != null && lastLastRecord != null) {          ❻
          if (lastRecord._2 < r._2 && lastRecord._2 < lastLastRecord._2) {
            results.+=(new PivotPoint(r._1.uniqueId,
              position,
              lastRecord._1.eventTime,
              lastRecord._2,
              false))
          } else if (lastRecord._2 > r._2 && lastRecord._2 > lastLastRecord._2) {
            results.+=(new PivotPoint(r._1.uniqueId,
              position,
              lastRecord._1.eventTime,
              lastRecord._2,
              true))
          }
        }
        lastUniqueId = r._1.uniqueId
        lastLastRecord = lastRecord
        lastRecord = r

    })

    results.iterator
  })

  // Format output
  pivotPointRDD.map(r => {                                           ❼
    val pivotType = if (r.isPeak) "peak" else "valley"
    r.uniqueId + "," +
      r.position + "," +
      r.eventTime + "," +
      r.eventValue + "," +
      pivotType
  } ).saveAsTextFile(outputPath)

}


class DataKey(val uniqueId:String, val eventTime:Long)
  extends Serializable with Comparable[DataKey] {
  override def compareTo(other:DataKey): Int = {
    val compare1 = uniqueId.compareTo(other.uniqueId)
    if (compare1 == 0) {
      eventTime.compareTo(other.eventTime)
    } else {
      compare1
    }
  }
}

class PivotPoint(val uniqueId: String,
                 val position:Int,
                 val eventTime:Long,
```

```
        val eventValue:Int,
        val isPeak:boolean) extends Serializable {}

}
```

❶ Nothing too interesting here: we're simply reading the input data and parsing it into easy-to-consume objects.

❷ This is where things get interesting. We're defining a partition here, just like defining a custom partitioner with MapReduce. A partition will help us to decide which records go to which worker after the shuffle process. We need a custom partitioner here because we have a two-part key: `primary_key` and `position`. We want to sort by both, but we only want to partition by the `primary_key` so we get output like that shown in Figure 4-3.

❸ This is the shuffle action that will partition and sort the data for us. Note that the 1.3 release of Spark provides a transformation called `repartitionAndSortWithin Partitions()`, which would provide this functionality for us, but since this is coded with Spark 1.2 we need to manually implement the shuffle.

❹ This `mapPartition()` method will allow us to run through the `primary_key` in the order of the position. This is where the windowing will happen.

❺ This is context information we need in order to find peaks and valleys and to know if we have changed `primary_keys`. Remember, to find a peak or a valley we will need to know of the record before and the one after. So we will have the `currentRow`, `lastRow`, and `lastLastRow`, and we can determine if the `lastRow` is a peak or valley by comparing it against the others.

❻ Perform comparisons to determine if we're in a peak or in a valley.

❼ And finally, this is the code that will format the records and write them to HDFS.

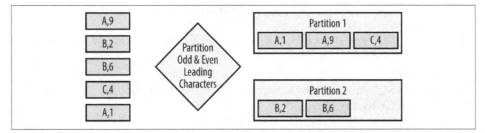

Figure 4-3. Partitioning in the peaks and valleys example—here we partition the sequences into two groups, so we can distribute the analysis on two workers while still keeping all events for each sequence together

Code Example: Peaks and Valleys in SQL

As in the previous example, we'll first create a table over our test data:

```
CREATE EXTERNAL TABLE PEAK_AND_VALLEY_TABLE (
  PRIMARY_KEY STRING,
  POSITION BIGINT,
  EVENT_VALUE BIGINT
)
ROW FORMAT DELIMITED FIELDS TERMINATED BY ','
STORED AS TEXTFILE
LOCATION 'PeakAndValleyData';
```

Now that we have our table we need to order the records and then use the lead() and lag() functions, which will provide the context of the surrounding records:

```
SELECT                              ❶
    PRIMARY_KEY,
    POSITION,
    EVENT_VALUE,
    CASE
     WHEN LEAD_EVENT_VALUE is null OR LAG_EVENT_VALUE is null THEN 'EDGE'
     WHEN
       EVENT_VALUE < LEAD_EVENT_VALUE AND EVENT_VALUE < LAG_EVENT_VALUE
     THEN
       'VALLEY'
     WHEN
       EVENT_VALUE > LEAD_EVENT_VALUE AND EVENT_VALUE > LAG_EVENT_VALUE
     THEN
       'PEAK'
     ELSE 'SLOPE'
    END AS POINT_TYPE
  FROM
  (
  SELECT                            ❷
   PRIMARY_KEY,
   POSITION,
   EVENT_VALUE,
   LEAD(EVENT_VALUE,1,null)
       OVER (PARTITION BY PRIMARY_KEY ORDER BY POSITION) AS LEAD_EVENT_VALUE,
   LAG(EVENT_VALUE,1,null)
       OVER (PARTITION BY PRIMARY_KEY ORDER BY POSITION) AS LAG_EVENT_VALUE
  FROM PEAK_AND_VALLEY_TABLE
  ) A
```

Although this SQL is not overly complex, it is big enough that we should break it down to explain what's going on:

❶   After execution of the subquery in step 2, we have the data organized in such a way that all the information we need is in the same record and we can now use that record to determine if we have one of the following: an edge, a point on the leftmost or rightmost part of the window timeline; a peak, a value that has a lower value before and after it; a valley, a value that has a higher value before and after it; or a slope point, a value that has a lower value either before or after it and a higher value either before or after it.

❷ The subquery is where we're doing all the windowing logic. This query is putting the values that appear before and after the current value in the same row. Figure 4-4 shows an example of the input and output of this subquery.

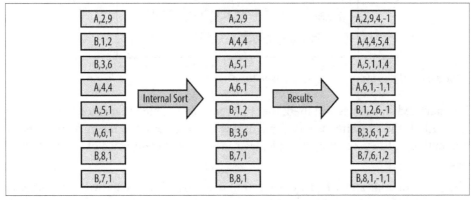

Figure 4-4. Input and output of the preceding subquery: the first step groups the events for each sequence together and sorts them by the order the events occurred; the second step adds to each event the values from the previous and following event, which is then used by the main query to detect peaks and valleys

Windowing and SQL

Even in this example the SQL code is more concise than Spark, and could be considered simpler. At the same time we need to consider the limitations; doing multiple complex windowing operations in SQL will mean an increase in complexity that will need to read and write to disk, which will increase I/O and lead to a corresponding decrease in performance. With Spark we only need to order the data once and then do N windowing operations on it, using the functionality provided by Java or Scala to hold information in memory and perform operations.

Pattern: Time Series Modifications

For our final example we are going to mix components from the first two examples. We will update records based on a primary key while also keeping all of the history.

This will allow a record to know when it was current and when it expired, providing information about an entity and a start and stop time, as shown in Figure 4-5.

Figure 4-5. The price of Apple stock over time

The start and stop times will mark the time range over which that record represented the truth. If the stop time is null, this means that the record is the current truth for that entity. In the preceding example, we can see the current price of Apple stock is $42.

The problem comes in when we need to update this table. As shown in Figure 4-6, when we add a new record of price 43, we need to close out the previous record with a new end time that equals the new record's start time. The darker cells are cells that need to be updated.

PKey	StartTime	EndTime	Value
Apple	12/05/2014	null	43
Apple	12/01/2014	12/05/2014	42
Apple	11/25/2014	12/01/2014	41
Apple	11/20/2014	11/25/2014	40

Figure 4-6. Adding a new record to Apple stock price table

At face value this looks like a very simple problem, but in fact, can be complex to implement when you are dealing with updates in large data sets. We'll discuss some of the challenges and approaches to address them in the following discussion.

Use HBase and Versioning

One common way of storing this information is as versions in HBase. HBase has a way to store every change you make to a record as versions. Versions are defined at a column level and ordered by modification timestamp, so you can go to any point in time to see what the record looked like.

The advantage to this approach is that modifications are very fast, as is getting the latest values. There is, however, some penalty in getting historical versions and a major disadvantage in performing large scans or block cache reads.

Large scans will suffer because they have to pass over all the versions of one record before reaching the next record. So the larger your version count, the slower your large scans will be.

Block cache reads are disadvantageous because when retrieving a record HBase pulls a whole 64 KB HFile block into memory, and if your history is large, it may be pulling into memory other versions instead of the actual record you want.

Lastly, this data model does have the start and stop time in the same record. You need to look at a couple of versions to figure out when a version started and ended.

Use HBase with a RowKey of RecordKey and StartTime

In order to have HBase include the start and stop time in the same record, we have to create a composite key of `RecordKey` and `StartTime`. Now the difference from the versioning solution is that the record will have a column for stop time.

Note that start time in the `RowKey` will need to be a reverse epoch number so that it can be sorted from newest to oldest.

So, to modify such a schema when a new version of a record is added, we will need to first do a single-record scan with the `RecordKey` as the start `RowKey`. This will return the most current version of the `RecordKey`. When we have that information we need to do two `put`s: one to update the stop time in the current record, and the other to add a new current record.

When we want to get a version for any given time, we just do a single-row scan of `RecordKey` and the reverse epoch of the time for the record we wish to fetch.

This solution still has the large scan and block cache problems, but now we can get a version quickly and have the stop time in the same row. Just remember this comes at the cost of an additional `get` and `put` upon insertion of the record.

Use HDFS and Rewrite the Whole Table

If we remove HBase from the picture and just do the simplest HDFS implementation, we would have all the data in HDFS and we'd refresh the table as we get new data on some periodic basis—for example, once daily.

This solution might seem very expensive, but with Hadoop we can re-write terabytes of data in a short period of time. As data sets get larger, there are techniques we can use to optimize the execution—for example, separate partitions for the most current records. We'll discuss that solution next.

Use Partitions on HDFS for Current and Historical Records

A smarter implementation on HDFS is to put the most current records in one partition and the historic records in another partition. This would allow you to rewrite just the latest version, not all the versions in history. Then we only append the new records to the older record's partition.

The big win here is that the execution time is fixed to the number of current records as opposed to getting longer and longer with every version of history added.

We'll provide an example of this technique next, again using Spark and SQL. For purposes of illustration, we'll use a simple, contrived data set composed of a unique ID, event time, and a random integer, but it should be easy to imagine how this technique could be extended to real-world, time-based data, such as the stock ticker example described earlier.

Data Generation for Time Series Example

Let's create our data set for our time series example, again using Scala and the HDFS FileSystem API:

```
def main(args: Array[String]): Unit = {
  if (args.length == 0) {
    println("{outputPath} {numberOfRecords} {numberOfUniqueRecords} {startTime}")
    return
  }

  val outputPath = new Path(args(0))
  val numberOfRecords = args(1).toInt
  val numberOfUniqueRecords = args(2).toInt
  val startTime = args(3).toInt

  val fileSystem = FileSystem.get(new Configuration())
  val writer =
      new BufferedWriter(new OutputStreamWriter(fileSystem.create(outputPath)))

  val r = new Random


  for (i <- 0 until numberOfRecords) {
    val uniqueId = r.nextInt(numberOfUniqueRecords)
    val madeUpValue = r.nextInt(1000)
    val eventTime = i + startTime
```

```
    writer.write(uniqueId + "," + eventTime + "," + madeUpValue)
    writer.newLine()
  }
  writer.close()
}
```

Looking at this data generator, you will note it is very close in design to the previous examples of data generation.

Code Example: Time Series in Spark

Now, we move on to our Spark code implementation to update our single partition of time series data with the updated start and stop times. You can find this code in the GitHub in the SparkTimeSeriesExecution Scala object. This is the largest example we have in this chapter, but we'll walk you through the code to explain what's going on.

```
object SparkTimeSeriesExecution {
  def main(args: Array[String]): Unit = {
    if (args.length == 0) {
      println("{newDataInputPath} " +
        "{outputPath} " +
        "{numberOfPartitions}")
      println("or")
      println("{newDataInputPath} " +
        "{existingTimeSeriesDataInputPath} " +
        "{outputPath} " +
        "{numberOfPartitions}")
      return
    }

    val newDataInputPath = args(0)
    val existingTimeSeriesDataInputPath = if (args.length == 4) args(1) else null
    val outputPath = args(args.length - 2)
    val numberOfPartitions = args(args.length - 1).toInt

    val sparkConf = new SparkConf().setAppName("SparkTimeSeriesExecution")
    sparkConf.set("spark.cleaner.ttl", "120000");

    val sc = new SparkContext(sparkConf)

    // Load data from HDFS
    var unendedRecordsRDD = sc.hadoopFile(newDataInputPath,       ❶
      classOf[TextInputFormat],
      classOf[LongWritable],
      classOf[Text],
      1).map(r => {
      val splits = r._2.toString.split(",")

      (new TimeDataKey(splits(0), splits(1).toLong),
        new TimeDataValue(-1, splits(2)))
```

```
  })

  var endedRecordsRDD:RDD[(TimeDataKey, TimeDataValue)] = null

  // Get existing records if they exist
  if (existingTimeSeriesDataInputPath != null) {                        ❷
    val existingDataRDD = sc.hadoopFile(existingTimeSeriesDataInputPath,
      classOf[TextInputFormat],
      classOf[LongWritable],
      classOf[Text],
      1).map(r => {
      val splits = r._2.toString.split(",")
      (new TimeDataKey(splits(0), splits(1).toLong),
        new TimeDataValue(splits(2).toLong, splits(3)))
    })

    unendedRecordsRDD = unendedRecordsRDD
      .union(existingDataRDD.filter(r => r._2.endTime == -1))

    endedRecordsRDD = existingDataRDD.filter(r => r._2.endTime > -1)
  }

  // Define our partitioner
  val partitioner = new Partitioner {                                  ❸
    override def numPartitions: Int = numberOfPartitions

    override def getPartition(key: Any): Int = {
      Math.abs(
        key.asInstanceOf[TimeDataKey].uniqueId.hashCode() % numPartitions)
    }
  }

  val partedSortedRDD =
    new ShuffledRDD[TimeDataKey, TimeDataValue, TimeDataValue](
      unendedRecordsRDD,
      partitioner).setKeyOrdering(implicitly[Ordering[TimeDataKey]])

  // Walk down each primaryKey to make sure the stop times are updated
  var updatedEndedRecords = partedSortedRDD.mapPartitions(it => {       ❹
    val results = new mutable.MutableList[(TimeDataKey, TimeDataValue)]

    var lastUniqueId = "foobar"
    var lastRecord: (TimeDataKey, TimeDataValue) = null

    it.foreach(r => {
      if (!r._1.uniqueId.equals(lastUniqueId)) {
        if (lastRecord != null) {
          results.+=(lastRecord)
        }
        lastUniqueId = r._1.uniqueId
        lastRecord = null
```

```
        } else {
          if (lastRecord != null) {
            lastRecord._2.endTime = r._1.startTime
            results.+=(lastRecord)
          }
        }
        lastRecord = r
      })
      if (lastRecord != null) {
        results.+=(lastRecord)
      }
      results.iterator
    })

    // If there were existing records union them back in
    if (endedRecordsRDD != null) {                                    ❺
      updatedEndedRecords = updatedEndedRecords.union(endedRecordsRDD)
    }

    // Format and save the results to HDFS
    updatedEndedRecords                                               ❻
      .map(r => r._1.uniqueId + "," +
      r._1.startTime + "," +
      r._2.endTime + "," +
      r._2.data)
      .saveAsTextFile(outputPath)
  }

  class TimeDataKey(val uniqueId:String, val startTime:Long)
      extends Serializable with Comparable[TimeDataKey] {
    override def compareTo(other:TimeDataKey): Int = {
      val compare1 = uniqueId.compareTo(other.uniqueId)
      if (compare1 == 0) {
        startTime.compareTo(other.startTime)
      } else {
        compare1
      }
    }
  }

  class TimeDataValue(var endTime:Long, val data:String) extends Serializable {}
}
```

❶ As in previous code examples, here we are just reading in the new data from HDFS.

❷ Unlike previous examples in this chapter, in this case we have the possibility of two inputs: the new data and the data from the existing table in HDFS. We're making the existing data set optional here, because the first time we add records we obviously won't have an existing data set. Note that we will filter out any records that already have `endTimes`. This is because we don't need them to go through the shuffle code and be transferred over the network and sorted. We will union these values back in later.

❸ Just as in the peak and valley example, we are going to need a custom partition and shuffle. This will be a common pattern we'll use whenever we need to traverse over a data set in order by a given key. The partitioning here is similar to previous examples: we want to partition on the `primaryKey` and sort on the combination of the `primaryKey` and the `startTime`.

❹ This is the code that will traverse each `primaryKey` and update records that need new stop times.

❺ Here is where we union in the existing records that already had `endTimes` with a `union()` method.

❻ And finally, this is where we write out the formatted results to HDFS.

Code Example: Time Series in SQL

As before, we need to first set up our source tables for Hive or Impala. In this example we are going to have two tables: one for the existing time series data and one for the new data:

```
CREATE EXTERNAL TABLE EXISTING_TIME_SERIES_TABLE (
  PRIMARY_KEY STRING,
  EFFECTIVE_DT BIGINT,
  EXPIRED_DT BIGINT,
  EVENT_VALUE STRING
  )
 ROW FORMAT DELIMITED FIELDS TERMINATED BY ','
 STORED AS TEXTFILE
 LOCATION 'ExistingTimeSeriesData';

CREATE EXTERNAL TABLE NEW_TIME_SERIES_TABLE (
  PRIMARY_KEY STRING,
  EFFECTIVE_DT BIGINT,
  EVENT_VALUE STRING
  )
 ROW FORMAT DELIMITED FIELDS TERMINATED BY ','
 STORED AS TEXTFILE
 LOCATION 'NewTimeSeriesData';
```

The two tables are very close except the new records don't have an expired date.

Note that in a real-world use case we would likely have multiple partitions in our data set—for example, for current and historic records. This is because we don't really need to read the existing expired records to perform this processing. We only need to read the existing active records to see if they have been expired with the addition of new records in the NEW_TIME_SERIES_TABLE.

Therefore, the current records would be rewritten, whereas the history would only be appended to.

Now let's take these two tables and populate a result table with the updated records:

```
SELECT
    PRIMARY_KEY,
    EFFECTIVE_DT,
    CASE
      WHEN LEAD(EFFECTIVE_DT,1,null)
        OVER
          (PARTITION BY PRIMARY_KEY ORDER BY EFFECTIVE_DT)
            IS NULL THEN NULL
      ELSE LEAD(EFFECTIVE_DT,1,null)
        OVER
          (PARTITION BY PRIMARY_KEY ORDER BY EFFECTIVE_DT)
    END AS EXPIRED_DT,
    EVENT_VALUE
    FROM (
      SELECT
        PRIMARY_KEY,
        EFFECTIVE_DT,
        EVENT_VALUE
      FROM
        EXISTING_TIME_SERIES_TABLE
      WHERE
        EXPIRED_DT IS NULL
      UNION ALL
      SELECT
        PRIMARY_KEY,
        EFFECTIVE_DT,
        EVENT_VALUE
      FROM NEW_TIME_SERIES_TABLE
    ) sub_1
UNION ALL
SELECT
  PRIMARY_KEY,
  EFFECTIVE_DT,
  EXPIRED_DT,
  EVENT_VALUE
FROM
  EXISTING_TIME_SERIES_TABLE
WHERE
  EXPIRED_DT IS NOT NULL
```

This is a fairly long query, so let's break it down. At the top level there are two main SELECTs that are unioned together. The first one handles updating existing current records and new records to see which records have expired. The second one is just moving over the existing expired records. If we used the partition strategy described earlier we wouldn't need this second top-level SELECT statement.

Focusing on the first SELECT, shown in the following snippet, notice that in the subquery there is a union of the two starting tables. Note that we are filtering out the existing expired tables from the EXISTING_TIME_SERIES_TABLE; this is because we don't want the extra work of resorting all those records in the windowing function:

```
SELECT
  PRIMARY_KEY
  EFFECTIVE_DT,
  EVENT_VALUE
FROM
  EXISTING_TIME_SERIES_TABLE
WHERE
  EXPIRED_DT IS NULL
UNION ALL
  SELECT
    PRIMARY_KEY,
    EFFECTIVE_DT,
    EVENT_VALUE
  FROM NEW_TIME_SERIES_TABLE
```

The results of that inner SELECT will be partitioned by the primary key and ordered by the effective date and time. This will allow us to ask, "Is there a record with a greater timestamp and the same primary key, and that also has an effective date?" If the answer is yes, this record is expired. Here is that portion of the query:

```
PRIMARY_KEY,
EFFECTIVE_DT,
CASE
  WHEN LEAD(EFFECTIVE_DT,1,null)
    OVER
      (PARTITION BY PRIMARY_KEY ORDER BY EFFECTIVE_DT)
        IS NULL THEN NULL
  ELSE LEAD(EFFECTIVE_DT,1,null)
    OVER
      (PARTITION BY PRIMARY_KEY ORDER BY EFFECTIVE_DT)
END AS EXPIRED_DT,
EVENT_VALUE
```

As you can see, this is a somewhat complex query, but it's still more concise than the Spark code. In this case Spark or SQL are both good choices, and your choice will likely be determined by comfort and familiarity with one or the other.

Conclusion

To wrap up this chapter, here are a few takeaways:

- We can do some pretty complex stuff with Spark and SQL in Hadoop.
- We don't have to abandon SQL when moving to Hadoop, and in fact SQL remains a powerful abstraction for processing and analyzing data in Hadoop, just as it is with more traditional data management systems.
- We can attack problems with different tools, each giving us a different approach to solving the problem.

It's likely that SQL-on-Hadoop will become an increasingly powerful tool with the introduction of new tools like Impala and Hive on Spark, but it's unlikely that SQL will replace Spark and other processing frameworks for solving a number of problems. Ultimately it will be necessary for well-rounded Hadoop developers to understand the available tools in order to evaluate the appropriate one to solve their particular problem.

## CHAPTER 5

Graph Processing on Hadoop

In Chapter 3, we talked about tools for processing data with Hadoop, but there's another class of data processing being done on Hadoop that we did not cover there: graph processing. We'll discuss graph processing with Hadoop separately in this chapter, since it's at the heart of many of the applications we use every day, and provides significant opportunities for implementing specific types of applications. Some common uses of graph processing are ranking pages in search engines, finding new friends on social networks, determining the underlying equities in our investment funds, planning routes, and much more.

What Is a Graph?

Before we go into the tools for graph processing, let's step back and first define what a graph is, in case you are new to this topic. Then we will go over what graph processing is and distinguish it from graph querying.

Needless to say, a graph can mean multiple things. It can mean a line, pie, or bar graph in tools like Excel. One author's second grader has to chart different-colored M&Ms on a bar graph, but that isn't the type of graph we're talking about in this chapter. The graphs we're talking about here only contain two types of objects called *vertices* and *edges*.

As you might have been taught in grade school, the points of a triangle are called vertices, and the lines that connect those points are edges, as shown in Figure 5-1. To provide some context, this is a good place to start.

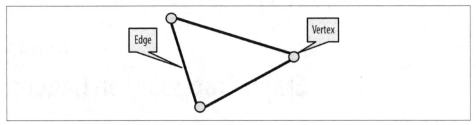

Figure 5-1. Edges and vertices

Now let's change the image a little and give each vertex some information. Let's say each vertex represents a person, and we want it to have some information about that person like his or her name and type (which in this case would be Person). Now for the edges, let's give them some information also describing the relationship of the two vertices they connect. We can use information like movies viewed, or relationships like brother, father, mother, and wife (see Figure 5-2).

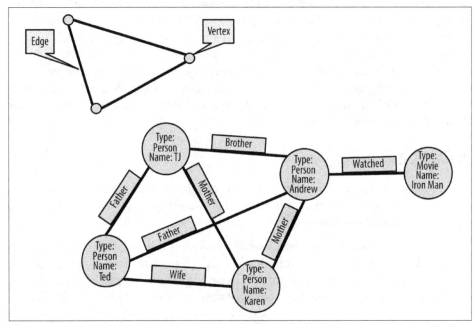

Figure 5-2. Adding information to vertices and edges

But this isn't enough information. We know that Karen is TJ's mother, but TJ can't also be Karen's mother, and we know that Andrew watched *Iron Man*, but *Iron Man* is not watching Andrew. So, we can fix this problem by giving our edges directions, which gives us an image, or graph, that looks like Figure 5-3.

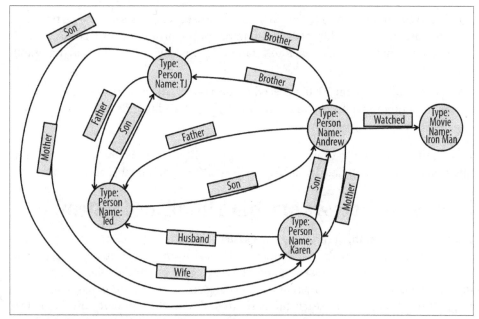

Figure 5-3. Edges showing directional relationships between vertices

This is more like it. We can show this graph to even a nontechnical person and he or she will still be able to figure out what we're trying to express.

What Is Graph Processing?

When we talk about graph processing, we are talking about doing processing at a global level that may touch every vertex in the graph. This is in contrast to the idea of *graph querying*. Graph querying is when you ask a question of the graph, like "Who's connected to Karen?" This query will execute the following steps:

1. Look up Karen and her edges.
2. Follow each edge and get those vertices.
3. Return the resulting list to the user.

Now, by *graph processing*, we mean something a little different that would be asking something like "What are the top five connections with a separation of five degrees?" This question is much larger in scale than the query and requires much more horsepower to process because it involves looking through a lot of people and all their connections. In contrast, the query focused on a single user could have been executed by a single client with a couple of hops to a data store such as HBase.

These concepts manifest in many real-world examples:

- The Web can be seen as a very large graph, where web pages are the vertices, and links are the edges. This leads to a number of opportunities for analysis, including algorithms such as PageRank, famously used by Google in ranking search results.

- As should be evident by the preceding discussion, social networks are a natural application of graph processing; for example, determining degrees of connection between users of a networking site.

It's these types of applications that this chapter will focus on; how do we ask these questions with Hadoop data in an effective way that is maintainable and performant?

How Do You Process a Graph in a Distributed System?

In order to perform this processing on a system like Hadoop, we can start with MapReduce. The problem with MapReduce is that it can only give us a one-layer join, which means we have to tackle a graph like peeling an onion. For those of you who don't peel onions, it is very different from peeling an apple. An onion has many layers to get through before you reach the core. In addition, that property of onions that makes your eyes water and makes the peeling experience less than joyful is similar to how processing a graph with MapReduce might reduce you to tears at a certain point. The graph in Figure 5-4 is an example of what we mean by "like peeling an onion." The center dot is our starting person, and every growing circle is yet another MapReduce job to figure out who is connected for each level.

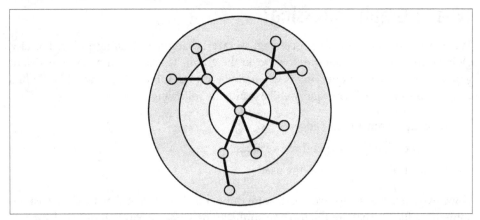

Figure 5-4. In MapReduce, tackling a graph is like peeling an onion

This hurts even more when we realize that with every pass we are rereading and rewriting the *whole* graph to disk.

Thankfully, once again some very smart people at Google decided to break the rules. In this case, it was the MapReduce rule that mappers are not allowed to talk to other mappers. This *shared nothing* concept is very important to a distributed system like Hadoop that needs sync points and strategies to recover from failure. So how did these very smart people solve this problem? Well, in short they found another way to get the same sync points and recovery strategies without the limitations of siloed mappers.

The Bulk Synchronous Parallel Model

So how do we maintain synchronous processing and still break the "no talking between mappers" rule? The answer was provided by a British computer scientist named Leslie Valiant of Harvard, who developed the Bulk Synchronous Parallel (BSP) model in the 1990s. This BSP model is at the core of the Google graph processing solution called Pregel (*http://bit.ly/pregel-sys*).

The idea of BSP is pretty complex, yet simple at the same time. In short, it is the idea of distributed processes doing work within a *superstep*. These distributed processes can send messages to each other, but they cannot act upon those messages until the next superstep. These supersteps will act as the boundaries for our needed sync points. We can only reach the next superstep when all distributed processes finish processing and sending message sending of the current superstep. There's then normally a single-threaded process that will decide if the overall process needs to continue with a new superstep. It's acceptable for this process to run in a single thread, since it does very little work in comparison to the worker threads and thus isn't a bottleneck.

BSP by Example

That was admittedly a short definition of a distributed processing model that took years of research. We'll help clarify with a short example of BSP. Scientists can use graph processing as a way to model the spread of a disease through a community. In this example, we illustrate this with zombies, who began as humans but changed after being bitten by another zombie.

Let's make a new graph and call it zombie bites. As you can see in Figure 5-5, in the start state we have one zombie and a bunch of people. The rule when the processing starts is that the zombie can bite every human it shares an edge with, and then when a vertex is bitten, it must turn itself into a zombie and continue by biting all of its edges. Once a zombie bites, it will not bite again because everyone around it will already have become a zombie, and we know from watching countless zombie movies that zombies never bite other zombies.

Figure 5-5 shows what the graph looks like in the different supersteps of our BSP execution model.

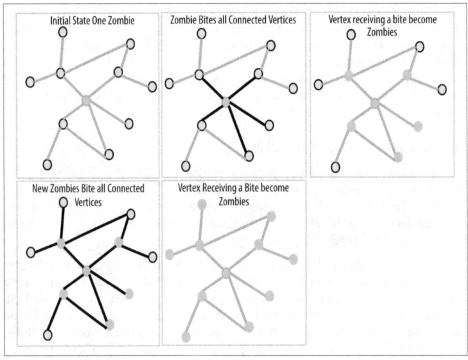

Figure 5-5. Supersteps for the zombie bites graph

We'll be introducing two graph processing tools, Giraph and GraphX, in this chapter to show implementations of this example. But before we do so, it is important to note that BSP is not the only solution. As we are learning as we dig deeper into Spark, the penalty for the onion approach has been hugely reduced from the days of MapReduce. The penalty of the I/O writes and reads in between onion layers has been largely mitigated by Spark, at least in the cases where the data can fit in memory. But with that said, the BSP model is very different in that it only has to send the messages between the distributed processes, whereas the onion joining will have to resend everything.

In the next two subsections we will dive into the two most popular graph processing frameworks for Hadoop today. First will be Giraph, which was born out of LinkedIn and used by Facebook as part of its graph search. Giraph is the more mature and stable system, with the claim of handling up to a trillion edges.

The second tool is the newer GraphX, which is part of the Apache Spark project. Spark GraphX gets a lot of its roots from GraphLab (*https://dato.com/products/create/open_source.html*), an earlier open source graph processing project, and is an extension built on Spark's generic DAG execution engine. Although still young and not as tuned and stable as Giraph, GraphX still holds a lot of promise because of its ease of use and integration with all other components of Spark.

Giraph

Giraph is an open source implementation of Google's Pregel. From the ground up, Giraph is built for graph processing. This differs from Spark's GraphX, which as noted, contains an implementation of the Pregel API built on the Spark DAG engine.

To get a simple view of Giraph, let's remove a lot of its details and focus on the three main stages of a Giraph program (see Figure 5-6):

1. Read and partition the data.
2. Batch-process the graph with BSP.
3. Write the graph back to disk.

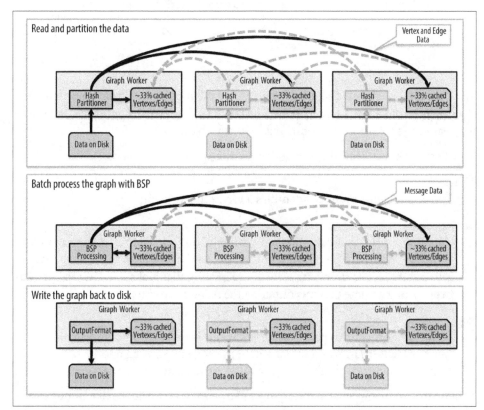

Figure 5-6. The three main stages of a Giraph program

There are many other details to Giraph that we can't cover here. Our intent is to provide enough detail for you to decide which tools belong in your architecture.

Let's dig into these stages in more detail and look at the code we will have to implement to customize these stages to our data and the zombie biting problem.

Read and Partition the Data

Just as MapReduce and Spark have input formats, Giraph has `VertexInputFormat`. In both cases, an input format takes care of providing the splits and the record or vertex reader. In our implementation we will stick with the default split logic and only override the reader. So our `ZombieTextVertexInputFormat` is as simple as the following:

```
public class ZombieTextVertexInputFormat extends
    TextVertexInputFormat<LongWritable, Text, LongWritable> {

    @Override
    public TextVertexReader createVertexReader(InputSplit split,
                                               TaskAttemptContext context)
        throws IOException {
      return new ZombieTextReader();
    }
}
```

The next thing we need is a `VertexReader`. The main difference from a normal MapReduce `RecordReader` is that a `RecordReader` is returning a key and value `Writable`, whereas the `VertexReader` is returning a `Vertex` object.

So, what is a `Vertex` object? It is made up of three parts:

Vertex ID
> This is an ID that uniquely identifies a vertex in our graph.

Vertex value
> This is an object that contains information about our vertex. In our example, it will store the state of our human or zombie and at which step he or she turned into a zombie. For simplicity we will use a string that looks like `"Human"` or `"Zombie.2"` for a zombie that was bitten on the second superstep.

Edge
> This is made up of two parts: the vertex ID of the source vertex and an object that can represent information about where the edge is pointing and/or what type of edge it is—for example, is the edge a relationship, a distance, or a weight?

So now that we know what a vertex is, let's see what a vertex looks like in our source file:

```
{vertexId}|{Type}|{comma-separated vertexId of "bitable" people}

2|Human|4,6
```

This is a vertex with the ID of 2 that is currently a human and is connected to vertices 4 and 6 with a directional edge. So, let's look at the code that will take this line and turn it into a `Vertex` object:

```
public class ZombieTextReader extends TextVertexReader {

    @Override
    public boolean nextVertex() throws IOException, InterruptedException {
        return getRecordReader().nextKeyValue();
    }

    @Override
    public Vertex<LongWritable, Text, LongWritable> getCurrentVertex()
            throws IOException, InterruptedException {
        Text line = getRecordReader().getCurrentValue();
        String[] majorParts = line.toString().split("\\|");
        LongWritable id = new LongWritable(Long.parseLong(majorParts[0]));
        Text value = new Text(majorParts[1]);

        ArrayList<Edge<LongWritable, LongWritable>> edgeIdList =
            new ArrayList<Edge<LongWritable, LongWritable>>();

        if (majorParts.length > 2) {
            String[] edgeIds = majorParts[2].split(",");
            for (String edgeId:  edgeIds) {
                DefaultEdge<LongWritable, LongWritable> edge =
    new DefaultEdge<LongWritable, LongWritable>();
                LongWritable longEdgeId = new LongWritable(Long.parseLong(edgeId));
                edge.setTargetVertexId(longEdgeId);
                edge.setValue(longEdgeId); // dummy value
                edgeIdList.add(edge);
            }
        }

        Vertex<LongWritable, Text, LongWritable> vertex = getConf().createVertex();

        vertex.initialize(id, value, edgeIdList);
        return vertex;
    }
}
```

There's a lot going on in this code, so let's break it down:

- Our `VertexReader` extends `TextVertexReader` so we are reading text files line-by-line. Note that we'd have to change our parent reader if we intend to read any other Hadoop file type.

- `nextVertex()` is an interesting method. If you drill down into the parent class, you'll see that it is using the normal `RecordReader` to try to read the next line and return if there is something left.

- The `getCurrentVertex()` method is where we parse the line and create and populate a `Vertex` object.

So as this method is firing, the resulting `Vertex` objects are being partitioned to the different distributed workers across the cluster. The default partitioning logic is a basic hash partition, but it can be modified. This is out of scope for this example, but just note you have control over the partitioning. If you can identify patterns that will force clumps of the graph to fewer distributed tasks, then the result may be less network usage and a corresponding reduction in speed.

Once the data is loaded in memory (or disk with the new spill-to-disk functionality in Giraph), we can move to processing with BSP in the next sub-section.

Before we move on, note that this is just an example of the `VertexInputFormat`. There are more advanced options in Giraph like reading in vertices and edges through different readers and advanced partitioning strategies, but that is out of scope for this book.

Batch Process the Graph with BSP

Of all the parts of Giraph, the BSP execution pattern is the hardest to understand for newcomers. To make it easier, let's focus on three computation stages: vertex, master, and worker. We will go through the code for these three stages soon, but check out Figure 5-7 first.

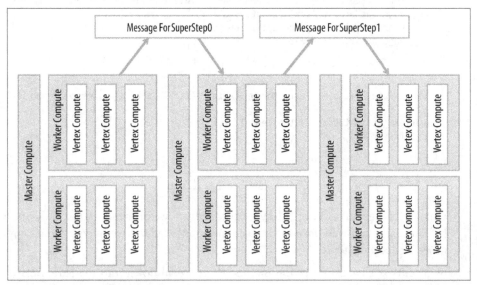

Figure 5-7. Three computation stages of the BSP execution pattern: vertex, master, and worker

Hopefully, from the image you can see that each BSP pass will start with a master computation stage. Then it will follow with a worker computation stage on each distributed JVM, followed by a vertex computation for every vertex in that JVM's local memory or local disk.

These vertex computations may process messages that will be sent to the receiving vertex, but the receiving vertices will not get those messages until the next BSP pass.

Let's start with the simplest of the computation stages, the master compute:

```
public class ZombieMasterCompute extends DefaultMasterCompute {

  @Override
  public void compute() {
    LongWritable zombies = getAggregatedValue("zombie.count");

    System.out.println("Superstep "+String.valueOf(getSuperstep())+
                       " - zombies:" + zombies);
    System.out.println("Superstep "+String.valueOf(getSuperstep())+
                       " - getTotalNumEdges():" + getTotalNumEdges());
    System.out.println("Superstep "+String.valueOf(getSuperstep())+
                       " - getTotalNumVertices():" +
                       getTotalNumVertices());
  }

  @Override
  public void initialize()
      throws InstantiationException, IllegalAccessException {
    registerAggregator("zombie.count", LongSumAggregator.class);
  }
}
```

Let's dig into the two methods in the `ZombieMasterCompute` class. First, we'll look at the `initialize()` method. This is called before we really get started. The important thing we are doing here is registering an `Aggregator` class.

An `Aggregator` class is like an advanced counter in MapReduce but more like the accumulators in Spark. There are many aggregators to select from in Giraph, as shown in the following list, but there is nothing stopping you from creating your own custom one.

Here are some examples of Giraph `aggregators`:

- Sum
- Avg
- Max
- Min
- TextAppend

- Boolean And/Or

The second method in the `ZombieMasterCompute` class is `compute()`, and this will fire at the start of every BSP. In this case we are just printing out some information that will help us debug our process.

On to the next bit of code, which is the `ZombieWorkerContext` class for the worker computation stage. This is what will execute before and after the application and each superstep. It can be used for advanced purposes like putting aggregated values at the start of a superstep so that it is accessible to a vertex compute step. But, for this simple example, we are doing nothing more than using `System.out.println()` so that we can see when these different methods are being called during processing:

```
public class ZombieWorkerContext extends WorkerContext {

    @Override
    public void preApplication() {
        System.out.println("PreApplication # of Zombies: " +
            getAggregatedValue("zombie.count"));

    }

    @Override
    public void postApplication() {
        System.out.println("PostApplication # of Zombies: " +
            getAggregatedValue("zombie.count"));
    }

    @Override
    public void preSuperstep() {
        System.out.println("PreSuperstep # of Zombies: " +
            getAggregatedValue("zombie.count"));

    }

    @Override
    public void postSuperstep() {
        System.out.println("PostSuperstep # of Zombies: " +
            getAggregatedValue("zombie.count"));

    }
}
```

Last and most complex is the vertex computation stage:

```
public class ZombieComputation
    extends BasicComputation<LongWritable,Text, LongWritable, LongWritable> {
    private static final Logger LOG = Logger.getLogger(ZombieComputation.class);

    Text zombieText = new Text("Zombie");
    LongWritable longIncrement = new LongWritable(1);
```

```java
@Override
public void compute(Vertex<LongWritable, Text, LongWritable> vertex,
                    Iterable<LongWritable> messages) throws IOException {

    Context context = getContext();
    long superstep = getSuperstep();

    if (superstep == 0) {
      if (vertex.getValue().toString().equals("Zombie")) {

        zombieText.set("Zombie." + superstep);
        vertex.setValue(zombieText);

        LongWritable newMessage = new LongWritable();
        newMessage.set(superstep+1);

        aggregate("zombie.count",longIncrement );

        for (Edge<LongWritable, LongWritable> edge : vertex.getEdges()) {
          this.sendMessage(edge.getTargetVertexId(), newMessage);
        }
      }
    } else {
      if (vertex.getValue().toString().equals("Human")) {

        Iterator<LongWritable> it = messages.iterator();
        if (it.hasNext()) {
          zombieText.set("Zombie." + superstep);
          vertex.setValue(zombieText);
          aggregate("zombie.count",longIncrement );

          LongWritable newMessage = new LongWritable();
          newMessage.set(superstep+1);

          for (Edge<LongWritable, LongWritable> edge : vertex.getEdges()) {
            this.sendMessage(edge.getTargetVertexId(), newMessage);
          }
        } else {
          vertex.voteToHalt();
        }

      } else {
        vertex.voteToHalt();
      }
    }
}
```

There is a lot of logic in this code, which we'll drill down into in a minute, but first let's clarify how the method is being called. The compute() method is called for each vertex and is given an iterator of all the messages sent to that vertex by the end of the last superstep.

The logic goes like this:

- If it is the first superstep and I'm a zombie, bite everyone around me.
- If it is after the first superstep and I'm a human that receives a bite message, turn myself into a zombie and bite everyone next to me.
- If I'm a zombie that gets bitten, do nothing.

Also note that we vote to halt in two places: if we are a zombie that gets bitten, or if we are a human that doesn't get bitten. We do this because these are the two possible end conditions:

- We could have everyone bitten and turned into a zombie, and at that point we need to stop processing.
- We could have some zombies but also some humans that don't have direct edges to them. So those humans will never become zombies.

Write the Graph Back to Disk

Now that we have infected our graph with zombies, it is time to write the results back to disk. We do that with the VertexOutputFormat. We won't go into detail here, but just notice it is the opposite of the input format:

```java
public class ZombieTextVertexOutputFormat
    extends TextVertexOutputFormat<LongWritable, Text, LongWritable> {

    @Override
    public TextVertexWriter createVertexWriter(TaskAttemptContext context)
        throws IOException, InterruptedException {
        return new ZombieRecordTextWriter();
    }

    public class ZombieRecordTextWriter extends TextVertexWriter {
        Text newKey = new Text();
        Text newValue = new Text();

        public void writeVertex(Vertex<LongWritable, Text, LongWritable> vertex)
            throws IOException, InterruptedException {
            Iterable<Edge<LongWritable, LongWritable>> edges = vertex.getEdges();

            StringBuilder strBuilder = new StringBuilder();

            boolean isFirst = true;
            for (Edge<LongWritable, LongWritable> edge : edges) {
                if (isFirst) {
```

```
          isFirst = false;
        } else {
          strBuilder.append(",");
        }
        strBuilder.append(edge.getValue());
      }

      newKey.set(vertex.getId().get() + "|" + vertex.getValue() + "|"
              + strBuilder.toString());

      getRecordWriter().write(newKey, newValue);
    }
  }
}
```

Putting It All Together

Now, just as with MapReduce, we need to set everything up and configure it in the
main method. Here's the code for that:

```
public class ZombieBiteJob implements Tool {
  private static final Logger LOG = Logger.getLogger(ZombieBiteJob.class);
  private Configuration conf;

  @Override
  public void setConf(Configuration conf) {
    this.conf = conf;
  }

  @Override
  public Configuration getConf() {
    return conf;
  }

  @Override
  public int run(String[] args) throws Exception {
    if (args.length != 3) {
      throw new IllegalArgumentException(
          "Syntax error: Must have 3 arguments " +
          " <numbersOfWorkers> <inputLocaiton> <outputLocation>");
    }

    int numberOfWorkers = Integer.parseInt(args[0]);
    String inputLocation = args[1];
    String outputLocation = args[2];

    GiraphJob job = new GiraphJob(getConf(), getClass().getName());
    GiraphConfiguration gconf = job.getConfiguration();
    gconf.setWorkerConfiguration(numberOfWorkers, numberOfWorkers, 100.0f);

    GiraphFileInputFormat.addVertexInputPath(gconf,
                                        new Path(inputLocation));
```

```
FileOutputFormat.setOutputPath(job.getInternalJob(),
                      new Path(outputLocation));

gconf.setComputationClass(ZombieComputation.class);
gconf.setMasterComputeClass(ZombieMasterCompute.class);
gconf.setVertexInputFormatClass(ZombieTextVertexInputFormat.class);
gconf.setVertexOutputFormatClass(ZombieTextVertexOutputFormat.class);
gconf.setWorkerContextClass(ZombieWorkerContext.class);

boolean verbose = true;
if (job.run(verbose)) {
  return 0;
} else {
  return -1;
}
}

public static void main(String[] args) throws Exception {
  int ret = ToolRunner.run(new ZombieBiteJob(), args);
  if (ret == 0) {
    System.out.println("Ended Good");
  } else {
    System.out.println("Ended with Failure");
  }
  System.exit(ret);
}
}
```

When Should You Use Giraph?

Giraph is very powerful, but as you can see from the concepts and the code required, it's not for the faint of heart. If your use cases are graphing, you have hard service-level agreements (SLAs), and you need a mature solution, Giraph may be your tool.

However, note that not all of the major Hadoop vendors are currently supporting Giraph in their distribution. That does not mean it won't work with your chosen distribution, but you may need to talk with your vendor to see if you can get support. At the very least you will likely have to build your own Giraph JARs for your distribution.

GraphX

We talked a lot about Spark in the last chapter for ETL as a replacement for MapReduce, but how did Spark get to be a contender in the graph processing world? Well, consider that Spark's GraphX removed the two main issues with MapReduce that Pregel and Giraph were designed to address: speed for iterative processing and data that's as close to in-memory as possible. Spark's GraphX also provides another advantage as a graph processing framework, which is that graphs are just another type of RDD.

This means that GraphX is a familiar programming model for developers who already know Spark.

 To be fair, graph processing on Spark is still new, and we will see that reflected in our code example, which you'll note is implemented in Scala. This is because the Java API wasn't available at the time of this writing.

Just Another RDD

There are a couple of root RDDs in Spark. The most common are RDD and PairRDD. As you might guess, to get to graph processing from normal Spark we just need to make an EdgeRDD and a VertexRDD, which are simply extensions of the normal RDD object.

We can get from any RDD to an EdgeRDD or VertexRDD with a simple map transformation function—no magic required. Then the last step from normal Spark to GraphX is putting these two new RDDs in a Graph object. The Graph object just contains a reference to these two RDDs and provides methods for doing graph processing on them.

As easy as it is to get into graph mode with GraphX, it's also easy to get out of graph mode. At any time we can grab the VertexRDD and EdgeRDD back out of our Graph object and start doing normal RDD functions on them.

There's really no easier way to explain this than just jumping into the code. The following code gets a Spark context and creates the two RDDs we need to get a graph:

```
val sc =
    new SparkContext(args(0), args(1), args(2), Seq("GraphXExample.jar"))

// Create an RDD for the vertices
val users: RDD[(VertexId, (String))] =
  sc.parallelize(Array(
      (1L, ("Human")),
      (2L, ("Human")),
      (3L, ("Human")),
      (4L, ("Human")),
      (5L, ("Human")),
      (6L, ("Zombie")),
      (7L, ("Human")),
      (8L, ("Human")),
      (9L, ("Human")),
      (10L, ("Human")),
      (11L, ("Human")),
      (12L, ("Human")),
      (13L, ("Human")),
      (14L, ("Human")),
```

```
        (15L, ("Human")),
        (16L, ("Zombie")),
        (17L, ("Human")),
        (18L, ("Human")),
        (19L, ("Human")),
        (20L, ("Human")),
        (21L, ("Human")),
        (22L, ("Human")),
        (23L, ("Human")),
        (24L, ("Human")),
        (25L, ("Human"))
        ))
// Create an RDD for edges

val relationships: RDD[Edge[String]] =
  sc.parallelize(Array(
        Edge(10L, 9L, "X"),
        Edge(10L, 8L, "X"),
        Edge(8L, 7L, "X"),
        Edge(8L, 5L, "X"),
        Edge(5L, 4L, "X"),
        Edge(5L, 3L, "X"),
        Edge(5L, 2L, "X"),
        Edge(9L, 6L, "X"),
        Edge(6L, 1L, "X"),
        Edge(20L, 11L, "X"),
        Edge(20L, 12L, "X"),
        Edge(20L, 13L, "X"),
        Edge(5L, 13L, "X"),
        Edge(20L, 14L, "X"),
        Edge(11L, 15L, "X"),
        Edge(20L, 16L, "X"),
        Edge(14L, 17L, "X"),
        Edge(1L, 17L, "X"),
        Edge(20L, 18L, "X"),
        Edge(21L, 18L, "X"),
        Edge(21L, 22L, "X"),
        Edge(4L, 23L, "X"),
        Edge(25L, 15L, "X"),
        Edge(24L, 3L, "X"),
        Edge(21L, 19L, "X")
        ))
// Define a default user in case there are relationship with missing user

val defaultUser = ("Rock")
// Build the initial Graph
val graph = Graph(users, relationships, defaultUser)
graph.triangleCount
```

Again, there's no magic here. The Spark context method `parallelize()` would be the same method we would use to create normal RDDs. Note that we're populating the

---

sample data in the code to make the example easier to understand, but we could have loaded this data from disk just as easily.

Before going on to the processing code, let's take a minute to talk about the `defaul tUser` variable. In the GraphX world we get an option for a catch-all vertex called default. So, if a message were sent to a nonexisting vertex, it would go to the default. In our example, if a zombie tries to bite someone who does not exist, our unfortunate zombie will trip and bite a rock. But don't worry—he's already dead, so it won't hurt.

GraphX Pregel Interface

Before we get into the code we need to discuss two considerations. First, the GraphX Pregel API is not like Giraph. Second, the code is in Scala, making it very compact, so we are going to have to take some time breaking it down. With that being said, however, it is important to note that the 300-plus lines we wrote in Giraph are now replaced with about 20 lines in Scala with GraphX:

```
//All the biting logic is right here
val graphBites = graph.pregel(0L)(
  (id, dist, message) => {
    if (dist.equals("Zombie")) {
      (dist + "_" + message)
    } else if (message != 0){
      "Zombie" + "_" + message
    } else {
      dist + "|" + message
    }
  }, triplet => {
    if (triplet.srcAttr.startsWith("Zombie") &&
        triplet.dstAttr.startsWith("Human")) {
      var stringBitStep =
          triplet.srcAttr.substring(triplet.srcAttr.indexOf("_") + 1)
      var lastBitStep = stringBitStep.toLong
      Iterator((triplet.dstId, lastBitStep + 1))
    } else if (triplet.srcAttr.startsWith("Human") &&
               triplet.dstAttr.startsWith("Zombie")) {
      var stringBitStep =
          triplet.dstAttr.substring(triplet.dstAttr.indexOf("_") + 1)
      var lastBitStep = stringBitStep.toLong
      Iterator((triplet.srcId, lastBitStep + 1))
    } else {
      Iterator.empty
    }
  },
  (a, b) => math.min(b, a))

graphBites.vertices.take(30)
```

If you can untangle that code with no help, then you probably already know more than the authors. Let's start breaking it down by first defining the `graph.pregel()` method.

`graph.pregel()` has two sets of parameters: the first set is values, and the second set is functions that will be executed in parallel.

Of the first set of parameters, we used only the first one, but here are the definitions:

- First message
- Max iterations (we used the default value and didn't use this parameter)
- Edge direction (we used the default value and didn't use this parameter)

So the first message we send is 0. Note that unlike with Giraph, we won't have access to a superstep number, so for our example we will keep track of the superstep in the message. This isn't the only way to do a superstep; we'll discuss more on this shortly.

We didn't set max iterations, because GraphX will stop when no more messages are sent and we want to go until we reach that point. We also didn't set edge direction because the default was fine for our processing.

The second set of parameters is a set of methods for processing:

`vprog()`
> This is a user-defined vertex program. In other words, it specifies what to do when a message reaches a vertex.

`sendMessage()`
> This contains logic for a vertex that may or may not want to send a message.

`mergeMessage()`
> This is a function that determines how messages going to the same vertex will be merged. This helps in cases where millions of vertices send a message to the same vertex.

vprog()

Now, let's dig into each of these methods in our GraphX code, starting with the `vprog()` method:

```
(id, dist, message) => {
  if (dist.equals("Zombie")) {
    (dist + "_" + message)
  } else if (message != 0){
      "Zombie" + "_" + message
  } else {
      dist + "|" + message
```

```
    }
  }
```

We can see that this method takes the ID of the vertex, the object that contains the vertex's information, and the message that is being sent to the vertex. In this method, we are determining if we need to modify the vertex's information object in response to the incoming message.

The logic in this code is pretty simple. If the message is 0 (meaning the first super-step), update the zombie to Zombie_0. If the message is greater than 0, change the human to a Zombie_{messageNUM}. Otherwise, there's no change to the vertex.

sendMessage()

The next method dictates when to send messages. The cool thing about GraphX as opposed to Giraph is at the time you plan to send messages out you have access to the destination vertex information. This prevents us from sending bites to other zombies and therefore wasting our bite.

You will see in this method we have access to the triplet object, which holds all the information we will need about the source vertex, the destination vertex, and the edge that connects them:

```
triplet => {
  if (triplet.srcAttr.startsWith("Zombie") &&
      triplet.dstAttr.startsWith("Human")) {
    var stringBitStep =
       triplet.srcAttr.substring(triplet.srcAttr.indexOf("_") + 1)
    var lastBitStep = stringBitStep.toLong
    Iterator((triplet.dstId, lastBitStep + 1))
  } else if (triplet.srcAttr.startsWith("Human") &&
             triplet.dstAttr.startsWith("Zombie")) {
    var stringBitStep =
       triplet.dstAttr.substring(triplet.dstAttr.indexOf("_") + 1)
    var lastBitStep = stringBitStep.toLong
    Iterator((triplet.srcId, lastBitStep + 1))
  } else {
    Iterator.empty
  }
}
```

The logic here is pretty simple: if the source is a zombie, and the destination is a human, then send a bite message.

mergeMessage()

The last method in our review is by far the easiest. All we are doing here is consolidating our messages so we only bite our humans once. More than one bite won't make them any more of a zombie, and it will only waste network bandwidth.

```
(a, b) => math.min(b, a)
```

Now in this example we did `math.min(b, a)`, but that isn't really needed here because b and a will always be the same value. We used `math.min()` to show that you can use methods in this function. The following will work just as well, but may be less clear:

```
(a, b) => a
```

GraphX versus Giraph

So when looking at GraphX and Giraph, you will notice that a lot is missing from GraphX, namely:

- Master compute
- Halting
- Worker compute
- Supersteps

When you're first learning GraphX, it is frustrating to find out all these tools you had in Giraph are gone, until you remember GraphX is graph processing with Spark. So what does that mean?

Remember the three stages in Giraph: read, process, and write. While in GraphX those stages are not explicitly available to the developer, with the Spark model you're free to mix processing types as necessary. So your application can perform Spark transformations to GraphX processing and back to Spark transformations. This ability to mix processing models in your application provides a great deal of power. So with GraphX these stages aren't explicitly exposed, but the Spark model provides you with greater flexibility in processing.

Which Tool to Use?

At the time of this writing, Giraph had a huge edge over GraphX in terms of maturity, but over time GraphX will close the gap. Over the short term, the decision point will be: if your use cases are 100% graph and you need the most robust and scalable solution, Giraph is your best option. If graph processing is just a part of your solution and integration and overall code flexibility is important, GraphX is likely a good choice.

Conclusion

Graphs have long been a core concept in computer science. With the integration of graph processing and Hadoop, we now have the ability to efficiently process extremely large graphs in orders of magnitude less time than with previous systems.

Although the graph processing ecosystem on Hadoop is still relatively young, it's maturing rapidly, and is an ideal fit for solving several classes of problems that require analysis of relationships between people, places, or things. This is especially true as the amount of data on these relationships continues to grow dramatically, requiring increasing amounts of storage and processing horsepower.

This chapter was intended to give you an idea of applications that are appropriate for graph processing, and provide an overview of current tools available for graph processing with Hadoop in order to guide you in selecting the right tool.

## CHAPTER 6

Orchestration

Workflow orchestration, sometimes referred to as *workflow automation* or *business process automation*, refers to the tasks of scheduling, coordinating, and managing workflows. *Workflows* are sequences of data processing actions. A system capable of performing orchestration is called an *orchestration framework* or *workflow automation framework*.

Workflow orchestration is an important but often neglected part of application architectures. It is especially important in Hadoop because many applications are developed as MapReduce jobs, in which you are very limited in what you can do within a single job. However, even as the Hadoop toolset evolves and more flexible processing frameworks like Spark gain prominence, there are benefits to breaking down complex processing workflows into reusable components and using an external engine to handle the details involved in stitching them together.

Why We Need Workflow Orchestration

Developing end-to-end applications with Hadoop usually involves several steps to process the data. You may want to use Sqoop to retrieve data from a relational database and import it to Hadoop, then run a MapReduce job to validate some data constraints and convert the data into a more suitable format. Then, you may execute a few Hive jobs to aggregate and analyze the data, or if the analysis is particularly involved, there may be additional MapReduce steps.

Each of these jobs can be referred to as an *action*. These actions have to be scheduled, coordinated, and managed.

For example, you may want to schedule an action:

- At a particular time
- After a periodic interval
- When an event happens (e.g., when a file becomes available)

You may want to coordinate an action:

- To run when a previous action finishes successfully

You may want to manage an action to:

- Send email notifications if the action succeeded or failed
- Record the time taken by the action or various steps of the action

This series of actions, or a workflow, can be expressed as a directed acyclic graph (DAG) of actions. When the workflow executes, actions either run in parallel or depend on the results of previous actions.

One of the benefits of workflow orchestration is that breaking down complex into simple reusable units is simply a good engineering practice. The workflow engine helps in defining the interfaces between the workflow components. The other benefits involve pushing concerns out of application logic by using features that are already a part of the orchestration system.

Good workflow orchestration engines will support business requirements such as metadata and data lineage tracking (the ability to track how specific data points were modified through multiple steps of transformation and aggregation), integration between various software systems in the enterprise, data lifecycle management, and the ability to track and report on data quality. They will also support operational functionality such as managing a repository of workflow components, scheduling flexible workflows, managing dependencies, monitoring the status of the workflows from a centralized location, being able to restart failed workflows, being able to generate reports, and being able to roll back workflows when issues have been detected.

Let's talk about what common choices are available to architects orchestrating a Hadoop-based application.

The Limits of Scripting

When first rolling out a Hadoop-based application, you might be tempted to use a scripting language like Bash, Perl, or Python to tie the different actions together. For short and noncritical workflows, this approach is fine and is usually easier to implement than the alternatives.

This usually looks like the bash script shown in Example 6-1.

Example 6-1. workflow.sh

```
sqoop job -exec import_data
if beeline -u "jdbc:hive2://host2:10000/db" -f add_partition.hql 2>&1 | grep FAIL
then
        echo "Failed to add partition. Cannot continue."
fi

if beeline -u "jdbc:hive2://host2:10000/db" -f aggregate.hql 2>&1 | grep FAIL
then
        echo "Failed to aggregate. Cannot continue."
fi
sqoop job -exec export_data
```

And you will usually execute this script, say every day at 1 a.m., using a crontab entry like Example 6-2.

Example 6-2. Crontab entry

```
0 1 * * * /path/to/my/workflow.sh > /var/log/workflow-`date +%y-%m-%d`.log
```

As this script moves to production and your organization relies on its results, additional requirements emerge. You want to handle errors more elegantly, be able to notify users and other monitoring systems of the workflow status, be able to track the execution time of the workflow as a whole and of individual actions, apply more sophisticated logic between different stages of the workflow, be able to rerun the workflow in whole or in part, and be able to reuse components among various workflows.

Attempting to maintain a home-grown automation script in the face of growing production requirements can be a frustrating exercise of reinventing the wheel. Since there are many tools that perform this part of the job, we recommend becoming familiar with one of them and using it for your orchestration needs.

Be aware that converting an existing workflow script to run in a workflow manager is not always trivial. If the steps are relatively isolated, as in Example 6-1 where each step uses the files the previous step wrote in HDFS, then conversion is fairly easy. If, on the other hand, the script passes information between steps using standard output or the local filesystem, things can get a bit more complex. It's important to take this into account both when choosing to start developing a workflow in a script versus a workflow manager and when planning the conversion.

The Enterprise Job Scheduler and Hadoop

Many companies have a standard framework for workflow automation and scheduling software that they use across the entire organization. Popular choices include ControlM, UC4, Autosys, and ActiveBatch. Using the existing software to schedule Hadoop workflows is a reasonable choice. This allows you to reuse existing infrastructure and avoid the learning curve of an additional framework when it is not necessary. This approach also makes it relatively easy to integrate in the same workflow actions that involve multiple systems, not just Hadoop.

In general, these systems work by installing an agent on each server where actions can be executed. In Hadoop clusters, this is usually the edge node (also called gateway nodes) where the client utilities and application JARs are deployed. When designing a workflow with these tools, the developer typically indicates the server where each action will execute and then indicates the command that the agent will execute on the server in question. In Example 6-1, those commands are `sqoop` and `beeline`, respectively. The agent will execute the command, wait for it to complete, and report the return status back to the workflow management server. When designing the workflow, the developer can specify rules of how to handle success or failure of each action and of the workflow as a whole. The same enterprise job scheduler can also be used to schedule the workflow to run at specific times or periodic intervals.

 Because these enterprise workflow automation systems are not Hadoop specific, detailed explanations of how to use each of them are beyond the scope of this book. We will focus on frameworks that are part of the Hadoop ecosystem.

Orchestration Frameworks in the Hadoop Ecosystem

There are a few workflow engines in the Hadoop ecosystem. They are tightly integrated within the Hadoop ecosystem and have built-in support for it. As a result, many organizations that need to schedule Hadoop workflows and don't have a standard automation solution choose one of these workflow engines for workflow automation and scheduling.

A few of the more popular open source workflow engines for distributed systems include Apache Oozie, Azkaban, Luigi, and Chronos:

- Oozie (*http://oozie.apache.org/*) was developed by Yahoo! in order to support its growing Hadoop clusters and the increasing number of jobs and workflows running on those clusters.

- Azkaban (*http://azkaban.github.io/*) was developed by LinkedIn with the goal of being a visual and easy way to manage workflows.

- Luigi (*https://github.com/spotify/luigi*) is an open source Python package from Spotify that allows you to orchestrate long-running batch jobs and has built-in support for Hadoop.

- Chronos (*http://mesos.github.io/chronos/*) is an open source, distributed, and fault-tolerant scheduler from Airbnb that runs on top of Mesos. It's essentially a distributed system that's meant to serve as a replacement for cron.

In this chapter, we will focus on Oozie and show how to build workflows using it. We chose Oozie because it is included with every Hadoop distribution. Other orchestration engines have similar capabilities, whereas the syntax and details are different.

When choosing a workflow engine, consider the following:

Ease of installation
How easy is it to install the workflow engine? How easy is it to upgrade it as newer versions are released?

Community involvement and uptake
How fast does the community move to add support for new and promising projects in the ecosystem? As new projects get added to the ecosystem (e.g., Spark being a fairly popular recent addition), you don't want the lack of support from your workflow engine preventing you from using a newer project in your workflows.

User interface support
Are you going to be crafting workflows as files or via UI? If files, how easy is it to create and update these files? If UI, how powerful and intuitive is the UI?

Testing
How do you test your workflows after you have written them?

Logs
Does the engine provide easy access to logs?

Workflow management
Does the engine provide the level of management you want? Does it track times taken by the workflow as a whole or in part? Does it allow the flexibility to control your DAG of actions (e.g., being able to make decisions based on the output of a previous action).

Error handling
Does the engine allow you to rerun the job or parts of it in case of failure? Does it allow you to notify users?

Oozie Terminology

Let's review Oozie terminology before we go further:

Workflow action
A single unit of work that can be done by the orchestration engine (e.g., a Hive query, a MapReduce job, a Sqoop import)

Workflow
A control-dependency DAG of actions (or jobs)

Coordinator
Definition of data sets and schedules that trigger workflows

Bundle
Collection of coordinators

Oozie Overview

Oozie is arguably the most popular scalable, distributed workflow engine for Hadoop. Most, if not all, Hadoop distributions ship with it. Its main benefits are its deep integration with the Hadoop ecosystem and its ability to scale to thousands of concurrent workflows.

Oozie has a number of built-in actions for popular Hadoop ecosystem components like MapReduce, Hive, Sqoop, and distcp. This makes it easy to build workflows out of these building blocks. In addition, Oozie can execute any Java app and shell script.

We'll provide a brief overview of Oozie here and then provide considerations and recommendations for its use.

The main logical components of Oozie are:

A workflow engine
Executes a workflow. A workflow includes actions such as Sqoop, Hive, Pig, and Java.

A scheduler (aka coordinator)
Schedules workflows based on frequency or on existence of data sets in preset locations.

REST API
Includes APIs to execute, schedule, and monitor workflows.

Command-line client

Makes REST API calls and allows users to execute, schedule, and monitor jobs from the command line.

Bundles

Represent a collection of coordinator applications that can be controlled together.

Notifications

Sends events to an external JMS queue when the job status changes (when a job starts, finishes, fails, moves to the next action, etc.). This also allows for simple integration with external applications and tools.

SLA monitoring

Tracks SLAs for jobs based on start time, end time, or duration. Oozie will notify you when a job misses or meets its SLA through a web dashboard, REST API, JMS queue, or email.

Backend database

Stores Oozie's persistent information: coordinators, bundles, SLAs, and workflow history. The database can be MySQL, Postgres, Oracle, or MSSQL Server.

Oozie functions in a client-server model. Figure 6-1 depicts Oozie's client-server architecture.

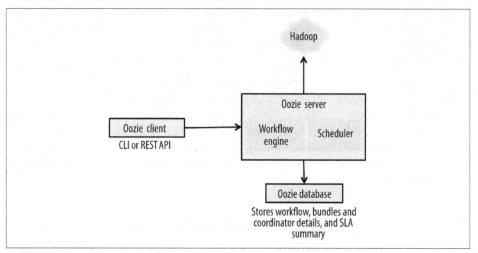

Figure 6-1. Oozie architecture

When you execute a workflow, the sequence of events shown in Figure 6-2 takes place.

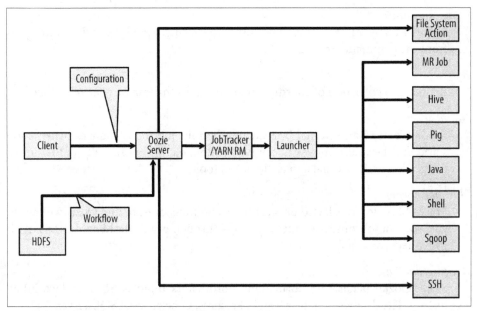

Figure 6-2. Oozie sequence of events during workflow execution

As you can see, the client connects to the Oozie server and submits the job configuration. This is a list of key-value pairs that defines important parameters for the job execution, but not the workflow itself. The workflow, a set of actions and the logic that connects them, is defined in a separate file called *workflow.xml*. The job configuration *must* include the location on HDFS of the *workflow.xml* file. It can also contain other parameters, and very frequently it includes the URIs for the NameNode, Job-Tracker (if you are using MapReduce v1 [MR1]), or YARN Resource Manager (if you are using MapReduce v2 [MR2]). These parameters are later used in the workflow definition. When the Oozie server receives the job configuration from the client, it reads the *workflow.xml* file with the workflow definition from HDFS. The Oozie server then parses the workflow definition and launches the actions as described in the workflow file.

Why Oozie Server Uses a Launcher

The Oozie server doesn't execute the action directly. For any action, the Oozie server launches a MapReduce job with only one map task (called a *launcher* job), which then launches the Pig or Hive action. This architectural decision makes the Oozie server lightweight and more scalable.

If all the actions were launched, monitored, and managed by a single Oozie server, all client libraries would have to exist on this server, making it very heavyweight and likely a bottleneck because all the actions would be executed by the same node. However, a separate launcher task enables Oozie to use the existing distributed MapReduce framework to delegate the launching, monitoring, and managing of an action to the launcher task and hence to the node where this launcher task runs. This launcher picks up the client libraries from the Oozie *sharedlib*, which is a directory on HDFS that contains all the client libraries required for various Oozie actions. The exceptions to this discussion are filesystem, SSH, and email actions, which are executed by the Oozie server directly.

For example, if you run a Sqoop action, the Oozie server will launch a single-mapper MapReduce job called sqoop-launcher; this mapper will run the Sqoop client, which will in turn launch its own MapReduce job called sqoop-action. This job will have as many mappers as Sqoop was configured to execute. In case of Java or shell actions, the launcher will execute the Java or shell application itself and will not generate additional MapReduce jobs.

Oozie Workflow

As mentioned earlier, workflow definitions in Oozie are written in an XML file called *workflow.xml*. A workflow contains action nodes and control nodes. Action nodes are nodes responsible for running the actual action, whereas a control node controls the flow of the execution. Control nodes can start or end a workflow, make a decision, fork and join the execution, or kill the execution. The *workflow.xml* file is a representation of a DAG of control and action nodes expressed as XML. A complete discussion of the schema of this XML file is beyond the scope of this book but is available in the Apache Oozie documentation (*http://bit.ly/oozie-schema*).

Oozie comes with a default web interface that uses ExtJS. However, the open source UI tool Hue (*http://www.gethue.com*) (Hadoop user experience) comes with an Oozie application that is a more commonly used UI for building and designing Oozie workflows. Hue generates a *workflow.xml* file based on the workflow designed via the UI.

Azkaban

Azkaban is an open source orchestration engine from LinkedIn. As with Oozie, you can write workflows (simply called *flows*) in Azkaban and schedule them. Oozie and Azkaban were developed with different goals in mind: Oozie was written to manage thousands of jobs on very large clusters and thus emphasizes scalability. Azkaban was developed with ease of use as its primary goal and emphasizes simplicity and visualization.

Azkaban ships as two services and a backend database; the services are Azkaban Web Server and Azkaban Executor. Each of these can run on different hosts. Azkaban web server is more than just a web UI; it is the main controller of all flows scheduled and run by Azkaban. It's responsible for their management, scheduling, and monitoring. The Azkaban executor is responsible for executing flows in Azkaban. Currently the web server is a single point of failure, while there is support for multiple executors—providing both high availability and scalability.

Both the web server and the executor talk to the backend MySQL database, which stores collections of workflows, workflow schedules, SLAs, the status of executing workflows, and workflow history.

Azkaban has built-in support for running only local UNIX commands and simple Java programs. However, you can easily install the Azkaban Job Types plug-in for enabling support for Hadoop, Hive, and Pig jobs. Azkaban Web Server includes a number of other useful plug-ins: HDFS Browser for browsing contents of HDFS (similar to Hue's HDFS browser), Security Manager for talking to a Hadoop cluster in a secure way, Job Summary for providing summaries of jobs run, Pig Visualizer for visualizing Pig jobs, and Reportal for creating, managing, and running reports.

Figure 6-3 shows Azkaban's architecture.

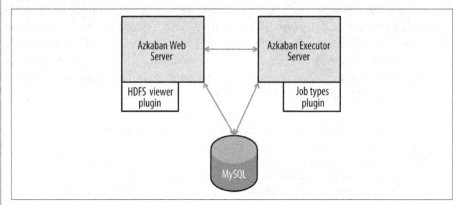

Figure 6-3. Azkaban architecture

Although Table 6-1 is not meant to provide an exhaustive comparison between Oozie and Azkaban, it lists some of their points of difference.

Table 6-1. Comparison between Oozie and Azkaban

Criteria	Oozie	Azkaban
Workflow definition	Uses XML, which needs to be uploaded to HDFS.	Uses simple declarative *.job* files. Needs to be zipped up and uploaded via web interface.

Criteria	Oozie	Azkaban
Scalability	Spawns a single map-only task called Launcher that manages the launched job. Makes for a more scalable system but adds an extra level of indirection when debugging.	All jobs are spawned via the single executor, which may cause scalability issues.
Hadoop ecosystem support	Offers very good support. Has support for running Java MapReduce, Streaming MapReduce, Pig, Hive, Sqoop, and Distcp actions.	Supports Java MapReduce, Pig, Hive, and VoldemortBuildAndPush (for pushing data to Voldemort key-value store) jobs. Other jobs have to be implemented as command job types.
Security	Integrates with Kerberos.	Supports Kerberos but has support only for the old MR1 API for MapReduce jobs on secure Hadoop cluster.
Versioning workflows	Offers easy workflow versioning by HDFS symlinks.	Provides no clear way of versioning workflows since they are uploaded via the web UI.
Integration outside of Hadoop ecosystem	Supports workflows on HDFS, S3, or a local filesystem (although local filesystem is not recommended). Email, SSH, shell actions are supported. Offers API for writing custom actions.	Does not require flows to be on HDFS; may be used completely outside of Hadoop.
Workflow parameterization	Supports workflow parameterization via variables and Expression Language (EL) functions (e.g., ${wf:user()}).	Requires flows to be parameterized via variables only.
Workflow scheduling	Supports time and data triggers.	Supports only supports time triggers.
Interaction with the server	Supports REST API, Java API, and CLI; has web interfaces (built-in and via Hue).	Has a nice web interface, can issue cURL commands to the web server trigger flows; no formal Java API or CLI.

Workflow Patterns

Now that we have a good understanding of the architecture of popular orchestration engines, let's go through some workflow patterns that are commonly found in the industry.

Point-to-Point Workflow

This type of workflow is common when you are performing actions sequentially. For example, let's say you wanted to perform some aggregation on a data set using Hive and if it succeeded, export it to a RDBMS using Sqoop.

When implemented in Oozie, your *workflow.xml* file would look the following:

```
<workflow-app xmlns="uri:oozie:workflow:0.4" name="aggregate_and_load">
    <global>
            <job-tracker>${jobTracker}</job-tracker>
            <name-node>${nameNode}</name-node>
    </global>

    <start to="aggregate" />

    <action name="aggregate">
        <hive xmlns="uri:oozie:hive-action:0.5">
            <job-xml>hive-site.xml</job-xml>
            <script>populate_agg_table.sql</script>
        </hive>
        <ok to="sqoop-export" />
        <error to="kill" />
    </action>

    <action name="sqoop_export">
        <sqoop xmlns="uri:oozie:sqoop-action:0.4">
            <arg>export</arg>
            <arg>--connect</arg>
            <arg>jdbc:oracle:thin:@//orahost:1521/oracle</arg>
            <arg>--username</arg>
            <arg>scott</arg>
            <arg>--password</arg>
            <arg>tiger</arg>
            <arg>--table</arg>
            <arg>mytable</arg>
            <arg>--export-dir</arg>
            <arg>/etl/BI/clickstream/aggregate-preferences/output</arg>
        </sqoop>
        <ok to="end" />
        <error to="kill" />
    </action>

    <kill name="kill">
        <message> Workflow failed. Error message
```

```
        [${wf:errorMessage(wf:lastErrorNode())}]</message>
    </kill>
    <end name="end" />
</workflow-app>
```

At a high level, this workflow looks like Figure 6-4.

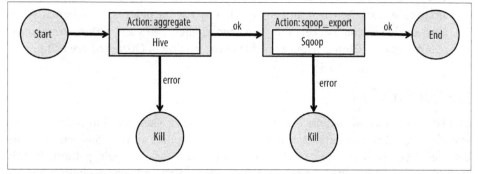

Figure 6-4. Point-to-point workflow

Now, let's dig into each of the XML elements in this workflow:

- The global element contains global configurations that will be used by all actions —for example, the URIs for JobTracker and NameNode. The job-tracker element is a little misleading. Oozie uses the same parameter for reading the Job-Tracker URI (when using MR1) and the YARN ResourceManager URI (when using MR2).

- The start element points to the first action to be run in the workflow. Each action has a name, and then a set of parameters depending on the action type.

- The first action element is for running the Hive action. It takes the location of the Hive configuration file and the location of the HQL script to execute. Remember, since the process issuing the Hive command is the launcher map task, which can run on any node of the Hadoop cluster, the Hive configuration file and the HQL scripts need to be present on HDFS so they can be accessed by the node that runs the Hive script. In our example, the *populate_agg_table.sql* script performs an aggregation via Hive and stores the aggregate results on HDFS at *hdfs://nameservice1/etl/BI/clickstream/aggregate-preferences/output*.

- The sqoop_export action is responsible for running a Sqoop export job to export the aggregate results from HDFS to an RDBMS. It takes a list of arguments that correspond to the arguments you'd use when calling Sqoop from the command line.

- In addition, each action contains directions on where to proceed if the action succeeds (either to the next action in the workflow or to the end), or if the action fails (to the "kill" node, which generates an appropriate error message based on the last action that failed, but could also send a notification JMS message or an email).

- Note that each action and the workflow itself has an XML schema with a version (e.g., xmlns="uri:oozie:sqoop-action:0.4"). This defines the elements available in the XML definition. For example, the global element only exists in uri:oozie:workflow:0.4 and higher. If you use an older XML schema, you'll need to define jobTracker and nameNode elements in each action. We recommend using the latest schema available in the version of Oozie you are using.

Fan-Out Workflow

The fan-out workflow pattern is most commonly used when multiple actions in the workflow could run in parallel, but a later action requires all previous actions to be completed before it can be run. This is also called a fork-and-join pattern. In this example, we want to run some preliminary statistics first and subsequently run three different queries for doing some aggregations. These three queries—for prescriptions and refills, office visits, and lab results—can themselves run in parallel and only depend on the preliminary statistics to have been computed. When all of these three queries are done, we want to generate a summary report by running yet another Hive query.

Here is the workflow definition in Oozie:

```
<workflow-app name="build_reports" xmlns="uri:oozie:workflow:0.4">

    <global>
        <job-tracker>${jobTracker}</job-tracker>
        <name-node>${nameNode}</name-node>
        <job-xml>${hiveSiteXML}</job-xml>
    </global>

    <start to="preliminary_statistics" />

    <action name="preliminary_statistics">
        <hive xmlns="uri:oozie:hive-action:0.5">
            <script>${scripts}/stats.hql</script>
        </hive>
        <ok to="fork_aggregates" />
        <error to="kill" />
    </action>

    <fork name="fork_aggregates">
        <path start="prescriptions_and_refills" />
        <path start="office_visits" />
        <path start="lab_results" />
    </fork>
```

```
<action name="prescriptions_and_refills">
    <hive xmlns="uri:oozie:hive-action:0.5">
        <script>${scripts}/refills.hql</script>
    </hive>
    <ok to="join_reports" />
    <error to="kill" />
</action>

<action name="office_visits">
    <hive xmlns="uri:oozie:hive-action:0.5">
        <script>${scripts}/visits.hql</script>
    </hive>
    <ok to="join_reports" />
    <error to="kill" />
</action>

<action name="lab_results">
    <hive xmlns="uri:oozie:hive-action:0.5">
        <script>${scripts}/labs.hql</script>
    </hive>
    <ok to="join_reports" />
    <error to="kill" />
</action>

<join name="join_reports" to="summary_report" />

<action name="summary_report">
    <hive xmlns="uri:oozie:hive-action:0.5">
        <script>${scripts}/summary_report.hql</script>
    </hive>
    <ok to="end" />
    <error to="kill" />
</action>

<kill name="kill">
    <message> Workflow failed. Error message
              [${wf:errorMessage(wf:lastErrorNode())}]</message>
</kill>
<end name="end" />
</workflow-app>
```

In this workflow, the first action, `preliminary_statistics`, computes the preliminary statistics. When this action has finished successfully, the workflow control moves to the fork element, which will enable the next three actions (`prescrip tions_and_refills`, `office_visits`, and `lab_results`) to run in parallel. When each of those actions has completed, the control proceeds to the `join` element. The *join* element stalls the workflow until all the three preceding Hive actions have completed. Note that the assumption here is that the action following the join depends on the results of all actions that are part of the fork, so if even one of these actions fails, the entire workflow will be killed. When the three forked actions have completed successfully, the control proceeds to the last action, `summary_report`. The Workflow will finish when the last action completes.

Note that since all workflows use the same Hive definitions, the `<job-xml>` is defined once, in the `<global>` section.

Figure 6-5 shows the fan-out workflow.

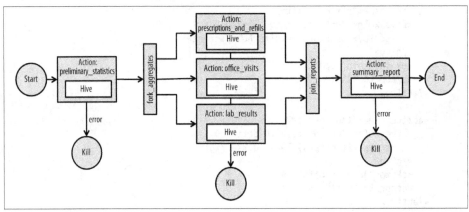

Figure 6-5. Fan-out workflow

Capture-and-Decide Workflow

The capture-and-decide workflow is commonly used when the next action needs to be chosen based on the result of a previous action. For example, say you have some Java code in the main class `com.hadooparchitecturebook.DataValidationRunner` that validates incoming data into Hadoop. Based on this validation, you want to proceed to processing this data by running the main class `com.hadooparchitecture book.ProcessDataRunner`, if there are no errors. However, in case of errors, you want your error handling code to put information about the errors into a separate errors directory on HDFS by running the main class `com.hadooparchitecturebook.Move OutputToErrorsAction` and report that directory back to the user.

Here is the *workflow.xml* file for implementing such a workflow in Oozie:

```
<workflow-app name="validation" xmlns="uri:oozie:workflow:0.4">

    <global>
        <job-tracker>${jobTracker}</job-tracker>
        <name-node>${nameNode}</name-node>
    </global>

    <start to="validate" />

    <action name='validate'>
        <java>
```

```xml
        <main-class>com.hadooparchitecturebook.DataValidationRunner
        </main-class>
        <arg>-Dinput.base.dir=${wf:conf('input.base.dir')}</arg>
        <arg>-Dvalidation.output.dir=${wf:conf('input.base.dir')}/dataset
        </arg>
        <capture-output />
    </java>
    <ok to="check_for_validation_errors" />
    <error to="fail" />
</action>

<decision name='check_for_validation_errors'>
    <switch>
        <case to="validation_failure">
            ${(wf:actionData("validate")["errors"] == "true")}
        </case>
        <default to="process_data" />
    </switch>
</decision>

<action name='process_data'>
    <java>
        <main-class>com.hadooparchitecturebook.ProcessDataRunner</main-class>
        <arg>-Dinput.dir=${wf:conf('input.base.dir')}/dataset</arg>
    </java>
    <ok to="end" />
    <error to="fail" />
</action>

<action name="validation_failure">
    <java>
        <main-class>com.hadooparchitecturebook.MoveOutputToErrorsAction
        </main-class>
        <arg>${wf:conf('input.base.dir')}</arg>
        <arg>${wf:conf('errors.base.dir')}</arg>
        <capture-output />
    </java>
    <ok to="validation_fail" />
    <error to="fail" />
</action>

<kill name="validation_fail">
    <message>Input validation failed. Please see error text in:
            ${wf:actionData("validation_failure")["errorDir"]}
    </message>
</kill>

<kill name="fail">
    <message>Java failed, error message[${wf:errorMessage
            (wf:lastErrorNode())}]</message>
</kill>
```

```
    <end name="end" />

  </workflow-app>
```

Figure 6-6 shows a high-level overview of this workflow.

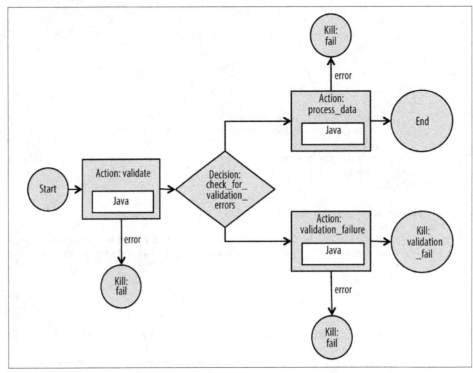

Figure 6-6. Capture-and-decide workflow

In this workflow, the first action, `validate`, runs a Java program to validate an input data set. Some additional parameters are being passed to the Java program based on the value of the `input.base.dir` parameter in the Oozie configuration. Note that we use the `<capture-output />` element to capture the option of this action, which will then be used in the next decision node, `check_for_validation_errors`. Java, SSH, and shell actions all support capture of outputs. In all cases, the output has to be in Java property file format (*http://bit.ly/property-file*), which is basically lines of key-value pairs separated by newlines. For shell and SSH actions, this should be written to standard output (stdout). For Java actions, you can collect the keys and values in a `Properties` object and write it to a file. The filename must be obtained from the `oozie.action.output.properties` system property within the program.

In the preceding example, we are checking for the value of the errors property from the output of the validate action. Here's an example of how you'd write errors=false for the output to be captured in Java:

```
File file = new File(System.getProperty("oozie.action.output.properties"));
Properties props = new Properties();
props.setProperty("errors", "false");

OutputStream os = new FileOutputStream(file);
props.store(os, "");
os.close();
```

The captured output is then referenced in the decision node via wf:action Data("_action_name_")["_key_"] where _action_name_ is the name of the action and _key_ is the property name. The decision node then contains a switch statement, which directs the control to the validation_failure node if the errors property was set to true in the captured output of the validate action, or to the process_data data action otherwise.

The process_data action simply calls another Java program to process the data, passing the location of the data set as a property to the program. In case of validation errors, the validation_failure action calls another Java program, passing two parameters to it. This time, however, the parameters are passed in as command-line arguments instead of properties (notice the lack of -D <property=value> syntax). This program is expected to put information about the validation errors in a directory and pass the name of this directory back to the workflow using the capture-output element. The name of the errors directory is passed as the errorsDir property, which is read by the next action, validation_fail, which in turn reports the location of the directory back to the user.

Parameterizing Workflows

Often, there is a requirement to run the same workflow on different objects. For example, if you have a workflow that uses Sqoop to import a table from a relational database and then uses Hive to run some validations on the data, you may want to use the same workflow on many different tables. In this case, you will want the table name to be a parameter that is passed to the workflow. Another common use for parameters is when you're specifying directory names and dates.

Oozie allows you to specify parameters as variables in the Oozie workflow or coordinator actions and then set values for these parameters when calling your workflows or coordinators. Apart from enabling you to quickly change values when you need to without having to edit code, this also allows you to run the same workflow on different clusters (usually dev, test, and production) without redeploying your workflows. Any parameters specified in Oozie workflows can be set in any of the following ways:

- You can set the property values in your *config-defaults.xml* file, which Oozie uses to pick default values for various configuration properties. This file must be located in HDFS next to the *workflow.xml* file for the job.

- You can specify the values of these properties in the *job.properties* file or the Hadoop XML configuration file, which you pass using the `-config` command-line option when launching your workflow. However, this method has some risk since the user may accidentally make other changes when editing the file, and many times the same file is used for multiple executions by different users.

- You can specify the values of these properties on the command line when calling the workflow or coordinator using the `-D <property=value>` syntax.

- You can pass in the parameter when calling the workflow from the coordinator.

- You can specify a list of mandatory parameters (also called formal parameters) in the workflow definition. The list can contain default values. When you submit a job, the submission will be rejected if values for those parameters are missing. You specify this list in the beginning of the workflow, before the `<global>` section:

```
<parameters>
    <property>
        <name>inputDir</name>
    </property>
    <property>
        <name>outputDir</name>
        <value>out-dir</value>
    </property>
</parameters>
```

These parameters can then be accessed in workflows as `${jobTracker}` or `${wf:conf('jobTracker')}`. If the parameter name is not a Java property (i.e., contains more than just `[A-Za-z_][0-9A-Za-z_]*`), then it can only be accessed by the latter method, `${wf:conf('property.name')}`.

In addition, we've already seen how many actions themselves pass arguments to the code they call within the workflow. Shell actions may pass the arguments to the shell command, Hive actions may take in the name of the Hive script as a parameter or additional arguments for parameterizing the Hive query, and Sqoop actions may take arguments to parameterize Sqoop import or export. The following example shows how we pass a parameter to a Hive action that is then used in the query:

```
<workflow-app name="cmd-param-demo" xmlns="uri:oozie:workflow:0.4">
    <global>
        <job-tracker>${jobTracker}</job-tracker>
        <name-node>${nameNode}</name-node>
    </global>
```

```
    <start to="hive-demo" />

    <action name="hive-demo">
        <hive xmlns="uri:oozie:hive-action:0.5">
            <job-xml>${hiveSiteXML}</job-xml>
            <script>${dbScripts}/hive1.hql</script>
            <param>MYDATE=${MYDATE}</param>
        </hive>
        <ok to="end" />
        <error to="kill" />
    </action>

    <kill name="kill">
        <message>Action failed, error message
        [${wf:errorMessage(wf:lastErrorNode())}]</message>
    </kill>

    <end name="end" />
</workflow-app>
```

In this workflow, we have a parameter called ${MYDATE} that is then passed to the
Hive query as the parameter MYDATE. The Hive query can then use the parameter, as
shown in Example 6-3.

Example 6-3. hive1.hql

```
INSERT INTO test SELECT * FROM test2 WHERE dt=${MYDATE}
```

Classpath Definition

Oozie actions are typically small Java applications that Oozie executes for us. This
means that the dependencies for the actions must be available in the classpath when
the action executes. Oozie handles some of the details of the dependency management for us by allowing you to define a shared location for libraries used by predefined actions (this location is called the *sharelib*), and it also provides multiple
methods for developers to add libraries specific to their applications to the classpath.
Such libraries can include dependencies for Java actions or user-defined functions for
Hive actions.

> The following section has been adapted from Cloudera's blog post
> *How-to: Use the ShareLib in Apache Oozie (http://bit.ly/oozie-
> sharelib).*

All Hadoop JARs are automatically included in the classpath, and the *sharelib* directory includes JARs for the built-in actions (Hive, Pig, Sqoop, etc.).

You create the *sharelib* directory by running `oozie-setup sharelib create -fs HDFS:\\host:port`. To enable a workflow to use *shareLib*, simply specify `oozie.use.system.libpath=true` in the `job.properties` file, and Oozie will know to include the JARs in *shareLib* with the necessary actions in your job.

If you need to add custom JARs for an action (this includes your own JARs for Map-Reduce or Java actions, or JDBC drivers or connectors for a Sqoop action), there's a few ways to do this:

- Set `oozie.libpath=/path/to/jars,another/path/to/jars` in *job.properties*. This is useful if you have many workflows that all need the same JAR; you can put it in one place in HDFS and use it with many workflows. The JARs will be available to all actions in that workflow.

- Create a directory named *lib* next to your *workflow.xml* file in HDFS and put JARs in there. This is useful if you have some JARs that you only need for one workflow.

- Specify the `<archive>` tag in an action with the path to a single JAR; you can have multiple `<archive>` tags. This is useful if you want some JARs only for a specific action, not all actions in a workflow.

- Add the JAR to the *sharelib* directory. This is not recommended for two reasons: first, the JAR will be included in every workflow, which may lead to unexpected results. Second, if you upgrade *sharelib*, the JAR will be removed and you'll need to remember to add it again.

Scheduling Patterns

So far, we have learned that various actions and decisions about those actions can be put together in a workflow, which can then be run by an orchestration system. However, workflows are *time-agnostic*; that is, they don't have any notion of when or how they will be run. You can run these workflows manually, but you can also schedule them to run when certain predicates hold true. Oozie makes use of coordinators that allow you to schedule a workflow using an XML file (or via the Hue Oozie UI), whereas Azkaban provides scheduling options when you're executing the workflow via its UI.

For Oozie, the coordinator is defined in XML format in a file called *coordinator.xml*, which is then passed to the Oozie server for submission. The Oozie coordinator engine works in UTC but supports various time zones and Daylight Saving Time (DST) for coordinator applications.

Whereas Oozie supports a fairly large number of scheduling use cases, Azkaban's latest version at the time of this writing supports only the first scheduling use case we'll discuss called *frequency scheduling*.

Frequency Scheduling

Frequency scheduling is the simplest kind of scheduling; it allows you to execute a workflow in a periodic manner. For example, if you want to execute a workflow every 60 minutes to do some hourly aggregation, your Oozie *coordinator.xml* file would look like:

```
<coordinator-app name="hourly-aggregation" frequency="${coord:minutes(60)"
start="2014-01-19T08:00Z" end="2014-01-20T08:00Z" timezone="America/Los_Angeles"
xmlns="uri:oozie:coordinator:0.4">
   <action>
      <workflow>
         <app-path>hdfs://nameservice1/app/workflows/hourly-aggregation
         </app-path>
      </workflow>
   </action>
</coordinator-app>
```

In this coordinator example and the ones that follow, the Z suffix at the end symbolizes that the timestamp is in UTC.

The preceding coordinator, called `hourly-aggregation`, runs the `hourly-aggregation` workflow every 60 minutes (the default unit for the `frequency` attribute being minutes). The first instance of this workflow runs at 8 a.m. UTC on 2014-01-19 and the last instance run happens at 7 a.m. UTC on 2014-01-20 (one hour before the end; there is no run at the end time). The workflow definition being run is expected to be located in a file called *workflow.xml* under HDFS directory *hdfs:// nameservice1/app/workflows/hourly-aggregation*. Because the `start` and `end` fields differ by exactly one day (i.e., 24 hours), this workflow would run exactly 24 times. Oozie also supports *cron* syntax, which is very flexible and readable.

Time and Data Triggers

Often times, you need a workflow to run at a certain time but only if a particular data set or a particular partition in the data set is available. Oozie coordinators can be configured to only trigger a workflow if a specific data set or its partition exists. If the data set doesn't exist, the coordinator would check for its existence periodically until the specified timeout period. If `timeout=0` is specified, the coordinator discards the workflow (i.e., doesn't run it) if the data doesn't exist and doesn't check for its existence again until the entire coordinator gets triggered again based on the `frequency` listed in `coordinator-app`. The default timeout is `-1`, in which case the Oozie server keeps the coordinator in the waiting state in the queue until all required conditions are met—in other words, until the required instance of the data set becomes available.

Let's say your Hadoop cluster and Oozie server are all located in California and in your use case, on any given day at 1 a.m., you want to aggregate the data on an hourly basis from the previous day. However, if the data set is delayed due to an issue upstream, you only want to trigger the workflow when the data set arrives. Here is an example of how to implement such a coordinator in Oozie:

```
<coordinator-app name="hourly-aggregation" frequency="${coord:days(1)}"
start="2014-01-19T09:00Z" end="2015-01-19T10:00Z" timezone="America/Los_Angeles"
xmlns="uri:oozie:coordinator:0.1">
    <dataset name="logs" frequency="${coord:days(1)}"
            initial-instance="2014-01-15T06:15Z" timezone="America/Los_Angeles">
    <uri-template>
        hdfs://nameservice1/app/logs/${YEAR}${MONTH}/${DAY}
    </uri-template>
    <done-flag>_DONE</done-flag>
    </dataset>
    <input-events>
    <data-in name="input" dataset="logs">
        <instance>${coord:current(-1)}</instance>
    </data-in>
    </input-events>
    <action>
        <workflow>
            <app-path>hdfs://nameservice1/app/workflows/hourly-aggregation
            </app-path>
        </workflow>
    </action>
</coordinator-app>
```

This coordinator triggers every day starting 2014-01-19 at 1 a.m. Pacific time (which is 09:00 in UTC). The dataset field describes the data set that needs to be checked before the workflow is run.

 We are denoting start and end times in UTC even though the coordinator is running in the Pacific time zone. Oozie executes everything in UTC, and specifying start and end times in other time zones will result in submission errors. The time zone field is only used for DST values when calculating frequency.

The frequency denotes the rate, in minutes, at which the data set is periodically written. Oozie uses this when checking for the presence of nth instance of the data set in the past. Instead of specifying the *frequency* as *1440* (number of minutes in a day), we use ${coord:days(1)}, because the number of minutes in a day changes when DST kicks in or out. The initial-instance field refers to the first instance of the data set that exists. The presence of any instances that occur before the initial-instance would be ignored. The path to the data set's directory on HDFS is defined by the uri-template field. The URIs will resolve to */app/logs/2014/06/19*, */app/logs/2014/06/20* and so on. In particular, the coordinator will look for the presence of a file named *_DONE* in these HDFS directories to determine if that directory is ready for processing or not. The name of this file is provided by the done-flag field. If done-flag is set to an empty string, Oozie will look for the existence of the directory itself. The YEAR, MONTH, and DAY variables used in the URI template are based on the time instance in UTC, for which Oozie does the conversion automatically if needed. If the coordinator app was first triggered at 2014-01-19T09:00Z (i.e., 9 a.m. UTC on 2014-01-19) YEAR, MONTH, and DAY map to 2014, 01, and 19, respectively. Also, note that this is the time when the coordinator app gets triggered (9 a.m. California time), not necessarily when the workflow runs (which may have to wait for the input data set to become available).

> Because the uri-template field relies only on YEAR, MONTH, and DAY, the hour and minute part of initial-instance (i.e., 06:15) is inconsequential. Whether it's 06:15 or 06:16, it would map to the same instance and the same URI for the first instance. As long as the initial instance maps to the same URI in UTC time (YEAR, MONTH, DATE, and similar variables are evaluated in UTC time), the hour and minute parts of initial-instance don't matter in this example.

The input-events field defines the inputs that are required in order to execute the workflow. In our example, we declare the logs data set as a required input. We also specify which instance of this logs data set is the one that's required. In our case, we want the instance from the day before, so we specify ${coord:current(-1)}. This normalized time instance would be converted to UTC, which would be used to automatically populate the variables YEAR, MONTH, DAY, and so on.

Because no timeout was specified in the preceding example, if the data set instance is not available, the Oozie server will wait indefinitely until the data set instance becomes available to run the workflow. In such cases, it becomes important to set the concurrency, throttling, and execution strategy for your coordinator job. *Concurrency* refers to how many instances of the same job can be running at any given time, and the default value is 1. *Throttle* refers to the number of jobs that can be waiting for execution at the same time. *Execution* refers to the order of execution if two or more instances of the job are queued, and the default is FIFO (first in, first out; i.e., the first job triggered would be run first). Other options include LIFO (last in, first out; i.e., the last job triggered would be run first) and LAST_ONLY (only the last job triggered would be run).

If your workflow only refers to data from one day at a time, it may make sense to allow for multiple jobs to run at the same time in a FIFO order. The *coordinator.xml* file with such settings would look like:

```
<coordinator-app ...>
  <controls>
    <timeout>1440</timeout>
    <execution>FIFO</execution>
    <concurrency>5</concurrency>
    <throttle>5</throttle>
  </controls>
  <dataset ....>
  .
  .
  .
</coordinator-app>
```

Alternatively, if you'd like the Oozie server to only keep checking the data set for availability for at most two hours before giving up, you can set the `timeout` to 120 minutes.

Here is an example of *coordinator.xml* with such settings:

```
<coordinator-app ...>
  <controls>
    <timeout>120</timeout>
  </controls>
  <dataset ....>
  .
  .
  .
</coordinator-app>
```

If you'd like to not wait at all for the data set instance to become available if it's not available already, you can set the `timeout` to 0. This will make the coordinator exit right away if the data is not available instead of waiting for the timeout period.

Also, it is possible to depend on multiple data sets by specifying more than one data-in dependency. So far, we have been talking about data sets that are written daily. However, let's now see an hourly example. If the data set is being written every hour and you need 24 hours of data to process up until the last complete hour, you can enforce presence of all instances between start and end instances of the data set. Assuming this coordinator triggers at the 10th minute of every hour, the coordinator job would look like:

```
<coordinator-app name="hourly-aggregation" frequency="${coord:hours(1)}"
start="2014-01-19T09:10Z" end="2015-01-19T10:10Z" timezone="America/Los_Angeles"
xmlns="uri:oozie:coordinator:0.1">
  .
  .
  .
  <input-events>
      <data-in name="coordInput1" dataset="input1">
```

```
            <start-instance>${coord:current((coord:tzOffset()/60) - 24)}
            </start-instance>
            <end-instance>${coord:current(coord:tzOffset()/60) - 1}</end-instance>
        </data-in>
    </input-events>
        .
        .
        .
```

Here, we are using ${coord:current((coord:tzOffset()/60) - 24)} as the start
instance. Let's ignore the -24 part for a moment. coord:tzOffset() gives the offset
between the nominal time zone and UTC in minutes. coord:tzOffset()/60 gives the
same in hours. For California, this would usually be –8 during regular time and –7
during DST. If we simply use ${coord:current()}, the instance corresponding to the
trigger time of 2014-01-19T09:10Z would be YEAR=2014, MONTH=01, DAY=19, HOUR=09.
However, because our data set is being generated in Pacific time zone, that instance
doesn't exist yet given that it's only 1 a.m. in California. To pick the relevant instance,
we have to take into account the relevant time zone offset, which we do with $
{coord:current(coord:tzOffset()/60)}. Since we want 24 instances including the
last full hour, we subtract one to get the end instance and 24 to get the first instance.
Also note, we didn't have to take care of time zone offset in our previous example,
since our data set was being written daily. Technically, we could have used $
{coord:current(coord:tzOffset()/1440) - 1} there (1440, since our data set is
written daily) instead of just ${coord:current(-1), but we know from geography
class that all time zone offsets are always less than 1,440 minutes (24 hours), so that
value would have always amounted to 0.

You may need to pass the hour timestamp to the workflow for it to make use of it.
Oozie provides a set of functions that can be used in coordinators to generate and
format timestamps and pass them on to the workflows. Such an example coordinator
would look like:

```
<coordinator-app name="hourly-aggregation" frequency="${coord:hours(1)}"
start="2014-01-19T09:10Z" end="2015-01-19T10:10Z" timezone="America/Los_Angeles"
xmlns="uri:oozie:coordinator:0.1">
    <action>
        <workflow>
            <app-path>hdfs://nameservice1/app/workflows/hourly-aggregation
            </app-path>
            <configuration>
             <property>
                    <name>dateHour</name>
                    <value>${coord:formatTime(coord:nominalTime(),'yyMMdd_HH')}
             </property>
            </configuration>
        </workflow>
    </action>
</coordinator-app>
```

`coord:nominalTime()` returns the time when this coordinator was triggered in UTC. In this case, the workflow will receive a parameter named `dateHour` whose value is a formatted string with the current hour. This parameter can then be used in the aggregation action just like the parameters we showed earlier in the section "Parameterizing Workflows" on page 201.

Executing Workflows

To execute a workflow or a coordinator, first you place the XML defining them in HDFS. Also place any JARs or files that the workflow depends on in HDFS, as explained in the section "Classpath Definition" on page 203. The next step is to define a properties file, traditionally named *job.properties*. This file should include any parameters you want to use in your workflow. You *must* specify `oozie.wf.applica tion.path`, the URL of the workflow definition XML file. That is typically `${name Node}/user/${user.name}/myworkflow`. It is also very common to specify:

nameNode
:   The URL of the NameNode; it should be similar to `hdfs://hadoop1:8020`.

jobTracker
:   The URL of the JobTracker; this is similar to `hadoop1:8021`.

In addition, if your workflow includes Hive, Pig, or Sqoop actions, Oozie will require access to those libraries. These may already be in HDFS as part of your Oozie installation (referred to as Oozie *sharelib*), but you will need to specify that you wish to use them by adding `oozie.use.system.libpath=true` to your properties file. See the section "Classpath Definition" on page 203 for details.

If you are executing a coordinator, you'll also need to include `oozie.coord.applica tion.path`, the URL of the coordinator definition XML (for example, `${nameNode}/user/${user.name}/myworkflow/coord.xml`).

Conclusion

If you are developing applications on Hadoop for any nontrivial dependency management of various actions, you'll require a workflow management system. If you already have an enterprise orchestration engine, we suggest you explore its support for Hadoop. You can always roll your own, but we recommend against it for anything nontrivial. You can use one of the existing engines, such as Oozie, which we have discussed in detail. The one you choose will depend on your use case.

If most of your orchestration is centered on Hadoop and you are OK with putting workflow and coordinator definitions in HDFS, Oozie makes a really strong case—especially if you are using a distribution that comes with it—along with offering installation and management support. Other open-source options you can explore include Azkaban, Luigi and Chronos.

## CHAPTER 7

Near-Real-Time Processing with Hadoop

Through much of its development, Hadoop has been thought of as a batch processing system. The most common processing pattern has been loading data into Hadoop, followed by processing of that data through a batch job, typically implemented in MapReduce. A very common example of this type of processing is the extract-transform-load (ETL) processing pipeline—loading data into Hadoop, transforming it in some way to meet business requirements, and then moving it into a system for further analysis (for example, a relational database).

Hadoop's ability to efficiently process large volumes of data in parallel provides great benefits, but there are also a number of use cases that require more "real time" (or more precisely, near-real-time, as we'll discuss shortly) processing of data—processing the data as it arrives, rather than through batch processing. This type of processing is commonly referred to as *stream processing*.

Fortunately, this need for more real-time processing is being addressed with the integration of new tools into the Hadoop ecosystem. These stream processing tools include systems like Apache Storm, Apache Spark Streaming, Apache Samza, or even Apache Flume via Flume interceptors. In contrast to batch processing systems such as MapReduce, these tools allow you to build processing flows that continuously process incoming data; these flows will process data as long as they remain running, as opposed to a batch process that operates on a fixed set of data. The systems in this category seeing the widest use with Hadoop currently are Storm and Spark Streaming, and they are the tools we'll examine in this chapter. We'll also examine how Flume can be leveraged in a stream processing architecture.

Some examples that call for this type of processing are:

- Analyzing social media feeds (e.g., detecting trends in updates from users of a social media site)

- Analyzing financial feeds (e.g., anomaly detection in a user's account activity)
- Analyzing video game usage feeds (e.g., watching the player's behavior to guard against strategies that provide an unfair advantage to some players)
- Analyzing machine data feeds (e.g., raising alerts in the case of anomalies or errors in application logs)

What About Tools Like Apache Kafka?

A possible source of confusion is how a tool like Kafka fits into real-time processing. The answer is that Kafka is a distributed message bus; its main use is reliable message delivery in architectures that require consuming high rates of events. Kafka is a powerful tool, but it does not provide functionality to transform, alert on, or count data in flight.

It's important to note that while it's not a stream processing system, Kafka is often a key part of many architectures that involve stream processing. As we'll see in the discussion of Storm, the data delivery guarantees provided by Kafka make it a good choice as a complement to Storm. It's also common to have Kafka as part of an architecture to ingest events into Hadoop.

Another thing to note is that, although Flume is also often thought of as an ingestion mechanism, we can use the Flume interceptor functionality for event-level operations. Flume interceptors allow us to do some very common stream processing activities like enrichment and validation/alerting. We'll explore this further in the section "Flume Interceptors" on page 246.

Before we get started, there are a couple of items we should note. The first is to more precisely define what we mean by *real time*. The term tends to be overused and is often imprecisely defined. For the purposes of our discussion, we'll consider the processing discussed in this chapter to be more precisely defined as *near-real-time (NRT)*, or processing that needs to occur in multisecond ranges down to the hundreds of milliseconds. If your applications require processing faster than 50–100 milliseconds, the tools we discuss in this chapter will not be able to reliably meet your needs.

The other thing to mention is what we *won't* discuss in this chapter: query engines such as Cloudera Impala, Apache Drill, or Presto. These systems are often referred to in an NRT context, but they are really low-latency, massively parallel processing (MPP) query engines. We discussed these query engines in Chapter 3 when we explored processing data on Hadoop.

Figure 7-1 shows how these tools should be viewed in a real-time context. The light gray boxes indicate the systems we'll be discussing in this chapter. The dark gray boxes show where tools will fit in terms of execution time, even though we're not specifically covering them in this chapter.

Note the box on the left marked "Custom." Although there may be cases for which Storm or Flume can operate on data faster than 50 milliseconds or so, generally speaking when processing requirements get to this category it may mean custom applications implemented in C/C++.

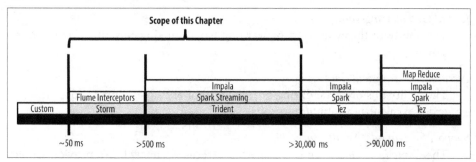

Figure 7-1. Near-real-time processing tools

We'll also explore how HBase fits into an NRT architecture, since it will often act as a persistence layer for stream processing, and will provide functionality to aid in decision making or data enrichment.

We start by giving an overview of the stream processing engines Storm (and the related Trident project) and Spark Streaming, followed by a comparison of these tools. Then we'll explore when you might want to use a stream processing tool, as well as why you might choose one tool over the other.

Stream Processing

As we noted before, stream processing refers to systems that continuously process incoming data, and will continue to process that incoming data until the application is stopped. Stream processing is not a new concept; applications that perform stream processing have been around since long before Hadoop. This includes commercial offerings like StreamBase and open source tools such as Esper. Newer tools like Storm, Spark Streaming, and Flume interceptors bring the ability to perform distributed stream processing integrated with Hadoop.

In discussing these streaming frameworks, we'll explore how they handle the following common functions that are required by a number of NRT use cases:

Aggregation
> The ability to manage counters. A simple example of this is the classic word count example, but counters are required by a number of use cases, such as alerting and fraud detection.

Windowing averages
  Support for keeping track of an average over a given number of events or over a given window of time.

Record level enrichment
  The ability to modify a given record based on rules or content from an external system such as HBase.

Record level alerting/validation
  The ability to throw an alert or warning based on single events arriving in the system.

Persistence of transient data
  The ability to store state during processing—for example, counts and averages in order to calculate continuous results.

Support for Lambda Architectures
  The *Lambda Architecture* is a somewhat overused concept. We provide a fuller definition in the upcoming sidebar, but briefly we'll consider it a means to bridge the gap between imprecise streaming results and more accurate batch calculations.

Higher-level functions
  Support for functions like sorting, grouping, partitioning, and joining data sets and subsets of data sets.

Integration with HDFS
  Ease and maturity of integration with HDFS.

Integration with HBase
  Ease and maturity of integration with HBase.

The Lambda Architecture

We touch on the Lambda Architecture througout this chapter, so let's provide a brief overview of what it actually is. The Lambda Architecture, as defined by Nathan Marz and James Warren and described more thoroughly in their book *Big Data* (Manning), is a general framework for scalable and fault-tolerant processing of large volumes of data.

The Lambda Architecture is designed to provide the capability to compute arbitrary functions on arbitrary data in real time. It achieves this by splitting the architecture into three layers:

Batch layer
> This layer stores a master copy of the data set. This master data is an immutable copy of the raw data entering the system. The batch layer also precomputes the *batch views*, which are essentially precomputed queries over the data.

Serving layer
> This layer indexes the batch views, loads them, and makes them available for low-latency querying.

Speed layer
> This is essentially the real-time layer in the architecture. This layer creates views on data as it arrives in the system. This is the most relevant layer for this chapter, since it will likely be implemented by a streaming processing system such as Storm or Spark Streaming.

> New data will be sent to the batch and speed layers. In the batch layer the new data will be appended to the master data set, while in the speed layer the new data is used to do incremental updates of the real-time views. At query time, data from both layers will be combined. When the data is available in the batch and serving layers, it can be discarded from the speed layer.

> This design provides a reliable and fault-tolerant way to serve applications that require low-latency processing. The authoritative version of the data in the batch layer means that even if an error occurs in the relatively less reliable speed layer, the state of the system can always be rebuilt.

We'll start by providing an overview of Storm and examine how it meets our criteria for a stream processing system. After discussing Storm we'll provide an overview of Trident. Trident is an abstraction over Storm that provides higher-level functionality as well as other enhancements to the core Storm architecture through microbatching.

Apache Storm

Apache Storm is an open source system designed for distributed processing of streaming data. Many of the design principles on which Storm is built will be very familiar to Hadoop users. The Storm architecture was created with the following design goals:

Simplicity of development and deployment
> Similar to the way MapReduce on Hadoop reduces the complexity to implement distributed batch processing, Storm is designed to ease the task of building streaming applications. Storm uses a simple API and a limited number of abstractions to implement workflows. Storm is also designed to be easy to configure and deploy.

Scalability
> Like Hadoop, Storm is designed to efficiently process large volumes of messages in parallel and scales simply through the addition of new nodes.

Fault tolerance
> Again like Hadoop, Storm is architected with the assumption that failure is a given. Similar to tasks in Hadoop jobs, Storm processes are designed to be restartable if a process or node fails, and will be automatically restarted when they die. However, it is important to note that this fault tolerance won't extend to locally persisted values like counts and rolling averages. An external persistence system will be required to make those fault-tolerant. We'll examine how Trident can address this gap later on.

Data processing guarantees
> Storm guarantees every message passing through the system will be fully processed. On failure, messages will be replayed to ensure they get processed.

Broad programming language support
> Storm uses Apache Thrift in order to provide language portability when implementing workflows.

A full overview of Storm is out of scope for this book, so we'll focus on integration of Storm with Hadoop. For more detail on Storm, refer to the Storm documentation (*http://storm.apache.org/documentation/Home.html*). For a good, practical introduction to using Storm, refer to *Storm Applied* by Sean T. Allen, et al. (Manning).

Microbatching versus Streaming

We'll pause again here to touch on a term we use frequently in this chapter: *microbatching*. Storm is an example of a pure streaming tool, while Spark Streaming and Trident provide a microbatching model, which is simply the capability to group events into discrete transactional batches for processing. We'll discuss this concept in more detail as we talk about the different tools and use cases, but the important thing to note is that microbatching is not necessarily a better approach than streaming. As with many decisions around designing an architecture, the choice of microbatching versus streaming will depend on the use case. There are cases where reduced latency makes streaming the appropriate choice. There are other cases where the better support for exactly-once processing makes microbatch systems the preferred choice.

Storm High-Level Architecture

Figure 7-2 shows a view of the components in the Storm architecture.

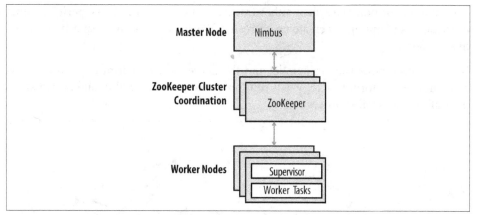

Figure 7-2. Storm high-level architecture

As shown in this image, there are two types of nodes in a Storm cluster:

- The master node runs a process called *Nimbus*. Nimbus is responsible for distributing code around the cluster, assigning tasks to machines, and monitoring for failures. You can think of the Nimbus process as being similar to the JobTracker in the MapReduce framework.

- Worker nodes run the *Supervisor* daemon. The Supervisor listens for work assigned to the node, and starts and stops processes that Nimbus has assigned to the node. This is similar to the TaskTrackers in MapReduce.

- Additionally, *ZooKeeper* nodes provide coordination for the Storm processes, as well as storing the state of the cluster. Storing the cluster state in ZooKeeper allows the Storm processes to be stateless, supporting the ability for Storm processes to fail or restart without affecting the health of the cluster. Note that in this case, "state" is the operational state of the cluster, not the state of data passing through the cluster.

Storm Topologies

Applications to process streaming data are implemented by Storm *topologies*. Topologies are a graph of computation, where each node in the topology contains processing logic. Links between the nodes define how data should be passed between nodes.

Figure 7-3 shows a simple example of a Storm topology, in this case the classic word count example (*http://bit.ly/storm-wce*). As shown in this diagram, *spouts* and *bolts* are the Storm primitives that provide the logic to process streaming data, and a network of spouts and bolts is what makes up a Storm topology. Spouts provide a source of *streams*, taking input from things like message queues and social media feeds. Bolts consume one or more streams, (either from a spout or another bolt), perform some processing, and optionally create new streams. We'll talk more about spouts and bolts in a moment.

Note that each node runs in parallel and the degree of parallelism for a topology is configurable. A Storm topology will run forever or until you kill it, and Storm automatically restarts failed processes.

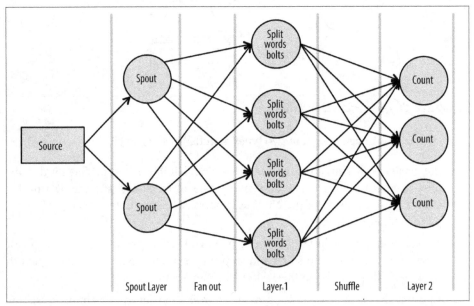

Figure 7-3. Storm word count topology

We'll provide a more detailed walkthrough of Storm code in an upcoming example. In the meantime, the following code shows what Figure 7-3 would look like in terms of the Storm code to set up the word count topology:

```
builder.setSpout("spout", new RandomSentenceSpout(), 2);
builder.setBolt("split", new SplitSentence(), 4).shuffleGrouping("spout");
builder.setBolt("count", new WordCount(), 3).
    fieldsGrouping("split", new Fields("word"));
```

We'll soon see that the code to set up a Storm topology is very different from the other systems we explore in this chapter, such as Trident (see "Trident" on page 233 for more details) and Spark Streaming (see "Spark Streaming" on page 237 for more details). In Storm you are building a topology that is solving a problem. In Trident and Spark Streaming you are expressing how to solve a problem, and the topology is constructed for you behind the scenes. This is similar to the way that Hive provides an abstraction layer over MapReduce.

Tuples and Streams

Tuples and *streams* provide abstractions for the data flowing through our Storm topology. Tuples provide the data model in Storm. A tuple is an ordered, named list of values (see Figure 7-4). A field in a tuple can be of any type; Storm provides primitive types, strings, and byte arrays. You can use other types by implementing a custom serializer. Every node in a topology declares the fields for the tuples it emits.

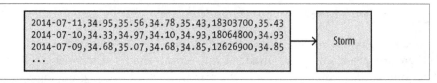

Figure 7-4. Storm tuples

The stream is the core abstraction in Storm. A stream is an unbounded sequence of tuples between any two nodes in a topology (see Figure 7-5). A topology can contain any number of streams.

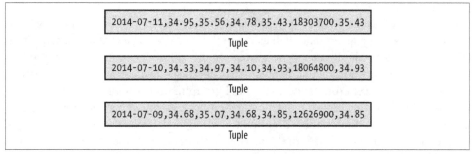

Figure 7-5. Storm stream

Spouts and Bolts

As we mentioned earlier, the other core components in the Storm architecture are spouts and bolts, which provide the processing in a Storm topology:

Spouts

As noted, spouts provide the source of streams in a topology. If you're familiar with Flume, you can think of spouts as loosely analogous to Flume sources. Spouts will read data from some external source, such as a social media feed or a message queue, and emit one or more streams into a topology for processing.

Bolts

Bolts consume streams from spouts or upstream bolts in a topology, do some processing on the tuples in the stream, and them emit zero or more tuples to downstream bolts or external systems such as a data persistence layer. Similar to chaining MapReduce jobs, complex processing will generally be implemented by a chain of bolts.

One important thing to note about bolts is they process a single tuple at a time. Referring back to our discussion of microbatching versus streaming, this design can be an advantage or disadvantage depending on specific use cases. We'll explore this topic more later.

Stream Groupings

Stream groupings tell Storm how to send tuples between sets of tasks in a topology. There are several groupings provided with Storm, and it's also possible to implement custom stream groupings. A few of the commonly used stream groupings are:

Shuffle grouping
> Tuples are emitted to instances of a bolt randomly, with the guarantee that each bolt instance will receive the same number of tuples. A shuffle grouping is appropriate where each tuple can be processed independently.

Fields grouping
> Provides control for how tuples are sent to bolts based on one or more fields in the tuples. For a given set of values the tuples will always be sent to the same bolt. Comparing to MapReduce processing, you can think of this as somewhat analogous to the partitioning that happens in order to send values with the same key to the same reducer. You would use a field grouping in cases where tuples need to be treated as a group—for example, when aggregating values. It's important to note, however, that unlike MapReduce for which unique keys go to unique reducers, with Storm it's entirely possible for a single bolt to receive tuples associated with different groups.

All grouping
> Replicates stream values across all participating bolts.

Global grouping
> Sends an entire stream to a single bolt, similar to a MapReduce job that sends all values to a single reducer.

For a complete overview of stream groupings, refer to the Storm documentation (*http://bit.ly/storm-docs*).

Stream grouping is an important feature of Storm, and in combination with the ability to define topologies, it is why Storm is more suited for tasks like counting and rolling averages than a system like Flume. Flume has the ability to receive events and perform enrichment and validation on them, but doesn't have a good system for grouping those events and processing them in different partition groupings. Note that Flume does have the ability to partition, but it has to be defined at a physical level, whereas with Storm it is defined at a logical topology level, which makes it easier to manage.

Reliability of Storm Applications

Storm provides varying levels of guarantees for processing tuples with a fairly minimal increase in implementation complexity for the different levels. These different levels of guarantee are:

At-most-once processing
> This is the simplest implementation, and is suitable for applications where some message loss is acceptable. With this level of processing we ensure that a tuple never gets processed more than once, but if an issue occurs during processing tuples can be discarded without being processed. An example might be where we're performing some simple aggregations on incoming events for alerting purposes.

At-least-once processing
> This level ensures that each tuple is processed successfully at least once, but it's also acceptable if tuples get replayed and processed multiple times. An example of where tuples might be reprocessed is the case where a task goes down before acknowledging the tuple processing and Storm replays the tuples. Adding this level of guarantee only requires some fairly minor additions to the code that implements your topology. An example use case is a system that processes credit cards, where we want to ensure that we retry authorizations in the case of failure.

Exactly-once processing
> This is the most complex level of guarantee, because it requires that tuples are processed once and only once. This would be the guarantee level for applications requiring idempotent processing—in other words, if the result from processing the same group of tuples always needs to be identical. Note that this level of guarantee will likely leverage an additional abstraction over core Storm, like Trident. Because of this need for specialized processing, we'll talk more about what's required for exactly-once processing in the next section.

Note that the ability to guarantee message processing relies on having a reliable message source. This means that the spout and source of messages for a Storm topology need to be capable of replaying messages if there's a failure during tuple processing. Kafka is a commonly used system with Storm, since it provides the functionality that allows spouts to request replay of messages on failure.

Exactly-Once Processing

For cases where exactly-once processing is required, Storm offers two options:

Transactional topologies (http://bit.ly/tran-tops)

In a transactional topology, tuple processing is essentially split into two phases:

- A processing phase in which batches of tuples are processed in parallel.

- A commit phase, which ensures that batches are committed in strict order. These two phases encompass a transaction and allow for parallel processing of batches, while ensuring that batches are committed and replayed as necessary. Transactional topologies have been deprecated in more recent versions of Storm in favor of Trident, which we'll discuss next.

Trident

Similar to transactional topologies, Trident (*http://bit.ly/trident-tu*) is a high-level abstraction on Storm that provides multiple benefits, including:

- Familiar query operators like joins, aggregations, grouping, functions, etc. For developers who work with Pig, the programming model should be very familiar.

- Most importantly for this topic, Trident supports exactly-once processing semantics.

As we noted, Trident is now the preferred method for implementing exactly once processing. We will walk through Trident at a high level in its own section below, since it looks and performs very differently from Storm. In terms of the programming model Trident is very much like Spark Streaming, as we'll see later.

Fault Tolerance

In addition to guaranteed processing of tuples, Storm provides facilities to ensure processing in the eventuality of process or hardware failures (*http://bit.ly/storm-fault*). These capabilities will be very familiar to Hadoop users:

- If workers die, the Supervisor process will restart them. On continued failure, the work will be assigned to another machine.

- If a server dies, tasks assigned to that host will time out and be reassigned to other hosts.

- If the Nimbus or a Supervisor process dies, it can be restarted without affecting the processing on the Storm cluster. Additionally, the worker processes can continue to process tuples if the Nimbus process is down.

Integrating Storm with HDFS

As noted before, Storm is really intended as a standalone processing system, although it can be easily integrated with external systems as both data sources and data sinks. There's an HDFS bolt (*http://bit.ly/hdfs-bolt*) now included with the Storm project that does provide the ability to write text and sequence files to HDFS. It should be noted though that this bolt provides fairly basic integration with Hadoop, as opposed to the richer functionality supported by the Flume HDFS sink (*http://bit.ly/hdfs-sink*).

For example, a couple of things to be aware of when using the HDFS bolt in your architecture:

- At the time of writing, the implementation of the HDFS bolt supports writing a tuple at a time, along with the ability to specify how often to sync files to HDFS based on the number of tuples processed. However, this option comes with the possibility of data loss—for example, if the bolt dies after tuples have been acknowledged but before they're synced to HDFS.

- Also at the time of writing, the HDFS bolt lacks support for formats other than text or sequence files (e.g., Avro).

It's important to note that these are not limitations in the Storm framework itself, and will likely be addressed as HDFS integration improves.

Integrating Storm with HBase

The same considerations we discussed for the HDFS integration apply to how Storm interacts with HBase (*https://github.com/ptgoetz/storm-hbase*). As with the HDFS bolt, make sure to read the documentation and examine the source code to make sure you are doing batch puts to HBase, not just single puts. If you're only doing single puts, then on every put the write-ahead log has to sync to disk on three different nodes in HDFS. The result of this is a large performance hit for your HBase writes. Table 7-1 shows the performance of simple tests on a small test cluster. These results are not intended to mirror what you would see on a production cluster, but are simply intended to show the relative performance impact of different batch sizes.

Table 7-1. Relative performance of different batch sizes

Cluster type	Key bytes	Value bytes	Batched puts	Threads	Puts per second
3 low-powered VMs	32	1,024	1	4	3,180
3 low-powered VMs	32	1,024	10	4	5,820
3 low-powered VMs	32	1,024	100	4	38,400

Cluster type	Key bytes	Value bytes	Batched puts	Threads	Puts per second
3 low-powered VMs	32	1,024	1,000	4	120,000
4 bare metal boxes	32	1,024	1	10	28,533
4 bare metal boxes	32	1,024	1,000	10	389,385

Returning to the discussion of microbatching versus streaming, this is a good example of where microbatching has the advantage in terms of HBase throughput.

Storm Example: Simple Moving Average

Before turning to an evaluation of Storm, let's look at an example—in this case, a small application to calculate simple moving averages (SMAs) over stock tick records. We implement an SMA by calculating the average of the last N values in a stream of values, where N is a specific period—essentially calculating an average over a specific window of values.

As an example, given a stream of stock prices, and a window size of 3, our input and output would look like the following:

```
Next value = 33.79, SMA = 33.79
Next value = 35.61, SMA = 34.7
Next value = 35.70, SMA = 35.03
Next value = 35.43, SMA = 35.58
Next value = 34.93, SMA = 35.35
Next value = 34.85, SMA = 35.07
Next value = 34.53, SMA = 34.77
```

With a window size of 3 the average is always calculated over the last 3 values in the stream, with any previous values discarded. Essentially we have a moving window over our incoming stream of values, hence the name *moving average*.

Our example implementation uses stock ticker data with the following format:

```
stock symbol, date, opening price, daily high, daily low, closing price, volume,
adjusted close
```

We'll use the closing prices as the values for our SMA calculation. For simplicity, the resulting records from processing will contain the following fields:

```
ticker, SMA
```

In addition to calculating moving averages, the example uses the HDFS bolt to persist the raw records to HDFS, providing an example of how to integrate a Storm topology with Hadoop. Our topology to implement this example looks like Figure 7-6.

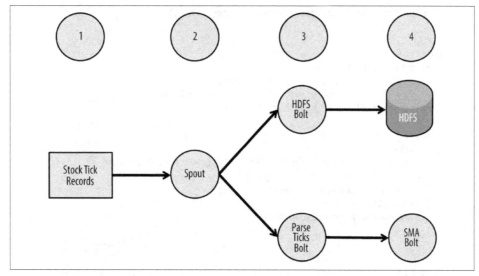

Figure 7-6. Storm simple-moving average topology

Let's walk through the steps in this diagram:

1. Our source data is daily stock tick records. For example purposes, the records will be read from a file on local disk. In a real-world application, records would likely be coming through a reliable event source such as a message queue, Kafka, or Flume.

2. The stock tick records will be emitted into our topology through our Storm spout.

3. Our spout will emit tuples to two different bolts: an instance of the HDFS bolt to persist raw records to HDFS, and a bolt that will parse out the fields needed to calculate the moving averages.

4. The output tuples from the parsing bolt will stream to the bolt that will calculate moving averages.

Let's walk through the code implementing this example.

We'll start by looking at the StockTicksSpout, which provides the entry point into our topology. For example purposes, StockTicksSpout is a simple spout implementation that just reads data from a local file:

```
public class StockTicksSpout extends BaseRichSpout {
  private SpoutOutputCollector outputCollector;
  private List<String> ticks;

  @Override
  public void declareOutputFields(OutputFieldsDeclarer outputFieldsDeclarer) {
```

```
        outputFieldsDeclarer.declare(new Fields("tick"));          ❶
    }

    @Override
    public void open(Map map,
                     TopologyContext context,
                     SpoutOutputCollector outputCollector) {
        this.outputCollector = outputCollector;

        try {
            ticks =
                IOUtils.readLines(ClassLoader.getSystemResourceAsStream( ❷
                    "NASDAQ_daily_prices_A.csv"),
                    Charset.defaultCharset().name());
        } catch (IOException e) {
            throw new RuntimeException(e);
        }
    }

    @Override
    public void nextTuple() {
        for (String tick : ticks) {
            outputCollector.emit(new Values(tick), tick);          ❸
        }
    }
}
```

❶ Define field names for tuples emitted by this spout. In this case we're emitting each input record as a tuple named `tick`.

❷ Read each record in the file into a `List` object.

❸ The `nextTuple()` method will get called when Storm is ready to read the next tuple. Note also in the `emit()` method that we're explicitly *anchoring* each tuple by assigning a message ID to each one we emit. In this case we're simply using the tuple itself as the ID. Performing this anchoring ensures reliability by allowing downstream components to acknowledge the processing of each tuple. We'll see this acknowledgment (*http://bit.ly/process-m*) when we look at the bolt example code in a moment.

As shown in Figure 7-6, the tuples will be sent to two different bolts for processing: `ParseTicksBolt`, which will parse out the required fields from the incoming tuples, and an HDFS bolt, which will persist the incoming tuples to HDFS. The `ParseTicks Bolt` class looks like the following:

```
public class ParseTicksBolt extends BaseRichBolt {

    private OutputCollector outputCollector;
```

```
    @Override
    public void prepare(Map config,
                        TopologyContext topologyContext,
                        OutputCollector collector) {
      outputCollector = collector;
    }

    @Override
    public void declareOutputFields(OutputFieldsDeclarer declarer) {
      declarer.declare(new Fields("ticker", "price"));            ❶
    }

    @Override
    public void execute(Tuple tuple) {
      String tick = tuple.getStringByField("tick");               ❷
      String[] parts = tick.split(",");                           ❸
      outputCollector.emit(new Values(parts[0], parts[4]));       ❹
      outputCollector.ack(tuple);                                 ❺
    }
  }
}
```

❶ Define the field names for tuples emitted by this bolt.

❷ Get a tick record from the input stream.

❸ Split each tick record.

❹ Emit a new tuple composed of the ticker symbol and closing price.

❺ Acknowledge processing of this tuple. This is enabled by the explicit anchoring of tuples in the upstream spout.

And here's the code for our HDFS bolt:

```
RecordFormat format = new DelimitedRecordFormat()              ❶
  .withFieldDelimiter("|");
SyncPolicy syncPolicy = new CountSyncPolicy(100);              ❷

FileRotationPolicy rotationPolicy =                            ❸
  new FileSizeRotationPolicy(5.0f, Units.MB);

FileNameFormat fileNameFormat = new DefaultFileNameFormat()    ❹
  .withPath("stock-ticks/");

HdfsBolt hdfsBolt = new HdfsBolt()                             ❺
  .withFsUrl("hdfs://localhost:8020")
  .withFileNameFormat(fileNameFormat)
  .withRecordFormat(format)
  .withRotationPolicy(rotationPolicy)
  .withSyncPolicy(syncPolicy);
```

```
    return hdfsBolt;
```

❶ Define the format for saving data to HDFS.

❷ Sync to HDFS after every 100 tuples.

❸ Rotate files once they reach 5 MB.

❹ Save files into HDFS in a directory called *stock-ticks* in the user's home directory.

❺ Create the bolt with the parameters we've just defined.

When the input tuples are parsed, the bolt that will do the work of calculating the moving averages is CalcMovingAvgBolt:

```
public class CalcMovingAvgBolt extends BaseRichBolt {

    private OutputCollector outputCollector;
    private Map<String, LinkedList<Double>> windowMap;          ❶
    private final int period = 5;

    @Override
    public void prepare(Map config,
                        TopologyContext topologyContext,
                        OutputCollector collector) {
      outputCollector = collector;
      windowMap = new HashMap<String, LinkedList<Double>>();
    }

    @Override
    public void declareOutputFields(OutputFieldsDeclarer declarer) { ❷
    }

    /**
     * For each ticker in input stream, calculate the moving average.
     */
    @Override
    public void execute(Tuple tuple) {
      String ticker = tuple.getStringByField("ticker");          ❸
      String quote = tuple.getStringByField("price");

      Double num = Double.parseDouble(quote);
      LinkedList<Double> window = (LinkedList)getQuotesForTicker(ticker); ❹
      window.add(num);                                            ❺

      // Print to System.out for test purposes. In a real implementation this
      // would go to a downstream bolt for further processing, or persisted, etc.
      System.out.println("----------------------------------------");  ❻
      System.out.println("moving average for ticker " + ticker + "=" +
                         getAvg(window));
```

```
      System.out.println("-------------------------------------");
    }

    /**
     * Return the current window of prices for a ticker.
     */
    private LinkedList<Double> getQuotesForTicker(String ticker) {        ❼
      LinkedList<Double> window = windowMap.get(ticker);
      if (window == null) {
        window = new LinkedList<Double>();
        windowMap.put(ticker, window);
      }
      return window;
    }

    /**
     * Return the average for the current window.
     */
    public double getAvg(LinkedList<Double> window) {                     ❽
      if (window.isEmpty()) {
        return 0;
      }

      // Drop the oldest price from the window:
      if (window.size() > period) {
        window.remove();
      }

      double sum = 0;

      for (Double price : window) {
        sum += price.doubleValue();
      }

      return sum / window.size();
    }
  }
```

❶ Create a map to hold the window for each ticker. As we discussed earlier, we can use a fields grouping to ensure that all values for a ticker go to the same bolt, but we can't guarantee that a single bolt will only get the values for a single ticker. We'll use a map keyed by ticker symbol so we can manage windows over multiple tickers in instances of our bolt.

❷ For testing purposes we're just going to print to standard output, so we don't need to declare output fields. In an actual implementation we'd probably send tuples to a downstream bolt or a persistence layer, for instance.

❸ Retrieve the ticker and price values from the input tuple.

❹ Retrieve the list of values (the current window) associated with the ticker.

❺ Add the current value to the window.

❻ Call the method that calculates the average for the current window, and output the result.

❼ The `getQuotesForTicker()` method will retrieve the current window for the requested ticker. If the window doesn't exist, create a new one.

❽ Return the average for the current window. Note that we make sure to move the window forward before calculating the average.

The topology is configured in the `buildTopology()` method of the `MovingAvgLocal TopologyRunner` class. This method looks like the following:

```
private static StormTopology buildTopology() {

    TopologyBuilder builder = new TopologyBuilder();                    ❶

    builder.setSpout("stock-ticks-spout", new StockTicksSpout());       ❷

    builder.setBolt("hdfs-persister-bolt", createHdfsBolt())            ❸
        .shuffleGrouping("stock-ticks-spout");

    builder.setBolt("parse-ticks", new ParseTicksBolt())               ❹
        .shuffleGrouping("stock-ticks-spout");

    builder.setBolt("calc-moving-avg", new CalcMovingAvgBolt(), 2)     ❺
        .fieldsGrouping("parse-ticks", new Fields("ticker"));

    return builder.createTopology();                                    ❻
}
```

❶ The `TopologyBuilder` class will be used to wire our bolts and spouts into a topology.

❷ Define our spout.

❸ Define our HDFS bolt.

❹ Define our bolt to parse ticks.

❺ Define our bolt that does the actual work of calculating the moving averages. Note that we use a fields grouping to ensure that all values for a ticker go to the same bolt.

❻ Create the topology.

Evaluating Storm

We've talked about Storm's integration with Hadoop, so let's see how Storm stacks up on the other criteria we defined at the beginning of this chapter.

Support for aggregation and windowing

Tasks like counting and calculating windowing averages is easy to implement in Storm, both because there is existing examples of bolt implementations for many common operations, and because the topology and grouping functionality in Storm supports this type of processing well.

However, there are also two potential downsides: first, the local storage of the counters and historical information needed to perform continuous counting and rolling averages is not fault-tolerant. So on the loss of a bolt process, we lose any locally persisted values. This makes aggregations created by Storm unreliable, hence the need for a batch job for more accuracy.

The second issue is the throughput Storm can achieve with external persistence systems like HBase or Memcached to persist the counts and averages. As we noted before, single puts means more disk syncs and also additional round-trips on the network.

Enrichment and alerting

As we discussed, Storm bolts allow very low-latency access to events, which allows developers to implement event enrichment and alerting functionality. This functionality is similar to what we can get with Flume interceptors. The main difference is if there is an intention to persist the enriched data in a system like HBase or HDFS, Flume has options for much higher throughput interactions with these systems with similar latencies.

Lamdba Architecture

Note there is no 100% reliable streaming solution. There's always the possibility of duplicates or lost data. Systems that must ensure accurate data warrant running batch jobs in conjunction with Storm processing. The code to implement such batch processes will normally be implemented with something like MapReduce or Spark.

Trident

As mentioned previously, Trident is a higher-level abstraction over Storm that addresses some of the shortcomings of processing a single event at a time. Rather than build an entirely new system, the designers of Trident chose to wrap Storm in order to provide support for transactions over Storm. In contrast to Storm, Trident follows a declarative programming model similar to SQL—in other words, Trident expresses topologies in terms of *what* rather than *how*.

A Trident application replaces the Storm spout with a Trident spout, but rather than defining bolts to process tuples, Trident *operations* are used for processing. As you'll see in the upcoming example, rather than define an explicit topology to process our streams as with Storm, we chain these operations together to create our processing flow. Trident provides a number of operation types such as filters, splits, merges, joins, and groupings. Most of these will look familiar to anybody who's used SQL or abstractions such as Pig or Cascading. This also means that Trident applications need to be implemented with only the provided operations, although, as we'll see shortly, there's some flexibility in the processing that occurs within operations.

Of course, another primary difference between Storm and Trident is that Trident follows a microbatching model—streams are handled as batches of tuples rather than individual tuples, providing a model where exactly-once semantics can be more easily supported.

A core feature of Trident that supports reliable exactly-once processing is functionality that allows reading tuples from and writing tuples to stateful sources such as memory or HDFS. This provides the ability to replay tuples in the event of failure, and Trident provides management of batches to ensure that tuples are processed exactly once.

Trident Example: Simple Moving Average

We'll provide a simple example to give you an idea of a Trident application. Although we don't show it in this example, note that the HDFS bolt we used before also provides support for Trident.

As with the previous example, we'll calculate moving averages over stock ticker data. Unlike the previous example, for simplicity our incoming stream will contain records for only a single ticker. These records will have the following format:

```
date, opening price, daily high, daily low, closing price, volume, adjusted close
```

Let's start by looking at the main class for the example, `MovingAvgLocalTopologyRun ner`:

```
public class MovingAvgLocalTopologyRunner {

  public static void main(String[] args)
      throws Exception {

    Config conf = new Config();
    LocalCluster cluster = new LocalCluster();
```

```
    TridentTopology topology = new TridentTopology();

    Stream movingAvgStream =
      topology.newStream("ticks-spout", buildSpout()) ❶
      .each(new Fields("stock-ticks"), new TickParser(), new Fields("price")) ❷
      .aggregate(new Fields("price"), new CalculateAverage(),
                new Fields("count")); ❸

    cluster.submitTopology("moving-avg", conf, topology.build()); ❹
  }
}
```

❶ Create a new spout to emit batches of tick tuples into our topology. In this case
we're just using a simple spout that reads records from a local file and emits
batches containing five tuples. The buildSpout() method is a utility method
defined in the FixedBatchSpoutBuilder class (see the next code block), which
simply reads our stock data from a file and emits batches of five records at a time.

❷ For each tuple in the input stream, parse out the price field using the TickParser
class.

❸ Calculate the average using an *aggregation* operation. We'll look at this code next.

❹ Start our topology.

Before moving on to our aggregate operation, here's the code for our FixedBatch
SpoutBuilder utility class:

```
public class FixedBatchSpoutBuilder {
  public static FixedBatchSpout buildSpout() {
    List<Values> ticks = new FixedBatchSpoutBuilder().readData();
    FixedBatchSpout spout = new FixedBatchSpout(new Fields("stock-ticks"), 5,
        ticks.toArray(new Values[ticks.size()]));
    spout.setCycle(false);
    return spout;
  }

  public List<Values> readData() {
    try {
      BufferedReader reader = new BufferedReader(
          new InputStreamReader(getClass().getResourceAsStream(
            "/AAPL_daily_prices.csv")));

      List<Values> ticks = new ArrayList<Values>();
      String line = null;
      while ((line = reader.readLine()) != null) ticks.add(new Values(line));

      return ticks;
    } catch (IOException e) {
```

```
      throw new RuntimeException(e);
    }
  }
}
```

As we noted, the class that performs the calculation of averages is an implementation of an aggregation operation; in this case we're implementing `Aggregator` from the Trident API. This class looks like the following:

```
public class CalculateAverage
    extends BaseAggregator <CalculateAverage.AverageState> {

  static class AverageState {
    double sum = 0;
  }

  @Override
  public AverageState init(Object batchId, TridentCollector collector) {  ❶
    return new AverageState();
  }

  @Override
  public void aggregate(AverageState state,
                        TridentTuple tuple,
                        TridentCollector collector) {             ❷
    state.sum = state.sum + Double.valueOf((Double)tuple.getValue(0));
  }

  @Override
  public void complete(AverageState state, TridentCollector collector) {  ❸
    collector.emit(new Values(state.sum/5));
  }
}
```

❶ The `init()` method will get called before each batch is processed. In this case we'll just create a new object that maintains state within the object. Here, the state is simply a running sum of closing prices in the batch.

❷ The `aggregate()` method gets called for each tuple in the batch, and will simply update the sum of closing prices.

❸ The `complete()` method gets called when all tuples for the batch have been processed, and emits the calculation of the average for the batch.

Although this is a somewhat simpler example than our Storm example, it's clear that the Trident code is much more concise than the Storm code; rather than writing multiple lines of code to define a topology, we simply define the operations to perform our processing with the following code:

```
Stream movingAvgStream =
  topology.newStream("ticks-spout", buildSpout())
  .each(new Fields("stock-ticks"), new TickParser(), new Fields("price"))
  .aggregate(new Fields("price"), new CalculateAverage(), new Fields("count"));
```

We did need to write some custom code to calculate the moving average, but Trident also includes many built-in operations that facilitate implementation of common processing tasks.

We've given a very brief overview of Trident here, so for more on Trident see the online documentation (*http://bit.ly/storm-docs*), or *Storm Applied*.

Evaluating Trident

Now that we have an idea of how Trident works, let's look at how it relates to our streaming evaluation criteria.

Support for counting and windowing

Trident marks a large improvement over core Storm. We now can persist to external storage systems to maintain state with higher throughput.

Enrichment and alerting

Here we should have similar functionality as core Storm. In the case of Trident, the batches are merely wrappers. This is unlike batches in Spark Streaming, which are true microbatches, meaning there is a delay before the first event is fired. Instead, Trident batches are nothing more than a marker at the end of a group of tuples.

Lamdba Architecture

Again, there is no completely reliable streaming solution, but we are in a much better place here than we were with Storm, although to support the Lambda Architecture we will still need to implement the batch process in something like MapReduce or Spark.

Spark Streaming

A more recent arrival in the stream processing space is Spark Streaming. Spark Streaming takes advantage of the power of Spark RDDs, and combines it with reliablity and exactly-once semantics, similar to Trident, to provide a streaming solution with very high throughput.

If your use cases allow for processing data in microbatches of 2–5 seconds, Spark Streaming provides the following features:

- Reliable persistence of intermediate data for your counting and rolling averages.

- Supported integration with external storage systems like HBase.
- Reusable code between streaming and batch processing.
- The Spark Streaming microbatch model allows for processing patterns that help to mitigate the risk of duplicate events.

Overview of Spark Streaming

For those already familiar with Spark, Spark Streaming will be very similar in coding style and APIs. We'll start our exploration of Spark Streaming with the `StreamCon text`, which is a wrapper over the `SparkContext`; recall that the `SparkContext` is the basis of everything in standard Spark applications. The big addition the `StreamCon text` brings is a parameter called `batchDuration`. This duration will set the goal batch interval, which we will illustrate in a short bit.

Just like in core Spark where your initial RDDs are created with the `SparkContext`, in Spark Streaming your initial `DStreams` are created with the `StreamingContext`. A `DStream` is a wrapper over an RDD. The difference between the two is really what they represent. Whereas the normal RDD is a reference to a distributed immutable collection, the `DStream` is a reference to a distributed immutable collection in relation to a batch window. To put this into context, think of a `DStream` as being like a video, where what appears on screen is constantly changing, but underneath it's made up of static images. In this context, the RDDs are the unchanging (immutable) images, while the `DStream` is the video that appears to be mutable, being made up of a series of immutable RDDs.

This is a complex idea, so let's look at some examples in Spark Streaming and then diagram what is happening.

Spark Streaming Example: Simple Count

We'll first start with an example that creates an `InputDStream` with the `StreamingCon text` and then does a simple filter and count. Figure 7-7 shows what this looks like.

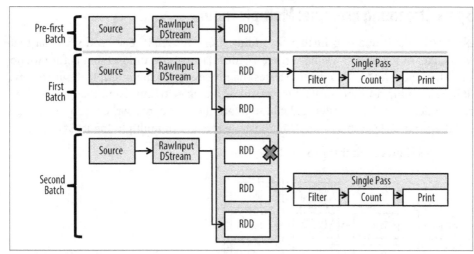

Figure 7-7. Spark Streaming simple count example

Let's dig into this image a little bit and call out some important points:

- Everything is batch based, and the image shows the same system but at different points in time.
- The InputDStream is always collecting data and putting it into a new RDD to be processed.
- The DStream that gets executed on is no longer taking in data. It is an immutable DStream at the point of execution. We will talk about this later, but this ensures that if the batch is replayed it will be replayed perfectly.
- Execution runs on the same engine as Spark.
- RDDs within the context of the DStreams are removed when they are no longer needed. Although the image makes it look like RDDs are removed as soon as the next step is executed, this is an oversimplification of how this works. The main point to take away is that old, unused RDDs are cleaned up.

Under the hood the code looks like the following. This example counts the lines sent every second to Spark Streaming that contain the word *the*:

```
val sc = new SparkContext(sparkConf)
val ssc = new StreamingContext(sc, Seconds(1))
val rawStream = ssc.socketTextStream(host, port, StorageLevel.MEMORY_ONLY_SER_2)
rawStream.filter(_.contains("the")).count().print()
ssc.start()
```

Spark Streaming Example: Multiple Inputs

Now, let's take it one step further by adding more InputDStreams and see what that looks like. In Figure 7-8, we have three InputDStreams and union them before we do our filter and counts. This demonstrates the process of taking multiple input streams and performing a union so we can treat it as a single stream. Note that it would be more efficient to do the filter and count before the union, but we're trying to change as little as possible in this example to illustrate the idea of multiple InputDStreams.

Figure 7-8 shows what this process looks like.

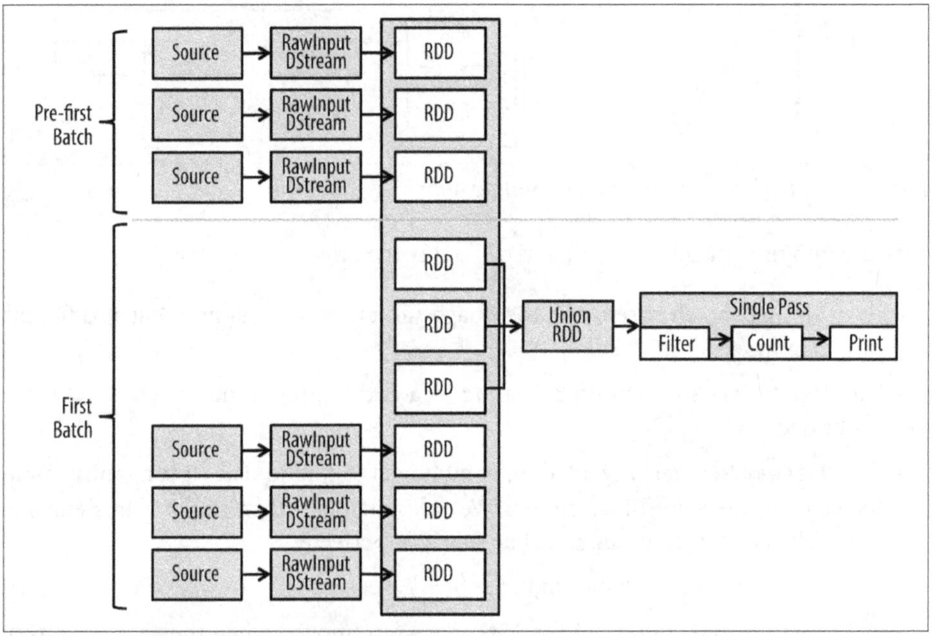

Figure 7-8. Spark Streaming multiple stream

And the following is an example of what the code looks like:

```
val sc = new SparkContext(sparkConf)
val ssc = new StreamingContext(sc, Seconds(1))
val rawStream1 =
  ssc.socketTextStream(host1, port1, StorageLevel.MEMORY_ONLY_SER_2)
val rawStream2 =
  ssc.socketTextStream(host2, port2, StorageLevel.MEMORY_ONLY_SER_2)
val rawStream = rawStream1.union(rawStream2)
rawStream.filter(_.contains("the")).count().print()
ssc.start()
```

There's not much new here—we just added another input that can add more streams that we have the option to union and work with in a single microbatch. That doesn't mean that joining streams always makes sense. When you're dealing with large data volumes, it may make sense to never join the streams in order to prevent increased latencies.

There are many design patterns where the incoming data may have been partitioned —for example, if the input stream was coming from different Kafka partitions. Note that unioning or joining across partitions is expensive, so avoid it if your application doesn't require it.

Spark Streaming Example: Maintaining State

The next example demonstrates the idea of how we maintain state between intervals, such as when we are doing continuous counting. Figure 7-9 shows what that looks like.

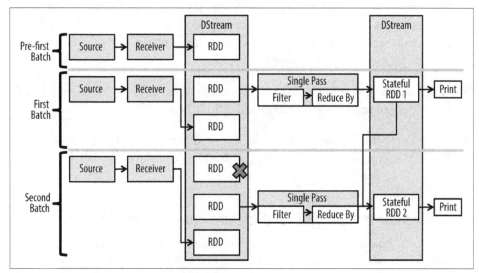

Figure 7-9. Maintaining state in Spark Streaming

And here's the code:

```
val sc = new SparkContext(sparkConf)
val ssc = new StreamingContext(sc, Seconds(1))
val rawStream = ssc.socketTextStream(host, port, StorageLevel.MEMORY_ONLY_SER_2)

val countRDD = rawStream.filter(_.contains("the"))
  .count()
  .map(r => ("foo", r))

countRDD.updateStateByKey((a: Seq[Long], b: Option[Long]) => {  ❶
  var newCount = b.getOrElse(0l)
  a.foreach( i => newCount += i)
  Some(newCount)                                                 ❷
```

```
}).print()

ssc.checkpoint(checkpointDir)                                    ❸

ssc.start()
```

This is our first example of a DStream crossing over into batch processing. Here, the totals from one batch are used to join with the new totals to generate a new DStream with the new totals in it.

Let's dig into a few aspects of this code:

❶ First, note that the function for updateStateByKey() is based on a key, so only the values are passed in, although how they're passed in is unique to Spark. The first value is a Seq[Long], which contains all new possible values for this key from this microbatch. It is very possible that this batch didn't include any values and this will be an empty Seq. The second value is an Option[Long], which represents the value from the last microbatch. The Option allows it to be empty because no value may have existed.

❷ Note that the return is an Option[Long]. This allows us the option to remove values populated in past microbatches with a Scala None.

❸ Finally, note that we have added a *checkpoint* folder. This is to help us restore our RDDs that cross microbatches along with supplying additional data loss protection.

How the Immutability of DStreams Provides Fault Tolerance

This is a good point to talk about how Spark Streaming does recovery in the case of failure. In the examples so far, we've seen that all the DStreams are made up of many immutable RDDs over time—meaning they cannot change after they have been created.

The stateful DStream in the updateStateByKey() call is a great example of this. The results in batch two are joined with the stateful DStreams RDD of the previous batch to make the new stateful DStream.

In the case of failure Spark has two options: the stateful DStream flushes to a *check point* directory every *N* microbatches, with *N* being configurable. So, if it is configured to write on every microbatch, we can recover from the *checkpoint* directory. If *N* is set to a value greater than every batch, then we need to recreate the state from the RDDs used to create it.

There is a trade-off here in disk I/O (which is distributed, so it isn't that large a trade-off in practice), or the use of extra memory to store the recreation path. Note that

---

there are options on the drawing board to make failure recovery even more optimal, but at the time of writing this is the state of things.

Notice how this stateful DStream is similar to the Trident state, but at the same time different. It is still in Spark Streaming and fault-tolerant. With Trident you need to replay on an external persistent system to achieve this same functionality and provide fault tolerance, whereas in Spark Streaming the DStream is fault-tolerant.

Spark Streaming Example: Windowing

Now, let's say we wanted to have a rolling count over a period of time. The following code shows how this would be implemented:

```
val sc = new SparkContext(sparkConf)

val ssc = new StreamingContext(sc, Seconds(2))
val rawStream = ssc.socketTextStream(host, port, StorageLevel.MEMORY_ONLY_SER_2)

val words = rawStream.flatMap(_.split(' '))
val windowCount = words.countByValueAndWindow(Seconds(20), Seconds(6))
windowCount.count.print()

ssc.checkpoint(checkpointDir)

ssc.start()
```

So how does this work? As we can see in Figure 7-10 Spark Streaming will store a bunch of DStreams and use them to build the first result until we reach the sixth pass. On that pass, we will add the last results and the new values and remove the oldest values. This makes it scale to a window of 20, 30, 100, with a fixed execution time.

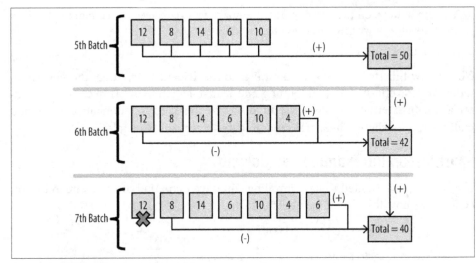

Figure 7-10. Spark Streaming windowing example

Spark Streaming Example: Streaming versus ETL Code

In this next example, we will go through code differences between Spark Streaming and Spark. Using word count again as an example, let's say we want to run it in a stream mode and in a batch mode. Let's look at what the code looks like in Spark Streaming and Spark, and what differences there are in execution.

Here is the Spark Streaming code:

```
val lines = ssc.textFileStream(args(0))
val words = lines.flatMap(_.split(" "))
val wordCounts = words.map(x => (x, 1)).reduceByKey(_ + _)
wordCounts.print()
```

And the Spark code:

```
val lines = ssc.textFileStream(args(0))
val words = lines.flatMap(_.split(" "))
val wordCounts = words.map(x => (x, 1)).reduceByKey(_ + _)
wordCounts.print()
```

Needless to say, this reinforces the idea that Spark and Spark Streaming share a common programming model. With that being said, there are possible scenarios where the code and flow will execute differently in batch than in streaming. However, even in those cases the majority of the code will be in the transformation functions.

The following provides an example where this would be different. Both of the preceding code snippets do the same thing, one for a batch and the other for a fixed set of input events. But what if we want to compare a continuous word count? Then, we would see code like the following:

```
val words = lines.flatMap(_.split(" "))
val wordCounts = words.map(x => (x, 1)).updateStateByKey[Int](_ + _)
wordCounts.print()
```

Even though the code is not identical, the underlying engine remains the same. The code itself has minor differences, and still leverages function reuse.

There's much more to Spark Streaming functionality than we can go into here, but hopefully the previous examples provide a good idea of the basics.

To explore Spark Streaming further, visit the Spark documentation (*http://bit.ly/ spark-docs*) or check out *Learning Spark* (*http://bit.ly/learning-spark*).

Also note that with every release more and more of Spark's functionality is being opened to Spark Streaming, so that means tools like GraphX and MLlib can be part of your NRT solution, which will provide greater opportunities for supporting different streaming use cases.

Spark Streaming Fault Tolerance

Spark Streaming utilizes a write-ahead log (WAL) for the driver process, similar to HBase, so in the case of failure of the driver process, another driver process can be started up and gather the state from the write-ahead log. Using this WAL makes data loss unlikely with Spark Streaming since the DStreams are built on RDDs, and RDDs are by design resilient. The level of resilience will be definable by the developer as with standard Spark jobs.

With the data being protected in case of failure, Spark Streaming will know which transformations or actions need to be rerun. This is a big advantage for microbatch systems in terms of performance, in that they only need to keep track of the success or failure of the batch, not every event. Event-level monitoring can have a large impact on systems like Storm.

Evaluating Spark Streaming

Now that we have a basic understanding of how the plumbing of Spark Streaming works, let's review our Spark Streaming functionality and see how it stacks up.

Support for counting and windowing

Counting, windowing, and rolling averages are straightforward in Spark Streaming. There are some differences in comparison to a system like Storm:

- The latency is on average more than 0.5 milliseconds to get a count or aggregate to increment.
- The counts are more stable in that they will survive a worker failure.

- Microbatching will help throughput in terms of persisting counts and averages to systems like HBase because it allows for batch puts or increments.
- The acknowledgment associated with microbatching will also help reduce duplicates being created by Spark Streaming.

Enrichment and alerting

In terms of enrichment and alerting, Spark Streaming can be implemented in the same simple manner as Flume or Storm. It may even have performance throughput advantages if it requires lookup from external systems like HBase to execute the enrichment and/or alerting.

The major downside here is the latency. As we said before, Spark Streaming is microbatching, so if your requirements are for alerting under 500 milliseconds, this is not your tool.

Lambda Architecture

Yes, you guessed it: there is no perfect streaming solution. Although Spark Streaming is not perfect, it does provide some advantages, such as code reuse. The code used for Spark Streaming will be very similar to the ETL code implemented in Spark. This will reduce the maintenance cost, which is the bane of every development organization.

Flume Interceptors

We won't go into too much detail about Flume here since we have more in-depth discussions about it elsewhere in this book. The scope of this chapter is just the source and the interceptor components of Flume, as shown in Figure 7-11.

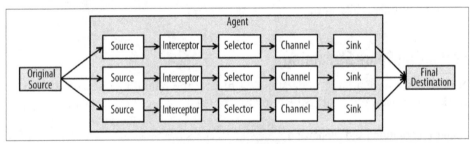

Figure 7-11. Flume interceptors for stream processing

Because the interceptor comes before the channel, the event is processed as soon as it is collected, or when a predetermined number of events in a batch is defined.

A large consideration in selecting Flume over the other solutions in this chapter is that it is highly tuned for ingestion. This is important for cases of validation and alerting because these normally come with a persistence requirement. Take, for example, alerting on fraud; it is normal to have a requirement that every event and the alert decision on that event needs to be recorded in HDFS for later review.

Which Tool to Use?

We've discussed a number of solutions here and details of their advantages and disadvantages. Note that each of these systems has merit depending on use case. These are different engines with slightly different optimizations and focus. The appropriate tool will depend on your requirements, so rather than try to provide hard-and-fast rules we'll discuss some example scenarios and explore different ways we can leverage these tools to implement solutions.

We'll focus on solving for three different use cases:

1. Low-latency enrichment, validation, and alerting on events, followed by ingestion.

2. NRT counting, rolling averages, and iterative processing such as machine learning.

3. More complex data pipelines. This is basically all of the above: enrichment, validation, alerting, counting and rolling averages, and finally ingestion.

Low-Latency Enrichment, Validation, Alerting, and Ingestion

We'll look at two options to explore different approaches to this task. Both of these designs have been used in real-world applications and each approach has merits. An example where you might require this functionality is fraud detection, which we discuss in more detail in Chapter 9.

Solution One: Flume

Figure 7-12 shows a Flume workflow to address this functionality. As you can see, this is a fairly simple workflow composed of a custom interceptor and an HDFS sink. The Flume channel provides a customizable level of data protection, as we talked about previously when discussing Flume. Since the interceptor is before the channel, we'll also get minimal latency in processing events.

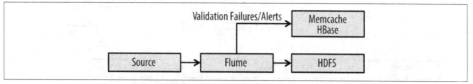

Figure 7-12. Use case one with Flume

Solution Two: Kafka and Storm

Our second approach, shown in Figure 7-13, uses Storm for processing in conjunction with Kafka for event delivery. Kafka provides reliable event delivery, while Storm provides reliable processing of those events.

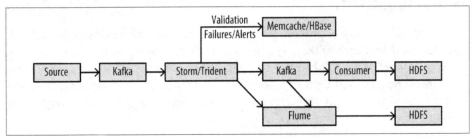

Figure 7-13. Use case one with Storm and Kafka

Note that we're using Kafka not just for event delivery to Storm, but also for ingestion into HDFS, either alone or optionally with Flume. We could have used an HDFS bolt to write directly to HDFS from the Storm/Trident topology. This would probably be more efficient, but Kafka and Flume are more mature and provide more functionality in terms of HDFS integration at this point.

NRT Counting, Rolling Averages, and Iterative Processing

For this case we don't have a great low-latency option. As we discussed, Storm provides a good low-latency solution, but the complexity to build a huge topology with batching may be difficult. Even if we get past the initial development, it may be difficult to maintain and modify in comparison to Spark Streaming or Trident.

So, we can build this use case in Storm, Trident, or Spark Streaming. Figure 7-14 shows how this would look with each solution.

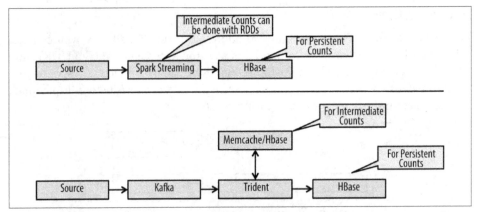

Figure 7-14. Use case two with Trident and Spark Streaming

Some considerations when deciding which option is preferable here:

Same programming model for batch and streaming
> If having the same programming model for streaming and batch is important to you, then Spark Streaming is a strong contender in this case. Being able to use the same language and model for the streaming and processing code provides benefits in training, administration, and maintenance.

Throughput per node
> Not surprisingly, there are a number of benchmarks available that show advantages for one tool or another. We're not going to make claims about superiority of one tool or another in terms of performance. Each tool may perform better depending on the use case, so the best approach is to try a prototype to determine for yourself whether a particular tool provides adequate performance.

Advanced functionality
> Here, Spark Streaming has the advantage, which is growing every day because of its larger base of contributors.

Complex Data Pipelines

This is the all-of-the-above requirement for your implementation—in this case, a more complex data flow requiring all of the processing functionality we've discussed for the previous two use cases. As we'll see, the answer here is pretty much just adding the answers from the last two use cases together. Let's first look at the Flume and Spark Streaming solution in Figure 7-15.

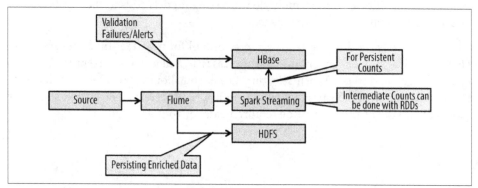

Figure 7-15. Use case three with Spark Streaming

The main thing to note here that's new is the integration between Flume and Spark Streaming.

Now let's look at what the Storm/Trident version looks like in Figure 7-16.

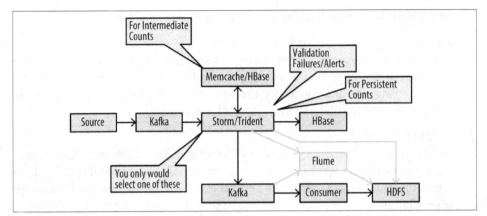

Figure 7-16. Use case three with Storm/Trident

The only thing that is changing here is we are adding together the topologies of the two use cases.

Conclusion

As we've seen once again in this chapter, Hadoop is rapidly becoming a big data plat-form supporting multiple processing models. In addition to the ability to efficiently process large data volumes in batch, Hadoop can now act as a platform for continu-ous processing of data with new tools such as Storm, Trident, and Spark Streaming. We also explored how the tried-and-true Flume can be leveraged for some NRT func-tionality. The ability to support multiple processing models adds to the capabilities of Hadoop as the hub for an enterprise's data.

As we've also seen in this chapter, the choice of tool for near-real-time processing on Hadoop will be very dependent on your use cases as well as your current toolset, lan-guage choices, and so on. When selecting a tool, you should take all these considera-tions into account, and ensure that you do appropriate performance testing with your tool of choice to ensure it meets the requirements for your application.

## PART II

Case Studies

## CHAPTER 8

Clickstream Analysis

Clickstream analysis commonly refers to analyzing the events (*click data*) that are collected as users browse a website. Such an analysis is typically done to extract insights into visitor behavior on your website in order to inform subsequent data-driven decisions.

You can use clickstream analysis to figure out how users interact with your online presence, which geographic regions or time zones your traffic originates from, what devices and operating systems are most commonly used to access your site, what the common paths are that your users take before they do something that's of interest to you (usually referred to as a *goal*—e.g., register for the mailing list, sign up for an account, or add an item to the shopping cart), and so on. You can correlate such click data with your marketing spend to do further analysis like the return on investment (ROI) of various marketing channels (organic search, paid search, social media spending, etc.). You can also, optionally, join click data with your ODS (Operational Data Store) or CRM (Customer Relationship Management) data to do further analysis based on additional information about your users.

Although this chapter uses analysis on clickstream data to show how to put together the various pieces described in Part I for a given use case, the concepts described here are applicable to any "batch" processing system that operates on machine-generated data. Examples of such data include but are not limited to ad impressions data, performance or other machine logs, network logs, and call logs.

Defining the Use Case

Suppose you are an online retailer selling bike parts. Users visit your website to browse bike parts, read reviews, and hopefully make a purchase. Whenever users view a page or click a link, this gets logged by your website application. The logs generated by the website, in many cases, are plain old Apache web server or Nginx logs, but in some cases could be custom logs generated by web analytics tools tracking your website. Regardless, all these clicks are logged in strictly increasing order of time.

As an online retailer, you'd like to gain a better understanding of your users and streamline your sales and marketing efforts. To accomplish these goals, you'd like to answer questions like the following:

- What is the total number of pages viewed on my website last month? How does it compare to previous months?
- How many unique visitors visited my website in the past month? How does it compare to previous months?
- How much time on average do visitors spend shopping on my website?
- What is the bounce rate of my website? In other words, how many users leave the website without visiting any other page except the one they landed on?
- For each landing page, what is the probability that a new user who landed at that page will end up buying something from the website in that session?
- For each landing page, what is the probability that a new user who landed at that page will end up buying something from the website within the next seven days?
- For each user who ends up buying something, to which marketing channel (direct, organic search, paid search, etc.) can that purchase be attributed?

To answer these questions and more, you would need to scan, process, and analyze data logged by your web servers.

For the purposes of subsequent discussion, we will assume the web logs are in a commonly used web log format known as *combined log format* (*http://bit.ly/combine-log*). Each individual log entry in this log format looks like (note that due to space constraints, the following example is shown on multiple lines; however in an actual log entry, this code would appear on one continuous line):

```
127.0.0.1 - frank [10/Oct/2000:13:55:36 -0700] "GET /
apache_pb.gif HTTP/1.0" 200 2326 "http://www.example.com/start.html"
"Mozilla/4.08 [en] (Win98; I ;Nav)"
```

Breaking the log entry down into various parts, we get:

`127.0.0.1`
This is the source IP (i.e., the IP address of the device where the click came from).

The second field, represented by a hyphen in this example, is intended to be the identity of the client, but in practice is considered unreliable and is simply disregarded by the server.

`frank`
This is the username (if applicable) as identified by HTTP authentication.

`10/Oct/2000:13:55:36 -0700`
This specifies the time at which the server finished processing the request, along with the associated time zone.

`GET /apache_pb.gif HTTP/1.0`
This is the type of request and page requested by the client.

`200`
This indicates the status code returned by the web server to the client.

`2326`
This is the size of the object returned to the client, minus any response headers.

`http://www.example.com/start.html`
This represents the referrer (if applicable)—that is, the page that brought the user to the site.

`Mozilla/4.08 [en] (Win98; I ;Nav)`
This is the user agent string identifying the browser and operating system on the device from which the click was made.

Using Hadoop for Clickstream Analysis

A very active website can generate several gigabytes of web server logs per day. Storing and analyzing this sheer volume of data requires a robust distributed system. Also, log data arrives at a very high velocity. Typically, logs need to be rotated several times a day—often, several times in an hour—and analysts want to know the latest micro and macro trends as soon as possible. Moreover, log data is semistructured; it may have user agent strings that need to be parsed, or additional parameters that might be added to and later removed from log records, such as parameters added for testing. All these characteristics make Hadoop a very good candidate for doing analytics on clickstream data.

In this chapter, we will show how you can implement an application for collecting, processing, and analyzing web server clickstream data using Apache Hadoop and related ecosystem projects.

Design Overview

We can break the high-level design of our example into five main sections—storage, ingestion, processing, analyzing, and orchestration:

- Storage refers to decisions around the storage system (HDFS or HBase), data formats, compression, and data models.

- Ingestion refers to getting click data from the web servers and secondary data (e.g., CRM, ODS, marketing spend data) and loading it into Hadoop for processing.

- Processing refers to taking the raw data ingested into Hadoop and transforming it into data set(s) that can be used for analysis and querying. Processing here may refer to, but is not limited to, deduplication of data, filtering out "bad" clicks, converting the clicks into columnar format, sessionization (the process of grouping clicks made by a single user in a single visit by associating a session ID representing that visit to each click made as a part of the visit), and aggregation.

- Analyzing refers to running various analytical queries on the processed data sets to find answers and insights to the questions presented earlier in the chapter.

- Orchestration refers to automating the arrangement and coordination of various processes that perform ingestion, processing, and analyzing.

Figure 8-1 depicts an overview of such a design.

In our design implementation, we will use HDFS to store the data, Flume for ingesting Apache logs, and Sqoop for ingesting other secondary data (e.g., CRM, ODS, marketing spend) into Hadoop. We will use Spark for processing and Impala for analyzing the processed data. By connecting a BI tool to Impala, we will be able to perform interactive queries on the processed data. We will use Oozie to orchestrate multiple actions into a single workflow.

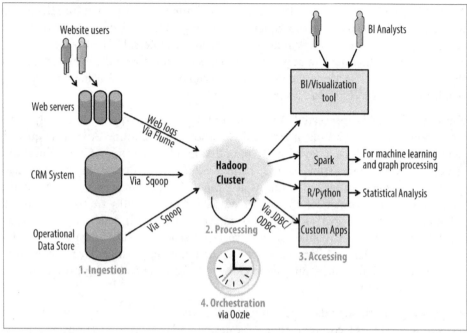

Figure 8-1. Design overview

Next, we will dive into a detailed description of our design. This will include details of file formats and data models, how to instrument a web application to send click-stream information to Flume, and how to configure Flume to store these events in text format. We will also discuss various processing algorithms involved—in particular, the sessionization algorithm and how it can be implemented—and how Impala (or another SQL-on-Hadoop tool) can be used to efficiently perform aggregations over large data sets. Where applicable, we will also discuss the cadence of the automated processes (ingestion, processing, etc.) being run on the data. We will also discuss why each tool was chosen over the alternatives.

Let's go through the aforementioned sections of our design one by one.

Storage

As we discussed in the previous section, our application will take raw data ingested via Flume, perform several steps of transformation, and prepare a cleaned and enriched data set for analysis. To begin this process, we need to decide how to store the raw data, the intermediate results of the transformations, and then the final data set. Because each of these data sets serves a different purpose, we want to make sure our storage decisions—data formats and models—will fit the purpose of the data set.

To start, we will store the raw data ingested via Flume in text format on HDFS. We will use HDFS because the subsequent processing calls for batch transformations across multiple records. As we discussed in previous chapters, HDFS is a better fit for batch operations that need to scan large amounts of data efficiently. We chose text as the file format because it's simple to handle and can be used with any log type without requiring extra processing in Flume.

However, after data is processed, we will be running aggregate queries and analysis on large chunks of data at a time, mostly only on a subset of columns. Analytical queries require scanning at least a day's worth, and often months' worth, of data as efficiently as possible, which means that HDFS is still a good choice. Because many analytical queries only select a subset of columns at a time, a columnar format is a very good choice for storage format for the processed data. Consequently, we use Parquet—a columnar format—for storing the processed (i.e., sessionized) data that will be analyzed later on. We will compress the processed data set with Snappy due to its improved CPU efficiency. For a complete discussion of all possible file and compression formats, and guidelines on how to choose the best file and compression format, please see Chapter 1.

We plan to store the raw data indefinitely, rather than removing it after we are done processing it. This is a common choice for designing Hadoop applications because of several benefits:

- It allows us to reprocess data easily in case of bugs or failures in ETL processing.
- It allows us to analyze the raw data for interesting features we may have neglected to extract into the processed data set. This is also useful in data discovery and exploration in which raw data is explored in the design of the ETL pipeline—in particular, for deciding what features need to be included in the processed data set.
- It is also useful for auditing purposes.

To store the data sets, we are going to use the directory structure introduced in the section "HDFS Schema Design" on page 14. Moreover, because our analysis would be over chunks of at least a day in duration (or a multiple thereof), we decided to partition our click data sets by date where one leaf-level partition corresponds to one day of click data. For click data, here is the directory structure we will use to store raw and processed click data:

/etl/BI/casualcyclist/clicks/rawlogs/year=2014/month=10/day=10
    Raw clicks as they arrive from Flume. This is the *raw* data set.

/data/bikeshop/clickstream/year=2014/month=10/day=10
    Cleaned, sessionized data, ready for analyzing. This is the *processed* data set.

As you see, we use three levels of partitions (year, month, and day) to partition both the data sets by date.

Size of the Processed Data Set

The processed data set is often smaller than that of the raw data set. This is true especially when the processed data set is stored in a more compression-friendly format (e.g., a columnar format like Parquet). Because the processed data set is smaller, the average size of each leaf-level partition (i.e., a partition representing one day of data) may be too small for efficient use of Hadoop. As mentioned in Chapter 1, the average size of each partition should be at least a few multiples of the HDFS block size (the default HDFS block size being 64 MB) to make efficient use of Hadoop's processing capabilities. If you find that the average size of the daily partitions in your processed set is smaller than that, we recommend you get rid of the day partitions in the processed data set and have only year and month as the two levels of partitions. The raw data set can still stay partitioned by year, month, and day.

For the rest of this chapter, we assume that the daily data in the processed data set is large enough to warrant day being a third-level partition column.

Also, oftentimes you will see a single-level partitioning scheme like `dt=2014-10-10` being used instead of the three-level partitioning scheme `year=2014/month=10/day=10`. This alternate one-level partitioning scheme is another valid choice for partitioning the raw and processed data sets and has only one partition column (of type string: `dt`) instead of having three partition columns (of type int: `year`, `month`, and `day`). The one-level partitioning scheme creates fewer total partitions, even though the number of leaf-level partitions remains the same. Fewer number of partitions means less logical metadata about these partitions that needs to be stored in the metastore, which may lead to a small performance gain when you're querying the data set using tools that access metadata like Hive, HCatalog, and Impala. However, the one-level partitioning scheme offers less flexibility with querying the data sets as compared to the three-level partitioning scheme. For example, if you were doing yearly analysis on the data set with three-level partitioning scheme, we could simply use `WHERE year=2014` instead of `WHERE dt LIKE '2014-%'`.

At the end of the day, they are both reasonable partitioning schemes and are used equally. Choosing one over the other is likely more of a matter of preference and style. In this chapter, we will use the three-level partitioning scheme.

Figures 8-2 and 8-3 show the three-level and one-level partition scheme, respectively.

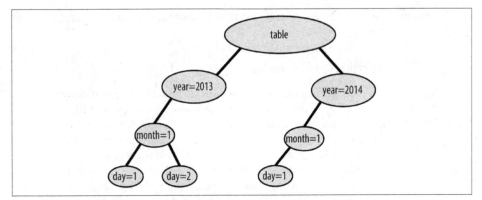

Figure 8-2. Three-level partitioning scheme

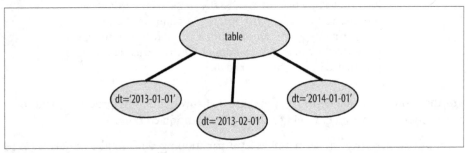

Figure 8-3. One-level partitioning scheme

For a more complete discussion of schema design in HDFS and Hive, please refer to *Programming Hive* (*http://bit.ly/prog-hive*).

Ingestion

As we discussed in Chapter 2, we have several options for getting data into Hadoop. Let's evaluate these options and see how they fit with the requirements for our architecture:

File transfer
> This option is appropriate for one-time transfers of files, but not for reliable ingestion of large volumes of clickstream data.

Sqoop
> Sqoop is an excellent tool for moving data to and from external data stores such as a relational database management system, but it's clearly not a fit for ingesting log data.

Kafka

As we discussed in Chapter 2, Kafka's architecture makes it an excellent solution for reliably moving large volumes of log data from our web servers to various consumers, including HDFS. We'll consider Kafka a strong contender for the ingestion part of our architecture.

Flume

Like Kafka, Flume is also an excellent choice for reliably moving large volumes of event data such as logs into HDFS.

So our top contenders for ingesting our logs are Kafka and Flume. Both provide the reliable, scalable ingestion of log data we require. Because our application only requires ingesting the log data into HDFS, we'll select Flume, because it's purpose-built for HDFS—the built-in components tailored for HDFS mean that we won't have to do any custom development in order to build our Flume pipeline. Flume also supports *interceptors*—the ability to perform small transformations of the data, such as filtering fake clicks from search crawlers, while the data is being ingested and before it is written to Hadoop.

If we needed to build a more general-purpose ingestion pipeline supporting multiple data sinks in addition to HDFS, then we'd likely want to consider Kafka.

Now that we've selected our tool, let's discuss our options for getting data into our Flume pipeline:

- If we're working with a web application written in Java that uses Log4j for logging, we can use the Flume Log4j appender to send data to a Flume Avro source. This is one of the simplest ways to send events to Flume, and requires just the addition of a single file to the application classpath (`flume-ng-sdk-*.jar`) and a few modifications to Log4j properties. Unfortunately, in this case we're working with a third-party application where we may not have access to modify the code, or it may be written in a language other than Java, so the Log4j appender won't be suitable.

- In cases such as this in which the Log4j appender isn't suitable, there are other good options available. You can use the Avro or Thrift sources to send Avro or Thrift messages to Flume. Flume can also pull messages from a JMS queue. Another option is to send JSON messages to the HTTP source. The choice of integration point depends on the frameworks you are using in your application. Having the choice of multiple integration options allows you to use something that works well with your existing infrastructure. For example, if you are already sending events to a JMS queue, it makes sense to integrate Flume with this queue. If you are not already using a JMS queue, there is no need to introduce it just for Flume integration, and you can choose a more convenient option. Again, none of these will be appropriate choices for ingesting logs from disk.

- Flume provides a *syslog source*, which can read events from a syslog stream and convert them into Flume events. Syslog is a standard tool for capturing and moving system logs. The Apache HTTP server has some support for sending log output to syslog, but currently error logs only. We'd need to implement a workaround for the access logs, such as piping them to syslog.

- In our case, because we're working with a third-party application and don't have the flexibility to add clickstream instrumentation into the application itself, and we need to work with logfiles already written to disk, we'll look at Flume's *spooling directory source*. This source will read files from a directory and turn every line into a Flume event. Note that some examples found on the Web show how to use the *exec source* to tail a logfile. This is highly discouraged because it is not a reliable solution. Tail does not track the last place it read, and if the Flume agent crashes it will either read duplicate records or miss them, both of which are, of course, undesirable. By contrast, the spooling directory source will only read complete files, so in case of failure it will retry the entire file and mark files successfully read so they will not be ingested twice. This creates a much more reliable solution for ingesting data from files.

After we've selected the Flume source to get events into our Flume pipeline, we need to consider the appropriate Flume channels throughout our tiers. As we discussed in Chapter 2, the memory channel is the best choice when performance is more important than reliability, and the file channel is recommended when reliability is more important. In this example, reliability is very important. If the memory channel is losing clicks, it is more likely to do so during times of peak activity, leading to potential data loss when your site is under heavy load. We'll therefore use the file channel in all of our Flume tiers.

The choice of the terminal sink is pretty obvious: we want to store the data in HDFS, and will therefore use the HDFS sink. In particular, we will store the data in text format for reasons that will become clear in the processing section. Data will be partitioned by timestamp within our HDFS directories; we'll discuss this in more detail when we dig into the ingestion architecture in a moment. This partitioning by date and time will allow us to minimize disk I/O during processing, making our data processing jobs more efficient.

Now that we've made these architectural decisions for our ingestion layer, let's dig deeper into the architecture of our Flume pipeline. We'll start with a higher-level view, and then we'll drill down into the configuration details of the individual tiers in our ingestion pipeline. Figure 8-4 shows the high-level view of our ingestion workflow. You'll note that we're using the fan-in pattern (as discussed in Chapter 2) in this flow.

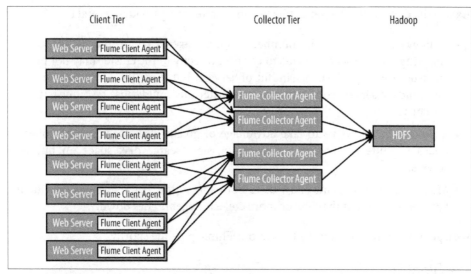

Figure 8-4. High-level view of our Flume ingestion architecture

In this diagram, you'll see that we have three primary tiers in our pipeline:

Client tier

In this example, our client tier is composed of the web servers generating the logs that need to be ingested into HDFS so we can use them for the required analysis. An important thing to note here is that each of our web servers hosts a Flume agent, which is responsible for taking the log events generated by the web server running on that host, and sending them to the collector tier.

Collector tier

These hosts aggregate the events coming from the client tier and pass them on to the final destination, in this case HDFS. In this example, we're assuming the collector agents are running on cluster edge nodes—these are nodes within the cluster network that have a Hadoop client configuration so they can communicate with the Hadoop cluster in order to submit Hadoop commands, write data to HDFS, and so on.

HDFS

This is our terminal destination. The Flume agents on the collector tier will be responsible for persisting the events to files in HDFS. As part of this persistence, the Flume agents are configured to ensure the files are partitioned and named appropriately on disk.

In this configuration, our Flume agents run on the web servers and collector tiers—note that we don't run a Flume agent on HDFS, but instead the agents on the collector tier leverage the Hadoop client to write the events to HDFS.

As we talked about in Chapter 2, this fan-in architecture provides several benefits:

- It allows us to control the number of Flume agents connecting to the cluster. Allowing the web server agents to connect directly to the cluster may not present an issue if we only have a handful of servers, but if we have hundreds or even thousands of servers connecting to our cluster this could cause resource issues on the cluster.

- It potentially allows us to take advantage of greater disk space on the collector nodes to buffer events, and preserve possibly scarce disk space on our web servers.

- Multiple collector agents allow us to both spread the load as well as provide for failover in the event that one or more collector agents goes down.

We'll get into more detail on the tiers in our Flume pipeline shortly.

The Client Tier

Figure 8-5 shows the details of our client-tier Flume agents.

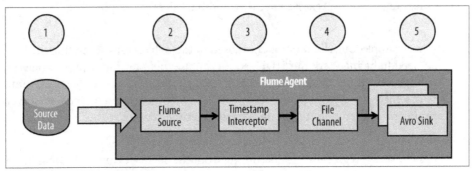

Figure 8-5. Client-tier detail

The following list describes the individual components in the client agents:

Source data
> This is the incoming events to our Flume pipeline, in this case Apache log records. As mentioned, for purposes of this example we're using the spooling directory source, so in this case our source data will be pulled from a specific directory on each web server host.

Flume source
> This is the spooling directory source, which will read files for ingestion from a directory on disk, convert them into events, and then rename logs when processing is completed.

Timestamp interceptor

This interceptor simply inserts a timestamp into the header of each of our Flume events. We'll use this timestamp downstream in the HDFS sink in order to partition the resulting files in HDFS by date.

Channel

We use a file channel here for maximum durability.

Avro sinks

The Avro sinks, in combination with Avro sources, provide the serialization mechanism to transmit our events between Flume tiers. The important thing to note here is that we're configuring multiple sinks to provide the failover functionality that we spoke about earlier, using a load balancing sink group processor to spread the load across all available sinks.

 Our choice of the Flume Avro source has little to do with the format that the data will be stored on HDFS, via the HDFS sink. As mentioned in Chapter 1, Avro is a serialization format that can be used when we're transferring data from one process or another or when storing data on a filesystem, say HDFS. In this case, the Avro sinks and sources are just acting as a serialization mechanism to move our event data over the wire. The format of the click data stored in HDFS will be determined by the terminal Flume sink.

The following shows an example Flume configuration file for the client Flume agents. This configuration would be deployed on all of our web servers:

```
# Define spooling directory source:
client.sources=r1
client.sources.r1.channels=ch1
client.sources.r1.type=spooldir
client.sources.r1.spoolDir=/opt/weblogs
# Use the Timestamp interceptor to add a timestamp to all event headers:
client.sources.r1.interceptors.i1.type=timestamp
client.sources.r1.interceptors=i1
# Define a file channel:
client.channels=ch1
client.channels.ch1.type=FILE
# Define two Avro sinks:
client.sinks=k1 k2
client.sinks.k1.type=avro
client.sinks.k1.hostname=collector1.hadoopapplicationarch.com
# Compress data before sending across the wire:
client.sinks.k1.compression-type=deflate
client.sinks.k1.port=4141
client.sinks.k2.type=avro
client.sinks.k2.hostname=collector2.hadoopapplicationarch.com
client.sinks.k2.port=4141
```

```
client.sinks.k2.compression-type=deflate
client.sinks.k1.channel=ch1
client.sinks.k2.channel=ch1
# Define a load balancing sink group to spread load over multiple collectors:
client.sinkgroups=g1
client.sinkgroups.g1.sinks=k1 k2
client.sinkgroups.g1.processor.type=load_balance
client.sinkgroups.g1.processor.selector=round_robin
client.sinkgroups.g1.processor.backoff=true
```

The Collector Tier

Figure 8-6 shows the details of our collector tier Flume agents.

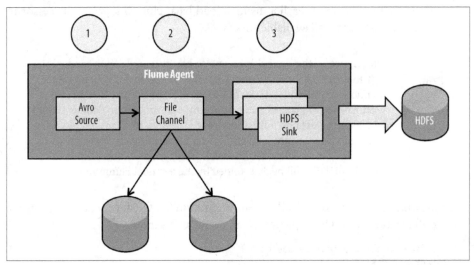

Figure 8-6. Collector tier detail

Following are the descriptions of the components in our collector-tier agents:

Avro source
> As we noted in the discussion of the Avro sink, this provides the other end of our serialization hop from the client tier to the collector tier.

Channel
> Here again, we use a file channel to ensure the reliability of event delivery. To further increase reliability, note that we take advantage of multiple disks on the edge nodes, as discussed in Chapter 2.

HDFS sink
> This is the end of the line for our Flume pipeline; this is where we're taking the log events and persisting them to HDFS. Some things to note in the configuration of the HDFS sink are the use of the hdfs.path, hdfs.filePrefix, and

`hdfs.fileSuffix` parameters to partition the resulting files by date, with a defined filename. With the parameters shown in the upcoming configuration, our resulting files will be written to a path that looks like *weblogs/access/YEAR/ MONTH/DAY/access.EPOCH_TIMESTAMP.log*. Also, note that we're writing the files as plain text using the `hdfs.fileType=DataStream` and `hdfs.writeFor mat=Text` parameters to the HDFS sink.

The following shows what our configuration file for the collector agents looks like. In our architecture, this configuration will be deployed to each of our edge nodes that's part of the collector tier:

```
# Define an Avro source:
collector.sources=r1
collector.sources.r1.type=avro
collector.sources.r1.bind=0.0.0.0
collector.sources.r1.port=4141
collector.sources.r1.channels=ch1
# Decompress the incoming data:
collector1.sources.r1.compression-type=deflate
# Define a file channel using multiple disks for reliability:
collector.channels=ch1
collector.channels.ch1.type=FILE
collector.channels.ch1.checkpointDir=/opt/flume/ch1/cp1,/opt/flume/ch1/cp2
collector.channels.ch1.dataDirs=/opt/flume/ch1/data1,/opt/flume/ch1/data2
# Define HDFS sinks to persist events to disk as text.
# Note the use of multiple sinks to spread the load:
collector.sinks=k1 k2
collector.sinks.k1.type=hdfs
collector.sinks.k1.channel=ch1
# Partition files by date:
collector.sinks.k1.hdfs.path=/weblogs/combined/%Y/%m/%d
collector.sinks.k1.hdfs.filePrefix=combined
collector.sinks.k1.hdfs.fileSuffix=.log
collector.sinks.k1.hdfs.fileType=DataStream
collector.sinks.k1.hdfs.writeFormat=Text
collector.sinks.k1.hdfs.batchSize=10000
# Roll HDFS files every 10000 events or 30 seconds:
collector.sinks.k1.hdfs.rollCount=10000
collector.sinks.k1.hdfs.rollSize=0
collector.sinks.k1.hdfs.rollInterval=30
collector.sinks.k2.type=hdfs
collector.sinks.k2.channel=ch1
# Partition files by date:
collector.sinks.k2.hdfs.path=/weblogs/combined/%Y/%m/%d
collector.sinks.k2.hdfs.filePrefix=combined
collector.sinks.k2.hdfs.fileSuffix=.log
collector.sinks.k2.hdfs.fileType=DataStream
collector.sinks.k2.hdfs.writeFormat=Text
collector.sinks.k2.hdfs.batchSize=10000
collector.sinks.k2.hdfs.rollCount=10000
collector.sinks.k2.hdfs.rollSize=0
```

```
collector.sinks.k2.hdfs.rollInterval=30
collector.sinkgroups=g1
collector.sinkgroups.g1.sinks=k1 k2
collector.sinkgroups.g1.processor.type=load_balance
collector.sinkgroups.g1.processor.selector=round_robin
collector.sinkgroups.g1.processor.backoff=true
```

Before wrapping up the discussion of data ingestion, let's talk about ingesting secondary data into Hadoop. If you are joining click data with data from CRM, ODS, or similar systems, you would need to ingest data from secondary data sources into Hadoop. While the exact choice of ingestion method would depend on what these data sources look like in your organization, in this chapter we will assume they are traditional relational databases. As discussed in Chapter 2, Sqoop is the best choice for transferring data from relational databases into Hadoop. CRM and ODS data sets are very small compared to the click data and don't grow (or change) as fast as click data. This makes them ideal candidates for a batch Sqoop job, say once a day or several times a day, to import the data from CRM and ODS databases into Hadoop. If these data sets are small enough, it may make sense to simply delete and re-create them on every Sqoop job. However, if they're big enough, an incremental Sqoop import would make more sense.

Processing

Figure 8-7 shows the processing section of the architecture.

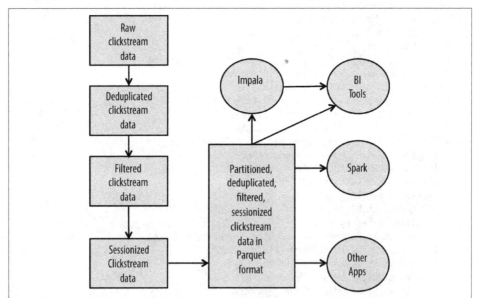

Figure 8-7. Processing design

As explained in the previous section, the click data is ingested into HDFS via Flume. However, this is *raw* data from the web servers that needs to be cleaned up. For example, we may need to remove incomplete and invalid log lines. Furthermore, there may be some log lines that have been duplicated that you will have to deduplicate. Then, we may also need to sessionize this data (i.e., assign unique session IDs to each of the clicks). We may also decide to do some further preaggregations or pre-analysis on the data. This may include doing daily or hourly aggregates/roll-ups on the clicks for faster querying later on, performing marketing ROI or attribution analysis by joining the data with your marketing spend data, or joining click data with your CRM or other data sources so you can analyze your website activity based on additional attributes from those data sources. Essentially any processing that you don't want to be done on the fly when running your interactive BI queries will fall into this category of preprocessing. Finally, we want the processed data to be in a format that can be queried in a performant manner.

Therefore, to summarize, we have the following four goals for the processing pipeline:

1. *Sanitize* and clean up the raw data.
2. *Extract* the interesting data from the raw clickstream events.
3. *Transform* the extracted data to create processed data set(s). In our example, we will create a sessionized data set.
4. *Load* (i.e., store) the results in a data format in Hadoop that supports high-performance querying.

As you might have noticed, barring the preliminary sanitization step, the other three steps represent each of the extract, transform, and load steps of an ETL pipeline, thereby illustrating Hadoop's use as an ETL tool replacement.

For the sanitization step, first we need to remove incomplete and invalid log lines. This can be simple logic written either in MapReduce or with tools like Hive or Pig to ensure that each record (i.e., log line) has all the fields and optionally does some quick validation on a few or all the fields. This is also where you could add logic to ignore any clicks that you believe are from spam bots by checking for particular IP addresses or referrers.

Then, we also need logic for deduplicating the log lines. This is because we are using Flume's file channel for ingesting logs. In the rare event of a Flume agent crash, Flume guarantees that all the log records being ingested will end up in Hadoop. However, there is no guarantee that each of these records would be stored exactly once. In the case of a Flume agent crash, you may end up with some of the log records duplicated, hence the need for deduplicating them. You will learn more about deduplication in the section "Data Deduplication" on page 270.

Hive, Pig, Spark, and MapReduce are candidates for tools for deduplicating data. Since both Hive and Pig are higher-level languages, they allow for a simpler and more readable implementation than MapReduce. Therefore, we recommend using Hive or Pig for implementing deduplication; both are reasonable choices. The main considerations for choosing between the two will be the developer skill set, fit with other technologies used by the team, or any other specific project requirements. Regardless of the language, we recommend writing the deduplicated data into a temporary table and then moving it to a final table, to avoid clobbering the original data set.

For the extract step, we will extract the timestamp (in seconds since epoch), the referrer address, user agent string (containing browser and operating system version), IP address, language, and the URL. We chose these fields because we think they are sufficient for doing the analysis presented by the questions earlier in the chapter. You may decide to simply extract all fields without filtering any, if your subsequent analysis may use all of them.

For the transform step, we will perform sessionization of the clicks and create a new sessionized data set. You will learn more about sessionization in the section "Sessionization" on page 272.

For secondary data like ODS or CRM data, you may not need to sanitize it since the data coming from relational databases has already been cleaned before it was ingested there. Consequently, you may be able to directly ingest it into a queryable location on HDFS. The directory structure could look like:

- */data/bikeshop/ods*: data from ODS
- */data/bikeshop/crm*: data from CRM

Also, there is typically no need to partition the secondary data since it's usually much smaller in size.

Now that you have an overview of all the processing steps required, let's look in detail at how we will implement two of those steps: deduplication and sessionization.

Data Deduplication

As explained, in the case of a Flume agent crash, you may see some of the log records duplicated.

Hive, Pig, and MapReduce are good candidates for deduplicating data. As we've mentioned, because both Hive and Pig are higher-level languages, they allow for a simpler and more readable implementation than MapReduce, and are therefore our tools of choice. Hive requires creating an external table for the source raw data and another table for storing the deduplicated data on which further processing will be done. Pig, on the other hand, doesn't require creating extra tables for writing the deduplicated data. Again, the choice between Hive and Pig will be determined by the developer skill set, fit with other technologies used by the team, or any other specific project requirements.

Deduplication in Hive

Here is some example code performing deduplication of clicks in Hive and inserting into a daily partition:

```
INSERT INTO table $deduped_log
SELECT
  ip,
  ts,
  url,
  referrer,
  user_agent,
  YEAR(FROM_UNIXTIME(unix_ts)) year,
  MONTH(FROM_UNIXTIME(unix_ts)) month
FROM (
  SELECT
    ip,
    ts,
    url,
    referrer,
    user_agent,
    UNIX_TIMESTAMP(ts,'dd/MMM/yyyy:HH:mm:ss') unix_ts
  FROM
    $raw_log
  WHERE
    year=${YEAR} AND
    month=${MONTH} AND
    day=${DAY}
  GROUP BY
    ip,
    ts,
    url,
    referrer,
    user_agent,
    UNIX_TIMESTAMP(ts,'dd/MMM/yyyy:HH:mm:ss')
) t;
```

Other than extracting the month and day information for the partitioning, notice that the only operation we do here is to group the data set by all its columns. If two rows are duplicated, they will be identical in all their columns, and after the GROUP BY operation we will be left with a single copy.

Deduplication in Pig

Deduplicating in Pig is very straight forward and requires little explanation:

```
rawlogs = LOAD '$raw_log_dir';
dedupedlogs = DISTINCT rawlogs;
STORE dedupedlogs INTO '$deduped_log_dir' USING PigStorage();
```

Sessionization

An important part of clickstream analysis is to group clicks made by a single user in a single visit by associating a session ID that represents that visit to each click made as a part of the visit. This process is known as sessionization.

You can then analyze these sessions to figure out what people are doing on your website during a visit: are they buying things, how are their visits being initiated (e.g., organic search, paid search, links on partner websites). Some tools and marketing analysts use the terms *session* and *visit* interchangeably.

Sessionization can be done by the web server itself, in which case it assigns a session ID to each of the clicks, representing which session a click is a part of. However, if this session ID is not reliable or if you want to use your own custom logic to sessionize clicks, you can write your own sessionization algorithm.

In order to perform sessionization, you have to figure out two things:

- Given a list of clicks, determine which clicks came from the same user. It is tough to gauge which clicks came from the same user just by looking at the information in the clicks. Some websites drop cookies on their users' browsers when they visit the website (or an affiliate site) for the first time. These cookies are logged in the web server logs, which can then be used to identify clicks from the same user. Keep in mind that cookies are not 100% reliable since users may delete their cookies often, even in the middle of a visit. Alternatively, or if the cookies are not present, IP addresses can be used to identify clicks that came from the same user. IP addresses, like cookies, are not 100% reliable either, because many companies use network address translators to share IPs between multiple workstations and therefore multiple users may be treated as one user. Your application may take additional parameters, such as the user agent and language, into account to differentiate between such users. In our design, we simply use IP address to identify clicks from the same user.

- Given a particular user's clicks, determine if a given click is a part of a new visit to the website or a continuation of the previous visit. If a user has three consecutive clicks within five minutes of each other, it's reasonable to say that the clicks were all part of the same browsing session. However, if first two clicks were within five minutes of each other while the third one came an hour later, it is reasonable to assume that the third click was a part of a separate visit from the user and hence a separate session. Most marketing analytics tools consider a click to be a part of a new session if more than 30 minutes has elapsed since the last click from the same user. Also, in our implementation, and as is the case with many marketing analytics tools, we consider all sessions terminated at the end of the day. Doing so leads to a slight margin of error, but it's very well worth the simplicity. For example, we could resessionize the data for a particular day, without it impacting the sessionization of any of the days before or after the day in question. It also makes the implementation of the sessionization process much simpler.

In this section, we show examples of implementing sessionization using various tools. MapReduce, Hive, Pig, Spark, MapReduce, Impala, and many other tools in the Hadoop ecosystem are good choices for performing sessionization, and Chapter 3 discusses them in depth. You will typically only use one of these options for sessionization. Since nearly every framework used in Hadoop will be a good fit here, the main considerations for choosing the right tool for your workload are developer skill set, fit with other technologies used by the team, or other specific project or performance requirements.

In general, any sessionization algorithm will have to perform the following steps:

1. Go over the data set and for each click, extract the relevant columns as we discussed earlier (IP address in our case, cookies if you choose to).

2. Collect all the events for a single user for a given day into a sequence, and sort that sequence by timestamp.

3. Go over the sequence for each user, and assign a session ID for each click event. Increment the session ID every time there is more than 30 minutes between consecutive clicks.

Now, let's see how each of these steps can be performed in various tools.

Sessionization in Spark

Spark is a new execution engine on Hadoop, which, in general, performs much better than MapReduce. We will create an RDD from the click data on HDFS. A map() function will be used to extract the important fields for each click, returning a key-value pair with the IP address as the key and an object with the extracted log fields as the value (step 1). Here is the sample code for that function:

```
JavaRDD < String > dataSet =
  (args.length == 2) ? jsc.textFile(args[1]) : jsc.parallelize(testLines);

JavaPairRDD<String,SerializableLogLine> parsed =
  dataSet.map(new PairFunction<String, String, SerializableLogLine>() {
    @Override
    public Tuple2<String, SerializableLogLine> call(String s)
      throws Exception {
        return new Tuple2<String,SerializableLogLine>(getIP(s),getFields(s));
      }
});
```

Then, we will group all the clicks that belong to the same IP address, sort them by timestamp (step 2), and use the `sessionize()` function to go over the sorted list of clicks and associate a session ID to each click (step 3). Here is the code for these steps:

```
// Sessionize function - take a sequence of events from one IP,
// sort by timestamp and mark all events less than 30 minutes apart as a session
public static List<SerializableLogLine> sessionize
        (Iterable<SerializableLogLine> lines) {
    List<SerializableLogLine> sessionizedLines = Lists.newArrayList(lines);
    Collections.sort(sessionizedLines);
    int sessionId = 0;
    sessionizedLines.get(0).setSessionid(sessionId);
    for (int i = 1; i < sessionizedLines.size(); i++) {
        SerializableLogLine thisLine = sessionizedLines.get(i);
        SerializableLogLine prevLine = sessionizedLines.get(i - 1);

        if (thisLine.getTimestamp() - prevLine.getTimestamp() > 30 * 60 * 1000) {
            sessionId++;
        }
        thisLine.setSessionid(sessionId);
    }

    return sessionizedLines;
    }

// This groups clicks by IP address
JavaPairRDD<String,List<SerializableLogLine>> grouped = parsed.groupByKey();

JavaPairRDD<String, Iterable<SerializableLogLine>> sessionized =
        grouped.mapValues(new Function<Iterable<SerializableLogLine>,
                Iterable<SerializableLogLine>>() {
@Override
public Iterable<SerializableLogLine> call
        (Iterable<SerializableLogLine> logLines) throws
        Exception {
    return sessionize(logLines);
    }
});
```

You can find the complete code for doing sessionization in Spark in this book's Git-Hub repository.

Sessionization in MapReduce

Sessionizing in MapReduce allows for a bit more control over code. The `map()` function will extract the relevant fields from the clicks (step 1, in the list of steps listed earlier). The `shuffle()` function will collect and group all events on a per-user basis, and we can use a custom comparator to sort the list of clicks by timestamp before it goes to the reducers (step 2). The `reduce()` function will then go over the list of sorted clicks per user and assign a session ID (step 3).

You can find the complete code for doing sessionization in MapReduce in this book's GitHub repository.

Sessionization in Pig

The popular DataFu library in Pig contains a `Sessionize` function. The `Session ize()` function expects as input a list of records belonging to a given user on a given day, where the first field of the each record is the timestamp and the list of clicks is sorted in ascending order of timestamps. The output of the `Sessionize()` function is a list of click records, with a session ID added to each record.

Sessionization in Hive

Although it is possible to do sessionization in pure SQL with the use of analytical (windowing) functions, the resulting query is challenging to maintain and debug. We don't recommend using Hive or Impala for this processing task.

Analyzing

After we have ingested and processed the data, we are ready to analyze it to find the answers to the questions we presented earlier in the chapter. There are several tools used by business analysts to explore and analyze data. We covered them in much detail in Chapter 3, but to recap, such tools can be divided into the following categories:

- Visualization and BI tools, such as Tableau and MicroStrategy
- Statistical analysis tools, such as R or Python
- Advanced analysis for machine learning, such as Mahout or Spark MLlib
- SQL—through Impala, for example

In our design, we will focus on SQL queries via Impala for accessing and analyzing the processed data.

For example, to answer how much time, on average, shoppers spend on your website, you can run a query like:

```
SELECT
  AVG(session_length)/60 avg_min
FROM (
  SELECT
    MAX(ts) - MIN(ts) session_length_in_sec
  FROM
    apache_log_parquet
  GROUP BY
    session_id
  ) t
```

You can find the *bounce rate* of your website—that is, the percentage of users who leave the website without visiting any other page except the one they landed on—using a query like:

```
SELECT
  (SUM(CASE WHEN count!=1 THEN 0 ELSE 1 END))*100/(COUNT(*)) bounce_rate
FROM (
  SELECT
    session_id,
    COUNT(*) count
  FROM
    apache_log_parquet
  GROUP BY
    session_id)t;
```

We can also connect Impala to a BI tool (for example, MicroStrategy or Tableau) via Impala's ODBC or JDBC drivers to perform further BI queries on the click data.

Orchestration

We have gone through how data will be ingested into Hadoop, the various kinds of processing we will do on the clickstream data, and how the processed data can be analyzed by the end users. The final data analysis happens on an ad hoc basis; however, the prior steps—ingestion and the various processing actions on the data—need to be automated, scheduled, and orchestrated. In this section, we will show you for how to orchestrate the various steps involved in doing clickstream analysis with Hadoop.

For ingestion, we'll use Flume to continuously stream the click data into the system. For processing, on the other hand, we decided to run the sessionization algorithm every day, because it's common to terminate all sessions at the end of the day. We decided running the sessionization algorithm once a day was a good trade-off between the latency and complexity of the sessionization algorithm. If we were to run the sessionization algorithm more frequently, it would require maintaining a list of running sessions throughout the day (because sessions can be arbitrarily long), making the algorithm more complicated. This is too slow for a near-real-time system, but not every system needs to be real time. Chapter 9 will show the details of how to create a near-real-time analysis system, and many of the techniques shown in Chapter 9 can be applied to clickstream analysis, if you desire.

To orchestrate the sessionization process, we will use Oozie as discussed in Chapter 6.

In our case, the Oozie workflow will do some pre-processing and then sessionization. Here's an example of the Oozie workflow, triggering deduplication using Pig, followed by sessionization in MapReduce:

```
<workflow-app xmlns="uri:oozie:workflow:0.4" name="process-clickstream-data-wf">
  <global>
```

```
    <job-tracker>${jobTracker}</job-tracker>
    <name-node>${nameNode}</name-node>
</global>
<start to="dedup"/>
<action name="dedup">
  <pig>
    <prepare>
      <delete path="${dedupPath}"/>
    </prepare>
    <script>dedup.pig</script>
    <argument>-param</argument>
    <argument>raw_log_dir='${wfInput}'</argument>
    <argument>-param</argument>
    <argument>deduped_log_dir='${dedupPath}'</argument>
  </pig>
  <ok to="sessionize"/>
  <error to="fail"/>
</action>

<action name="sessionize">
<java>
  <prepare>
    <delete path="${sessionPath}"/>
  </prepare>
  <main-class>com.hadooparchitecturebook.MRSessionize</main-class>
  <arg>${dedupPath}</arg>
  <arg>${sessionPath}</arg>
</java>
<ok to="end"/>
<error to="fail"/>
</action>

<kill name="fail">
  <message>Workflow failed:[${wf:errorMessage(wf:lastErrorNode())}]</message>
</kill>
<end name="end"/>

</workflow-app>
```

Notice that we are passing the parameters year, month, and day to populate the dedup
Path variable which contains the exact date for which we are sessionizing the clicks.
These parameters are generated by a coordinator job, which will also be responsible
for scheduling the workflow.

In our design, the coordinator triggers the workflow every day, during which it processes the data of the previous day. We need to ensure that all the data for the previous day has been collected before we start to sessionize it. Having such
synchronization before processing is a fairly common orchestration design pattern. It
avoids inconsistencies that can happen if we start to process data from the current
day while it is still being populated.

There are two common ways to achieve such synchronization:

- You can validate that Flume has started writing the data for the current day before kicking off the processing workflow.
- Alternatively, you can have Oozie wait until a file indicating that the data set finished arriving appears. This indicator flag is usually named _SUCCESS and indicates that the entire data set arrived successfully and that processing can begin. The coordinator supports rules that hold off the scheduled workflows until such a file appears in the designated directory (using the <done-flag> option).

In our design it's tough to make Flume provide us with an indicator file. It's easier to check to see if the current day's data has begun being written by simply checking for the existence of current day's partition. Therefore, it makes sense to go with the first option, which is depicted by the following coordinator code (you can see the non-truncated code in this book's repo):

```
<coordinator-app name="prepare-clickstream" frequency="${coord:days(1)}"
                 start="${jobStart}" end="${jobEnd}"
                 timezone="UTC"
                 xmlns="uri:oozie:coordinator:0.1">

  <datasets>
    <dataset name="rawlogs" frequency="${coord:days(1)}"
             initial-instance="${initialDataset}" timezone="America/Los_Angeles">
      <uri-template>/etl/BI/casualcyclist/clicks/rawlogs/year=${YEAR}/...
      <done-flag></done-flag>
    </dataset>
  </datasets>

  <input-events>
    <data-in name="input" dataset="rawlogs">
      <instance>${coord:current(0)}</instance>
    </data-in>
    <data-in name="readyIndicator" dataset="rawlogs">
      <!-- Since Flume doesn't set a readyness flag when it finishes writing
           to a directory we can just use the next directory as an input event,
           which instructs Oozie not to kick off a coordinator
           action until the next day of data starts being available. -->
      <instance>${coord:current(1)}</instance>
    </data-in>
  </input-events>

  <action>
    <workflow>
      <app-path>${workflowRoot}/processing.xml</app-path>
      <configuration>
        <property>
          <name>wfInput</name>
          <value>${coord:dataIn('input')}</value>
```

```
        </property>
        <property>
          <name>wfYear</name>
          <value>${coord:formatTime(coord:dateOffset(
          coord:nominalTime(), tzOffset, 'HOUR'), 'yyyy')}</value>
        </property>
        <property>
          <name>wfMonth</name>
          <value>${coord:formatTime(coord:dateOffset(
          coord:nominalTime(), tzOffset, 'HOUR'), 'MM')}</value>
        </property>
        <property>
          <name>wfDay</name>
          <value>${coord:formatTime(coord:dateOffset(
          coord:nominalTime(), tzOffset, 'HOUR'), 'dd')}</value>
        </property>
      </configuration>
    </workflow>
  </action>
</coordinator-app>
```

As you'll notice above, the `readyIndicator` instructs Oozie not to kick off the workflow until the next day of data starts being available, which, in turn, means that the
previous day's data has been fully ingested.

Conclusion

In this chapter, we walked through a very common Hadoop use case: analyzing
machine-generated data in batch mode. Hadoop is particularly good for such a use
case because of the sheer volume of data involved, the high velocity at which it
arrives, and the diversity of all the data that needs to be stored and processed.

In our architecture, we ingested the click data via Flume, and data sets from secondary data sources like CRM or ODS via Sqoop. We then discussed the different kinds
of processing that are usually done on click data. These include deduplication, filtering, and, most important, sessionization. We also illustrated how each of these processing needs can be solved in various execution engines available in the ecosystem.
Then, we showed several analytics queries, like finding the bounce rate of a website,
that you can do using the data sets stored in Hadoop. Finally, we demonstrated how
the entire workflow can be orchestrated through an orchestration tool like Oozie.

While this architecture was batch-oriented, an alternative architecture might perform
clickstream analytics in near-real-time and store the live stats in a no-SQL system like
HBase. Such an implementation is not discussed in this chapter; however, you can see
some sample architecture and code for such an implementation on the book's GitHub
repository (*http://bit.ly/haa-session*).

While this use case may not apply to you word for word, it's similar to other machine-data-processing use cases on Hadoop, and we hope that it connects the dots in helping you design your Hadoop applications.

## CHAPTER 9

Fraud Detection

What is fraud detection? Well, yes, it's a multibillion-dollar industry that touches every company with significant amounts of money to lose, but what is fraud detection *at its heart*? For the purpose of our discussion, we can view fraud detection as making a decision based on whether an actor (human or machine) is behaving as it should. There are two different points here: 1) knowing the difference between normal and abnormal behavior, and 2) being able to act on that knowledge.

An easy example to illustrate the first point is parents knowing when their child is telling a lie or hiding something. If you are a parent, you know how it is: you see your child every day and you know his normal behaviors and patterns. If one day he's a little quieter than normal or trying to avoid eye contact, your instincts kick in and you start asking questions until you find out he failed a test, got into a fight with a friend, or got bullied at school. You were able to detect the deception because of your close relationship and knowledge of your child. That close relationship is key to detecting changes in well-established patterns.

Continuous Improvement

Now, our example will rarely end in your child stealing millions from a bank or getting involved in money laundering, but, like the actors in those examples, the child is trying to hide something. Just as your child becomes better at deception as he grows older, scammers and hackers become more sophisticated as time goes on.

As humans we have different levels for processing new information and making decisions. For simplicity we'll break this into two different groups of processing: background processing and quick reactions. Background processing is useful for learning and improving our process, while quick reactions are used when we're taking action based on the existing process.

In our example, background processing is learning the normal behavior of our child: you do that by observing your child over time. It can happen consciously or unconsciously while you engage in activities with your child, or afterward in a retrospective way. This is where we will be reviewing our child's behavior and essentially building a profile of our child's normal behavior. Generally, it's this deeper review of events, typically done offline, where new insights are discovered.

A more relevant example of this is how credit card scammers have gotten better through the years. First, the credit card thieves would steal one or more credit card numbers and start buying things. After a while the card company would flag the card and find the thieves if they continued to use the card. The thieves adapted to only use the card a couple of times in a single, short burst. This worked for a while until banks developed new algorithms designed to detect those outliers from the original cardholders' normal behavior. Now, the card thieves have the power of computers and the Internet to make microtransactions that can make the fraudulent behavior even harder to detect. Consider scammers firing off microtransactions across many users. This approach can affect what is perceived as normal behavior for the actor, which hinders the ability to isolate it as something abnormal.

Getting back to our parenting example, to know one child or even a couple of children is totally different (in terms of scale) from knowing billions of actors like credit card holders, shoppers, bank account owners, video game players, or fans. This is where Hadoop provides valuable services by offering enough space to store all the information we need for all those actors, and the processing power to review all of that information and act on it.

Taking Action

Based on this background processing, we are ready to act when something seems a bit odd. The quick reaction in this scenario is the observation that your child is quieter than normal or is avoiding eye contact; this triggers your instinct that there may be something off. However, this quick reaction processing can only happen if you know the normal behavior to expect from your child. This allows us, the parents, to match the child's actions against this profile and react quickly, if and when it's necessary to detect that something's off.

It can be interesting to consider that successful fraud detection systems are modeled after our understanding of how the brain learns and reacts: the fraud detection system has to be able to react quickly and make tiny updates to its reactions based on incoming data, but offline processes are needed to find that insight. It's these insights that may change the rules that are firing in the fast reaction stage or uncover new patterns to which to react.

We've been talking about credit card transaction fraud in this discussion, but it should be noted that fraud detection cuts across industries and domains. As we noted before, any business for which there is something to gain by cheating is at risk. In the upcoming case study discussion, we use the example of a fraud detection system that can be used by a bank or a credit card company to detect fraud on a customer's account. However, similar architecture would apply fraud detection applications as well—for example, detecting fraud in trading currencies or goods in a massively multiplayer online game (MMOG).

Architectural Requirements of Fraud Detection Systems

Fraud detection systems are different than many other Hadoop use cases because they include the quick reaction component. A clickstream analysis system or a data warehouse may need to process billions of events, but it can take hours to do so. Fraud detection systems must respond to events in few milliseconds and be utterly reliable —all this in addition to handling millions of transactions per second and running large-scale data analysis in the background. The Hadoop ecosystem provides real-time components (such as Flume, Kafka, and HBase), near-real-time components (such as Spark Streaming), and Search components that can be used for background processing and analysis (such as Spark, Hive, and Impala).

Introducing Our Use Case

To help you understand the fraud detection architecture, we've created a simple example that implements fraud detection as it pertains to a bank account or a credit card.

The goal of the fraud detection in this example is to review a new transaction that comes in. If the transaction is a given multiple larger than the user's normal transaction amount per day, it will be flagged. The system will also check to see if the user location is different from the user's last 20 locations. If this is a web transaction system, this would mean checking the IP address against that of the user's last 20 logins. If it's from a physical point-of-sale system, that would mean checking the user's geographic location (say, city) against the user's last 20 locations and basing the decision on proximity. If the transaction originates from a new location (online or otherwise), the threshold of the amount over the average transaction value may be lowered further.

This is a simple example that uses a single profile table to hold information about account holders. It implements a simple local caching layer and uses HBase for the backend persistence. Although this is a simple use case, it should provide you with an understanding of how Hadoop is used to provide a solution for fraud detection as well as a concrete example of near-real-time processing on Hadoop.

Broad Relevance of Anomaly Detection Techniques

Note that we started the discussion by defining fraud detection as "making a decision based on whether an actor (human or machine) is behaving as it should." The ability to differentiate normal and abnormal events is also called *anomaly detection* or *outlier detection* and has wide implications in many industries, in addition to preventing financial fraud. The same techniques shown in this chapter can be used to detect intrusion into secure networks, early warning signs of failures in machines, customers who may abandon a service in order to retain them in time, or patients who go "doctor shopping"—an early indicator of a possible drug-abuse problem. No matter what industry you are in, anomaly detection is one of the most useful data analysis techniques in your arsenal.

High-Level Design

So, how can Hadoop help us implement such a system? There are a number of ways to build this system, but we'll start with a general design and then dig into different options for the components in order to demonstrate how the overall design can be tuned for specific use cases.

Figure 9-1 provides a high-level view of our system. There's a lot going on in this diagram, so let's break it up and take it piece by piece:

- Starting from the upper-left side, we have the client. In our example, the client is a web service responsible for receiving requests for credit card transactions and responding with an approval or rejection. There are multiple boxes because the web service could be distributed across multiple servers.

- To approve a transaction, the web service may retrieve the user's profile and transaction history from HBase. It also needs to record the current transaction in HBase as part of the user's history.

- The transaction, the decision on whether it was approved or rejected, and the reasons for the decision are sent to HDFS through Flume.

- When the data is in HDFS, it can be automatically processed by a near-real-time processing framework such as Spark or Spark Streaming. Spark Streaming can also process data directly from Flume. NRT processing can detect trends and events unfolding over a few minutes that you would not be able to see by inspecting each transaction in isolation (for example, suspicious activity across multiple users in the same geographical region or same retailer). The NRT process can then automatically update the profiles in HBase accordingly.

- The data can also be explored and analyzed by humans, using tools such as Impala, Spark, and MapReduce. They can discover additional behavior patterns and update both the client logic and the information in HBase.

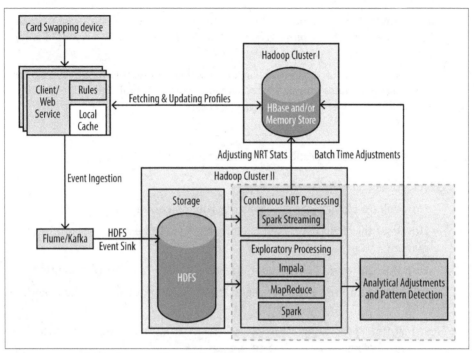

Figure 9-1. High-level view of fraud detection system

In this chapter, we will cover the architecture of the client, the HBase schema design, and the Flume-based ingestion framework in detail. We will give some suggestions regarding near-real-time processing and exploratory analysis, but specific machine-learning algorithms are outside the scope of this book.

Recommended Machine Learning Resources

Knowledge of machine-learning algorithms is obviously useful for anyone serious about implementing a fraud detection system. Here are some resources to help you get started:

- For an amusing and educational approach to data analysis, we recommend Analytics Made Skeezy (*http://analyticsmadeskeezy.com/*), a blog that explains essential methods and algorithms with an entertaining narrative about shady criminals.

- For a practical approach to machine learning, we recommend *Algorithms of the Intelligent Web* by Douglas G. McIlwraith, et al. (Manning), a book that explains the algorithms that power popular websites with easy-to-follow Java implementations.

- If you are looking for a practical introduction and prefer Python to Java, Sarah Guido's upcoming book *Introduction to Machine Learning with Python* (O'Reilly) is recommended.

- For a more in-depth theoretical background that still doesn't require a PhD in mathematics to understand, we recommend Stuart Russell and Peter Norvig's *Artificial Intelligence: A Modern Approach* (Pearson).

Here is a list of the high-level subsections we are going to drill into:

- Client architecture:
  — How will the client make decisions regarding incoming events?
  — How does the client use HBase to store, retrieve, and update user profile information?
  — How does the client deliver the transaction status to additional systems?
- Ingest: How do we use Flume to ingest the transaction data from the client into HDFS?
- Near-real-time processing: How do we learn from incoming data with low-latency processing?
- Background processing, reviewing, and adjustments: How do we learn from all our data and improve the process?

Although there are other solutions out there, which we will discuss in more detail at the end of the chapter, the architecture in this chapter was selected because it is easy, simple, scalable, and fast.

Let's now look into the subsystems in our architecture in more detail.

Client Architecture

In our architecture, the transaction approval logic is implemented in the client. The client itself can be a web server or a similar application. This is any system that an event hits requiring review and decision. For this discussion we'll assume this is a web server and one of its main jobs is to review incoming events and respond with approval or rejection.

How exactly does the client do all this reviewing and alerting? It can be broken down into three checks on each event:

Event validation

> This is validation of rules that fire off in the context of the event itself—for example, format or basic logical rules like "column A must be a positive number" and "column B says withdraw."

Global context validation

> This is validation of rules in the context of global information, such as thresholds of risk. An example would be: Is this URL safe? I might have a global list of IP address masks that have a risk rating, and the rule would say I'm only allowing IP addresses below a certain level of risk.

Profile content validation

> This version of validation raises the level of required information needed about the actors related to the event. A good example of this is bank transactions. If the user's last 100 transactions were in the states of Ohio and Michigan and then suddenly we get a transaction in Russia 22 minutes after a transaction in Ohio, that should give us reason to be alarmed.

Putting these together, each time the client application receives an event it retrieves the profile, executes fraud detection logic using the profile and the event, and returns a result.

Note that it's because of the global- and profile-level validations that we require Hadoop or HBase; if all we needed was the event validation, we could remove Hadoop and HBase entirely from the architecture. It is getting and updating profile information of potentially billions of actors that makes Hadoop and HBase a great fit.

Let's focus on how we're going to populate the client with the global and user profile information when it is needed.

Profile Storage and Retrieval

There are two challenges in storing user profiles and accessing them from the client. One is the sheer amount of information we need to store—potentially a long history of transactions about billions of users. The second challenge is fast retrieval of information. To react to fraud in a timely manner, we need to be able to look up the history of any user in few milliseconds. In this section, we will explore the options of using NoSQL databases and caches for quick retrieval of information. We will focus on HBase and show how to store the user profiles in HBase in ways that make the data fast to both retrieve and update.

Caching

The fastest way for the client to retrieve profile information is from local memory. If the profile is found in the local cache, we are looking at sub-microsecond latency to get the information ready for the validation logic.

A complete discussion on implementing a good caching layer is out of scope for this book, but we will give a quick high-level overview to provide the basic ideas behind implementing a caching framework.

At the heart of any caching framework is memory. Memory, of course, has limitations, and it's very possible that we won't have enough memory on a given host to hold all the data we need. We recommend a multi-layered approach, combining a local cache with a remote distributed cache.

Regardless of whether additional layers of caching are used, we recommend using the local cache at least for the most active users. Although this can complicate the architecture to some extent, the difference in latency between local memory (submicrosecond) and reading a profile over the network (at least a few milliseconds) is typically worth the additional complexity. To overcome the memory size limitation of the local cache, it is possible to partition the profile information between the clients so that each client holds a subset of records, and transaction approval requests are routed to the appropriate client. In our example, we use Google's Guava Cache library, which makes it very easy to create local caches (*http://bit.ly/guava-cache*) and we configure its get method to load the profile from HBase if it does not exist in the cache.

As for the remote cache layer, there are two possibilities:

- A distributed memory caching solution, such as *Memcached*, to distribute the data across a cluster of nodes.
- Setting up HBase so that all needed records can be found in the block cache. The block cache keeps data blocks in memory, where they can be quickly accessed.

Let's explore these options a little more in the following sections.

Distributed memory caching

A distributed memory solution like Memcached or Redis simplifies the work of developing a caching layer. In terms of performance, though, it still requires a network call, which can add a small amount of latency to requests. Request times should be in the 1- to 4-millisecond range. The advantage of this solution over the partitioning solution is that we won't have downtime when nodes fail, since we can set up the caching solution with multiple replicas of the data. The only downside of the distributed memory caching solution is you need enough memory to hold everything. If you can't hold everything, you need an additional persistence store backed by disk, which means an additional call when data is not in memory. As we'll see shortly, if we're utilizing HBase, there is little reason why you need to also use a distributed caching solution.

HBase with BlockCache

If configured correctly, HBase can give us a couple of millisecond response times when used as our caching layer, so long as we can keep the results we are looking for in memory. In this case, we'll be using the HBase BlockCache, which again is allowing us to keep recently used data blocks in memory. Note that previous versions of HBase had memory limitations that impacted the size of the BlockCache, but recent enhancements have reduced many of these limitations with advancements like off-heap block cache, compressed block cache, and improvements in Java's garbage collection (GC) system.

However, a core feature of HBase—strong consistency—presents a potential downside for near-real-time responses in our fraud detection system. As the CAP theorem notes, systems such as HBase with strong consistency and partition tolerance will likely not offer strong availability guarantees. And, indeed, when an HBase region server fails, there is a subsection of row keys that cannot be read or written for a period of time that could span minutes.

For this reason, in a production system utilizing HBase as a core component we'll need to introduce a mechanism to provide stronger availability. A full discussion of this is outside the scope of this book, but note that work is under way in the HBase project to provide capabilities to run multiple HBase clusters and keep the data in sync between them. This will allow for failover in the case of a failure in persisting or fetching data from a primary HBase cluster.

HBase Data Definition

To further explore how we should implement a solution with HBase, let's walk through what the data model and interaction with HBase looks like. In our example of credit card transaction fraud, we need a profile that will hold enough information for us to run our model against to determine if there is abnormal behavior.

The following is Java code that will represent our ProfilePojo class with the values we will be discussing. Note that we are separating the fields into few categories: values that rarely change, values that change often, values that count things, and values that capture historical events:

```
// Fields that rarely change:
  private String username;
  private int age;
  private long firstLogIn;
```

```
// Values that frequently change:
   private long lastLogIn;
   private String lastLogInIpAddress;

// Counters:
   private long logInCount;
   private AtomicLong totalSells;
   private AtomicLong totalValueOfPastSells;
   private AtomicLong currentLogInSellsValue;
   private AtomicLong totalPurchases;
   private AtomicLong totalValueOfPastPurchases;
   private AtomicLong currentLogInPurchasesValue;

// Historical fields:
   private Set<String> last20LogOnIpAddresses;
```

The different categories are important because each type may be stored in HBase differently. Let's see what options we have in terms of persisting and updating data fields in HBase.

Columns (combined or atomic)

The first two categories we will look at are the values that don't change a lot and the ones that do change a lot. With all these columns, we have the option to store them in a single column qualifier or to store them in their own column qualifiers.

Those coming from the RDBMS world would never consider storing multiple fields in a single column, but HBase is a little different because of how it stores the data on disk. Figure 9-2 shows the difference between storing these five values as a single column in HBase and storing them as individual columns.

RowKey	TimeStamp	Column	Value
42	123456789	c	JimS|80|123456789|123456788|1.0.0.127

RowKey	TimeStamp	Column	Value
42	123456789	un	JimS
42	123456789	ag	80
42	123456789	fLg	123456789
42	123456789	|Ln	123456788
42	123456789	|Lg|p	1.0.0.127

Figure 9-2. Single-column versus individual-column storage

As we can see from Figure 9-2, the benefit of using a single column is less space consumed on disk. Now, most of that extra information in the individual columns will be compressed away, but still there is the cost of decompressing and sending it over the network.

The downside to combining all the values is that you can no longer change them atomically. This is why this strategy of combining values is mostly reserved to columns that don't change much or always change together. That said, because this is a performance optimization, it's often best to keep things simple in initial development. A good design principle to follow is to have a method that encapsulates the persistence and serialization of objects to and from HBase so that the effect of any schema changes is localized in your code.

Using Short Column Names

One thing to call out is the short column names in Figure 9-2. Remember that column names are also stored on disk. This wouldn't be true for a normal RDBMS, but remember HBase doesn't have a fixed schema and can have different columns per record. Therefore, it needs to label the column names for each record. With that understanding, remember to keep your column names short.

Event counting using HBase increment or put

The HBase APIs provide an increment function that allows you to increment a numerical value stored in HBase and referenced by a row key, column family, and column qualifier. For example, if the value was originally 42 and you increment it by 2, it will be 44.

This is powerful because multiple applications can increment the same value with assurance that the value is correctly incremented in a thread-safe manner. If you are used to Java, the increment is like using an AtomicLong and the addAndGet() method, as opposed to a simple long++, which is not thread-safe.

So despite increment being thread-safe, there's still a potential concern—not with HBase, but with the client. It's easy to think of a case where a client will send the increment and then fail before getting acknowledgment of the original event. In that case, the client will try to recover and increment again. The result is a double increment, which means our number is wrong until the number is reset. This issue is even more pronounced if you try to update multiple HBase clusters: you could send the increment to the primary cluster and have the request take long enough that the client believes it has failed and then sends the increment to the failover cluster. If the first increment then completes successfully, we now have a double increment.

Given these potential issues, increment may not be the best option. Another option is to simply use HBase put, although there are limitations to puts that are actually addressed by the increment functions:

- The put requires the initial value. So, for example, if you're incrementing by 2, you first need to get the initial value, which in our example was 42. Then, we need to do the addition on the client before sending the value of 44 back to HBase.
- Because we need the original value, there is no way we can increment a value in a multithreaded manner.

A possible way to address these limitations would be a streaming solution like Spark Streaming. As we talked about in Chapter 7, Spark Streaming can store counts in an RDD that can be incremented in a reduce process. Then, you can put() these values into HBase. Although simple, this provides a powerful model. We don't need multithreading because we are partitioning and microbatching. Also, we don't need to get from HBase on every pass because we are the only system updating the values, so as long as we don't lose our RDD we don't need to re-get the latest values.

To summarize, HBase increment is simpler to use, but can have issues with duplicate increments. put does not have this issue, but can be a bit more complex to update in a consistent manner. In our example implementation we use put.

Event history using HBase put

In addition to simply counting events, we also want to store the complete transaction history for each user. Because an HBase record is uniquely described by its row, column, and version, we can store history for a user by simply putting new events for the user into the same row and column, and use HBase to keep track of the user history.

Like increments, HBase versioning provides a lot of power, but also has drawbacks:

- First off, the default number of versions stored per cell is one. For this use case we'll want to set the number of versions to a much higher number—at least 20 and possibly more. The number of versions is set at a column family level, not at a column level. So, if you want 20 versions only for one column of many in a row, you need to decide if you want all the columns to have 20 versions, or if you want to pay the extra cost of having two column families.
- If we decide to add 20 versions to all the columns, then we're adding overhead for the table. First, the scan times will slow down. Second, the amount of usable information going into the block cache will decrease, and the overall size of the table on disk will increase even after a compaction.

So is there another option? The answer is yes, and it's HBase puts again. The client will read the full history from HBase, add the new transactions, and then write the full history in a single put.

Unlike the increment and put solution, this one is not as easy to make a clear decision on. We may want to keep the last 100 IP addresses. In that case the put solution would involve a lot of updating. Also, the cost to retrieve this much history and store it in the local cache may be too great. You should consider your use case and performance of the two solutions carefully before locking down your schema design.

Let's look at how we will update profiles in HBase from our web service. Note that the example is a simplified code snippet; you'll find the full application in the book's GitHub repository (*https://github.com/hadooparchitecturebook/hadoop-arch-book*).

In this example, each profile has its own row, with the userId as the row key. The row has two columns: json, which stores the user profile in JSON format, and timestamp, which stores the time the profile was updated. Storing the profile in JSON is not our typical recommendation, because the Avro format has significant advantages (as discussed in previous chapters). In the case of low-latency stream processing, JSON takes less CPU to process and therefore increases the throughput of the web server.

The overall plan is to open a connection to HBase, instantiate a table, and then get and put profiles from the table:

```
static HConnection hConnection;

hConnection = HConnectionManager.createConnection(hbaseConfig);

byte[] rowKey = HBaseUtils.convertKeyToRowKey("profileCacheTableName", userId);
Get get = new Get(rowKey);

final HTableInterface table = hConnection.getTable("profileCacheTableName");

Result result = table.get(get); ❶
NavigableMap<byte[], byte[]> userProfile = result
                    .getFamilyMap("profile");


Put put = new Put(rowKey); ❷
put.add("profile",
        "json",
        Bytes.toBytes(profile.getKey().getJSONObject().toString()));
put.add("profile",
        "timestamp",
        Bytes.toBytes(Long.toString(System.currentTimeMillis())));

long previousTimeStamp = profile.getKey().lastUpdatedTimeStamp;

table.checkAndPut(rowKey,
                  "profile",
                  "timestamp",
                  Bytes.toBytes(Long.toString(previousTimeStamp)),put) ❸
```

❶ This code segment gets the profile from HBase. In the full application, it appears in the loadProfileFromHBase() method, which executes when we are looking for the profile in the cache, if it's not in the cache already.

❷ This code segment updates the profile in HBase. In the full application, it appears in HBaseFlusher. HBaseFlusher is a background thread that reads updated profiles from a queue and puts them into HBase as shown here.

❸ We are using the checkAndPut() method to avoid race conditions where we accidentally override a profile that was already updated by another web server. If the timestamp in HBase does not match the timestamp in our app, we have an outdated copy. We'll need to get a new copy from HBase, make our updates on it, and try writing it to HBase again. This line usually appears in a while() statement, so if the checkAndPut() fails, we reload the new profile, update it, and try again.

Delivering Transaction Status: Approved or Denied?

Now, let's discuss how to send notifications to systems when we have found fraud.

For the case in which our client has detected fraud, there could be actions that external systems need to take in response. With respect to the client, the number one external system is most likely the system sending the event to the client in the first place, with the requirement to know if the request or action was legitimate. In our simple architecture, having this method alert the original sender is as simple as populating the response to the sender's request.

The next group of external systems that may need to know about fraud detection outcomes are systems that are downstream and out of the real-time response window. We could send the detection events directly to these systems, but that would mean closely coupling these systems. Further, if there is more than one downstream system it would require multiple submissions of the same alert from the client, increasing the load on our NRT client solution. This is where Kafka or a message queue (MQ) system would be a perfect addition to our architecture. We could publish alerts to a topic on our Kafka or MQ system, allowing any downstream systems needing access to these alerts to subscribe to the appropriate topic.

Next, there most likely will be a need to log and learn from our fraud detection decisions. This will require us to send every event, its corresponding fraud detection decision (fraud, no fraud, or what kind of fraud), and the reasoning for the decision to HDFS for long-term storage and batch processing. In the long term, this will allow us to do a much deeper dive into the data with engines like Spark, Impala, and Map-Reduce. This long-term storage area and batch processing would be the deep thought process we previously discussed. We will look into how to do this next.

Lastly, the events and the decisions could also be sent to a stream processing system to get more up to the minute real-time learning done on the data. We will touch on that later in the chapter as well.

Ingest

Figure 9-3 highlights the subset of the architecture we will focus on when digging into the ingestion portion of our fraud application.

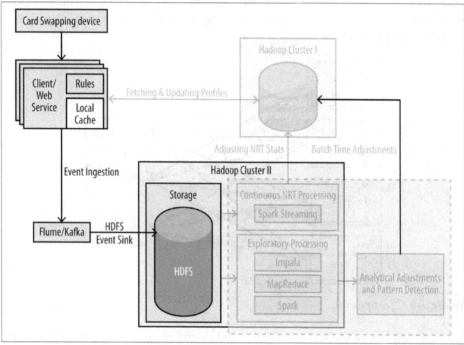

Figure 9-3. Ingest architecture

We'll use Flume here as the last leg before we hit HDFS or Spark Streaming, for all the reasons we talked about in Chapter 2: easy to configure, the ability to scale out, and maturity of the project.

In the next subsections we will focus on different approaches to connecting the client to Flume and approaches to deploy Flume alongside HDFS. There is a lot more that goes into building a Flume ingestion architecture, much of which we cover in Chapter 2.

Path Between the Client and Flume

We have many options for connecting the client to Flume, but for this discussion we'll focus on three: client push, logfile pull, and a message queue between the client and the final sink.

Client push

The first option is an easy one to start off with: putting a Flume client in the application that will batch up the messages and send them on their way to Flume. In this model the client will point straight to the Flume agents that will be doing the write to HDFS (see Figure 9-4).

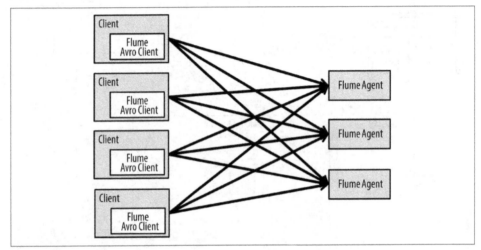

Figure 9-4. Client push

We could implement this easily using the NettyAvroRpcClient API in the web service, which would offer us the advantage of over-the-wire encryption, compression, and fine control of the batching and threads.

To use the NettyAvroRpcClient, you first need to get an instance from RpcClientFactory. You then create Flume events using EventBuilder and append the events to the NettyAvroRpcClient to send them to Flume. You can also call the appendBatch() function to send a list of events together; this method increases latency (because you are waiting for events to accumulate before sending them), but it increases throughput and we recommend using it for sending data to Flume.

For example, here's how we used an Avro client to send events from our fraud detection app to Flume (this is only a code snippet, the full application is available on our GitHub repository (*https://github.com/hadooparchitecturebook/hadoop-arch-book*)):

```java
public static class FlumeFlusher implements Runnable {

  int flumeHost = 0;

  @Override
  public void run() {

    NettyAvroRpcClient client = null;
    while (isRunning) {
      if (client == null) {
        client = getClient();  ❶
      }
      List<Event> eventActionList = new ArrayList<Event>();
      List<Action> actionList = new ArrayList<Action>();
      try {
        for (int i = 0; i < MAX_BATCH_SIZE; i++) {
          Action action = pendingFlumeSubmits.poll();  ❷

          if (action == null) {
            break;
          }

          Event event = new SimpleEvent();
          event.setBody(Bytes.toBytes(action.getJSONObject().toString()));
          eventActionList.add(event);
          actionList.add(action);  ❸
        }
        if (eventActionList.size() > 0) {
          client.appendBatch(eventActionList);  ❹
        }
      } catch (Throwable t) {
        try {
          LOG.error("Problem in HBaseFlusher", t);
          pendingFlumeSubmits.addAll(actionList);  ❺
          actionList.clear();
          client = null;
        } catch (Throwable t2) {
          LOG.error("Problem in HBaseFlusher when trying to return puts to " +
          + "queue", t2);
        }
      } finally {
        for (Action action: actionList) {
          synchronized (action) {
            action.notify();
          }
        }
      }
    }
    try {
      Thread.sleep(HBASE_PULL_FLUSH_WAIT_TIME);
    } catch (InterruptedException e) {
      LOG.error("Problem in HBaseFlusher", e);
```

```
    }
  }
```

❶ We start by initializing the Avro client with the address of the Flume agent to which we will send the data.

❷ We maintain a queue of actions (approve/deny decisions) that we want to send to Flume. We pick events out of the queue and convert them to Flume events.

❸ We add those events to a list, so we can send them to Flume in one batch.

❹ Here we send the list of events to Flume.

❺ If there was an error, we place the actions back in the queue so we can retry later.

This client connects to a Flume agent that has an Avro source listening to the port we used when initializing the client.

```
a1.sources.r1.channels = c1
a1.sources.r1.type = avro
a1.sources.r1.bind = 0.0.0.0
a1.sources.r1.port = 4243
```

There are some downsides to pushing events directly from the client to Flume:

- It assumes the client is implemented in Java.
- The Flume libraries would have to be included with your client application.
- It requires additional memory and CPU resources on the client.
- The client needs to be able to switch between Flume agents in the case where a Flume agent crashes.
- Clients will have different network latency between Flume agents depending on where they are located in relation to the Flume agents and the cluster. This will affect threading and batch sizing.

This is the recommended approach if you have full implementation control of the clients (which is something we assume in this use case), and if one of the client's primary jobs is ingesting data to Flume. Unfortunately, this is not always the case, so we need to consider additional options.

Logfile pull

The second option is one that is frequently seen in the real world, mainly because it's simple and usually easy to start with. Most applications are already using logfiles, so we can ingest events from the logfiles to Flume without modifying the client code. In this case, we're writing logs to disk and then using a Flume source to read log records into our ingest pipeline. Figure 9-5 illustrates this approach in a high-level way.

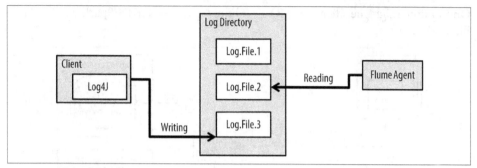

Figure 9-5. Logfile pull

Even though this is a common implementation, we do not recommend this solution for fraud detection. Using logfiles for ingest has some drawbacks compared to using the Avro client:

Performance

There is a performance hit in writing the logs to disk and then reading them back into Flume. Although the reading will hopefully benefit from OS disk-level caching, there is still the cost of writing, serialization, and de-serialization. There have even been cases where the reader is unable to keep up with the writers, leading to even bigger problems.

Data loss

It is not a simple task to tail logs that are changing quickly on disk, increasing the chance of losing data as files are rotated. A spooling directory source can be used to mitigate this problem, but this source will add latency since it only starts processing files after they've been closed by the application writing to them.

Flume has to know the client

Flume has to be knowledgeable of the application's log locations and file formats.

Because in this use case we assume that we are writing the client, we can use the preferred architecture and add the Avro client to the client. Compare this to the clickstream use case for which we assumed that the web server is a given and we can't modify it; in that case, we used Flume's spooling directory source to ingest from the logfiles.

Message queue or Kafka in the middle

This model is also pretty common. This solution decouples the client from Flume even more and allows third parties to get incoming messages. This solution could look different depending on how you set it up. Note that these are fairly complex options and were not included in our original high-level architecture where we aimed at a more straightforward approach.

One option might be client → MQ → Flume/Spark → HDFS/Spark as shown in Figure 9-6.

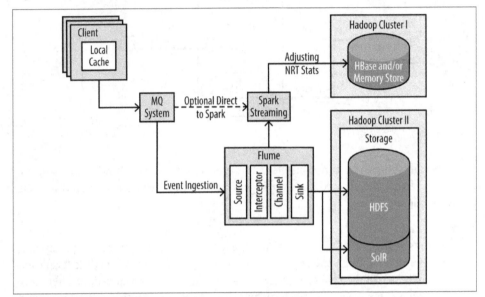

Figure 9-6. Client → MQ → Flume/Spark → HDFS/Spark

The advantage here is that we have decoupled our client from Flume and Spark. Note the two potential paths in this diagram where Spark can read from Flume or the MQ system. Both would work, but the advantage of having Spark receiving events from Flume is that we could have filtering before we send to Spark. This would allow us to reduce the load on our microbatching system.

This architecture is simple, and integrating Kafka can have advantages. So let's look at some of these options, starting with the client → Kafka → Flume/Spark, as shown in Figure 9-7.

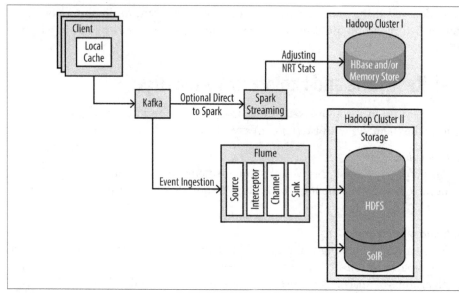

Figure 9-7. Client → Kafka → Flume/Spark

Like the last example, this option allows for decoupling from the client but still gives us all the functionality from Flume and Spark. Also, there is the big advantage of replaying the data here, which can come in handy for development and testing.

Figure 9-8 shows another option: client → Kafka → Flume sink/Spark.

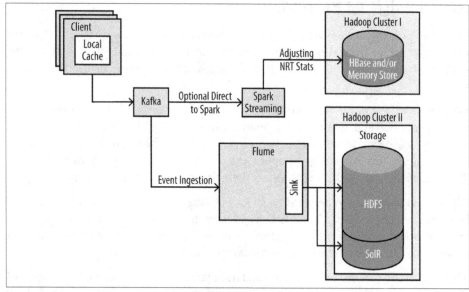

Figure 9-8. Client → Kafka → Flume sink/Spark

If you don't need the Flume interceptor and you don't want to do any mutation or filtering before events are sent to HDFS or Spark, then this is likely the cleanest option.

Near-Real-Time and Exploratory Analytics

As we described in the high-level architecture, in addition to the real-time decisions made by the client, we want two types of asynchronous data processing:

Near-real-time
> This type of processing is typically done seconds to a few minutes after the event occurred with the intention of finding trends that involve more than a single user.

Exploratory analytics
> This type of processing is typically done hours or days after the event occurred, with the intention of analyzing the event data to improve the fraud detection algorithms or analyzing the user behavior over long periods of time. This analysis can be done using any framework that is familiar to the analysts; MapReduce, Spark, and Impala are popular choices.

As we mentioned in the beginning of the chapter, we will discuss some possible uses of near-real-time and exploratory analytics in our architecture, but will not attempt to explore specific algorithms and their implementation.

Near-Real-Time Processing

Up to this point we have reviewed every event for fraud detection, we've stored all our decisions, and we have also sent that information to either HDFS or our streaming engine. Now let's use this information to add another layer of protection against fraud.

Let's assume we've put in the effort to craft models and rules to flag all known cases of fraud. The problem is that there are smarter people out there trying to commit fraud, and they're learning those models and rules we have crafted in order to catch them. They then use this knowledge to adjust their strategies in ways we hadn't imagined. This means that we need a way to detect their changed strategies.

So we need to be able to detect if behavior is changing. We'll do this not at an event level, but at a more macro level. If there is enough change, then this could be a sign that our original rules need to be adjusted, or, more important, that we need to shut down some activity before we risk significant loss to fraud.

Think of event processing or event-level validation as a very detailed and focused view of the world, whereas with near-real-time processing we are going to try to look at the larger picture. The problem is that we need to do it quickly, so in order to see everything we need to blur out the details a little bit. We will be looking at factors like totals, averages, and clusters of behavior to see if globally behavior is changing outside of our original expectations.

A good example of when a more global analysis of events is important is when thresholds for events change across a large group of users. Remember back when we talked about event validation for fraudulent activity, one of those checks is whether the user's behavior is within a global or relative threshold of normal behavior—for example, a threshold related to how much money is normally spent on electronics. In normal cases, if a user's spending on electronics increases by 100 times, that would be something to be concerned about, but if the event occurs on the same day the new iPhone comes out, what looks like something abnormal at the event level is normal at the global level.

In the same vein, we can also look for massive microfraud: here we are looking for spikes in macro activity that may signal fraud that is micro at an individual user level but is affecting many users. Think of a crime that takes 50 cents from a million users. This will go unnoticed at the event level, but at the macro level it can be singled out.

One common type of analysis that is done in near-real-time is windowing analysis— that is, looking at events over a finite timeframe (often seconds to minutes) or number of events, as illustrated in Figure 9-9:

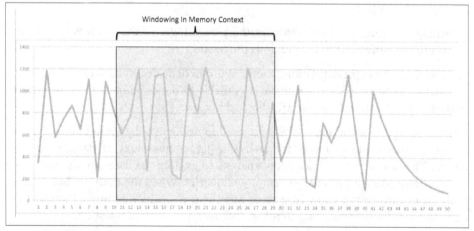

Figure 9-9. Windowing analysis

Windowing can be used, for example, to detect stock price manipulation. At an atomic event level it is near impossible to identify whether these patterns are taking place, but if we are allowed to view the market in a windowing fashion, we see the events happening in order and with the context of all the events around the same time.

We can do near-real-time analysis using stream processing frameworks such as Spark Streaming and Storm, or using a very fast batch framework such as Spark.

Spark and Spark Streaming would be our solution of choice here for a few reasons:

- The business rules are most likely complex and we want the focus on them, not on how to make the system work in a streaming implementation. Spark's high-level API and machine-learning libraries are likely to be useful.

- It is common to alternate between validating business rules in batch mode and running them in a streaming engine. Spark offers a very smooth transition from batch to streaming.

- Lastly, much of the fairly complex processing we need to do, such as continuous clustering or recommendations, is simplified with the APIs offered by Spark Streaming. Windowing, for example, is trivial to implement in Spark.

Exploratory Analytics

The final component in our architecture to discuss is exploratory analysis. This is often done by data analysts and fraud experts using SQL and visualization tools to find interesting patterns in the data. In addition, this step can also include automated pattern matching with machine-learning algorithms and model training for the algorithms used in real time.

Generally speaking, what differentiates the processing in this section is that it's not subject to the same SLAs as the previous processing.

After we load the event data (transactions, approve/deny decisions, and the causes for the decisions) to HDFS, we can make it available to nondevelopers such as business analysts via a SQL interface that will allow ad hoc querying.

This is the type of work that analysts are used to doing in a data warehouse, with the advantage that Hadoop allows for analyzing larger quantities of data faster than before. The fast response times allow analysts to explore the data rapidly: run a few queries, learn something, and then run more queries. When the analysts "learn something," they can use the knowledge to update the user profiles, improve the real-time algorithms, or modify the client to retain and use additional information.

In addition to analysts exploring the data, we can also apply common machine-learning algorithms to the data we store in HDFS. A few common approaches are:

Supervised learning on labeled data
> After a set of transactions is labeled as legitimate or fraudulent by a reliable source, an algorithm can determine what a fraudulent transaction looks like and

can assign risk scores to transactions. Support vector machines are a popular method of implementing this, as well as Bayesian networks.

Unsupervised learning

For example, clustering algorithms such as K-Means can find clusters of similar behaviors, and analysts can later assign specific clusters as possibly fraudulent.

Analysts will use historical data on HDFS to explore new algorithms and features that can be used with existing algorithms and train and validate their algorithms and rules. The results of the analysis will be used to improve the real-time and near-real-time fraud detection layers.

What About Other Architectures?

There are, of course, alternative architectures to solve this problem. Let's look at some of them to examine why we chose the preceding architecture to implement a solution. Figure 9-10 illustrates of our proposed design.

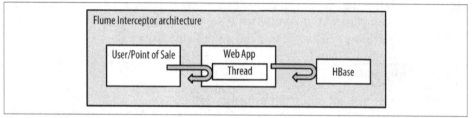

Figure 9-10. Our proposed architecture

Flume Interceptors

As we talked about in Chapter 7, we could implement the transaction approval logic in Flume interceptors, processing the events and updating profiles in HBase on the way to HDFS (Figure 9-11). This additional level of indirection would reduce load on the web service, because the activity of looking at the event, checking the profile in HBase, and deciding whether to approve will now be done in Flume rather than in the web service. This will assist in scaling the service even more. Flume interceptors will be able to handle the low latency requirements of the application. The downside is that it's not easy to return the answer to the requesting web server, because we've added another level of indirection. We will have to send the decision back to the client application through a callback URL or a messaging system.

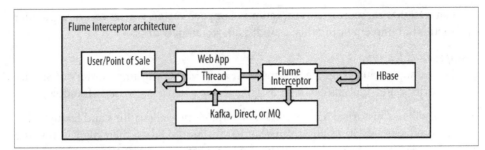

Figure 9-11. Flume interceptor architecture

Kafka to Storm or Spark Streaming

This architecture, shown in Figure 9-12, has similar benefits as Flume interceptors; it decouples event processing from the web service and improves scalability. In this architecture, the profile lookup, update, and approval will be done in Storm or in Spark Streaming workers. Note, this means that you have to go through two systems before you validate the event for fraud. When trying to build a fast system, minimizing hops and complexity is always better. Also, you have the same problem as with the Flume interceptors when returning the result to the requester.

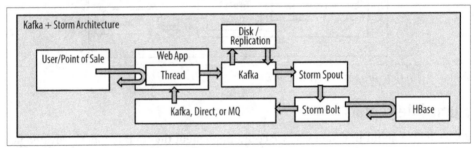

Figure 9-12. Kafka + Storm architecture

External Business Rules Engine

Another possibility is to use an external system to perform business rule processing as shown in Figure 9-13. The client will send a request to this system and get a response to return to the end requester. The benefits here are that the business rules engine is decoupled from the application and can support models that update throughout the day as new information comes in. This solution adds to the complexity of implementation by introducing an additional component. Not to mention, business rules engines are outside the scope of this book.

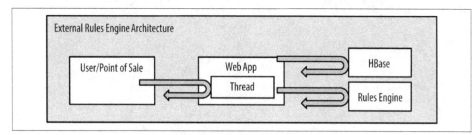

Figure 9-13. External rules engine architecture

Note that in all these alternate architectures, the NRT and exploratory analytics can be implemented the same way as we explained earlier. However, when using Spark Streaming or Storm, you can do some of the NRT processing in the streaming engine itself.

Conclusion

Implementing a robust fraud detection system requires reliability and the ability to return quick answers in response to events, as well as the ability to handle large volumes of incoming data. Implementing an architecture that meets these requirements has a fairly high degree of complexity, but Hadoop and components in the Hadoop ecosystem provide significant benefits by supporting streaming and batch operations on extremely large data volumes.

We've shown one possible architecture for implementing a fraud detection system with Hadoop, but this is just one alternative for implementing such a system. In the real world, architectures will be driven by specific use cases and fraud scenarios faced by an organization. Hopefully, though, we've provided some ideas on how Hadoop can be leveraged for these types of use cases, as well as other types of applications that require near-real-time processing.

## CHAPTER 10

Data Warehouse

Organizations today are making their decisions based on data. A *data warehouse*, also known as an *enterprise data warehouse* (EDW), is a large collective store of data that is used to make such data-driven decisions, thereby becoming one of the centerpieces of an organization's data infrastructure. One of the most common applications of Hadoop is as a complement to an EDW architecture, often referred to as *data warehouse offload* or *data warehouse optimization*.

This data warehouse offload with Hadoop encompasses several areas, including:

ETL/ELT

> Extract-transform-load (ETL) refers to the process in which data is extracted from a source system, transformed, and then loaded into a target system for further processing and analysis. The transformations may include transforming based on business requirements, combining data with other data sources, or validating/rejecting data based on some criteria. Another common processing pattern is extract-load-transform (ELT). In the ELT model, data is loaded into a target system, generally a set of temporary tables, and then transformed. We'll get into more detail shortly on ETL and ELT processing in the traditional data warehouse world, and the benefits that Hadoop provides in offloading this processing from existing systems.

Data archiving

> Since traditional databases are often difficult and expensive to scale as data volumes grow, it's common to move historical data to external archival systems such as tape. The problem is that the archived data becomes inaccessible for analysis unless brought back online. This means that potentially valuable data will likely never be seen again. Moving this data to Hadoop provides an effective and inexpensive option to transfer that data from traditional data management systems such as the EDW, and ensure that it remains online and available for analysis.

Exploratory analysis

Hadoop provides an ideal sandbox to perform analysis on data that's not available in the EDW. This may be because the value of the data is unknown, because the data's structure or lack thereof may make it hard for it to fit in an EDW, or simply because the data volumes make it prohibitive to load into the EDW. This capability provides access to potentially valuable data that would otherwise be unavailable.

Many organizations are using these Hadoop capabilities to enhance their existing data infrastructure. With recent advances, Hadoop also has the functionality required of a data warehouse, including reliable data storage and the low-latency query capabilities required to run user reports and queries. Hadoop can store and process semi-structured and unstructured data very well, and that data can then be joined with the traditional structured data. This can be of particular interest when you are analyzing customer feedback or social media data in conjunction with the EDW data. Hadoop also provides integration with many popular third-party BI and visualization tools.

The case study in this chapter will provide an example of both using Hadoop as a complement to a data warehouse, as well as offloading many of the traditional functions of a data warehouse. But first let's look at an example of a traditional data warehouse architecture to provide a starting point before we dive into our case study. Our goal here isn't to provide a comprehensive introduction to data warehousing, but rather set the stage for the case study to follow.

 For a more comprehensive introduction to the data warehouse architecture there are many excellent texts available, including *The Data Warehouse Toolkit* by Ralph Kimball and Margy Ross (Wiley).

Figure 10-1 shows a high-level view of the main components in a typical EDW architecture; this architecture consists of the following components:

- The operational source systems are the online transactional processing databases (OLTP) and operational data stores that capture the transactions of a business. For example, an ecommerce site would be backed by OLTP databases that capture all orders, returns, and other transactions that customers make when they visit the site. These systems are generally optimized for single-record queries, which in practice will usually mean highly normalized and indexed schemas.

- The staging area acts as a temporary storage area and as a platform for ETL/ELT processing. Data is extracted from operational source systems and moved into the staging area, where it's transformed before being loaded into the final data warehouse schemas. These transformations might include actions like deduplicating data, normalizing data, cleansing data, enriching data, and so forth. Note that what we're referring to as the staging area is not a fixed architecture, but rather will vary depending on tools used, processing model, and similar factors. For example, in the ETL model the staging area may be a set of relational tables external to the data warehouse, flat files, or a vendor-specific infrastructure. In the ELT model, the staging area will generally be a set of tables in the data warehouse itself where transformations occur before the data is loaded to the final tables. Regardless of the physical implementation of the staging area, note that this area is strictly for data processing—users never access the data in the staging area for querying, reporting, and the like.

• The data warehouse is where data is made available to users for analysis, reporting, and so on. As opposed to the normalized schemas typical of the source systems, schemas in the data warehouse are designed for data analysis, which typically involves accessing multiple records. This often means using dimensional schemas such as a star schema, which we'll see in practice when we walk through our example later.

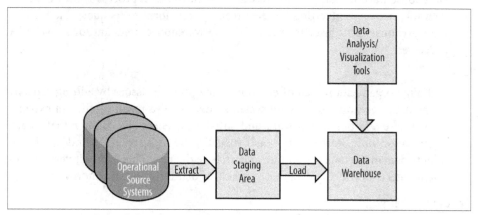

Figure 10-1. High-level data warehouse architecture

The tasks to move data between the layers in this architecture and perform the transformations are commonly implemented with *data integration* (DI) tools. There are many vendors providing these DI tools, such as Informatica, Pentaho, Talend, SAP, IBM, and others. Many of these DI vendors provide solutions for Hadoop in addition to traditional data management systems. Although the focus in this chapter is on tools in the open source ecosystem, many organizations already using one of these DI tools will choose to use that tool with Hadoop as well in order to leverage existing skill sets and investments.

Using Hadoop for Data Warehousing

Since this is a robust architecture that served organizations well for many years, why are many of these organizations integrating Hadoop into their data management infrastructures? As you might expect, the answer is the growing volume and complexity of data that many organizations are facing now. This leads to challenges such as:

Missed SLAs

As the volume and complexity of data grow, the time to process also grows. Many organizations are struggling to complete their ETL processing within required time constraints. This means either missing SLAs, or adding further capacity to their data warehouse infrastructure.

Excessive load on the data warehouse

Especially in case of ELT processing, data warehouse users querying the data warehouse have to compete for resources with the ELT process running on the data warehouse—converting the data from its raw form to its queryable form in the warehouse. This leads to frustrated data warehouse users and/or slower ELT processes.

Expense

Although organizations can often address the previous issues by adding capacity to the data warehouse or staging systems, this can also mean significant expense to purchase additional hardware and software licenses. To counter that, many organization only store a very small (usually, the most recent) window of full-fidelity data in the data warehouse and archive the rest. This makes it very expensive to query full-fidelity data that's outside of that most recent window.

Lack of flexibility

As requirements change, often new reports need to be created, or existing schemas and reports need to be updated. However, many organizations are unable to quickly respond to such changes due to the lack of flexibility of their data warehouse infrastructure. This issue has prevented many organizations from being able to join increasingly disparate sources of data (social media, images, etc.) with traditional structured data.

Many organizations are turning to Hadoop to address these challenges. Hadoop provides benefits as a complement to a data warehouse by:

- Offloading data transformations from existing systems to Hadoop. Hadoop provides a cost-effective platform for data processing, and because it's designed to efficiently process large volumes of data in parallel, it can often provide significant improvements in processing time and performance, allowing organizations to once again meet their SLAs.

- Moving processing to Hadoop can free up resources on the data warehouse, making these resources available for serving user queries.

Additionally, using Hadoop has three very powerful side effects:

- Making the data available in Hadoop can provide an exploratory sandbox for analysts to discover potentially valuable data that might otherwise never be available in the data warehouse.

- Using Hadoop as an online archive can free up valuable space and resources in the data warehouse, and avoid the need for expensive scaling of the data warehouse architecture.

- Flexibility of Hadoop allows for evolving schemas and handling semistructured and unstructured data, which enables fast turnaround time when changes to downstream reports or schemas happen.

Figure 10-2 shows a high-level view of an architecture where Hadoop complements the data warehouse.

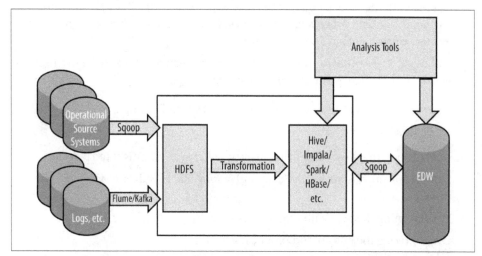

Figure 10-2. High-level Hadoop data warehouse architecture

Let's walk through this architecture:

- On the left-hand side we still have our operational source systems, such as our OLTP databases. It's also common to see additional multistructured sources of data being introduced with Hadoop, such as web logs, machine data, or social media feeds. These data sources are often difficult to manage with a traditional data warehouse architecture, but they're well suited for Hadoop. For our traditional data sources the ingestion mechanism will often be Sqoop, while for our event-based data we'll commonly use a tool like Flume or Kafka.

- Hadoop has now replaced our staging layer in the previous architecture. Our source data will be ingested into HDFS before being transformed and loaded into target systems. Transformations will occur through one of the processing frameworks supported on Hadoop, such as MapReduce, Spark, Hive, or Pig.

- Once transformed, data will be moved into target systems. In our example, this includes hosting the data in Hadoop via a SQL-like interface such as Hive or Impala, or exporting into our data warehouse for further analysis. Additionally, Figure 10-2 also shows that we'll often move data from the data warehouse back into Hadoop—for example, for archival purposes or as an exploratory sandbox for offloading analysis from the data warehouse.

- Figure 10-2 also shows the data being accessed by analysis tools such as BI, analytics, and visualization tools. One contrast with our traditional data warehouse architecture is that with the previous architecture, analysis tools never access the data in the staging area. In our new architecture, data analysis is commonly run against both the data warehouse and the data in Hadoop. Since Hadoop provides a general, big-data processing framework, it's easy to support multi workloads on a single cluster, such as ETL and analysis.

- Although it's not shown in this figure, our processing will likely be orchestrated by a workflow management tool such as Oozie.

The case study in this chapter will provide an end-to-end example of data warehouse offload with Hadoop, including:

- Using Sqoop to extract data from operational source systems into Hadoop
- Storage considerations for the data on Hadoop, such as data models and file formats
- Transforming the data with tools on Hadoop
- Orchestrating the end-to-end processing via Oozie
- Analyzing the data in Hadoop via tools like Impala

We'll begin the discussion of our example with an introduction to the data set we'll be using for our use case.

Defining the Use Case

For the purposes of this chapter, we will use a movie rating system as a use case. This rating system contains a listing of movies along with additional information about them like release date and IMDb URL (*http://imdb.com*). Users can sign up in order to rate movies, so this rating system also contains demographic information about them (e.g., age, occupation, and zip code, etc.). Users rate movies on a scale of 1 to 5, and this system stores these ratings. A user may rate no movies, all movies, or any number in between.

Once the system is implemented, we want to be able to answer questions like the following:

- What's the average rating for a given movie or a given set of movies?
- What's trending this week; that is, what movie ratings are increasing the most since the start of the week?
- What percentage of female users between the ages of 21 and 30 gave a rating of 3 or more to the movie *Dead Man Walking (1995)*?
- What percentage of users update their rating of a movie within three months of first rating it? Even more interestingly, what percentage of ratings get updated after being submitted, and of those that do get updated, how is the time period for the update distributed?

We will use the MovieLens (*http://grouplens.org/datasets/movielens/*) with some additions for our use case. On the MovieLens website, you can find data with 100k, 1 million, and 10 million entries, and their schema and structure is slightly different. We will be basing our discussion on the 100K MovieLens data set. If you download the data set, you will see many files; the ones of most interest to us are:

Ratings data
　　Located in a file called *u.data* that contains all the ratings for the movies. Movies and users in this file are represented by simple IDs.

Movies data
　　Located in a file called *item* that contains additional information about the movies (title, release date, etc.) mapped to the movie ID.

User data
　　Located in a file called *u.user* that contains demographic information about the users, mapped to the user ID.

We will use this use case to discuss how an organization running such a movie rating system would store and process the related data using a combination of Hadoop and the data warehouse. As we walk through this use case, we will first discuss what a potential OLTP schema for a system that generates the data set in question would look like. Then, we discuss what a possible representation and architecture of this data would look like when transferred to Hadoop and to the data warehouse.

OLTP Schema

While the data set is only available as files, a possible OLTP implementation for it is represented by the entity relationship diagram (ERD) in Figure 10-3.

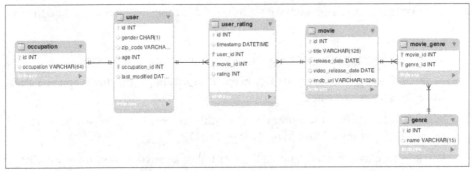

Figure 10-3. Example OLTP implementation for MovieLens data set

The goal of an OLTP schema usually is to normalize the data so as to reduce redundancy and provide data integrity. It allows you to easily and atomically create, delete, or update a given field in just one table and have it automatically propagated thereafter.

In Figure 10-3, you'll find a *user* table that contains information about each of the users. It contains the user's ID, gender, occupation, zip code, and age. The list of users' occupations is stored in a separate table called occupation. In our schema, we have slightly modified the user table from the original MovieLens schema by adding a column called last_modified. This column stores the timestamp for when the user information was last updated.

You'll also find a *movie* table, which stores information about each of the movies that can be rated. The movie table has an ID, which is the primary key of the table; the title of the movie; its release date and video release date, if any; and its IMDb URL. Each movie is associated with one or more genres. The available genres are stored in the genre table. Each movie is mapped to one or more genres by the movie_genre table.

There's also a *user_rating* table, which stores the ratings given by various users to various movies. This table maps a user ID (user_id) to a movie ID (movie_id) along with the rating given by the user and the timestamp when the rating was given. This table has a synthetic primary key called id, which is autogenerated whenever a new rating is entered.

Data Warehouse: Introduction and Terminology

Traditional data warehouse design usually involves a variant of one of two common approaches for data modeling: the *dimensional* model (also known as *star schema*) or the *normalized* model.

A dimensional model starts with a fact table—immutable values or measurements about entities in the database. Examples of such facts can be: a phone call in a telcom use case, a sale in a retail use case, or a prescription in a health care use case. In our use case, this is a rating given to a movie by a user.

To this fact table, the dimensional approach adds dimensions—tables with details about the entities in the system that give context to the facts. In a retail example, a fact can be the sale of an item for a specific price. The dimensions will include the item, the customer purchasing, the date of purchase, and the location of purchase. The item dimension table will contain details about the item, such as its weight, the name of the manufacturer, and the date it arrived to the warehouse. In our use case this is the information about the movies (the release date, URL, etc.) and the users (their age, occupation, zip code, etc.).

A normalized approach to data warehousing, on the other hand, involves a design very similar to an OLTP database. Tables are created by entity and designed to preserve the third normal form—attributes depend on the primary key in its entirety. In the retail example, an items table will contain the item name (since it depends completely on the item ID), but not the manufacturer name (which does not). As a result, queries on a normalized DWH schema usually involve long chains of joins.

In general, the dimensional approach is easier and faster when you're performing analytical queries, while the normalized approach makes updating information easier.

In our movie ratings example, we'll focus on a data warehouse architecture designed with the dimensional model, since it tends to be a better fit for analysis in Hadoop, for reasons we will explore in detail in a moment.

Let's quickly review a few fundamentals of dimensional design that will be useful when you're designing an ETL process or data warehouse in Hadoop:

Grain
> Grain refers to the level of granularity of the fact table. What does a single fact represent? A sale that may contain multiple items? A single item that may be part of a larger order? All facts in the fact table must be of the same grain for consistent analytics. The grain should be as granular as possible to allow users to answer unexpected questions by analyzing available data. In our use case, the grain is the rating of a movie by a user.

Additivity

Facts can be additive (such as sales amount in dollars) or non-additive (such as movie ratings). Additive facts can be summed, while non-additive facts are typically counted or averaged. In our use case, the ratings fact table is not additive but can and will often be averaged.

Aggregate fact tables

These are roll-ups of the fine-grained fact tables built to accelerate queries. Aggregates and granular fact tables are both presented to BI tools so the users can choose the level of granularity appropriate to the analysis. In our use case, an aggregate fact table is one that contains the up-to-date average rating of each of the movies.

Fact tables

These have one or more foreign keys (FK) that connect them to dimension tables. The primary key (PK) of a fact table is typically a composite of foreign keys that uniquely identify a fact. In our use case, the user_id, movie_id, and timestamp uniquely identify a fact.

Dimension tables

These are the source of all query constraints (users between the ages of 10 and 23, for example) and report labels.

Calendar dimension

This is a special dimension type attached to most fact tables and some dimensions—this is added to enrich simple dates. For example, in our use case, instead of trying to calculate when Christmas occurs in SQL so we can analyze if movie ratings go up during the holiday season, it is easier to dynamically look this information up in a calendar object.

Slowly changing dimensions

Some dimensions will get modified over time—users change addresses, manufacturers close down, production lines change names and so on. There are multiple ways of handling these changes, but the most common ones involve either modifying the existing value or adding a new row with the new value and marking it as current and pre-existing row(s) as obsolete. The former means that we would have overwrite in place, requiring us to rebuild aggregates. However, the latter means that we would not have to change history or rebuild aggregates. In our use case, the user data set is a slowly changing dimension and we use both of the aforementioned approaches. We have a user data set where we apply the updates to user information by modifying existing values. We also have a user_history data set, which contains a new row with the new value for every update. We use both approaches to provide optimal access to different usage patterns: the user data set for those interested in latest information about users and the user_history data set for those interested in historical information about users.

Data Warehousing with Hadoop

At the end of the day, Hadoop stores the same data that is stored in the OLTP database. However, this data is stored differently because the access patterns for the data in Hadoop are very different than those in the OLTP database.

In an OLTP database, you want quick and atomic insert/update/delete operations while maintaining data integrity. You are usually only operating in the context of one record at a time. In many cases, you want to minimize the number of tables you'd have to touch on every update or delete that comes from the application. Therefore, the data is stored in a highly normalized form, as you saw in the section "OLTP Schema" on page 316.

As explained in "Data Warehouse: Introduction and Terminology" on page 317, you can store data in a data warehouse using the dimensional approach or the normalized approach. We will store the data in Hadoop using the dimensional approach.

High-Level Design

Figure 10-4 shows the high-level design of our Hadoop data warehousing infrastructure.

For data warehousing purposes, we have to import three logical data sets from the OLTP database: the listing of movies that can be rated, the list of users who can rate the movies, and the ratings of movies given by various users. The import job for the movie data set is a Sqoop job that imports all information about all movies every run and simply overwrites the existing movie data set. The import jobs for users and ratings, on the other hand, only import new records and updates to existing records. These are called *incremental imports* since they only import incrementally based on what has previously been imported. Both these data sets have two variants: one that contains all of the history (user_rating_fact for ratings data and user_history for user data) where each update appends a new record, and another that contains the updates merged in place (user_rating for ratings data and user for user data). The variants that contain all history are populated first by the Sqoop incremental import jobs. The merged variants are then updated to include the incremental updates received in the latest run into the history variants.

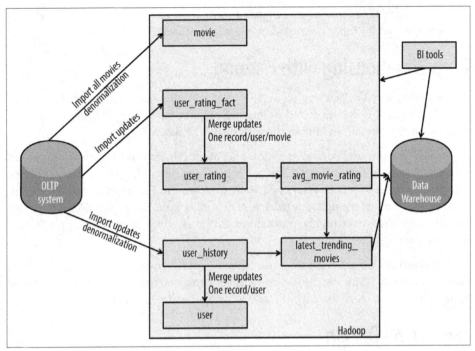

Figure 10-4. High-level infrastructure design

After all these data sets have been populated, they are used to populate some aggregate data sets in Hadoop. Examples of such aggregate data sets, as discussed in "Aggregations" on page 341, include data sets that store the up-to-date average rating for all movies, or data sets that store the number of times users rate a particular movie. These aggregate tables are then exported to the EDW for ease of access by various tools and users across the organization. All the processing can be orchestrated by an orchestration tool like Oozie. BI tools can also be used to directly query the full-fidelity data in Hadoop that was not exported to the data warehouse.

We will now walk through various considerations for modeling, storing, denormalizing, processing, and orchestrating data in Hadoop in the context of this use case.

Data Modeling and Storage

In this section, we will discuss how to model and store the MovieLens data set in Hadoop.

Choosing a storage engine

The first consideration is whether we choose to use HDFS or HBase for storage. The answer to this question mostly depends on the access patterns of the data as described in Chapter 1. For data warehousing, you'd be using Hadoop to offload some of the work of the ETL tool. In most data warehouse implementations, ETL is a batch job—data collected during an entire day is extracted out of the OLTP system, processed in batches, and bulk-loaded into the data warehouse. There are two main reasons for batch-processing ETL. The first is that one of the activities done during the ETL process is data aggregation, which by its nature requires data for the entire time period being aggregated. The other is that bulk processing is simply more efficient and reduces the overall duration of the ETL process.

Moreover, any queries that the BI analysts may run directly on Hadoop are also likely to be aggregation-style queries and complex analytics—that is, queries that require reading full table data and performing an aggregation on it. For the MovieLens data an example query might be "How many female users between the ages of 21 and 30 gave a rating of 3 or more to the movie *Dead Man Walking (1995)*?" This requires reading data for all females between the ages of 21 and 30, typically far too much data to effectively retrieve through indexes and random access to the table.

This access pattern is particularly suited for storing data on HDFS because of the need for higher scan performance instead of random read performance. Consequently, we will store our data warehouse data on HDFS.

Denormalizing

As mentioned earlier in the book, data is often denormalized when being brought into Hadoop. As a side effect, you pay the price of some redundancy, but it comes at the benefit of faster analysis. Having too many joins, especially with really small dimension tables, in a system like Hadoop is often suboptimal.

Let's take an example. In our use case, the occupation table is small and rarely changes, and most queries requiring this table would also query the users table. Therefore, we have two options:

- We can simply have a separate user and occupation data set in Hadoop.
- We can denormalize those two tables, essentially eliminating the need for the occupation.id column and have occupation embedded directly in the user data set in Hadoop.

We will go with the latter approach—denormalizing the two tables into a single user data set—because the overhead of storing occupation as a string instead of an ID in Hadoop is pretty small and is outweighed by the performance improvements of not having to join using the occupation.id column.

Let's talk about the movie table now. Associated with the movie table, we have movie_genre and genre tables as well. The genre table, similar to the occupation table, is a small dimensional table. More importantly, it will mostly be queried in conjunction with the movie and movie_genre tables. We have two options when it comes to the movie data:

- We can have three data sets in Hadoop: movie, movie_genre, and genre. The benefit of this option is that it keeps our ingest pipeline very simple since we are copying over the tables directly from OLTP database. However, the downside is that during querying we will almost always have to have a join with all three tables.

- We can denormalize the movie, movie_genre, and genre tables into one data set on Hadoop. We will have to have an additional step in our ingest pipeline or a follow-on job that merges these tables in Hadoop. However, it will make querying faster since all the data is stored in the same data set in Hadoop. Since a movie can have multiple genres associated with it, we will likely leverage a derived data type like an array (or a comma-separated genre list) to store all genres for a movie.

We will choose the latter approach—denormalizing the movie, movie_genre, and genre tables into one data set on Hadoop—to make querying simpler and faster.

At this point, we have two data sets in Hadoop: user, which contains all information about the users, including a string field that contains their occupation; and movie, which contains all information about each of the movies, including a composite column that contains information about all its genres. Now, let's move on to the next and only remaining table, user_ratings. You may be thinking, *where do we stop when it comes to normalization?* Technically, we have two options now as well:

- We can have three data sets—user, movie, and user_ratings—and we would need to join them during many of our queries.

- We can have just one data set in Hadoop: user_rating. We will denormalize everything (i.e., every rating from a user about any movie would come with all information about that movie and all information about the user in the same record). It will make our querying easier because no joins would be required, but it would complicate the ingest pipeline. Sounds extreme, no?

This time, we will choose the former and not denormalize. We will have three separate data sets: user, movie, and user_ratings. There are a few reasons why we chose to keep the data sets separate:

- Denormalizing gives the best bang for the buck when small tables are being denormalized (i.e., merged) into a larger data set. This was the case with our first two choices—occupation being merged into user, and genre and movie_genre being merged into movie. However, with user_ratings, user and movie are potentially fairly large tables for which the merge process on its own would take a long time to rationalize the time savings when querying.

- Updates to information would become very painful with denormalization. If a user updated her age, we would have to update every single rating she has ever submitted to reflect her updated information—that's a lot of touch points and hard to rationalize.

 We are not saying that joins should be avoided at any cost when you're using Hadoop. All we are saying is that joins are costly compared to having data in the same table, so if and where it makes sense, denormalizing (i.e., preaggregation) should be given consideration. The exact choice, however, would depend on the schema, distribution, and size of the data sets, along with the tools being used. Part of the reason joins are expensive is that when you have two data sets there are no guarantees that corresponding records (i.e., records with the same join key) across the two data sets will be present on the same node of your cluster—streaming these data sets across the network takes time and resources. Having the data in the same data set implies that it's guaranteed that the various fields of a record would be present on the same node.

So, in our architecture now, we will have three data sets in Hadoop: user, movie, and user_ratings. Even though Hadoop is not a data warehouse and an ERD doesn't precisely apply, Figure 10-5 shows an ERD representative of the data model in Hadoop. Important things to note are that the occupation table has been denormalized into user, and the movie_genre and genre tables have been denormalized into movie.

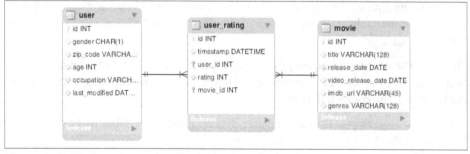

Figure 10-5. Hadoop data model for MovieLens data set

This is, however, not the final architecture. There is more to it, as you will soon find out.

Tracking updates in Hadoop

In this section, we will talk about how to capture changes to data and store them in Hadoop. Our OLTP schema allows for updates to the records. For example, the user may update her zip code or her rating of a movie she's rated before. It's important that our corresponding data model in Hadoop allows for such updates. We cannot, however, simply overwrite the updated records in place in Hadoop for a couple of reasons:

- We are storing our data in HDFS, which doesn't allow in-place updates. Some logic needs to be added to make the updates happen.

- We lose track of when the updates happened. For example, say you wanted to look back and see how many users, as a percentage, update their rating of a movie within three months of first rating it. You can't perform such an analysis since you updated the data in place, which implies that you have no record of when the rating updates actually happened.

Let's talk about the updateable data sets one by one. The user data set has a last_modified column, which stores the last time a given user's information was updated. The other updateable data set—user_rating—has a timestamp column, which stores the last time the rating was updated. If the rating has never been updated, it stores the time the rating was first given. For both these data sets, whenever an update is made, the column storing this last updated information is updated. Now, if we could track updates to this column, we'd be able to track updates to various records over time.

One approach is that in Hadoop, instead of overwriting the entries in place, we create tables where we only append, not overwrite. For the user data set, let's call this append-only data set user_history since it stores the history of all the users over time. For the rating data set, let's call this append-only data set user_rating_fact since it represents an immutable granular version of the data, referred to as a *fact* in data warehouse terminology.

On every run of the data ingest job, we retrieve a list of new records that either need to be inserted or updated to the Hadoop data set. These new records get appended to the bottom of the Hadoop data set.

Let's look at an example. Let's say the user data set looked like Table 10-1 in the OLTP database on day 1.

Table 10-1. User table in OLTP database before update

id	gender	zip_code	age	occupation_id	last_updated
1	M	85711	24	20	1412924400
2	F	94043	53	14	1412924410

The corresponding data set in Hadoop would look like Table 10-2.

Table 10-2. User data set in Hadoop before update

id	gender	zip_code	age	occupation	last_updated
1	M	85711	24	technician	1412924400
2	F	94043	53	other	1412924410

Now, let's say the user with ID 1 updated his zip code and a new user with ID 3 got added the next day. The new table in OLTP database would look like Table 10-3 on day 2.

Table 10-3. User table in OLTP database after update

id	gender	zip_code	age	occupation_id	last_updated
1	M	94301	24	20	1413014400
2	F	94043	53	14	1412924410
3	M	32067	23	21	1413014420

Notice that the zip_code column for the user with ID 1 has been updated in place from 85711 to 94301, and the last_updated column for the same user has been updated from 1412924400 to 1413014400. Also, note that a new user has been added with ID 3.

In Hadoop, however, the new updated user_history data set would now look like Table 10-4.

Table 10-4. user_history data set in Hadoop after update

id	gender	zip_code	age	occupation	last_updated
1	M	85711	24	technician	1412924400
2	F	94043	53	other	1412924410
1	M	94301	24	technician	1413014400
3	M	32067	23	writer	1413014420

Notice that two new records were added to the Hadoop data set. The first new record represents an update to the user with ID 1, and the second new record adds a new user with ID 3. This is similar to how databases maintain a transaction log of all transactions that happen on the data; we similarly track all updates and inserts to the data.

As you may have already guessed, while this approach preserves history, it makes it harder to query this data set in Hadoop. For example, if you wanted to execute a query to find the zip code for the user with ID 1, you would have to potentially go through the entire data set and then pick the latest entry based on the last_updated column. This makes queries slow to run and cumbersome to write. At the same time, however, we need this full-fidelity data to track the updates that happen to the users table and be able to track changes in user data down the road. Similarly, if you wanted to see the rating of a movie by a given user you'd have to go through all ratings of that movie by that user and then pick the latest rating based on the time it was given.

The solution we recommend for this is to have two copies of specific data sets in Hadoop. For the user data set, the first copy, called user_history, would store user data in Hadoop, the way we have described so far. It will be an append-only data set that will keep track of every single row that gets updated or added to the user table. The second copy, called user, would store only one record per user, which would correspond to its most recent state. Similarly for the rating data set, the first copy, called user_rating_fact, would store all the ratings, including any updates. The second copy, called user_rating, would store only the latest rating record per movie per user. The other option, instead of a fully materialized copy, would be have an unmaterialized view. However, the performance benefits of this preaggregation tilt the odds toward maintaining a preaggregated copy of the data sets.

The user_history and user_rating_fact data sets would be used for queries that require knowledge of the lineage of changes in user and rating data, respectively. The user and user_rating data sets would be used for queries that don't require the granularity of when the user data or rating was modified and only require the most recent information about the user or rating when that query was run. Both copies would have the same schema, they will just have different semantics of what's stored in those tables.

The reason for two copies of the data is that there are two different access patterns when it comes to querying an updatable data set like user or user_rating:

- Querying the data set as of today. Such queries may want to find out the current information about the user, for example.
- Querying the history. Such queries may want to find out if and how often the user has changed occupations or zip codes.

Our assumption is that queries from the as-of-today access pattern outweigh the number of queries from the history access pattern. In a typical data warehouse, you wouldn't maintain a copy of the table for faster access, especially a fact table like user_rating_fact, because storage is expensive. However, in Hadoop, storage is relatively much cheaper, and having a duplicate data set that can make the majority of queries faster can be a very worthy investment.

The workflow of having two data sets each for user data and rating data is represented in Figure 10-6.

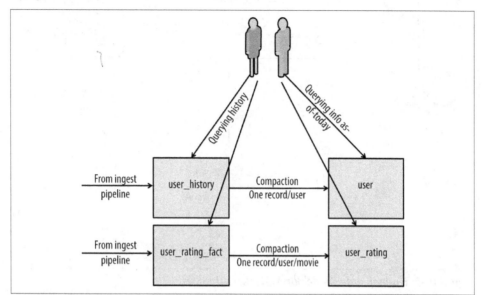

Figure 10-6. Workflow of having two data sets for user and rating data

The data ingest pipeline will add the new inserts/updates to user_history and user_rating_fact data sets on every run. After that, a separate process will be triggered to run a merge (or compaction job) that takes the new inserts/updates and merges them into the existing user and user_rating data sets, respectively, to populate a new data set with the inserts/updates applied to it. You can learn more about compactions and merges in Chapter 4.

Note that the movie table in the OLTP schema doesn't have a last_updated or similar column. This implies either that updates are not supported on that data or that, even if they are, it's fairly hard to track them. Therefore, for the movie data set in Hadoop we don't track updates to movies. For the new movies that get added to the OLTP database, we simply append them to the movie data set in Hadoop.

Our final schema in Hadoop would look like Figure 10-7.

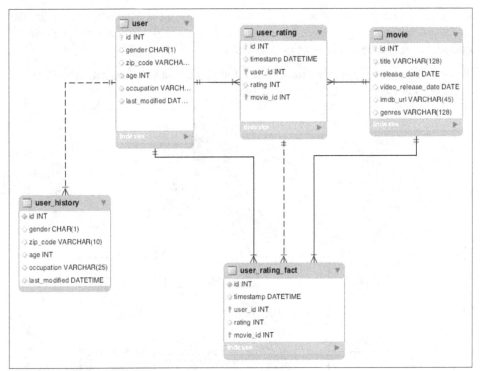

Figure 10-7. Hadoop data model for MovieLens data set

Selecting storage format and compression

Now we move on to deciding what file format and compression to use for our data sets in HDFS. Since relational data is typically structured in tables, the obvious candidates are CSV, Avro, and Parquet. As we've seen in Chapter 1, CSV is a suboptimal choice in terms of performance, compression, and schema management, all of which are critical for data warehouses. The choice between Avro and Parquet is far less obvious. Both are binary formats that contain schemas describing the data.

Avro has the advantage of supporting schema evolution. This means that our ETL process will not break when the OLTP schema is modified. Failed ETL processes due to schema maintenance that was not coordinated properly are a major concern for ETL developers and administrators, so this advantage can be quite important.

Parquet, on the other hand, has a significant performance advantage. Fact tables in data warehouses are typically very wide, since the data relates to many dimensions. But each analytical query or aggregation typically requires only a small subset of the columns. Our query regarding female users between ages of 21 and 30 will not access any of the genre columns. As a columnar format, Parquet will allow queries to skip blocks containing data from unused columns. In addition, Parquet tables compress very well, which leads to significant space savings.

The recommendation for formats is based on how a particular data set would be accessed. The rule of thumb here is to use Avro for everything that makes sense to be stored in a row-major manner and Parquet for everything that needs to be stored in a column-major manner.

For the data sets that get appended to (i.e., user_history and user_rating_fact), we recommend using Avro. These data sets get populated by the ingest pipeline and are then used to populate the compacted user and user_rating data sets. For these data sets, on every run, we will only be retrieving the updates and inserts that happened between the last run and this run, and more importantly we will be accessing the entire record for those updates/inserts. Therefore, it makes sense to store them in Avro.

> The recommended block size for Parquet data in HDFS is 256 MB. Therefore, if the size of your compressed user data set is not at least an order of magnitude larger than the recommended block size, it may make more sense to simply store the user data set in Avro as well.

For the user_rating data set, we recommend using Parquet since it is a large fact table. This table would grow at a fast pace, and you'd often want to do queries on it that involve aggregations over a subset of the columns for which Parquet is well suited.

For the user and movie data sets, we recommend using the Parquet format as well. This is because a subset of columns for these data sets would be queried for aggregations. For example, if you were trying to answer the question of how many female users between the ages of 21 and 30 gave a rating of 3 or more to the movie *Dead Man Walking (1995)*, you would be querying the entirety of the user data set, only retrieving the id and age column for your analysis.

For compression, as we saw in Chapter 1, Snappy is one of the most used compression codecs. We'd recommend using Snappy compression for all data sets whether they are stored in Avro or Parquet.

To summarize, Table 10-5 shows the storage formats and compression codecs to be used for various data sets. The data sets being queried frequently for a subset of columns in a data warehouse are better stored in columnar format, hence the use of Parquet. The data sets that are being appended to—user_rating_fact and user_history—are mostly used in the ETL pipeline (even though they can be queried directly as well) to populate the corresponding compacted tables; therefore, it makes sense to store them in Avro format since it's row major.

Table 10-5. Storage formats for various data sets

Data set	Storage format	Compression Codec
movie	Parquet	Snappy
user_history	Avro	Snappy
user	Parquet	Snappy
user_rating_fact	Avro	Snappy
user_rating	Parquet	Snappy

Partitioning

The next consideration is if we should partition any of our Hadoop data sets and, if so, by which columns. Correctly partitioning the data can eliminate large amounts of unnecessary I/O operations by allowing execution engines to skip parts of the data that are not necessary to execute the query.

Correctly partitioning depends on knowing the data access patterns. We have five data sets in total that we have to consider for partitioning: movie, user, user_history, user_rating, and user_rating_fact.

Let's talk about the append data sets, user_history and user_rating_fact, first. These are populated on every run of the ingest pipeline with new updates and inserts. However, typically when we query them we only want to retrieve the updates/inserts that were added to these tables in the last run. Partitioning them is quite important since we don't want to query historical data when we only want to retrieve the last run's results. Therefore, we decide to partition these data sets (assuming there is enough data to rationalize partitioning, especially in the case of user_history) by day. Depending on the data sizes, this may need to be adjusted.

Usually you want the average partition size to be at least a few multiples of the HDFS block sizes. Common block sizes for HDFS are 64 MB or 128 MB and based on the preceding analysis, a good canonical number for average partition size is 1 GB. If the number of ratings is much more than 1GB or so in a given day, then it may make sense to partition it by hour. On the other hand, if the number of user additions/updates is much less than 1 GB per day, it may make sense to partition the user data set weekly or monthly.

Now, let's talk about the other three data sets that are queried by end users: movie, user, and user_rating.

For movies, for example, it is very likely that we are more interested in ratings for new movies, so it may make sense to partition the movie data set according to the movie release dates. However, assuming the number of movies that gets released every year is somewhere between 10,000 and 20,000, the size of data for movies released in a given year would be of the order of several hundred megabytes at most (assuming a 10K average record size per movie multiplied by 10,000 movies, totaling 100 MB), which is not enough to fill a partition on its own. Therefore, given the small size of the movie data set, we recommend to not partition it at all.

The next question is whether we should partition the user data set and, if so, by what. The user table is likely too small to be partitioned, so we will leave it unpartitioned.

Next, let's move on to our last and arguably largest data set, user_rating. We have a few options here:

- We can leave user_rating unpartitioned. This means that on every query we will be doing I/O on the entirety of the data set, which is not optimal. Also, on every batch run to update this table, we will be rewriting all of this data set rather than a few partitions that were updated. So the I/O overhead at both read and write time is too much to rationalize this approach, especially given the size of the table.

- We can partition user_rating by day based on the timestamp on which a rating was first given. If most of the queries are going to be based on the day the rating was first given (e.g., the number of new ratings in the past seven days), then partitioning based on the day the rating was first given makes sense. However, there is a possibility that on every run, older partitions may need to be updated if a user updated his rating of a given movie since the last run.

- We can partition user_rating by day based on the timestamp on which rating was last updated. If most of the queries are going to be based on the day the rating was last updated (e.g., the average rating given to all movies in the past seven days), then partitioning based on the day the rating was last updated makes sense. There is still a possibility that on a given run, older partitions may need to be updated. This is because the table only contains one record per user per movie. This record stores the latest rating from that user for that movie. When a user updates her rating for a movie, this record needs to be moved from its older partition to the most recent new partition, since the movie was rerated.

The choice between the last two options is not an obvious one. The decision depends on how you are going to access the data in most cases. In our use case, we think that ratings will mostly be accessed based on the time they were last updated. Therefore, we'll go with the last option—to partition user_rating based on the timestamp when a user last updated her rating for a movie.

To summarize, we list the partitioning strategies for all our data sets in Table 10-6.

Table 10-6. Partitioning strategy for various data sets

Data set	Partitioned vs. Unpartitioned	Partitioning column	Notes
movie	Unpartitioned	N/A	Too small to be partitioned
user_history	Partitioned by day	Timestamp when the user information was last updated	For reduced I/O when using this data set to populate the user data set
user	Unpartitioned	N/A	Too small to be partitioned
user_rating_fact	Partitioned by day	Timestamp when the user last updated his rating for the movie	For reduced I/O when using this data set to populate the user_rating data set
user_rating	Partitioned by day	Timestamp when the user last updated his rating for the movie	For reduced I/O when querying data set based on the latest ratings given by users

Since all five data sets can be accessed by end users, the sets will reside under */data* (*/data/movielens*, to be precise).

Ingestion

Just as traditional ETL processes take data out of OLTP databases and load it to a data warehouse, we expect the majority of our data to arrive from an OLTP data store. This section goes into the details of ingesting data from our OLTP data store to Hadoop. In addition, Hadoop makes it possible to ingest nonrelational data relevant to our use case, such as movie reviews out of websites or comments from Twitter, and integrate them into our data analysis.

For the purpose of this example we will focus on ingesting relational data. Chapters 9 and 10 cover data ingest from streaming sources such as web logs and credit card purchases.

There are multiple options for ingesting data from relational databases to Hadoop. Sqoop is by far the most popular option and the one we will focus on in this chapter. We discussed how Sqoop works in Chapter 2, and shared some tips on how to use it. We will see here how Sqoop will be used in this specific case. Additional options are traditional ETL tools that integrate with Hadoop, such as Informatica or Pentaho. Change data capture systems, such as Oracle Golden Gate, can be used very effectively to replicate large tables that change very frequently.

Another option some Hadoop users attempt is to dump data from the relational databases to files and load these files to Hadoop. If a daily data dump from the OLTP system already exists, this allows "piggy backing" on an existing process and using it to load data to Hadoop. But if such a process does not already exist, there is no benefit to adding it; Sqoop itself will use the same data dump tools (such as mysqldump or Teradata fast export) to import data from the database and will do it in a way that is optimized, easy to use, and well tested. Therefore, if you are starting from scratch we recommend simply using Sqoop.

With Sqoop as our tool of choice, let's dive into the details of data import.

There are a few types of tables we will need to load:

Tables that rarely change
> We can extract these to Hadoop once and reimport on an as-needed. In our example, all the dimensions change on a regular basis—users change their profiles and new movies are released. So we will not include an example for this table type.

Tables that are modified regularly, but are relatively small
> We can extract these to Hadoop in full daily, without worrying about tracking changes depending on the exact size and available bandwidth. In our example, the movie table may be small enough to fit in this category. The movie data set falls in this category.

Tables that are modified regularly and are large enough that extracting them in full every day is infeasible
> For these tables we need a way to find the modifications done in the last day and extract only these modifications to Hadoop. These tables may be append-only (without updates), in which case we simply need to add the new rows to the table in Hadoop. Or they may have updates, in which case we will need to merge the modifications. The user_rating_fact and user_history data sets falls in this category.

The first and second types of tables are typically dimensions, although not all dimensions are small enough or change rarely enough to belong in this category. These tables will be extracted in the same way—the only difference is in how often we schedule the Sqoop job to run.

Note that we will not import these tables to Parquet since these are small tables with few columns. We will import them to Avro rather than CSV to avoid possible parsing problems when we need to access the data. Of course, with small tables we don't worry about partitioning either.

Now, let's see an example to import the movie data set into Hadoop from OLTP via Sqoop. Since the movie data set is small enough, we simply want to copy it over every run from the OLTP database to Hadoop. However, keep in mind that the schema of the movie data set in OLTP and Hadoop is different. In particular, the genre and movie_genre tables have been denormalized to become a part of the movie data set in Hadoop. We need to do a join between the movie, movie_genre, and genre tables to denormalize them into one data set. For that, we have two options:

- We can do the join in the Sqoop job, which will lead to the join being performed on the OLTP database. The data will then land in Hadoop in its denormalized form.

- We can do the join in Hadoop. We can simply import the movie, movie_genre, and genre tables from OLTP as exact copies from the OLTP database and then run a follow-on Hadoop job to join these three tables into a single denormalized data set.

The question is how do we decide which option to go with? In general, Sqoop allows free-form query imports (i.e., Sqoop import jobs that contain arbitrary SQL—in our case, a join). However, this is limited to simple queries that don't contain any ambiguous projections or OR clauses in the where clause. In such cases, you have to specify some additional parameters like --split-by in order to correctly parallelize the query, but it definitely saves the hassle of having to write and maintain an (albeit simple), follow-on job to do the join in Hadoop. On the other hand, in some environments the OLTP system may be short on resources, and using Sqoop to perform the join there would be considered too risky. Our recommendation is to use the free-form Sqoop import when the free-form SQL query to be run at the source database is simple and the OLTP database has the resources to execute it safely, but run a follow-on job in Hadoop for anything more complicated or when the OLTP system is at its capacity limits.

In our case, since we have a simple join, we will specify the join in the Sqoop job itself:

```
#!/bin/bash
# All nodes need to have access to the source database

# Cleanup if necessary. Script should continue even if
# this next rm command fails, hence the last || :
sudo -u hdfs hadoop fs -rm -r /data/movielens/movie || :

sqoop import --connect jdbc:mysql://mysql_server:3306/movielens
--username myuser --password mypass --query \
'SELECT movie.*, group_concat(genre.name)
FROM movie
JOIN movie_genre ON (movie.id = movie_genre.movie_id)
JOIN genre ON (movie_genre.genre_id = genre.id)
WHERE ${CONDITIONS}
GROUP BY movie.id' \
--split-by movie.id --as-avrodatafile --target-dir /data/movielens/movie
```

This command imports a denormalized version of the movie data set by running a join on the OLTP database. The data set is then stored in Avro format under */data/movielens/movie* on HDFS.

After importing the data, we want to create a matching Hive table, which we will later use for transformations. This requires getting the Avro schema for the files we just ingested and using them in the Hive table:

```
#!/bin/bash
# Clean up the destination schema file, if it exists.
# The last ||: ensures that we carry on the script even
# when the destination doesn't exist.
sudo -u hdfs hadoop fs -rm /metadata/movielens/movie/movie.avsc ||:
hadoop jar ${AVRO_HOME}/avro-tools.jar getschema \
/data/movielens/movie/part-m-00000.avro | \
hadoop fs -put - /metadata/movielens/movie/movie.avsc

hive -e "CREATE EXTERNAL TABLE IF NOT EXISTS movie
ROW FORMAT SERDE 'org.apache.hadoop.hive.serde2.avro.AvroSerDe'
STORED AS
INPUTFORMAT 'org.apache.hadoop.hive.ql.io.avro.AvroContainerInputFormat'
OUTPUTFORMAT 'org.apache.hadoop.hive.ql.io.avro.AvroContainerOutputFormat'
LOCATION '/data/movielens/movie'
TBLPROPERTIES ('avro.schema.url'='/metadata/movielens/movie/movie.avsc')"
```

Note that we always create tables as EXTERNAL. There is no performance drawback, and this allows us to drop or modify the table without losing the data. Also, note that in the preceding CREATE TABLE statement, we don't specify a schema when creating the Hive table. Instead, we specify the Avro schema using the avro.schema.url property, and the Hive schema is derived from the Avro schema. This way, we don't have to maintain two different schemas for the data, one in Avro and one in Hive. Here they share the same schema, as defined in Avro.

The third type has a few more requirements:

- First, we need to extract the entire table once and create a partitioned Hive table.
- Then, each day we need to extract the latest modifications and either append them to the Hive table or merge them.

Sqoop supports incremental imports. This means that if we have a column that can indicate whether the row contains new data—either a timestamp or an ID that gets incremented—Sqoop can store the value of the previous execution and use it on the next execution to make sure it only fetches new or modified rows.

To use this feature, we need to create a Sqoop metastore, which will be used to store the state of the Sqoop jobs. How to start the Sqoop metastore depends on your method of installation. If you are using packages, you can use the service command like so:

```
sudo service sqoop-metastore start
```

Alternatively, if you are using tarballs, you can use a command like the following:

```
mkdir -p /var/log/sqoop
nohup "/usr/bin/sqoop" metastore > /var/log/sqoop/metastore.log 2>&1 &
```

If you are using an administration tool, you should be able to start the Sqoop metastore via that tool.

After you have started the metastore, you can run your incremental import job as follows:

```
#!/bin/bash
SQOOP_METASTORE_HOST=localhost
# Delete the job if it already exists. If it doesn't exist, the last ||:
# ensures, the exit code is still success and the script continues on.
sqoop job --delete user_rating_import --meta-connect \
jdbc:hsqldb:hsql://${SQOOP_METASTORE_HOST}:16000/sqoop || :

# Need to explictly export HIVE_HOME before this command if Hive
# is not present under /usr/lib/hive
# No need to do so if you are using Apache Sqoop 1.4.6 or later
sqoop job --create user_rating_import --meta-connect \
jdbc:hsqldb:hsql://${SQOOP_METASTORE_HOST}:16000/sqoop \
-- import --connect jdbc:mysql://mysql_server:3306/movielens \
--username myuser \
--password-file hdfs://${NAMENODE_HOST}/metadata/movielens/.passwordfile \
--table user_rating -m 8 --incremental lastmodified \
--check-column timestamp --append --as-parquetfile --hive-import \
--warehouse-dir /data/movielens --hive-table user_rating_fact
```

This script creates a new Sqoop job called user_rating_import and stores the job in the Sqoop metastore. It imports the user_rating table from the MySQL OLTP database, specifying the user-name on the command line and password to connect in a password file on HDFS. It does an incremental import, based on the last value of the timestamp column that was imported in the last run, and appends the imported data to the destination Hive table, which stores the data in Parquet format. Every subsequent run will only extract rows with a timestamp higher than on the previous execution, which will only be the ratings that were added or updated since the last run.

To execute the job, simply run:

```
sqoop job -exec user_rating_import --meta-connect \
jdbc:hsqldb:hsql://${SQOOP_METASTORE_HOST}:16000/sqoop
```

If the original table is insert-only, we are done. The Sqoop job will append new data to a Hive table called user_rating every time we run the job. However, there are a few additional subsequent tasks we may need to perform:

- Partition the fact table according to the last update of the rating.

- In the scenario where data in the table can be modified and not just added—the users table, for example—we need to merge new updates into the existing table. In our example, we do this by having follow-on Hadoop jobs that take the recently appended data from user_rating_fact and merge it into the user_rating data set. You will read more about these jobs in "Data Processing and Access" on page 337.

- We may even want to run some aggregations in advance so later reports will execute faster.

Data Processing and Access

Now that we have discussed how we are going to model and ingest the data sets in Hadoop, we will discuss how to process the stored data.

Partitioning

There are three different types of data partitioning steps that may be required:

- Partitioning an existing table
- Loading data into multiple partitions in a table
- Adding data that was imported into a directory as a new partition to a table

To partition an existing table, we will need to create a new partitioned table, and then read the data from the existing table and load it into the correct partitions in the new table. The last step here is identical to what we will do when loading data into an existing partitioned table.

Let's start by creating a partitioned version of user_rating that is partitioned by year, month, and day. This table is otherwise identical to the original user_rating table:

```
#!/bin/bash
sudo -u hdfs hadoop fs -mkdir -p  /data/movielens/user_rating_part
sudo -u hdfs hadoop fs -chown -R ${USER}: /data/movielens/user_rating_part
hive -e "CREATE EXTERNAL TABLE IF NOT EXISTS user_rating_part(
  user_id INT,
  movie_id INT,
  rating INT,
  last_modified TIMESTAMP)
PARTITIONED BY (year INT, month INT, day INT)
ROW FORMAT SERDE 'parquet.hive.serde.ParquetHiveSerDe'
STORED AS
INPUTFORMAT 'parquet.hive.DeprecatedParquetInputFormat'
OUTPUTFORMAT 'parquet.hive.DeprecatedParquetOutputFormat'
LOCATION '/data/movielens/user_rating_part'"
```

The next step is to load the rating data into the correct partitions in the new table:

```
#!/bin/bash
hive -e "
SET hive.exec.dynamic.partition.mode=nonstrict;
SET hive.exec.dynamic.partition=true;
SET hive.exec.max.dynamic.partitions.pernode=1000;
INSERT INTO TABLE user_rating_part PARTITION (year, month, day)
SELECT
  *,
  YEAR(last_modified),
  MONTH(last_modified),
  DAY(last_modified)
FROM
  user_rating"
```

If the data was imported into a new directory and we just need to add this directory as a new partition, we can do this by:

```
#!/bin/bash
hive -e "ALTER TABLE user_rating_part
ADD PARTITION (year=2014, month=12, day=12)
LOCATION '/data/newdata'"
```

Merge/update

In some cases, it is not enough to add new facts to an existing table. Sometimes we actually want to modify existing information—for example, when we have "type 0" slowly changing dimension. Let's assume that when users modify their information, (e.g., their occupation), we have to update the user data set (in addition to updating the history in the user_history data set). In this section, we will focus on how to merge the updates into the user data set.

Remember that HDFS is a write-once filesystem. After we have the data in HDFS, we can't just modify the file a bit to update the records. What we need to do is read all the existing records from the file, and copy them to a new file with the modifications we need to make. As a last step, we update the Hive metastore so the table will now point at the new updated file.

As you can imagine, if the table is very large, reading all of it to make modifications can be slow and inefficient. There are three ways to handle this:

- Perhaps a large table can be partitioned and modifications are only needed on a subset of the partitions. For example, if sales can only be canceled up to 90 days following the date of sales, only partitions containing the last 90 days of data need to be copied and modified.

- Remember that Hadoop is not always fast, but it is very scalable. If you need to copy and modify large tables faster, perhaps the easiest solution is to add nodes to the cluster to achieve the required I/O and processing capacity.

- If the "slowly changing" dimension is actually large and rapidly changing, perhaps HDFS is not the best storage for it. Consider storing rapidly changing tables in HBase instead. Both Hive and Impala are capable of joining HBase and HDFS tables. Note that this will optimize updates at the expense of possibly slowing down some of the queries—HBase is slower than HDFS at large scan operations that are typical in a data warehouse.

Let's assume that we have decided to store the data in HDFS, and that for our user table example we need to update the entire table with new records we Sqooped from our OLTP system. After the incremental Sqoop job is finished, we have two directories with interesting data:

/data/movielens/user
    The existing table.

/etl/movielens/user_upserts
    New records—some are completely new, and some should replace records in the existing table. *Upsert* is a word derived from update + insert. In this context, this data set contains records that we need to *update* or *insert*.

The ingest query for user_upserts would look something like this:

```
#!/bin/bash
sqoop job --create user_upserts_import --meta-connect \
jdbc:hsqldb:hsql://${SQOOP_METASTORE_HOST}:16000/sqoop \
-- import --connect jdbc:mysql://mysql_server:3306/movielens \
--username myuser --password mypass \
-m 8 --incremental append --check-column last_modified --split-by last_modified \
--as-avrodatafile --query \
'SELECT
user.id,
user.age,
user.gender,
occupation.occupation,
zipcode,
last_modified
FROM user
JOIN occupation
ON (user.occupation_id = occupation.id)
WHERE ${CONDITIONS}' \
--target-dir /etl/movielens/user_upserts
```

We then create a Hive table that simply provides a tabular view on top of these records that we need to upsert:

```
#!/bin/bash
hive -e \
"CREATE EXTERNAL TABLE IF NOT EXISTS user_upserts(
  id INT,
  age INT,
```

```
  occupation STRING,
  zipcode STRING,
  last_modified BIGINT)
STORED AS AVRO
LOCATION '/etl/movielens/user_upserts'"
```

All we have to do at this point is to write a query that merges user_upserts with the existing user data set and overwrites the user table with the result of the merge. However, this INSERT OVERWRITE operation is not atomic in Hive. For a non-atomic insert, there may be times when users see an inconsistent view of the table. Therefore, we have to create a temporary user table, (say, user_tmp), insert the merge results into it, and atomically change the user table to pick up the new data.

Here are the CREATE TABLE statements for the user and user_tmp table:

```
#!/bin/bash
hive -e \
"CREATE EXTERNAL TABLE IF NOT EXISTS user(
  id INT,
  age INT,
  occupation STRING,
  zipcode STRING,
  last_modified TIMESTAMP)
ROW FORMAT SERDE 'parquet.hive.serde.ParquetHiveSerDe'
STORED AS
INPUTFORMAT 'parquet.hive.DeprecatedParquetInputFormat'
OUTPUTFORMAT 'parquet.hive.DeprecatedParquetOutputFormat'
LOCATION '/data/movielens/user'"

DT=$(date "+%Y-%m-%d")
hive -e \
"CREATE EXTERNAL TABLE IF NOT EXISTS user_tmp(
  id INT,
  age INT,
  occupation STRING,
  zipcode STRING,
  last_modified TIMESTAMP)
ROW FORMAT SERDE 'parquet.hive.serde.ParquetHiveSerDe'
STORED AS
INPUTFORMAT 'parquet.hive.DeprecatedParquetInputFormat'
OUTPUTFORMAT 'parquet.hive.DeprecatedParquetOutputFormat'
LOCATION '/data/movielens/user_${DT}'"
```

Notice that the table definitions for user and user_tmp are exactly the same except for the location part.

The goal now is to read the existing table, read the new records, and create a new table that merges the two. The new table will contain all the existing records (except where they conflict with new records) and all the new records.

In this example, the table is unpartitioned, but if the original user table were partitioned, we'd partition this table the exact same way. Note that we specify a location for the table and we include the current data in the location. This allows us to store a history of the user table and easily revert our changes.

The next step is the actual merge:

```
#!/bin/bash
hive -e "
INSERT OVERWRITE TABLE user_tmp
  SELECT
    user.*
  FROM
    user
    LEFT OUTER JOIN
    user_upserts
    ON (user.id = user_upserts.id)
  WHERE
    user_upserts.id IS NULL
  UNION ALL
  SELECT
    id, age, occupation, zipcode, TIMESTAMP(last_modified)
  FROM
    user_upserts"
```

This query, which may seem complex at first, takes all the records from user that are not replaced by records in user_upserts (we join the tables and only pick the records where `user_upserts.id` is null, which means there's no new record for this ID), and then we add all the new records (`UNION ALL SELECT * FROM USER_UPSERTS`). We then insert the results into the user_tmp data set:

```
#!/bin/bash
hive -e "ALTER TABLE user SET LOCATION '/data/movielens/user_${DT}'"
```

Now the user table will show the merged data from the current location. We can now safely drop user_upserts and perhaps a few days later delete the previous *user*${DT}_ directory.

Aggregations

Very frequently, the whole point of performing ETL in Hadoop is to support aggregations that are very expensive to perform in a relational database. When we discuss complex aggregations, people often think of advanced analytics. They frequently fail to notice that the best optimization opportunities occur when the aggregation involves very simple aggregations (sum, count, and average) performed for a very large number of entities. These types of aggregations are known as *embarrassingly parallel* and are a fantastic fit for Hadoop, where it's cheaper and more scalable to bring in large amounts of resources to perform the aggregation within SLAs. Examples of this type of aggregation include telecommunication companies aggregating error counts for all their installed equipment, or agricultural companies averaging moisture level for every square yard of every field they service.

In our case, an example would be counting the number of times a given user rated a particular movie. When the fact table is large, this can be a very large query, but it will execute remarkably fast on a large Hadoop cluster because each user-movie count can be done independently in parallel.

You can aggregate in Hive or Impala using the "CREATE TABLE AS SELECT" (or CTAS) pattern:

```
#!/bin/bash
hive -e "
CREATE TABLE user_movie_count AS
SELECT
  movie_id,
  user_id,
  COUNT(*) AS count
FROM
  user_rating_fact
GROUP BY
  movie_id,
  user_id"
```

A more useful aggregation in our case would be the average rating per movie:

```
#!/bin/bash
hive -e "
CREATE TABLE avg_movie_rating AS
SELECT
  movie_id,
  ROUND(AVG(rating), 1) AS rating
FROM
  user_rating_part
GROUP BY
  movie_id"
```

Note that although we used Hive or Impala for our examples, you can use any Hadoop processing tool. Some aggregations involve either specialized algorithms that are either not available in SQL (for example, geospatial functions) or are complex to express in SQL (for example, the sessionization example we explored in Chapter 8). It's good to remember that unlike ELT systems, where transformations are limited to what can be done in SQL, Hadoop gives you a huge range of tools to apply to any problem. If you choose to use a different tool for aggregation, it is a simple matter of creating an external table on the results, and users can access them through Impala.

Or, as we'll see in the next section, no matter how you generated the aggregated data set, you can use Sqoop to load the results to a relational data warehouse where it's accessible to all your BI tools.

Data Export

After the data is processed, we need to decide what to do with the results. One option is to simply keep it in Hadoop, and query it using Impala and BI tools that integrate with it. Hive may be used for this purposes as well; however, given the low-latency requirements of access, Impala may be a better fit.

But in many cases the business already has large investments in applications, either home-grown or third-party, that are using the existing relational data warehouse. Transitioning all of them to Hadoop is a significant investment and one that doesn't always makes sense.

In that case we need an efficient way to export the processed data from Hadoop to the relational data warehouse. There are several options here. ETL tools that integrate with Hadoop, such as Informatica and Pentaho, can be used. Some database vendors, most notably Oracle, have proprietary optimized connectors for loading data from Hadoop to their database. The most popular option is still Sqoop.

Using Sqoop to transfer data to a relational database is fairly straightforward. Instead of running `sqoop import` we run `sqoop export`, which works by inserting rows in batches and committing data to the database every few batches. This means that there will be multiple databases commits while data is exported, and if the export fails halfway through, there may be rows remaining in the database that can be challenging to clean up. That's why we recommend configuring Sqoop to import to a staging table and only move the data to the actual table when all the data has been successfully exported.

Another thing to note is that exporting data can involve both inserting and updating rows. Sqoop supports insert-only, update-only, or a mixed mode. Make sure you choose the correct one for your use case. Updates require an update key, which is a unique key for the table. This key is used to identify when Sqoop is actually updating an existing row, so it must be identical between Hadoop and the relational data warehouse.

Here's an example of Sqoop export to a staging table, with both inserts and updates:

```
#!/bin/bash
# The destination table in the data warehouse has to exist before this
# is run along with appropriate write permissions to the user running
# the Sqoop job
# Something like this should do:
# CREATE TABLE avg_movie_rating(movie_id INT, rating DOUBLE);

sqoop export --connect \
jdbc:mysql:/mysql_server:3306/movie_dwh --username myuser --password mypass \
--table avg_movie_rating --export-dir /user/hive/warehouse/avg_movie_rating \
-m 16 --update-key movie_id --update-mode allowinsert \
--input-fields-terminated-by '\001' --lines-terminated-by '\n'
```

A final recommendation is to always use an optimized Sqoop connector if one is available for your database. These connectors support bulk loading, reduce locks in the database, and significantly improve export rates.

Orchestration

After the entire ETL process was developed, it is time to automate the workflow. As we discussed in previous chapters, the orchestration can be done through Oozie (if you choose to use an open source solution) or with orchestration tools that are already used in your organization (Autosys, Activebatch, and UC4 are popular choices).

If you decide to use Oozie, the workflow is likely to include:

- A Sqoop action for retrieving the data
- A Hive action to join, partition, or merge the data sets
- Multiple Hive or MapReduce actions for aggregation
- A Sqoop action for exporting the results to a data warehouse

We've seen examples of Hive and MapReduce actions when we discussed the click-stream use case. Let's look at a quick example of a Sqoop action:

```
<action name="import_facts">
    <sqoop xmlns="uri:oozie:sqoop-action:0.4">
        <job-tracker>${jobTracker}</job-tracker>
        <name-node>${nameNode}</name-node>
        <command>job -exec user_rating_import \
        --meta-connect jdbc:hsqldb:hsql://edgenode:16000/sqoop</command>
        <archive>/tmp/mysql-connector-java.jar#mysql-connector-java.jar</archive>
        <file>/tmp/hive-site.xml#hive-site.xml</file>
    </sqoop>
    <ok to="end"/>
    <error to="kill"/>
</action>
```

Note that because we are executing a job stored in the Sqoop metastore, we only need to tell Sqoop which job to execute (and to make sure all cluster nodes can connect to the metastore). We do this through the <command> parameter. Note that we also need to tell Sqoop and Oozie where to find the JDBC driver and Hive configuration, which is done in the <archive> and <file> parameters.

Note that the workflow will include multiple Sqoop actions (one for each table), multiple partition or merge steps, multiple aggregations, and so on. We can implement this through the fork-and-join pattern described in Chapter 6.

Figure 10-8 shows what the overall workflow may look like.

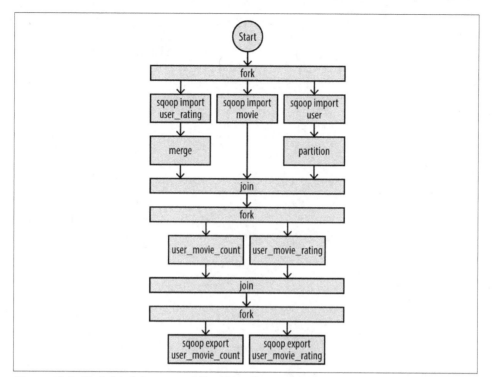

Figure 10-8. High-level Oozie workflow for ETL process

Conclusion

In this chapter, we learned about some of the challenges of the existing enterprise data warehouse deployments. We saw how Hadoop can complement EDWs to meet ETL SLAs, reduce excessive load on the EDW, and serve as an active archive for full-fidelity data and an excellent platform for doing exploratory analysis. We took the example of the MovieLens data set to illustrate how such a data set would look in an OLTP system, how it would get imported to Hadoop, and what transformations on that data in Hadoop would look like. Then, we showed some example aggregations that can be done on that MovieLens data in Hadoop and exported those aggregations to a data warehouse. We also showed how an orchestration tool like Oozie can be used to orchestrate all the import, processing and export processing. Similarly, you can join semi-structured or unstructured data with the traditional structured data in the EDW.

We hope that with the knowledge gained in this chapter, you will be able to use Hadoop to complement your EDW and derive more value from your data than you could before, due to constraints on your existing infrastructure.

Joins in Impala

We provided an overview of Impala and how it works in Chapter 3. In this appendix, we look at how Impala plans and executes a distributed join query. At the time of this writing, Impala has two join strategies: *broadcast joins* and *partitioned hash joins*.

Broadcast Joins

The broadcast join is the first and the default join pattern of Impala. In a broadcast join Impala takes the smaller data set and distributes it to all the Impala daemons involved with the query plan. Once distributed, the participating Impala daemons will store the data set as an in-memory hash table. Then each Impala daemon will read the parts of the larger data set that are local to its node and use the in-memory hash table to find the rows that match between both tables, (i.e., perform a hash join). There is no need to read the entire large data set into memory, so Impala uses a 1 GB buffer to read the large table and perform the joining part by part.

Figures A-1 and A-2 show how this works. Figure A-1 shows how each daemon will cache the smaller data set. While this join strategy is simple, it requires that the join occur with at least one small table.

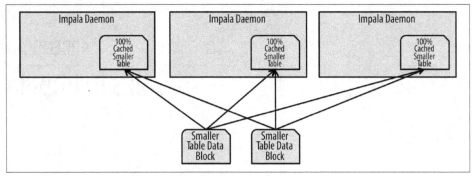

Figure A-1. Smaller table caching in broadcast joins

It's important to note that:

- The smaller data set is now taking up memory on every node. So if you have three nodes with 50 GB of Impala memory, the smaller data set in a broadcast join is limited to a little over 40 GB, even though the cluster has 150 GB total for Impala.

- The data buffered in memory is not the entire small table—it's a hash of the join columns together with other columns used in the query. If the query only uses a small subset of the columns from the smaller table, only this amount of memory will be used.

- The smaller table has to reach every Impala daemon. This means the data will need to go over the network, limiting the query throughput to that of the cluster bandwidth.

- Impala uses a cost-based optimizer to estimate the table size and decide whether to perform a broadcast join, which table is smaller, and how much memory the hash table will require. The cost-based optimizer can only come up with a reasonable execution plan if it knows the sizes of the tables involved in the query. Therefore, collecting statistics on the data on a regular basis is critical for achieving good performance with Impala.

After the data has been broadcast and cached, the larger data set has to be streamed across the in-memory hash map of the smaller data set. Each Impala daemon takes a portion of the larger data set, scans it in, and runs it through the hash join function, as shown in Figure A-2.

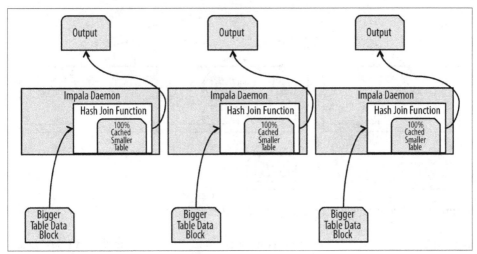

Figure A-2. Broadcast joins in Impala

The larger data set will typically be read by the Impala daemon from the local disk, reducing network utilization. Since the smaller data set is cached on each node, the only network transmission at this phase will occur only if the results go to another join in the query plan. Figure A-2 assumes a single join query.

Partitioned Hash Join

The partitioned hash join requires more network activity, but allows joining large data sets without requiring an entire table to fit into the memory of a single node. The partitioned hash join is used either when the table statistics indicate that the table is too large to fit into the memory of a single node or when a query hint is used to indicate the use of a partitioned hash join.

To perform a partitioned hash join (also known as a *shuffle join*), each Impala daemon reads the local data of the smaller of the two joined tables, partitions it using a hash function, and distributes each partition to a different Impala daemon.

As shown in Figure A-3, now each node only stores a subset of the data instead of the entire data set as happens in broadcast join. This allows more efficient use of cluster memory.

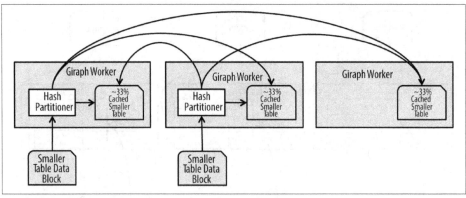

Figure A-3. Smaller table caching in partitioned hash joins

Figure A-4 illustrates how the join is implemented. To make the diagram less complex, we will focus on just one of the three Impala daemons, but understand that all Impala daemons are executing the same actions.

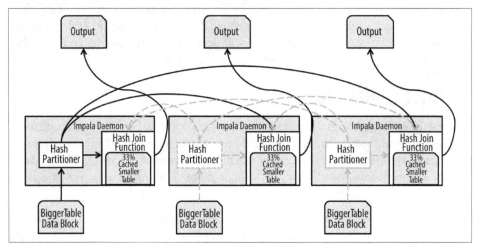

Figure A-4. Partitioned hash joins in Impala

As you can see in this diagram, the larger table is also partitioned via the same hash function and partitions are sent to the nodes, where they can be joined with matching data from the smaller table. Note that unlike the broadcast join where data is sent over the network only once, in a partitioned join the data from both tables has to be distributed between the nodes, causing higher network utilization.

To summarize, Impala has two types of joining strategies: a broadcast join, which requires more memory and is therefore suited only for smaller tables, and a partitioned join, which uses more network resources and is therefore slower, but is suitable for large tables.

Impala allows you to select the joining strategy with the hints of [BROADCAST] or [PAR TITION] in a SQL statement. Here is a simple coding example:

```
select
from foo f join [BROADCAST] bar b
on f.bar_id = b.bar_id
```

However, we recommend against using hints, since this means the join strategy is now hardcoded in your query. If a table started small and grew, the [BROADCAST] hint is no longer appropriate. One of the most common reasons Impala queries fail due to lack of memory is when a broadcast join is used on tables that are too large and should have been joined with a partitioned join.

A better design is to allow Impala to select the joining strategy, which requires collecting statistics on the data. To collect statistics you need to run the following query:

```
ANALYZE TABLE <Ttable> COMPUTE STATISTICS;
```

This instructs Impala to scan the table and collect statistics on size and key distributions. This will allow Impala to select the best joining strategy to optimize performance. It is always recommended to run the compute `statistics` statement on tables that have been updated with more than 10% of their content.

Index

A

abnormal behavior, 281
abstractions, 104-126
    Cascading, 106, 115-119
    Crunch, 105, 110-115
    Hive, 119-126
    Pig, 105, 106-109
access patterns
    for Hadoop storage options, 43
    HBase versus HDFS, 43
accumulator variables, 99
action nodes (Oozie workflow), 191
actions
    in workflows, 183
    workflow actions in Oozie, 188
        classpath definitions for, 203
actions (Spark), 99, 100
ActiveBatch, 186
additivity, 318
agents (Flume), 63
aggregate fact tables, 318
aggregations, 215, 235
    in data warehousing example, 341-342
    Storm support for, 233
aggregators in Giraph, 169
agnostic compression, 6
alerting, 216
    solutions for, 247
    Spark Streaming, support for, 246
    Storm capabilities, evaluation of, 233
    Trident capabilities, evaluation of, 237
all grouping, streams in Storm, 222
ALTER TABLE command, 34
Amazon, Simple Storage System (S3), 4

analysis tools accessing Hadoop data warehouse and data, 314
analyzing (in clickstream analysis), 256, 275
anomaly detection, 284
Apache Crunch (see Crunch)
Apache Drill, 127
Apache Oozie (see Oozie)
Apache Pig (see Pig)
Apache Spark website, 96
Apache Sqoop (see Sqoop)
Apache Storm (see Storm)
Apache Tez, 104
/app directory, 17
appending data, 60
    in data ingestion, 42
    user history, in data warehousing example, 324
archiving data (see data archiving)
ArrayFiles, 6
at least once delivery semantics, 73
at most once delivery semantics, 73
at-least-once processing (Storm), 223
at-most-once processing (Storm), 223
Autosys, 186
availability
    HBase and, 289
    HBase BlockCache and, 289
    high availability for Hive metastore, 34
    high availability in Kafka, 71
averages
    rolling averages, solutions for, 248
    simple moving averages, Storm example, 226-233

channels (Kafka), 74
checkpoint directory, 242
Chronos, 186
classpath definitions (Oozie actions), 203
click data, 253
clickstream analysis, 253-280
  analyzing data, 275
  defining the use case, 253-255
  high-level design of example, 256
  ingestion, 260
  orchestration, 276
  processing design, 268
    deduplicating data, 270
    sessionization, 272
  storage, 257
  using Hadoop, 255
client architecture, fraud detection system, 286
client tier (Flume ingestion pipeline), 263
  details of, 264
clients
  connecting client to Flume in fraud system,
    296
    client push, 296
    logfile pull, 298
    message queue or Kafka in middle, 299
cloud-based storage systems, 4
cluster managers, 96
collections
  PCollections in Crunch, 114
  RDDs, 97
collector tier (Flume ingestion pipeline), 263
  components in collector tier agents, 266
  configuration file for collector agents, 267
column families (in HBase), 30
columnar formats, 9
  failure handling, 11
  using in Flume when ingesting data into
    HDFS, 65
  using Parquet in data warehousing example,
    329
columns (in HBase), 28
  combined or atomic, 290
  naming, 291
combined log format, 254
combiners (MapReduce), 86
command-line interface
  Impala, 130
  Pig, 109
compaction, 136

lower cost in HBase, using column families,
  30
time required for, HBase table regions and,
  28
compaction jobs, 43
complex data pipelines, solutions for, 249
compression, 12
  agnostic, 6
  columnar formats, 9
  formats available for Hadoop, 12
    bzip2, 13
    Gzip, 13
    LZO, 12
    Snappy, 12
  in Hadoop, recommendations for, 13
  of files ingested into Hadoop, 45
  options for data stored in Hadoop, 3
  row keys, with Snappy, 24
  SequenceFiles, 6
  splittable files, 5
  text data stored in Hadoop, 4
  using Snappy in data warehousing example,
    329
$CONDITIONS placeholder, use in Sqoop, 56
config-defaults.xml file (Oozie), 202
Configuration object, 84
connectors, database
  bottlenecks in ingestion pipeline, 59
  database-specific connectors, using, 57
consistency in HBase, 289
consumer groups (Kafka), 71
consumers (Kafka), 71
container formats, 4
  for binary data, 5
  for structured text data, 5
containers, data containers in Pig, 107
control nodes (Oozie workflow), 191
ControlM, 186
coordinators (Oozie), 188
  coordinator.xml file for frequency schedul-
    ing, 205
  coordinator.xml files for time and data trig-
    gers, 206
  executing, 210
  in sessionizing orchestration, 277
  scheduling workflows, 204
counting
  event counting using HBase increment or
    put, 291

exec source, 262
EXPLAIN keyword (SQL), 123, 130
exploratory analysis, 302
    in fraud detection system, 304
    in Hadoop data warehouse offload, 310
    moving warehoused data to Hadoop for, 313
exporting data from Hadoop, 76
    in data warehousing example, 343
external rules engine architecture, fraud system, 306
extract, transform, and load (see ETL processes)
extract-load-transform processing (see ELT processing)

F

F1 white paper (Google), 126
fact, 324
fact tables, 318
    using Parquet as storage format, 329
failure handling
    comparing for different file formats, 11
    in ingestion pipeline, 50
fair scheduler throttling, 57
fan-in architecture (Flume), 63, 264
fan-out workflows, 196
fault tolerance
    in Hive, 126
    in Kafka, 72
    in MapReduce, 82
    in Spark Streaming, 242, 245
    in Storm, 224
feature-rich Hive, 126
fields grouping, streams in Storm, 222
file channels (Flume), 68, 71, 262, 266
    number of, 69
    size of, 70
file formats, 2
    compression, 12
    considerations when ingesting data into HDFS with Flume, 65
    data stored in Hadoop, 3
    failure handling behavior, comparing, 11
    Hadoop, 5
        file-based data structures, 6
    original file type of ingested data, 45
    RecordReader implementations for, 84
    standard, storing in Hadoop, 4

binary data, 5
    structured text data, 5
    text data, 4
file transfers, 52-56
    clickstream data and, 260
    using for data imports, 52
    using HDFS client commands, 52
    using Sqoop, 56
    versus other ingest methods, 55
filenames, embedding metadata in, 35
filesystems
    alternatives to HDFS, 3
    ingesting data from, considerations, 44
filter() function (Spark), 99
filter-join-filter code example
    in Cascading, 116-118
    in Crunch, 110-115
    in Hive, 121-125
    in Pig, 106
    in Spark, 102
Flume
    architecture, 62
    as push or pull tool, 50
    defined, 61
    encrypting data sent between agents, 49
    file formats, 65
    ingesting files with, 55
    ingestion layer of fraud system, 295
        path between client and Flume, 296-302
    ingestion of log data in clickstream analysis, 261
    ingestion pipeline for clickstream analysis
        architecture, high-level view, 262
        client tier, 264
        collector tier, 266
    interceptors, 48, 213, 246
        architecture for fraud detection, 305
        stream processing with, 214
    Kafka versus, for ingest of streaming data into Hadoop, 74
    Log4J appender, 261
    patterns, 63
        fan-in architecture, 63
        partitioning data on ingest, 65
        splitting data on ingest, 64
    recommendations and best practices for, 66
    selectors, 48
    streaming ingestion, failure handling, 51
    use in complex data pipelines solution, 249

hash tables, operations supported by, 21
HBase
    compactions, 43, 136
    data source, support by Impala, 127
    event counting using increment function or
        put, 291
    event history using HBase put, 292
    in a near-real-time architecture, 215
    integrating Storm with, 225
    integration with, 216
    profile storage and retrieval
        columns, combined or atomic, 290
        HBase data definition, 289
        Hbase with BlockCache, 289
    schema design for, 21-31
        hops, 25
        row keys, 22
        tables and regions, 26
        timestamps, 25
        using column families, 30
        using columns, 28
    time series modifications and versioning,
        148
    using with RowKey of RecordKey and Start-
        Time, 149
HCatalog, 33
    interfaces to store, update, and retrieve met-
        adata, 34
    limitations of, 34
HDFS (Hadoop Distributed File System), 2
    access patterns, 44
    accessing from Pig command line, 109
    client commands, 52
    data ingestion and
        incremental updates, 42
        timeliness requirements, 41
    data source, support by Impala, 127
    HDFS sink in collector tier of Flume pipe-
        line, 266
    in clickstream analysis design, 256
    in Flume pipeline in clickstream analysis
        design, 263
    integrating Storm with, 225
    integration with, 216
    mountable HDFS, 53
    schema design for, 14-21
        bucketing, 18
        denormalizing, 20
        location of HDFS files, 16

    partitioning, 18
    storage of data in clickstream analysis, 258
    storing metadata in, 36
    using for storage in data warehousing exam-
        ple, 320
    using for time series modifications, 149
HFiles, 28
high availaility
    Hive metastore, problems with, 34
    Kafka, 72
higher-level functions, 216
Hive, 119-126
    aggregations in, 342
    creating tables matching Avro tables, 335
    deduplication of data, 270
        deduplicating click data, 271
        deduplicating in SQL, 139
    example, filter-join-filter code, 121-125
    fan-out workflow, running in Oozie, 196
    information resources for, 121
    ORC (Optimized Row Columnar) format
        and, 10
    overview, 119
    passing parameter to Hive action in a work-
        flow, 202
    performance issues, and changes in execu-
        tion engine, 119
    running a Hive action in Oozie, 195
    sessionization in, 275
    when to use, 125
        versus Impala, 131
Hive metastore, 32
    embedded, local, and remote modes, 33
    HCatalog acting as accessibility veneer, 33
    limitations of, 34
Hive metastore database, 33
Hive metastore service, 33
HiveServer2, 120
hops (in HBase design), 25
Hue tool, 191

I

IMDb, 314
Impala, 126-132
    aggregations in, 342
    example, 130
    joins, 347-351
    overview, 127
    speed-oriented design, 128

efficient execution engine, 129
efficient use of memory, 128
long-running daemons, 129
use of LLVM, 130
using to analyze data in clickstream analysis, 275
when to use, 131
impala-shell, 130
impalad, 127
importing data
considerations, 39-51
access patterns of the data, 43
failure handling, 50
incremental updates, 42
level of complexity, 51
network bottlenecks, 48
network security, 49
original source system and data structure, 44
push or pull tools, 49
timeliness of data ingestion, 40
transformations of imported data, 47
in Hadoop data warehousing design, 319
ingesting secondary data into Hadoop, 268
ingestion architecture of fraud system, 295
ingestion in clickstream analysis, 256
Flume architecture, 262
ingestion in data warehousing example, 332-337
options for, 51-76
file transfers, 52-56
using Flume, 61
using Kafka, 71-76
using Sqoop, 56
stream processing solutions for ingestion, 247
increment() function (HBase), 291
--incremental flag (sqoop), 61
incremental imports, 319
performing in Sqoop, 335
incremental updates, 40
incrementing counter (windowing analysis example), 141
indexes, HDFS and, 18
ingestion, 256
(see also importing data)
input formats
Giraph, VertexInputFormat, 166
in MapReduce, 88, 138

InputDStream object, 238
multiple, in Spark Streaming example, 240
InputFormat class, 83, 138
INSERT OVERWRITE TABLE statement, 341
inserts, 339
Sqoop export to staging table with, 343
interceptors (Flume), 48, 62, 261
(see also Flume)
recommendations for, 68
interprocess communications, 8
Isilon OneFS, 4
iterative processing
MapReduce and, 82
Spark, 104
stream processing soltions for, 248

J

Java
Cascading, 106, 115
Crunch, 105
HCatalog API, 34
launching Java actions on Oozie, 191
Oozie actions, classpath definition for, 203
property file format, 200
SequenceFiles support, 7
Spark APIs, 101
Java virtual machines (JVMs), 81
JDBC (Java Database Connectivity), 57
Hive, 120
JDBC channel (Flume), 69
JMS queues, 261
Job object, 89
job.properties file, 202, 210
jobs, setup code, MapReduce example, 90
JobTracker URI, 195
join() function (Spark), 100
joins
denormalizing versus, in Hadoop, 323
having too many, 321
join element in fork-and-join workflow, 197
join strategies in Crunch, 114
join strategies in Impala, 128, 347-351
joining data sets, 19
joining tables in ingestion phase, data warehousing example, 334
map-side, 19
nested-loops join, 94
repeated, avoiding in Hadoop, 20
JSON

Avro schemas, 9
files stored in Hadoop, 5
profiles stored in, 293
JVMs (Java virtual machines), 81

K

Kafka, 71-76
  connecting client to Flume in fraud system, 300
  data encryption and, 49
  fault tolerance, 72
  Flume versus, for ingest of streaming data into Hadoop, 74
  ingestion of log data in clickstream analysis, 261
  Kafka to Storm or Spark Streaming, fraud detection architecture, 306
  publishing alerts in fraud detection system, 294
  real-time processing and, 214
  use cases, 72
  using for streaming input data, 47
  using with Hadoop, 74
  using with Storm for stream processing, 248
keyBy() function (Spark), 100
Kite SDK, 36

L

Lambda Architecture
  machine-learning applications that use, 133
  overview, 216
  Spark Streaming, support for, 246
  Storm and, 233
  support by streaming frameworks, 216
  Trident and, 237
launcher job, 190
lazy transformations, 99
leaf-level partitions, 259
least recently used (LRU) cache, 23
lineage (RDDs), 97
LLLVM (low level virtual machine), 130
local caches, 288
Log4J, 261
logs, 255
  (see also web logs)
  for clickstream analysis, 253
  importing logfiles into Hadoop, 47
  logfile pull, using to connect client to Flume, 298

low-latency enrichment, validation, alerting, and ingestion, 247
  Flume solution for), 247
  Kafka and Storm, using, 248
low-latency query engines, 126
Luigi, 186
LZO compression, 12
LzoJsonInputFormat, 5

M

machine data, 313
machine learning
  advanced analysis for, 275
  learning resources, recommended, 285
  Mahout library, 133
  use in fraud detection system, 304
macro batches, 40
map() function
  in Spark, 99
  Spark deduplication example, 138
map-side joins, 19
MapFiles, 6
mappers, 81
  cleanup() method, 86
  example code for, 90
  map() method, 85
  no talking between mappers rule, 163
  number of, 83
  output format, calling, 88
  setup() method, 84
MapReduce, 80-94
  abstractions over, 104
  DAG model, 95
  example, 88-94
    job setup, 90
    mapper, 90
    partitioner, 92, 93
  file formats designed to work with, 6
  graph processing, 162
  Hive execution engine, 119
  information resources for, 82
  JobTracker and YARN Resource Manager URIs, 195
  limitations making it unsuitable for iterative algorithms, 82
  map phase, 83
    combiners, 86
    InputFormat class, 83
    Mapper.cleanup(), 86

Sqoop extracting data from, for import into
        Hadoop, 50
relations (Pig), 107
remote caches, 288
remote mode (Hive metastore), 33
repartitionAndSortWithinPartitions(), 145
REPL (read-eval-print loop), 102
resends during data ingest, 135
resilient distributed datasets (RDDs), 96
    defined, 97
    DStreams versus RDDs, 238
    graph processing RDDs, 175
    Spark Streaming, taking advantage of, 237
    storage of, 101
    transformations, 99
    within the context of DStreams, 239
resource managers (Spark), 101
REST API, HCatalog, 34
row formats, 9
row keys, 22
    ability to scan, 23
    block cache in HBase, 23
    compression with Snappy, 24
    distribution of records in HBase, 22
    readability, 24
    record retrieval in HBase, 22
    size of, 24
    uniqueness, 24
RowKey, 149

S

S3 (Simple Storage System), 4
salting (row keys), 23
sanitization of raw data sets, 269
Scala
    Spark deduplication example, 137
    Spark in, 101
scheduling patterns, 204
    frequency scheduling, 205
    time and data triggers, 205
schema evaluation, Avro support for, 9
Schema-on-Read, 1
Schema-on-Write, 1
schemas
    Avro, 8
    Avro and Parquet, 11
    fixed schema for metadata in Hive meta-
        store, 35
    in data warehouse data, 311

schema design for data stored in Hadoop, 2
schema design for HBase, 21-31
    hops, 25
    row keys, 22
    tables and regions, 26
    timestamps, 25
    using column families, 30
    using columns, 28
schema design for HDFS, 14-21, 258
    bucketing, 18
    denormalizing, 20
    location of HDFS files, 16
    partitioning, 18
    XML schema for actions and workflow in
        Oozie, 196
scripting, limitations of, for workflow orches-
    tration, 184
security, network security and data imports into
    Hadoop, 49
SELECT command, explaining in Hive, 123
selectors (Flume), 48, 62
sendMessage() method, 179
Sequence IDs, 60
SequenceFiles, 6
    block-compressed, 6
    failure handling, 11
    limited support outside of Hadoop, 7
    record-compressed, 6
    uncompressed, 6
    use case, as container for smaller files, 7
sequential execution, Sqoop tasks, 57
serialization, 7
serialization formats, 8
    Avro, 8
    Protocol Buffers, 8
    Thrift, 8
serving layer (Lambda Architecture), 217
sessionization, 272
    in Hive, 275
    in MapReduce, 274
    in Pig, 275
    in Spark, 273
    orchestration of, 276
sessions, 272
SetFiles, 6
shared nothing architectures, 80, 163
    Impala, 127
shared variables, 99
sharedlib, 191

HBase, and regions per table, 26
types of, ingestion in data warehousing
example, 333
text data
storing in Hadoop, 4
structured text data, 5
using text files in Flume to ingest data into
HDFS, 65
TextInputFormat object, 83, 138
TextVertexInputFormat, 166
Tez, 104
Hive-on-Tez project, 119
third normal form, 20
threads
number of threads in Flume, 70
use by Flume sources, 67
three-level partitioning scheme, 259
Thrift, 8
client connections in Hive, 120
Impala connections via, 127
time series modifications, 147-156
data generation for example, 150
Spark time series, code example, 151
using HBase and versioning, 148
using HBase with RowKey or RecordKey
and StartTime, 149
using HDFS and rewriting the whole table,
149
using partitions on HDFS for current and
historical records, 150
time triggers for workflow scheduling, 205
time-agnostic (workflows), 204
time-to-live (TTL), in HBase, 30
timeliness of data ingestion, 40
transformations and, 48
timestamps
HBase, 25
in RDBMS data ingested into Hadoop with
Sqoop, 61
using in Flume when ingesting data into
HDFS, 262
/tmp directory, 16
topologies, 219
transactional topologies (in Storm), 224
transformations
in data warehouse operations, 310
in Hadoop data warehouse data, 314
in Spark, 99

repartitionAndSortWithinPartitions(),
145
of data being imported into Hadoop, 47
offloading to Hadoop by data warehouses,
312
RDD lineage, 97
Spark transformations to GraphX processing, 180
trasformation functions in Pig, 107
Trident, 224, 233-237
evaluation of
counting and windowing support, 237
enrichment and alerting, 237
example, simple moving average, 234-237
NRT counting, rolling averages, and iterative processing, 248
use in complex data pipelines solution, 249
troubleshooting
diagnosing bottlenecks in ingestion pipeline
between Hadoop and RDBMS, 59
finding Flume bottlenecks, 70
Tuple object, 139
tuples, 107
in Storm topologies, 221
type conversions, text data stored in Hadoop, 4

U

UC4, 186
unsupervised learning, in fraud detection analytics, 305
updates
data on Hadoop ingested from RDBMS, 60
incremental, 42
Sqoop export to staging table with, 343
stored data in data warehousing example,
338
tracking, MovieLens data warehousing
example, 324
upserts, 339
/user directory, 16
UTC time, 207

V

validation
global context validation, 287
in stream processing, 216
profile content validation, 287
stream processing solutions, 247
variables, shared, 99

About the Authors

Mark Grover is a committer on Apache Bigtop and a committer and PMC member on Apache Sentry (incubating) and a contributor to Apache Hadoop, Apache Hive, Apache Sqoop, and Apache Flume projects. He is also a section author of O'Reilly's book on Apache Hive, *Programming Hive*.

Ted Malaska is a Senior Solutions Architect at Cloudera helping clients be successful with Hadoop and the Hadoop ecosystem. Previously, he was a Lead Architect at the Financial Industry Regulatory Authority (FINRA), helping build out a number of solutions from web applications and service-oriented architectures to big data applications. He has also contributed code to Apache Flume, Apache Avro, Yarn, and Apache Pig.

Jonathan Seidman is a Solutions Architect at Cloudera working with partners to integrate their solutions with Cloudera's software stack. Previously, he was a technical lead on the big data team at Orbitz Worldwide, helping to manage the Hadoop clusters for one of the most heavily trafficked sites on the Internet. He's also a co-founder of the Chicago Hadoop User Group and Chicago Big Data, technical editor for Hadoop in Practice, and he has spoken at a number of industry conferences on Hadoop and big data.

Gwen Shapira is a Solutions Architect at Cloudera. She has 15 years of experience working with customers to design scalable data architectures. She was formerly a senior consultant at Pythian, Oracle ACE Director, and board member at NoCOUG. Gwen is a frequent speaker at industry conferences and maintains a popular blog.

Colophon

The animal on the cover of *Hadoop Application Architectures* is a manatee (family Trichechidae), of which there are three extant species: the Amazonian, the West Indian, and the West African.

Manatees are fully aquatic mammals that can weigh up to 1,300 pounds. The name *manatee* is derived from the Taíno word *manatí*, meaning "breast." They are thought to have evolved from four-legged land mammals over 60 million years ago; their closest living relatives are elephants and hyraxes.

Though they live exclusively underwater, manatees often have coarse hair and whiskers. They also have thick wrinkled skin and a prehensile upper lip that is used to gather food. Manatees are herbivores and spend half the day grazing on fresh- or saltwater plants. In particular, they prefer the floating hyacinth, pickerel weeds, water lettuce, and mangrove leaves. The upper lip is split into left and right sides that can move independently of one another, and the lip can even help in tearing apart plants to aid in chewing.

Manatees tend to be solitary animals except when searching for a mate or nursing their young. They emit a wide range of sounds for communication, and are similar to dolphins and seals in how they retain knowledge, engage in complex associative learning, and master simple tasks.

In the wild, manatees have no natural predators. Instead, the greatest threats to manatees come from humans—boat strikes, water pollution, and habitat destruction. The problem of boat strikes is so pervasive in the manatee population of the middle Atlantic that in 2008, boats were responsible for a quarter of manatee deaths. Additionally, a large portion of that population had severe scarring and sometimes mutilation from encounters with watercraft. All three species of manatee are listed as vulnerable to extinction by the World Conservation Union.

Many of the animals on O'Reilly covers are endangered; all of them are important to the world. To learn more about how you can help, go to *animals.oreilly.com*.

The cover image is from the *Brockhaus Lexicon*. The cover fonts are URW Typewriter and Guardian Sans. The text font is Adobe Minion Pro; the heading font is Adobe Myriad Condensed; and the code font is Dalton Maag's Ubuntu Mono.

Get even more for your money.

Join the O'Reilly Community, and register the O'Reilly books you own. It's free, and you'll get:

- $4.99 ebook upgrade offer
- 40% upgrade offer on O'Reilly print books
- Membership discounts on books and events
- Free lifetime updates to ebooks and videos
- Multiple ebook formats, DRM FREE
- Participation in the O'Reilly community
- Newsletters
- Account management
- 100% Satisfaction Guarantee

Signing up is easy:

1. Go to: oreilly.com/go/register
2. Create an O'Reilly login.
3. Provide your address.
4. Register your books.

Note: English-language books only

To order books online:
oreilly.com/store

For questions about products or an order:
orders@oreilly.com

To sign up to get topic-specific email announcements and/or news about upcoming books, conferences, special offers, and new technologies:
elists@oreilly.com

For technical questions about book content:
booktech@oreilly.com

To submit new book proposals to our editors:
proposals@oreilly.com

O'Reilly books are available in multiple DRM-free ebook formats. For more information:
oreilly.com/ebooks

Have it your way.

CPSIA information can be obtained
at www.ICGtesting.com
Printed in the USA
JSHW041734211020
8883JS00005B/151

9 781491 900086